STONES, BONES, AND THE SACRED

EARLY CHRISTIANITY AND ITS LITERATURE

David G. Horrell, General Editor

Editorial Board:
Warren Carter
Amy-Jill Levine
Judith M. Lieu
Margaret Y. MacDonald
Dale B. Martin

Number 21

STONES, BONES, AND THE SACRED

Essays on Material Culture and Ancient Religion
in Honor of Dennis E. Smith

edited by

Alan H. Cadwallader

**PRESS**

Atlanta

Copyright © 2016 by SBL Press

All rights reserved. No part of this work may be reproduced or transmitted in any form or by any means, electronic or mechanical, including photocopying and recording, or by means of any information storage or retrieval system, except as may be expressly permitted by the 1976 Copyright Act or in writing from the publisher. Requests for permission should be addressed in writing to the Rights and Permissions Office, SBL Press, 825 Houston Mill Road, Atlanta, GA 30329 USA.

Library of Congress Control Number: 2016956217

Printed on acid-free paper.

Contents

Abbreviations vii
Preface..xix

The Scholarship of Dennis E. Smith
    Hal E. Taussig..1

Embodied Inequalities: Diet Reconstruction and Christian Origins
    Steven J. Friesen...9

Food Crises in Corinth? Revisiting the Evidence and Its Possible
Implications in Reading 1 Cor 11:17–34
    Ma. Marilou S. Ibita 33

Don't Take It Lying Down: Nondining Features of the Omrit
Temple Excavations
    Daniel N. Schowalter 55

Eating Words in the New Testament
    Keith Dyer..69

Ancient Drinking in Modern Bible Translation
    Jorunn Økland...85

Making Men in Rev 2–3: Reading the Seven Messages in the
Bath-Gymnasiums of Asia Minor
    Lynn R. Huber...101

At the Origins of Christian Apologetic Literature: The Politics of
Patronage in Hadrianic Athens
    William Rutherford..129

One Grave, Two Women, One Man: Complicating Family Life
at Colossae
Alan H. Cadwallader 157

The Corinthian καιναὶ κτίσεις? Second Corinthians 5:17 and
the Roman Refoundation of Corinth
Dominika Kurek-Chomycz and Reimund Bieringer 195

Women as Leaders in the Gatherings of Early Christian
Communities: A Sociohistorical Analysis
Valeriy A. Alikin..221

The Political Charges against Paul and Silas in Acts 17:6–7: Roman
Benefaction in Thessalonica
Jeffrey A. D. Weima..241

Paul's Walk to Assos: A Hodological Inquiry into Its Geography,
Archaeology, and Purpose
Glen L. Thompson and Mark Wilson...269

The Baptists of Corinth: Paul, the Partisans of Apollos, and the
History of Baptism in Nascent Christianity
Stephen J. Patterson..315

A Response
Dennis E. Smith...329

List of Contributors..335
Index of Ancient Sources..339
Index of Place Names...352
Index of Modern Authors...355
Index of Subjects..361

Abbreviations

Primary Texts

1 Apol.	Justin, *Apologia i*
1 En.	1 Enoch
Ab urbe cond.	Livy, *Ab urbe condita*
Acts Paul Thecl.	Acts of Paul and Thecla
Acts Pet.	Acts of Peter
Aem.	Plutarch, *Aemilius Paullus*
Aen.	Virgil, *Aeneid*
A.J.	Josephus, *Antiquitates judaicae*
Ann.	Tacitus, *Annales*
Ant.	Josephus, *Jewish Antiquities*
Apol.	Tertullian, *Apologeticus*
Att.	Cicero, *Epistulae ad Atticum*
Aug.	Suetonius, *Divus Augustus*
Autol.	Theophilus, *Ad Autolycum*
Bapt.	Tertullian, *De baptismo*
Bell. civ.	Appian, *Bella civilia*
Bib. hist.	Diodorus Siculus, *Bibliotheca historica*
B.J.	Josephus, *Bellum judaicum*
Brut.	Plutarch, *Brutus*
Caes.	Plutarch, *Caesar*
Carm.	Horace, *Carmina*
Cels.	Origen, *Contra Celsum*
Char.	Theophrastus, *Characteres*
Chron.	Eusebius, *Chronicon*
Claud.	Suetonius, *Divus Claudius*
Coll. med.	Oribasius, *Collectiones medicae*
Cyr.	Xenophon, *Cyropaedia*
Deipn.	Athenaeus, *Deipnosophistae*

Descr.	Pausanius, *Graeciae descriptio*
Diatr.	Epictetus, *Diatribai*
Did.	Didache
Dig.	Digesta
Ecl.	Virgil, *Eclogae*
Ep.	Pliny, *Epistulae*
Epig.	Martial, *Epigrams*
Epit. Caes.	Pseudo-Aurelius Victor, *Epitome de Caesaribus*
ESG	Greek book of Esther
Eth. nic.	Aristotle, *Ethica nicomachea*
Fac.	Plutarch, *De facie in orbe lunae*
Font.	Cicero, *Pro Fonteio*
Frat. amor.	Plutarch, *De fraterno amore*
Gall.	Life of Gallienus
Geogr.	Ptolemy, *Geographia*; Strabo, *Geographica*
Gyn.	Soranus, *Gynecology*
Hist. Aug.	Historia Augusta
Hadr.	Life of Hadrian
Haer.	Irenaeus, *Adversus haereses*
Hell.	Xenophon, *Hellenica*
Herm. Sim.	Shepherd of Hermas, Similitude
Hist.	Polybius, *Historiae*; Tacitus, *Historia*; Velleius Paterculus, *History of Rome*
Hist. adv. Paganos	Orosios *Historiarum adversus Paganos*
Hist. eccl.	Eusebius, *Historia ecclesiastica*
Hist. rom.	Dio Cassius, *Historiae romanae*
Il.	Homer, *Ilias*
Jub.	Jubilees
Jul.	Suetonius, *Divus Julius*
LAB	Liber antiquitatum biblicarum
Leg.	Athenagorus, *Legatio pro Christianis*; Cicero, *De legibus*; Plato, *Leges*
Marc.	Tertullian, *Adversus Marcionem*
Mart. Pol.	Martyrdom of Polycarp
Met.	Apuleius, *Metamorphoses*
Mos.	Philo, *De vita Mosis*
Nat.	Pliny the Elder, *Naturalis historia*; Tertullian, *Ad nationes*
Nat. an.	Aelian, *De natura animalium*

ABBREVIATIONS

Noct. att.	Aulus Gellius, *Noctes atticae*
Oct.	Minucius Felix, *Octavius*
Od.	Homer, *Odyssea*
Opif.	Philo, *De opificio mundi*
Or.	Dio Chrysostom, *Orations*; Isaeus, *Orations*
Pan.	Epiphanius, *Panarion*
Peregr.	Lucian, *De morte Peregrini*
Pol.	Ignatius, *To Polycarp*
Polior.	Aeneas Tactitus, *Poliorcetica*
Praescr.	Tertullian, *De praescriptione haereticorum*
Prot.	Plato, *Protagoras*
Protr.	Galen, *Protrepticus*
Quaest. conv.	Plutarch, *Quaestionum convivialum libri IX*
Ran.	Aristophanes, *Ranae*
Rom.	Plutarch, *Romulus*
Sent.	Julius Paulus, *Sententiae*
Sib. Or.	Sibylline Oracles
Sol.	Plutarch, *Solon*
Strom.	Clement of Alexandria, *Stromateis*
Tib.	Suetonius, *Tiberius*
Usu part.	Galen, *De usu partium*
Trad. ap.	*Traditio apostolica*
Vesp.	Suetonius, *Vespasianus*
Virg.	Tertullian, *De virginibus velandis*
Vir. ill.	Jerome, *De viris illustribus*
Vit. Apoll.	Philostratus, *Vita Apollonii*
Vit. soph.	Philostratus, *Vitae sophistarum*
VP	Iamblichus, *Vita Pythagorae*

Secondary Resources

AB	Anchor Bible
ABD	*The Anchor Bible Dictionary*. Edited by David Noel Freedman. 6 vols. New York: Doubleday, 1992.
ADPF	Association pour la diffusion de la pensée française
AE	*L'Année épigraphique*. Edited by René Cagnat et al. Paris: Presses universitaires de France, 1888–.
AJA	*American Journal of Archaeology*
AJPA	*American Journal of Physical Anthropology*

ALA	*Aphrodisias in Late Antiquity: The Late Roman and Byzantine Inscriptions Including Texts from the Excavations at Aphrodisias Conducted by Kenan T. Erim.* Edited by Charlotte Roueché and Joyce Maire Reynolds. London: Society for the Promotion of Roman Studies, 1989.
AltHierapolis	*Altertümer von Hierapolis.* Edited by Carl Humann, Conrad Cichorius, Walther Judeich, and Franz Winter. Berlin: Reimer, 1898.
AmJT	*American Journal of Theology*
ANF	*The Ante-Nicene Fathers: Translations of the Writings of the Fathers down to A.D. 325.* Edited by Alexander Roberts and James Donaldson. 10 vols. Grand Rapids: Eerdmans, 1980–1983.
ANRW	*Aufstieg und Niedergang der römischen Welt: Geschichte und Kultur Roms im Spiegel der neueren Forschung.* Part 2, *Principat.* Edited by Hildegard Temporini and Wolfgang Haase. Berlin: de Gruyter, 1972–
AnSt	*Anatolian Studies*
ArchEph	*Archaiologikē Ephēmeris*
ASCSA	American School of Classical Studies at Athens
Athēna	*Athēna: Syngramma periodikon tēs en Athēnais epistēmonikes hetaireias*
BAR	*Biblical Archaeology Review*
BCH	*Bulletin de correspondance hellénique*
BCHSup	Supplement to *Bulletin de correspondance hellénique*
BCL	Bohn's Classical Library
BDAG	Danker, Frederick W., Walter Bauer, William F. Arndt, and F. Wilbur Gingrich. *Greek-English Lexicon of the New Testament and Other Early Christian Literature.* 3rd ed. Chicago: University of Chicago Press, 2000.
BECNT	Baker Exegetical Commentary on the New Testament
BETL	Bibliotheca Ephemeridum Theologicarum Lovaniensium
BGU	*Aegyptische Urkunden aus den Königlichen Staatlichen Museen zu Berlin, Griechische Urkunden.* 15 vols. Berlin: Weidmann, 1895–1937.
BHAK	Beiheft zur Halbjahresschrift Antike Kunst

Bibel 2000	*Bibel 2000: Ester enligt den grekiska texten.* Uppsala: Svenska Bibelsällskapet, 2000.
BiTS	Biblical Tools and Studies
BJS	Brown Judaic Studies
BMC	British Museum Collection
BNTC	Black's New Testament Commentaries
BSGRT	Bibliotheca Scriptorum Graecorum et Romanorum Teubneriana
BZNW	Beihefte zur Zeitschrift für die neutestamentliche Wissenschaft
CBET	Contributions to Biblical Exegesis and Theology
CB	*The Cities and Bishoprics of Phrygia: Being an Essay of the Local History of Phrygia from the Earliest Times to the Turkish Conquest.* William Mitchell Ramsay. 2 vols. Oxford: Clarendon, 1895–1897.
CBQ	*Catholic Biblical Quarterly*
CIG	*Corpus Inscriptionum Graecarum.* Edited by August Boeckh. 4 vols. Berlin: 1828–1877.
CIJ	*Corpus Inscriptionum Judaicarum.* Edited by Jean-Baptiste Frey. 2 vols. Rome: Biblical Pontifical Institute, 1936–1952.
CIL	*Corpus Inscriptionum Latinarum.* Berlin: Reimer, 1862–1974.
CIRB	*Corpus Inscriptionum Regni Bosporani.* Leningrad: Nauka; Saint Petersburg: Bibliotheca Classica Petropolitana, 1965. Repr., 2004.
CMG	*Corpus Medicorum Graecorum.* Leipzig: Teubner, 1915–
CNRS	Centre National de la Recherche Scientifique
COMCAR	Colloquium on Material Culture and Ancient Religion
CRAI	*Comptes rendus des séances de l'Académie des inscriptions et belles-lettres*
CTR	*Criswell Theological Review*
DNP	*Der neue Pauly: Enzyklopädie der Antike.* Edited by Hubet Cancik and Helmuth Schneider. Stuttgart: Metzler, 1996–.
Douay-Rheims	*The Vulgate Bible: Douay-Rheims Translation.* Edited by Swift Edgar and Angela M. Kinney. 4 vols. Cambridge: Harvard University Press, 2010–2013.

EA	*Epigraphica Anatolica*
EAD	*Exploration archéologique de Délos: Faite par l'Ecole française d'Athènes.* Paris: de Boccard, 1909–2007.
ECHC	Early Christianity in Its Hellenistic Context
EDNT	*Exegetical Dictionary of the New Testament.* Edited by Horst Balz and Gerhard Schneider. ET. 3 vols. Grand Rapids: Eerdmans, 1990–1993.
EPHMS.PT	Epistēmonikai pragmateiai. Hetaireia Makedonikōn Spudōn. Philology and Theology
ESV	English Standard Version
EvT	*Evangelische Theologie*
FRLANT	Forschungen zur Religion und Literatur des Alten und Neuen Testaments
GIBM	*The Collection of Ancient Greek Inscriptions in the British Museum.* Edited by Charles T. Newton, Gustav Hirschfeld, Frederik H. Marshall, and Edward L. Hicks. Oxford: Clarendon, 1874–1916. Repr., 1974.
GRBS	*Greek, Roman, and Byzantine Studies*
HesperiaSup	Hesperia Supplement Series
Historia	*Historia: Zeitschrift für alte Geschichte*
HNT	Handbuch zum Neuen Testament
HSCP	*Harvard Studies in Classical Philology*
HTR	*Harvard Theological Review*
HTS	Harvard Theological Studies
HvTSt	*Hervormde teologiese studies*
IArykanda	*Die Inschriften von Arykanda.* Edited by Helmut Engelmann et al. Bonn: Habelt, 1972.
IAssos	*Die Inschriften von Assos.* Edited by Reinhold Merkelbach. IGSK 4. Bonn: Habelt, 1976.
IBoubon	*Boubon: The Inscriptions and Archaeological Remains, a Survey 2004–2006.* Edited by Christina Kokkinia. Meletemata 60. Athens: de Boccard, 2008.
ICC	International Critical Commentary
IDelos	*Inscriptions de Délos.* Edited by Félix Dürrbach, Pierre Roussel, Marcel Launey, André Plassart, and Jacques Coupry. 7 vols. Paris: 1926–1972.
IG	*Inscriptiones Graecae. Editio Minor.* Berlin: de Gruyter, 1924–.

IGBR	*Inscriptiones graecae in Bulgaria repertae.* Edited by Georgi Mihailov. Sophia: Academiae Litterarum Bulgaricae, 1956–1997.
IGRR	*Inscriptiones graecae ad res romanas pertinentes.* Edited by René Cagnat, J. Touvain, Pierre Jouguet, and Georges Lafaye. 4 vols. Paris: Leroux; Rome: Bretschneider, 1906–1964.
IHadrianoi	*Die Inschriften von Hadrianoi und Hadrianeia.* Edited by Elmar Schwertheim. Bonn: Habelt, 1987
IK	*Inschriften griechischer Städte aus kleinasien.* Edited by Helmut Egelmann. Bonn: Habelt, 1972–
IKilikiaBM	*Journeys in Rough Cilicia, 1964–1963.* Edited by George E. Bean and Terence B. Mitford. 2 vols. Vienna: Böhlaus, 1965–1970
IKorinthKent	Kent, John H. *The Inscriptions, 1926–1950.* Vol. 8.3 of *Corinth: Results of Excavations Conducted by the American School of Classical Studies at Athens.* Princeton: American School of Classical Studies at Athens, 1966.
IKorinthMeritt	Meritt, Benjamin D., ed. *Greek Inscriptions 1896–1927.* Vol. 8.1 of *Corinth: Results of Excavations Conducted by the American School of Classical Studies at Athens.* Cambridge: Harvard University Press, 1931.
IKorinthWest	West, Allen Brown, ed. *Latin Inscriptions, 1896–1926.* Vol. 8.2 of *Corinth: Results of Excavations Conducted by the American School of Classical Studies at Athens.* Cambridge: American School of Classical Studies at Athens, 1931.
IKyzikos	*Die Grabtexte.* Vol. 1 of *Die Inschriften von Kyzikos und Umgebung.* Edited by E. Schwertheim. Bonn: Habelt, 1980.
ILipara	*Le iscrizioni lapidarie greche e latine delle isole Eolie.* Vol. 12 of *Meligunis Lipára.* Edited by Luigi B. Brea, Madeleine Cavalier, and Lorenzo Campagna, with the collaboration of Filippo Famularo. Palermo: Publiscula, 2003.
ILS	*Inscriptiones latinae selectae.* Edited by Hermann Dessau. 3 vols. Berlin: Weidmann, 1892–1916.

IMT	*Inschriften Mysia und Troas.* Edited by Matthias Barth and Josef Stauber. Munich: Leopold Wenger-Institut, 1993.
IPerge	*Die Inschriften von Perge.* Edited by S. Şahin. 3 vols. Bonn 1992.
ISmyrna	*Die Inschriften von Smyrna.* Edited by Georg Petzl. Bonn: Habelt, 1982–1990.
IstMitt	*Istanbuler Mitteilungen*
JdI	*Jahrbuch des deutschen archäologischen Instituts*
JArS	*Journal of Archaeological Science*
JFSR	*Journal of Feminist Studies in Religion*
JHS	*Journal of Hellenic Studies*
JNG	*Jahrbuch für Numismatik und Geldgeschichte*
JÖAI	*Jahreshefte des Österreichischen archäologischen Instituts*
JRA	*Journal of Roman Archaeology*
JRASup	Journal of Roman Archaeology Supplement Series
JRS	*Journal of Roman Studies*
JRSMS	Journal of Roman Studies Monograph Series
JSNTSup	Journal for the Study of the New Testament Supplement Series
KEK	Kritisch-exegetischer Kommentar über das Neue Testament (Meyer-Kommentar)
KJV	King James Version
KJVA	*The Apocrypha: Or, Non-canonical Books of the Bible; The King James Version.* Edited by Manual Komroff. New York: Tudor, 1949.
LBW	Le Bas, Philippe, and W. H. Waddington. *Inscriptions grecques et latines recueillies en Gréce et en Asie Mineure.* 3 vols. Paris: Didot, 1870.
LCL	Loeb Classical Library
LGPN	*Lexicon of Greek Personal Names.* Edited by P. M. Fraser and E. Matthews. Oxford: Clarendon, 1987–.
LNTS	The Library of New Testament Studies
LSAM	*Lois sacrées de l'Asie Mineure.* Edited by Franciszek Sokolowski. Paris: de Boccard, 1955.
LSJ	Liddell, Henry George, Robert Scott, and Henry Stuart Jones. *A Greek-English Lexicon.* 9th ed. with revised supplement. Oxford: Clarendon, 1996.

LXX	Septuagint
MAMA	*Monumenta Asiae Minoris Antiqua.* Edited by W. M. Calder et al. London: Manchester University Press; Longmans, Green, 1928–.
MDAIA	*Mitteilungen des Deutschen Archäologischen Instituts, Athenische Abteilung*
MnemosyneSup	Mnemosyne Supplement Series
MT	Masoretic Text
NA27	*Novum Testamentum Graece,* Nestle-Aland, 27th ed.
NETS	*A New English Translation of the Septuagint.* Edited by Albert Pietersma and Benjamin G. Wright. New York: Oxford University Press, 2007.
NeuePaulySup	Neue Pauly Supplements
NewDocs	*New Documents Illustrating Early Christianity.* Edited by Greg H. R. Horsley and Stephen Llewelyn. North Ryde, NSW: The Ancient History Documentary Research Centre, Macquarie University, 1981–.
NICNT	New International Commentary on the New Testament
NIGTC	New International Greek Testament Commentary
NIDB	*New Interpreter's Dictionary of the Bible.* Edited by Katherine Doob Sakenfeld. 5 vols. Nashville: Abingdon, 2006–2009.
NIV	New International Version
NKJV	New King James Version
NLT	New Living Translation
NO 1988	*Det gamle testamentes apokryfiske bøker: De deuterokanoniske bøker.* Oslo: Norske Bibelselskap, 1988.
NovT	*Novum Testamentum*
NovTSup	Supplements to Novum Testamentum
NRSV	New Revised Standard Version
NTG	New Testament Guides
NTL	New Testament Library
NTOA	Novum Testamentum et Orbis Antiquus
OGIS	*Orientis graeci inscriptiones selectae.* Edited by Wilhelm Dittenberger. 2 vols. Leipzig: Hirzel, 1903–1905.
OIP	Oriental Institute Publications
PfuhlMöbius	Pfuhl, Ernst, and Hans Möbius. *Die Ostgriechischen Grabreliefs.* 2 vols. Mainz: von Zabern, 1977–1979.

PHI	Packard Humanities Institute
P.Lond.	*Greek Papyri in the British Museum*. Edited by F. G. Kenyon, H. I. Bell, W. E. Crum, and T. C. Skeat. 7 vols. London: British Museum, 1893–1974
PNEAS	*Publication of the Near East Archaeological Society*
PNTC	Pillar New Testament Commentary
P.Oslo.	*Papyri Osloenses*. Edited by Samson Eitrem and Leiv Amundsen. 3 vols. Oslo: Dybwad, 1925–1936.
P.Oxy.	*The Oxyrhynchus Papyri*. Edited by Bernard P. Grenfell and Arthur S. Hunt. London: Egypt Exploration Society, 1898–.
REG	*Revue des études grecques*
RevPhil	*Revue de philologie*
RGRW	Religions in the Graeco-Roman World
RIDA	*Revue internationale des droits de l'antiquité*
Ritti	Ritti, Tullia. *Museo Archeologico di Denizli-Hierapolis: Catalogo delle iscrizioni greche e latine; Distretto di Denizli*. Naples: Liguori, 2008.
RRA	Rhetoric of Religious Antiquity
RSV	Revised Standard Version
RTR	*Reformed Theological Review*
SB	*Sammelbuch griechischer Urkunden aus Ägypten*. Edited by Friedrich Preisigke, Friedrich Bilabel, Hans-Albert Rupprecht, and Andrea Jördens. Strasbourg: Trubner; Wiesbaden: Harrassowitz, 1915–.
SBLDS	Society of Biblical Literature Dissertation Series
SBLMS	Society of Biblical Literature Monograph Series
SBT	Studies in Biblical Theology
SC	Sources chrétiennes
SCS	Septuagint and Cognate Studies
SEG	*Supplementum epigraphicum graecum*. Leiden: Brill, 1923–.
SemeiaSt	Semeia Studies
SGO	*Steinepigramme aus dem griechischen Osten*. Edited by Reinhold Merkelbach and Josef Stauber. Stuttgart: Teubner, 1998–2004.
SHR	Studies in the History of Religions (supplements to *Numen*)

SIG	*Sylloge inscriptionum graecarum.* Edited by Wilhelm Dittenberger. 4 vols. 3rd ed. Leipzig: Hirzel, 1915–1924.
SMA	Studies in Mediterranean Archaeology
SNTSMS	Society for New Testament Studies Monograph Series
SNTW	Studies of the New Testament and Its World
SPP	*Studien zur Palaeographie und Papyruskunde.* Edited by Carl Wessely. Leipzig: Avenarius, 1901–1924.
SPbCU	St. Petersburg Christian University
StPatr	Studia Patristica
TAM	*Tituli Asiae Minoris.* Vienna: Hoelder-Pichler-Tempsky, 1901–.
TANZ	Texte und Arbeiten zum neutestamentlichen Zeitalter
TAPA	*Transactions of the American Philological Association*
TDNT	*Theological Dictionary of the New Testament.* Edited by Gerhard Kittel and Gerhard Friedrich. Translated by Geoffrey W. Bromiley. 10 vols. Grand Rapids: Eerdmans, 1964–1976.
TNTC	Tyndale New Testament Commentaries
TynBul	*Tyndale Bulletin*
UBS4	*The Greek New Testament,* United Bible Societies, 4th ed.
VC	*Vigiliae Christianae*
VCSup	Supplements to Vigiliae Christianae
WW	*Word and World*
WBC	Word Biblical Commentary
WUNT	Wissenschaftliche Untersuchungen zum Neuen Testament
YNER	Yale Near Eastern Researches
ZECNT	Zondervan Exegetical Commentary on the New Testament
ZNW	*Zeitschrift für die neutestamentliche Wissenschaft und die Kunde der älteren Kirche*

Preface

There is a restaurant in the square at the entrance to Anton Kallinger Caddesi in Selcuk, Turkey. It was one of the regular watering holes for the participants in the first Colloquium on Material Culture and Ancient Religion (COMCAR) based at the Crisler Library in 2008. One unknown Australian met up with the epitome of a Texas gentleman for lunch. I was the Aussie; Dennis Smith was the exemplary companion.

Dennis proceeded to attend with keen interest, good humor, and bucketloads of encouragement to my take on the Syro-Phoenician woman and her daughter. Of course, as the discussion unfolded, I realized that little by little he was both mining and stretching my ideas about the dining customs that the story in Mark's Gospel was playing with at its heart and climax. From that moment on, Dennis has never ceased to cultivate the friendship begun over a meal in Turkey and nurtured in similar fashion many times since. Always there have been attentiveness, good humor, and encouragement; always a gentle, critical question or insight that fosters new considerations.

Mine is far from an isolated story, but it does distill the man that so many have found who have joined the COMCAR gatherings. This explains the desire to offer this collection of essays. In appreciation of Dennis's contribution to teaching, research, and scholarly collaboration, members of COMCAR from across the world have agreed to bring some of their research into ancient material culture and religion to a collection fêted in his honor. The collection focuses on the intersection of material culture, ancient religion, and the texts and practices of early Christianity. As diverse as the subjects may be, the various essays demonstrate the immense value of the exchange between artifacts, text, and interpreter that arises from the in situ context of a collaborative gathering of scholars from around the world. From Ephesus to Corinth, Colossae to Athens, Omrit to Assos, the refrain of "digging in the dirt" yields new, sometimes startling insights into the ubiquity of religion in life in the ancient world, most especially in the fabric, circumstances, and symbolics of meals—the life-long preoccupations of the one for whom the collection is dedicated.

Thanks must be given to the organizers of COMCAR, to Christine Thomas, Steven Friesen, Dan Schowalter, and James Walters. Without their commitment, experience, and love of the investigation of material culture, COMCAR would not exist, and the many who have joined the cheers of congratulation to Dennis would never have had the joy of meeting him. We are all grateful as well to Bob Buller and the editors of SBL Press, who have not only recognized the importance of material culture to biblical interpretation—a long-standing commitment of North American scholarship—but have joined in saluting one of its most astute and endearing exponents, Dennis E. Smith.

So, as we all imagine ourselves again being invited to recline at a feast, we raise our cups to you, Dennis, in thanksgiving and in honor.

Alan H. Cadwallader

****

The following participants in the Colloquium on Material Culture and Ancient Religions (COMCAR) have celebrated in the collegiality, scholarship, and generosity of Dennis Smith. They join in honoring his unsurpassed contribution to their material experience and their critical reflections.

Valeriy A. Alikin
Richard S. Ascough
Vicky Balabanski
Reimund Bieringer
Jeffrey Brodd
Alan H. Cadwallader
Kelley Coblentz-Bautch
Kindalee Delong
Nicola Denzey
Beth Digeser
Terry Donaldson
David Downs
Ruben Dupertuis
Keith Dyer
Steven J. Friesen

Lynn R. Huber
Christopher Hutson
Marilou S. Ibita
David Janssen
Dominika Kurek-Chomycz
Peter Marshall
Roberta Mazza
Mark Nanos
Paolo Noguiera
Jorunn Økland
Stephen J. Patterson
Jeremy Punt
Jonathan Reed
Helen Rhee
Betsey Robinson

William Rutherford
Daniel N. Schowalter
Philip Sellew
Kirsi Siitonen
Greg Snyder
Barbette Spaeth
Kimberley Stratton
Christine Thomas

Glen L. Thompson
Trevor Thompson
Janet Tulloch
Zsuzsa Varhelyi
James C. Walters
Jeffrey A. D. Weima
Mark Wilson

The Scholarship of Dennis E. Smith

Hal E. Taussig

Some eleven years ago, I learned in the early fall directly from Dennis Smith that he had an aggressive cancer. He recovered fully from that cancer, and overall I suspect it has not counted as a particularly important time of his life.

I begin my reflection on the work and ongoing life of Dennis with this memory because it ended up saying volumes about the character of his life and the centrality of scholarly collegiality in his life. Since Dennis and I have always lived in different parts of the country, we have worked hard at having time together in person. In this case more than a decade ago, Dennis asked that we spend some extended time together around when we met at the Annual Meetings of the Society of Biblical Literature later in the fall. He asked me to contact another Society of Biblical Literature colleague, along with a seminary colleague, to join us for a private dinner together.

Indeed, such a lively conversation happened those eleven years ago. Lots of earnest queries, some difficult reflection, a decent measure of laughter and ribaldry, and some significant relaxation took place as the evening lingered. It turned out that—with the significant exception of his wife Barbara (who delighted in Dennis's claiming that he was her "luv slave")—Dennis had hardly told anyone else about his cancer. So he had saved up for this private Society of Biblical Literature "meals seminar" a good deal of revelation and cogitation.

As I reflect on Dennis's many scholarly accomplishments, the long and hardy accolades by several generations of his seminary students, the tender intimacy of his relationship to Barbara and their son Adam, and the sturdy and wide range of his service to Philips Theological Seminary, the Disciples of Christ denomination, and the broader academy, that understated, yet poignant, dinner at the Society of Biblical Literature meeting captures much about who and what he is.

Dennis works hard, thinks incisively, turns regularly toward collegiality, surprises us from silence with great humor, lets his silent love of the arts seep into his historical fervor, and bends regularly toward kindness. But he is rarely far from the company of biblical scholarship. It is more the exception than the rule that it is far from his consciousness. He wakes up regularly with a new theory or the end of the last evening's argument. Due to his diffident streak, he often corrals his own contradictory, passionate, and patient scholarly musings in his head before talking about them with the rest of us. That is, it is no surprise that some of the deepest stirrings of his person convene themselves in the arena of biblical scholarship or ancient history. No wonder thinking about his own life and death makes a stable home in the company of scholars and scholarship. During my times together with Dennis in the hospital in his more recent battle with cancer, we could barely wait for the medical clan to leave and us to start laying out some new textual theory or ancient historical puzzle. Almost every time I would call on the phone to check in on his health, we ended up talking mostly about his thoughts on what needed to happen next in the study of Greco-Roman meals or his ponderings on some matter emerging in the drama of biblical scholars' relationships with one other. Now, as I write in the spring of 2016, Dennis has just come back from his first major scholarly presentation since the beginning of his ongoing battle with fourth-stage leukemia.

My writing makes it clear in at least four of my books and in numerous articles that Dennis is one of the crucial architects of the present study of the first two early Christian centuries over the last twenty-five years. Although his own modesty and the guild's substantial myopia about the first 150 years of Christian worship have underplayed his work, there is no doubt that Smith's powerful scholarship, ground-breaking research, and persistent leadership have been the primary dynamic at work in the discovery of the Greco-Roman meal at the heart of the vast majority of early Christian gatherings through most of the first two centuries CE.

It was Dennis's thirty-five years of scholarship on the Greco-Roman meal that have uncovered this well-articulated communal form as the primary gathering of the first fifteen decades of Jesus and Christ people. Although Dennis's strong penchant for collegial scholarship and the important connections it had with Matthias Klinghardt's scholarship in Germany made Dennis much more than a lonely genius, it was indeed his 1982 dissertation and his coauthored 1990 book that unleashed and guided the twenty-five years of internationally established understanding of how these early Christians worshiped, built lives together, and shaped their new and central understandings of their signature "festive banquet." Now—without so much as a party—the guild turns steadily and almost in unison to acclaim his magisterial book, *From Symposium to Eucharist: The Banquet in the Early Christian World*.[1] Scholarship on early Christian meaning-making and the form of these formative communities will not know a similarly significant shift for quite some time in the future, nor understand completely how thoroughly, yet quietly, the shortcuts taken and the long-lasting caricatures fell apart when Dennis's discovery and naming of this meal came into consciousness.

The integrity of Dennis's central portrait of the long-obscured and poorly understood meal has much to do with his even-keeled, no-nonsense, self-effacing scholarly routine within the academy decade after decade. For him, working steadily with difficult texts, patiently laying out the basics of the first century for students, painstakingly editing numerous books for group projects, listening carefully and crediting colleagues at every turn, and doing more than his fair share of administrative duties simply belongs to being a scholar of the New Testament and of the ancient Mediterranean. He has known for more than three decades of the pivotal significance of these meals for the beginnings for Christianity, and year by year he has woven his daily tasks into incremental elaborations of this larger picture. It is true that very occasionally he and I talk of writing a trade book about the way these meals brought so much meaning and liveliness to what became Christianity and the strange ways in which church over the centuries virtually undid the meal within traditional worship. Even now, he actively ponders how he can further prompt scholarship, church, and public consciousness to realize the ways in which these meals form some of the deepest dimensions of the initial two centuries of the Christ movements. But in the end he usually takes extra time to rework his understanding of a key text, give a sermon to seminary chapel via skype, stare at an obscure fragment of an ancient vase, or make sure a former student gets the complexity of the subjunctive. Who knows whether we will ever write that book? Here's hoping.

---

1. Dennis E. Smith, *From Symposium to Eucharist: The Banquet in the Early Christian World* (Minneapolis: Fortress, 2003).

Although Dennis's scholarship and leadership in meals studies is without a doubt his key contribution, his scholarship attracts much attention in two other fields. First, it is true that much of the public knows him almost exclusively for another long-term project with a significant public (and familial) face. He has been for the last twenty years one of key leaders in the study, elaboration, and performance of ancient biblical storytelling. With Michael E. Williams, he coauthored five of the thirteen volumes of the *Storytellers' Companion to the Bible*.[2] This major contribution to interpretation and study of the Bible for an audience that includes but is not defined by the scholarly guild expresses a larger performatory dimension to Dennis's work. Dennis's public work in storytelling and its interpretation includes more than being the luv slave of his wife and life partner, the nationally known storyteller Barbara McBride Smith. Again without any fanfare, with Williams, Dennis has built an entire structure of the narrative understanding of biblical texts in the scholarly, church, and public spheres.

Similar to the storytelling work, although lauded mostly among technical scholars, is Dennis's leadership of the Westar Institute's Acts Seminar. In close collaboration with his cochair, Joseph B. Tyson, Dennis led a number of scholars in a study of the Acts of the Apostles that lasted for over ten years and only recently concluded with the publication of *Acts and Christian Beginnings: The Acts Seminar Report*.[3] This work, also coedited with Tyson, is so startling in its reworking of the dating and composition of Acts that it is still difficult to gauge what the larger scholarly assessment will be. Written by twelve leading Acts scholars, the book rethinks the relationship of Acts to Paul's letters and places Acts itself clearly in the second century. Proposing the Acts of the Apostles as a considerable second-century integration of diverse early Christ movements, this major book sees Acts as marking a significant move toward epic notions of Christianity. Dennis still is a leading guild spokesperson for Acts as a powerful and perhaps also dangerous voice of emerging dominant Christianity. His central role as advocate in the way *Acts and Christian Beginnings* points toward such second-century agency in the emergence of Christianity will stay with us for some time.

---

2. Dennis E. Smith and Michael E. Williams, eds., *The Storyteller's Companion to the Bible* (Nashville: Abingdon, 1996–2005), vols. 9–13.

3. Dennis E. Smith and Joseph B. Tyson, *Acts and Christian Beginnings: The Acts Seminar Report* (Salem, OR: Polebridge, 2013).

It is in this larger context of his articulated and embedded life's calling as a New Testament scholar and his central contribution of the study of meals to the history of early Christianity that the dominant archeological motif in the writings of this book are dedicated to Dennis. As early as his doctoral study at Harvard Divinity School, he was already a member of Helmut Koester's Research Team for New Testament and Archaeology. He was Area Supervisor in Field Archaeology for the Joint Expedition to Caesarea Maritima, Israel, during the summers of 1974 and 1976. His first published article, "The Egyptian Cults at Corinth," was a collection of archaeological data from Corinth.[4] His first Society of Biblical Literature presentation, "Forms of Dining Rooms in Greek Sanctuaries," in November 1978 was an illustrated archaeological survey and provided background data for his dissertation. He also wrote the excavation report on the Byzantine hippodrome, "Field H, 1973 and 1974."[5] He has told me that all of these archeological accomplishments while he was still a student "were fundamental to my development as a historical scholar with a competence in the interpretation of material as well as literary data."

On one level, archaeological study has always clearly belonged to Dennis's work. Some of the key discoveries in his larger accomplishments on early Christian meals came directly from his own and others' archaeological work. On another level, the determining role these important archeological scholars play in this book dedicated to Dennis has a more personal and anachronistic character in comparison to the many roles he has played on the New Testament/early Christian stage. Yes, Dennis is ever the archeologist and a larger figure in the New Testament/early Christian scholarly world. The poignancy of this book has much to do with the fondness that has accumulated over the decades of archeological work together. Dennis was always a companion to these fine scholars, but also a steady author. It is this deep connection of companionship and scholarship to which this book points. It is why, above my listing of his published work, I have begun with Dennis's official contribution to the field of archeology.

---

4. Dennis E. Smith, "The Egyptian Cults at Corinth," *HTR* 70 (1977): 201–31.

5. Dennis E. Smith, "Field H, 1973 and 1974," chapter 11 in *The Joint Expedition to Caesarea Maritima: Preliminary Reports in Microfiche*, edited by Robert J. Bull (Madison, NJ: Drew University for Archaeological Research, 1987).

Selected Works of Dennis E. Smith

On Meals

Books

From Symposium to Eucharist: The Banquet in the Early Christian World. Minneapolis: Fortress, 2003.
Many Tables: The Eucharist in the New Testament and Liturgy Today. Coauthored with Hal E. Taussig. London: SCM; Philadelphia: Trinity Press International, 1990. Reprint, Eugene, OR: Wipf & Stock, 2001.
Meals in the Early Christian World: Social Formation, Experimentation, and Conflict at the Table. Coedited with Hal E. Taussig. New York: Palgrave Macmillan, 2012.

Dictionary Articles

"Banquet Hall." *NIDB* 1:390.
"Communion." *NIDB* 1:711.
"Eucharist." *NIDB* 2:353–55.
"Food and Dining in Early Christianity." Pages 357–64 in *A Companion to Food in the Ancient World*. Edited by John Wilkins and Robin Nadeau. Malden, MA: Wiley-Blackwell, 2015.
"Feasting, Hellenistic and Roman Period." Pages 405–12 in *The Oxford Encyclopedia of the Bible and Archaeology*. Edited by Daniel Master. New York: Oxford University Press, 2013.
"Last Supper" *NIDB* 3:582–85.
"Meals." Pages 874–76 in *Eerdmans Dictionary of the Bible*. Edited by David Noel Freedman. Grand Rapids: Eerdmans, 2000.
"Meals." Pages 929–26 in *The Eerdmans Dictionary of Early Judaism*. Edited by John J. Collins and Daniel C. Harlow. Grand Rapids: Eerdmans, 2010.
"Meals." Pages 530–32 in *The Encyclopedia of the Dead Sea Scrolls*. Edited by Lawrence H. Schiffman and James C. VanderKam. 2 vols. New York: Oxford University Press, 2000.
"Meal Customs (Greco-Roman)." *ABD* 4:651–53.
"Meal Customs (Sacred Meals)." *ABD* 4:653–55.
"Messianic Banquet." *ABD* 4:788–91.
"Table Fellowship." *ABD* 6:302–4.

Other Notable Articles

"Before There Was a Eucharist: Worship in the House Church." In *Eucharist and Ecclesiology: Essays in Honor of Everett Ferguson*. Edited by Wendell Willis. Eugene, OR: Wipf & Stock, forthcoming.

"Hospitality, the House Church, and Early Christian Identity." Pages 103–17 in *Mahl und religiöse Identität im frühen Christentum*. Edited by Matthias Klinghardt and Hal E. Taussig. TANZ 56. Tübingen: Francke, 2012.

"The House Church as Social Environment." Pages 3–21 in *Text, Image, and Christians in the Graeco-Roman World: A Festschrift in Honor of David Lee Balch*. Edited by Aliou Cissé Niang and Carolyn Osiek. Eugene, OR: Wipf & Stock, 2012.

"The Messianic Banquet Reconsidered." Pages 64–73 in *The Future of Early Christianity: Essays in Honor of Helmut Koester*. Edited by Birger A. Pearson. Minneapolis: Fortress, 1991.

"Revisiting Associations and Christ Groups." In *Scribal Practices and Social Structures among Jesus Adherents: Essays in Honor of John S. Kloppenborg*. Edited by William E. Arnal et al. BETL 285. Leuven: Peeters, forthcoming.

"Table Fellowship and the Historical Jesus." Pages 135–62 in *Religious Propaganda and Missionary Competition in the New Testament World: Essays Honoring Dieter Georgi*. Edited by Lukas Bormann, Kelly del Tredici, and Angela Standhartinger. Leiden: Brill, 1994.

"Table Fellowship as a Literary Motif in the Gospel of Luke." *JBL* 106 (1987): 613–38.

Storytelling and the Bible

Coeditor (with Michael E. Williams). *The Storyteller's Companion to the Bible*. Vols. 9–13. Nashville: Abingdon, 1996–2005.

Acts

Acts and Christian Beginnings: The Acts Seminar Report. Coedited with Joseph B. Tyson. Salem, OR: Polebridge, 2013.

"Acts of the Apostles." In *Handbook of Early Christian Meals in the Greco-Roman World*. Edited by Soham Al-Suadi and Peter-Ben Smit. New York: Bloomsbury T&T Clark, forthcoming.

"The Acts of the Apostles and the Rewriting of Christian History: On the Critical Study of Acts." *Forum* 5 (2003): 7–32.

Other

Chalice Introduction to the New Testament. St. Louis: Chalice, 2004.

Noteworthy Scholarly Seminars

Acts Seminar, Meeting under the Auspices of the Westar Institute, Chair, 1999–2010.
Colloquium on Ancient Religion and Material Culture, Member, 2008–2013.
Jesus Seminar, A National Research Seminar on the Jesus Tradition Organized by Robert Funk's Westar Institute, Charter Member, 1985–present.
Society of Biblical Literature Group on Archaeology of the New Testament World, Steering Committee Member, 1988–1997.
Society of Biblical Literature Section on Meals in the Greco-Roman World, Cochair with Hal E. Taussig, 2011–2013.
Society of Biblical Literature Section on the Social History of Formative Christianity and Judaism, Steering Committee Member, 1981–1998.
Society of Biblical Literature Seminar on Ancient Myths and Modern Theories of Christian Origins, Member, 1995–2003.
Society of Biblical Literature Seminar on Meals in the Greco-Roman World, Cochair with Hal E. Taussig, 2002–2010.

Embodied Inequalities:
Diet Reconstruction and Christian Origins

Steven J. Friesen

1. Seeking Religion among the Isotopes

An odd set of exchanges sent me into exploration of a topic that is also a central concern in Dennis Smith's work: the consumption of food in the Roman Empire. Here is how it happened. In 2005, I spent some time at the Corinth Excavations of the American School of Classical Studies. One of my goals was to pester the resident archaeologists with questions about ancient poverty. But when I asked what objects archaeologists might find that would tell them about poverty, the pragmatically minded excavators mostly looked at me as though I were asking the wrong question. So I started asking about physical evidence for nonelite inhabitants of the Roman Empire, and I began to get better results. They told me I needed to look at graves and bones. "Bones?" I asked. It is possible, they said, to reconstruct information about average diets of residents of the Roman Empire with stable isotope analysis of their skeletal remains. With information about which people ate how much of which foods, it might be possible to address systemic questions such as why food was distributed and consumed unevenly and why some individuals had more and some less.[1]

In the decade since those conversations, the literature on diet reconstruction in the Roman Empire has grown. In the meantime I have also stopped looking for poverty—a difficult concept for analytical work[2]—and

---

1. I am particularly indebted to Sherry Fox and Sandra Garvey-Lok for their assistance in this research and to Guy Sanders for his encouragement and advice. I also thank Jaimie Gunderson for help with the bibliography and the preparation of the manuscript.
2. The term *poverty* has at least two disadvantages. One disadvantage is that it is

have begun looking instead at forms of inequality. The concept of inequality allows us to be more specific about different kinds of biased distributions: according to gender, according to economic resources, according to ethnicity, age, family, legal status, and so on. Moreover, the discussion of these inequalities takes us very quickly to core issues in human societies. For human communities are always composed of people with unequal resources bound together in unequal relationships.

I note, however, that I am not a physical anthropologist nor a sociologist. I work in the study of religion, with special interests in the early phases of the movement that came to be called Christian. So what do I hope that the isotopes will tell me for the study of religion? Three goals have kept me involved in this line of analysis.

First, I am looking for ways to understand religion that include material practices and not simply ideas. In general, people in the West tend to define religion as a system of beliefs or values.[3] We also tend to think of this system as an autonomous realm of ideas that is separate from economics, politics, biology, national life, and so on. By investigating diet, however, I am trying to move my study of religion into a discourse about the circulation of material objects as a religious practice. Moreover, diet reconstruction and isotopic analysis focus our attention on the material body and specifically on the absorption of material objects into the body. It is a crucial process by which religion participates in the continual remaking of the individual, a process that shapes the body and the self. In other words, I am looking for a way to move beyond the study of disembodied ideas.

Second, I hope the isotopes will help us understand the ways in which early churches mirrored some dominant discourses and challenged other discourses. If we can construct a convincing portrait of dominant society

---

difficult to define poverty in a way that is meaningful and measurable for the Roman imperial period. Another disadvantage is that a definition of poverty for the ancient world would include nearly everyone because so many had so little. Thus, the concept is too broad to allow for meaningful distinctions in a setting where 80–90 percent of the people could be considered poor; see Walter Scheidel and Steven J. Friesen, "The Size of the Economy and the Distribution of Income in the Roman Empire," *JRS* 99 (2009): 61–91.

3. For an analysis of this tendency, see Wilfred Cantwell Smith, *The Meaning and End of Religion* (New York: Harper & Row, 1978), esp. 15–50. More recently, the argument has been extended by Brent Nongbri, *Before Religion: A History of a Modern Concept* (New Haven: Yale University Press, 2013).

and its unequal distribution of food resources, we may be able to show ways in which the earliest churches distributed resources differently.[4] I expect that the earliest churches manifested their own patterns of unequal distribution. But it would be a significant finding to establish that the earliest churches promoted a system of inequalities that was different from the system of inequalities evident in the dominant society.

Third, a better understanding of diets in the Roman Empire might help us chart the evolution of the churches in the early centuries. Over the course of three centuries, the churches evolved from an odd assortment of Jewish messianic groups into a network of powerful institutions, some of which gained imperial support and influence while others did not. I hope that more careful attention to the carbon, nitrogen, and oxygen isotopes found in human bodily remains might help us understand how the distribution of food and resources changed over the course of three or four centuries, and how these shifts in embodied inequalities shaped the movement.

It would take much more than a chapter to explore all of these issues, and the state of our knowledge does not yet allow for broad reconstructions. It is possible, however, to survey current literature on the reconstruction of Roman diets, to highlight crucial topics, and to suggest some directions for future study.

2. Seeking Inequality among the Isotopes

Stable isotope analysis became a useful archaeological method beginning in the 1970s, and it is now deployed throughout the world for the examination of human remains from all chronological periods.[5] This is not the place for a technical description of stable isotope analysis, but a

---

4. At this point in the history of research, we are not able to make large-scale comparisons between the diets of Christian populations and their neighbors. For the early centuries it is impossible to identify the remains of Christians, and few studies are available for periods when identification becomes possible. An example that illustrates some of the problems is L. V. Rutgers et al., "Early Christian Catacombs of Ancient Rome: New Insights into the Dietary Habits of Rome's Early Christians," *JArS* 36 (2009): 1127–34. In this case, the argument is not convincing due to the paucity of comparative data. See below, n. 48, for further details.

5. For a brief survey of these developments, see Anastasia Papathanasiou and Sherry C. Fox, "Introduction," in *Archaeodiet in the Greek World: Dietary Reconstruction from Stable Isotope Analysis*, ed. Anastasia Papathanasiou, Michael P. Richards,

brief orientation is necessary since it is not yet well known in the study of Christian origins.[6]

The basis of stable isotope analysis is the process by which human bodies absorb chemicals from the food and beverages consumed by an individual. Bones and teeth preserve some of these chemicals in particular ways, providing a record of certain aspects of a person's diet. Bones regenerate themselves, and thus they record a rolling average of a person's diet.[7] Teeth, on the other hand, develop permanent structures at particular developmental stages and thus create a snapshot of aspects of the diet at a given age.

One of the main chemical elements involved in diet reconstruction is carbon, specifically the measurement of the carbon isotopic ratio $^{12}C/^{13}C$, which is noted as $\delta^{13}C$. The $\delta^{13}C$ measurement yields information about the consumption of marine and terrestrial protein because terrestrial plants absorb CO_2 from the air, while marine plants absorb carbon from water. When humans eat these different types of protein, the carbon isotopes leave different signatures in the skeletal material. The $\delta^{13}C$ measurement also has implications for the *type* of terrestrial plants in the diet because C_3 plants (about 95 percent of earth's plants, including wheat and barley) process CO_2 differently than C_4 plants do (about 3 percent of terrestrial plants, including

---

and Sherry C. Fox, HesperiaSup 49 (Princeton: American School of Classical Studies at Athens, 2015), 1-13, esp. 2-4.

6. For a general overview, see Margaret J. Schoeninger, "Stable Isotope Studies in Human Evolution," *Evolutionary Anthropology* 4 (1995): 83-98, esp. 83-88. For briefer and more recent descriptions, see Tracy L. Prowse et al., "Isotopic Evidence for Age-Related Variation in Diet from Isola Sacra, Italy," *AJPA* 128 (2005): 2-13, esp. 2-4; Oliver E. Craig et al., "Stable Isotopic Evidence for Diet at the Imperial Roman Coastal Site of Velia (1st and 2nd Centuries AD) in Southern Italy," *AJPA* 139 (2009): 572-83, esp. 572-74; and Colleen Cummings, "Meat Consumption in Roman Britain: The Evidence from Stable Isotopes," in *TRAC 2008: Proceedings of the Eighteenth Annual Theoretical Roman Archaeology Conference, Amsterdam 2008*, ed. Mark Driessen et al. (Oxford: Oxbow, 2009): 73-83, esp. 75-78. Regarding oxygen and strontium analysis, see Carolyn Chenery, Hella Eckardt, and Gundula Müldner, "Cosmopolitan Catterick? Isotopic Evidence for Population Mobility on Rome's Northern Frontier," *JArS* 38 (2011): 1525-36, esp. 1527.

7. The length of time for regeneration varies according to the bone and according to age. Researchers often target a particular bone for analysis since adult ribs regenerate completely in about ten years, while long bones take two to three decades. Children's bones regenerate much faster than those of adults.

millet, sorghum, and some grasses), and thus these types of plants also leave different chemical signatures in a skeleton after they are consumed.

The other main element in diet reconstruction is the nitrogen isotopic ratio $^{14}N/^{15}N$, recorded as $\delta^{15}N$. This measurement is used especially to distinguish relative amounts of plants and animals consumed as food. This is possible because most nitrogen in the diet comes ultimately from bacterial activity in the soil, which is then absorbed into a plant. When a human (or animal) eats the plants, the nitrogen is processed in a way that depletes the ^{14}N isotope more than the ^{15}N isotope, and this differential increases the $\delta^{15}N$.

The nitrogen isotopic ratio can also distinguish types of animals and fish consumed because the isotopic ratio is different in plants (nitrogen processed mostly from the soil), in herbivores (nitrogen processed a second time), and in carnivores (nitrogen processed a third time). These differences reflect a hierarchy referred to as trophic levels.

> Level 1. Primary producers: make their own food (e.g., plants and algae).
> Level 2. Primary consumers: herbivores that consume plants.
> Level 3. Secondary consumers: carnivores that eat herbivores.
> Level 4. Tertiary consumers: carnivores that eat carnivores.
> Level 5. Apex predators: eaten by no one.

So a level 2 individual who eats plants will have different $\delta^{15}N$ than one who eats level 3 or level 4 consumers. In this way, the $\delta^{15}N$ present in human osteological material reflects the kinds of animals and fish consumed, according to the place of those animals in the trophic levels.

With that all-too-brief overview, we can begin to consider the reconstruction of ancient diets and the possible connections to inequality. As I have looked at the secondary literature on Roman imperial diet reconstruction and consulted specialists, I have been both fascinated and perplexed by these possibilities. The fascination comes from the potential information we might glean from the ^{12}C, ^{13}C, ^{14}N, and ^{15}N isotopes in skeletal material. But I am also perplexed by the studies because conclusive theories from the patterns in the data sets have not yet emerged. So in this section of the paper I survey findings about diet and inequality from several Roman imperial sites to clarify the shape of the discussions. I proceed thematically.

2.1. Diet, Regionalism, and Imperial Influence

In the course of this survey it is important not to lose sight of the big picture: all of these studies come to the same general conclusion about diet. The average diet for average inhabitants of the Roman Empire was overwhelmingly based on cereals (esp. wheat and barley), which supplied about 70–75 percent of the caloric intake. Olives, wine, vegetables, legumes, and other plants supplied much of the rest of the diet. Meat and fish were supplemental and not a staple.[8] Using stable isotope analysis and archaeological finds, these studies show that the meat came mostly from domesticated animals. Pork was especially popular. Sheep and goat made up about 1/4 to 1/3 of the meat consumption, and beef was a minor part of the meat intake.[9] Such trends, however, could vary according to region and even according to locality. So even though we can begin to see the broad structures of food consumption in the Roman Empire, one crucial feature of that big picture is the local variation.[10]

The reference to pork also reminds us that there were various kinds of regional and ethnic differences in the Roman world, and isotopic analysis helps us begin to see some intersections between imperialism, regionalism, and culture. For example, pork was popular in the Roman diet but less so in Jewish diets. There are signs from places like Sagalassos in Pisidia, however, that one of the effects of Roman control was an increase in the consumption of pork and, to a lesser extent, of beef.[11] Such imperial influences would have been received differently by various social groups, even in specific locales.

Because stable isotope analysis is particularly sensitive to marine/terrestrial distinctions, it gives us more information on the increased consumption of fish as a possible marker of Roman influence in some regions. One of the unexpected results of a diachronic examination of diets in Greece over the course of millennia was that "marine foods have never

---

8. Craig et al., "Site of Velia," 579.

9. Tracy L. Prowse et al., "Isotopic Paleodiet Studies of Skeletons from the Imperial Roman-Age Cemetery of Isola Sacra, Rome, Italy," *JArS* 31 (2004): 261.

10. Gundula Müldner, "Stable Isotopes and Diet: Their Contribution to Romano-British Research," *Antiquity* 87 (2013): 137–49.

11. Brian T. Fuller et al., "Isotopic Reconstruction of Human Diet and Animal Husbandry Practices during the Classical-Hellenistic, Imperial, and Byzantine Periods at Sagalassos, Turkey," *AJPA* 149 (2012): 157–71.

been an important staple in Greek diets, in either prehistoric or historic times,"[12] and so seafood seems to correlate with Roman control. An early study suggesting an increased consumption of fish in the Roman imperial period examined burials from Poundbury Camp on the south coast of Britain. Thirteen pre-Roman burials (Iron Age through first century BCE) had consistently low $δ^{13}C$ and $δ^{15}N$ values with little variation among them, indicating a diet with little variety and minimal marine protein. Thirty-seven burials from the Late Roman period at the same site, however, show much more variety and quantity in the consumption of fish.[13]

The 37 skeletons from Poundbury Camp represent a small sample that is spread over several centuries, so an important study of 105 skeletons (first to third centuries CE) from Isola Sacra helps fill out the picture. Isola Sacra was a major necropolis for Portus, Rome's major harbor at the mouth of the Tiber, and for Ostia. This study showed, among other things, a surprising level of marine consumption at this port city. The level of marine consumption is surprising because the elevated $δ^{15}N$ values from the human remains suggested that inhabitants buried at Isola Sacra had been eating larger fish like tuna or salmon, not just garum sauce made of small, cheaper fish at a lower trophic level.[14] In fact, the average Isola Sacra marine consumption matched levels from the high end of the Poundbury Camp samples.

Not everyone in Isola Sacra ate equally well, however, and I will return to the question of food access below. At this point it is important to note that the Isola Sacra findings provided a benchmark for two more studies published in 2009. One of these dealt with another Italian site—Velia, a regional port city on the southern coast. Examination of 117 skeletons from the first and second centuries CE showed lower marine protein consumption at Velia than at Isola Sacra.[15] A study of the Tunisian port city of Leptiminus, on the other hand, showed more consumption of marine protein

---

12. Anastasia Papathanasiou and Michael P. Richards, "Summary: Patterns in the Carbon and Nitrogen Isotope Data through Time," in Papathanasiou, Richards, and Fox, *Archaeodiet in the Greek World*, 197.

13. Michael P. Richards et al., "Stable Isotope Analysis Reveals Variations in Human Diet at the Poundbury Camp Cemetery Site," *JArS* 25 (1998): 1247–52. Similar trends have since been noted across Roman imperial Britain, with more diet diversity in urbanized areas; Müldner, "Stable Isotopes and Diet," 139–43.

14. Prowse et al., "Paleodiet Studies," 267–68.

15. Craig et al., "Site of Velia," 581.

than at Isola Sacra. The Leptiminus study involved skeletal material from 99 individuals in four cemeteries spread across four centuries (second to fifth centuries CE), and so there is less temporal specificity. But overall, as at Isola Sacra, the heightened marine consumption at Leptiminus came from higher trophic level fish and not from smaller fish found in garum.[16]

Data from Roman Ephesus reveal a different pattern, which is as yet unexplained. We would expect significant consumption of marine protein at Ephesus because it was a major harbor, the capital of the most prestigious Roman province, and one of the largest cities in the empire. An examination of fifty-three Ephesian individuals from the second and third centuries CE, however, showed depleted $\delta^{15}N$ values, most likely due to low intake of fish.[17]

The reasons for these different levels of consumption are matters of debate. Was the increased overall consumption of fish a direct adoption of Roman status markers, that is, eating fish because Romans did? Or was the connection less direct? Maybe the evolving imperial economy increased employment in the fishing and transport industries, which gave people greater access to fish in this way. Those are difficult questions, but questions one can now consider as a result of these isotopic studies.

2.2. Gender

Another important question is whether stable isotope analysis demonstrates unequal access to food for women and men. Can we see patriarchy at work in the distribution of protein? The results so far are mixed. The most provocative study is a follow-up on the Isola Sacra materials that argued that women were disadvantaged with respect to dietary protein. The remains of 105 individuals allowed estimation of sex and age at death for 80 individuals. When placed into age groups,[18] there was a small but

---

16. Anne Keenleyside et al., "Stable Isotopic Evidence for Diet in a Roman and Late Roman Population from Leptiminus, Tunisia," *JArS* 36 (2009): 59.

17. Sandra Lösch et al., "Stable Isotope and Trace Element Studies on Gladiators and Contemporary Romans from Ephesus (Turkey, 2nd and 3rd Ct. AD): Implications for Differences in Diet," *PLOS ONE* 9.10 (2014): 1–17.

18. The age groups were: fifteen–thirty years, thirty–forty-five years, and over forty-five years of age.

statistically significant difference: higher $δ^{15}N$ values suggest that the men in each age group had better access to protein than did the women.[19]

Other studies have been less confident in making such assertions about food and gender. The study of Leptiminus, for example, found no significant differences in diet between women and men among their ninety-nine individuals.[20] Another study that found no evidence for unequal food access according to gender was based on human remains from two suburban cemeteries outside Rome.[21] Likewise, the Ephesian study mentioned above found no significant differences in diet between gladiators, nongladiator males, females, and infants.[22]

Two other studies, however, found ambiguous dietary differences according to sex. At the south Italian port of Velia, men consumed higher trophic levels than did women, but the differences all come from immigrant males, and so the statistical differences at Velia may be due to culture more than to gender.[23] Another study from Britain published in 2012 detected slightly higher $δ^{13}C$ readings among men of the imperial and late Roman periods at Glevum (modern Gloucester, on the western coast of Britain). The men had higher $δ^{13}C$ values than the women and similar $δ^{15}N$ values, suggesting that the men had access to more terrestrial protein-rich foods than did the women. But the authors think this difference might also be due to immigration,[24] for Glevum became a colony for retired military veterans in the late first century CE, and an earlier study of the site showed a correlation between immigrants and higher $δ^{13}C$ values.[25] So the better terrestrial protein for men at Glevum might be chemical signatures from their military diets.

---

19. Prowse et al. "Age-Related Variation," 6–7.
20. Keenleyside et al., "Diet," 60.
21. Kristina Killgrove and Robert H. Tykot, "Food for Rome: A Stable Isotope Investigation of Diet in the Imperial Period (1st–3rd Centuries AD)," *Journal of Anthropological Archaeology* 32 (2013): 28–38.
22. Lösch et al. "Stable Isotope and Trace Element Studies," 9–13. For an exception related to the diet of these gladiators, see the section on "Occupation" below.
23. Craig et al., "Site of Velia," 572–83.
24. Christina Cheung, Hannes Schroeder, and Robert E. M. Hedges, "Diet, Social Differentiation and Cultural Change in Roman Britain: New Isotopic Evidence from Gloucestershire," *Archaeology and Anthropological Sciences* 4 (2012): 70–71.
25. Carolyn Chenery et al., "Strontium and Stable Isotope Evidence for Diet and Mobility in Roman Gloucester, UK," *JArS* 37 (2010): 157–59.

On gender and diet, then, the jury is still out. Some studies are finding significant differences for women and men and others are not. Those that have found differences have also highlighted several factors that complicate interpretation.

2.3. Age

The Isola Sacra findings related to gender raised another issue: can we isolate differences in diet according to age? The authors of that study found that the differences between women and men decreased as individuals grew older, but they could not determine why the protein gap decreased with age. There appear to be two possibilities. One possibility is that diets changed over the life cycle: perhaps status increased as women and men grew older, and so their access to better food improved. The other possibility is that the diets did not change. If this is the case, then the people who survived into old age tended to be those who had eaten more protein throughout their lives.[26] Meanwhile, the studies of Velia and Leptiminus found no significant dietary differences among adults according to age.[27]

More often, when studies have noted diet differences according to age, it has been between adults and subadults (rather than between adult age groups). The same Isola Sacra study examined burials before the age of fifteen and found low values of both $\delta^{13}C$ and $\delta^{15}N$. This suggests that these subadults were eating almost all plants and very little meat, with less olive oil and wine than adults. In the late teen age groups, the subadult diets converged with those of adults.[28]

Weaning provided different nourishment for most children in the first months or years of life, but only a few isotopic analyses for the Roman period have been devoted to this topic. The basis for such analysis is the observation that the consumption of breast milk has effects similar to those of eating higher trophic level foods, so that the infant's $\delta^{15}N$ value is higher than that of the mother.[29] Kwok and Keenleyside used materials from Apollonia Pontica on the Black Sea Coast (modern Bulgaria) from

---

26. Prowse et al., "Age-Related Variation," 10–11.
27. Craig et al., "Site of Velia"; Keenleyside et al., "Diet."
28. Prowse et al., "Age-Related Variation," 10. Since these subadults are the ones who did not survive into adulthood, it is possible that their diets were somewhat less healthy than the norm for their age cohort.
29. Brian T. Fuller et al., "Detection of Breastfeeding and Weaning in Modern

the fifth to third centuries BCE to examine these issues. They combined stable isotope, paleopathological, archaeological, and textual analysis, and concluded that for classical period Apollonia, infants showed signs that weaning began around six months of age and ended between the ages of two to four years, which matches literary instructions in Greek and Roman medical texts. Their findings for diet during and after weaning line up well with the results from Ostia: weaning foods were mostly dairy products and cereals, and after weaning, children still consumed dairy, cereals, fruits, and vegetables, but relatively little meat.[30]

Findings from Leptiminus also detected a difference for children under the age of three. These infants had a higher $\delta^{13}C$ and $\delta^{15}N$ compared to the mean value for adult females, but the children's isotopic levels came down into the normal range around age three. The authors concluded that the early elevated $\delta^{13}C$ and $\delta^{15}N$ in infants was due to breastfeeding.[31]

Thus a general pattern in the studies is emerging, although one that varies greatly among individuals. Infant diets were affected primarily by breast milk. Normally, weaning began in the first year of life and was completed around three years of age. Children tended to have a lower protein diet than adults until late in the second decade of life.

2.4. Migration

Analysis of oxygen isotopes in tooth enamel allows specialists to deduce conclusions about migration. Such calculations are possible because local

---

Human Infants with Carbon and Nitrogen Stable Isotope Ratios," *AJPA* 129 (2006): 279–93. I thank Sandra Garvie-Lok for this reference.

30. Cynthia S. Kwok and Anne Keenleyside, "Stable Isotope Evidence for Infant Feeding Practices in the Greek Colony of Apollonia Pontica," in Papathanasiou, Richards, and Fox, *Archaeodiet in the Greek World*, 147–70.

31. Other isotopic studies have shown that the weaning process began around the age of six months and usually ended around age three: Keenleyside et al., "Diet," 60. The remains of a two-year-old from Rome (third to fifth centuries CE) shows similar heightened $\delta^{15}N$ and $\delta^{13}C$ measurements; see Rutgers et al., "Early Christian Catacombs." Another study also suggested that enriched oxygen isotopic ratios ($\delta^{18}O$) in tooth enamel probably reflects breastfeeding; see Tracy L. Prowse et al., "Stable Isotope and Mitochondrial DNA Evidence for Geographic Origins on a Roman Estate at Vagnari (Italy)," in *Roman Diasporas: Archaeological Approaches to Mobility and Diversity in the Roman Empire*, ed. Hella Eckardt, JRASup 78 (Portsmouth, RI: Journal of Roman Archaeology, 2010), 175–97.

water is a major source of oxygen in the body through the consumption of beverages and food. The significant measurement here is $\delta^{18}O$ ($=^{18}O/^{16}O$). The $\delta^{18}O$ of local water varies according to rainfall, temperature, humidity, elevation, and distance from the coast,[32] and this isotopic signature determines the composition of the oxygen in body tissue and in teeth. The $\delta^{18}O$ measurement in skeletal remains should reflect the isotopic ratio of local water if an individual consumed local water for several years before death, because bones continually rebuild themselves.

Teeth, on the other hand, create permanent enamel at a specific age that preserves oxygen isotopes, and this yields clues about migration. If the $\delta^{18}O$ in early teeth does not match the $\delta^{18}O$ of the local water, the individual lived somewhere else when the tooth formed. The most useful teeth in this regard are first permanent molars (crown formed by 2.5–3 years of age), second permanent molars (formed between 2.5 and 8 years of age), third molars (begins forming at ages 7–12 and is complete between 10 and 17.5 years of age), and deciduous teeth (formed before birth but replaced by permanent teeth).[33]

The results from such methods indicate the variegated character of migration in the empire.[34] Researchers working with the Isola Sacra skeletal material (first to third centuries CE) found that one-third of the individuals did not grow up in the region around Rome, reflecting perhaps the need for labor at this busy international harbor.[35] Another study analyzed individuals from 76 burials at the Roman village at Vagnari in southern Italy. Here twenty-three individuals had molars suitable for analysis, and the results showed that 26 percent of the individuals (six out of twenty-three) came from elsewhere. Three of the six individuals had readings suggesting that they grew up further inland at a higher elevation, but the other three were probably raised further away, perhaps elsewhere in the Mediterranean region.[36]

---

32. Kristina Killgrove, "Identifying Immigrants to Imperial Rome Using Strontium Isotope Analysis," in Eckhardt, *Roman Diasporas*, 162.

33. For technical descriptions and discussions, see Tracy L. Prowse et al., "Isotopic Evidence for Age-Related Immigration to Imperial Rome," *AJPA* 132 (2007): 510–14; Prowse et al., "Stable Isotope and Mitochondrial DNA," 179–81.

34. Killgrove ("Identifying Immigrants to Imperial Rome," 157–74) laid out theoretical considerations regarding types of migration and factors at work in the relocation of people.

35. Prowse et al., "Age-Related Immigration," 510–19.

36. Prowse et al., "Roman Estate at Vagnari," 184–85.

A third study used strontium isotopic ratios ($^{87}Sr/^{86}Sr$) in tooth enamel to examine samples from nonelite cemeteries in Rome itself.[37] This research showed that only about 7 percent of the individuals (7/105) were not local: a male about age fifteen; an adolescent age eleven–thirteen, sex unknown; another adolescent age fourteen–sixteen, sex unknown; a child age seven–nine, sex unknown; a male in his thirties; a male in his forties; and a male in his fifties. Moreover, it appears that these were short-distance immigrants, perhaps part of a rural-to-urban movement that drew individuals to the imperial capital.

Other migration studies have used both $\delta^{18}O$ and $^{87}Sr/^{86}Sr$. One such study from Britain reveals a provincial pattern of mixed local and distant immigration. Here a late Roman cemetery from a regional capital in southern England (modern Winchester) yielded forty individuals suitable for such analysis. Twenty-one had oxygen and strontium signatures consistent with a childhood at Winchester and eight others had strontium signatures outside the Winchester range but a $\delta^{18}O$ consistent with a childhood in the British Isles. Thus, at least 25 percent of the individuals (11/40) appear to have come from outside Britain, perhaps as far as the Hungarian Basin and the Southern Mediterranean.[38]

2.5. Occupation

Occupational differences are difficult to determine through analyses based on diet reconstruction. It is sometimes possible to suggest vocation based on types of trauma to bones or on signs of muscle movement that wears bones, but the connection of diet and occupation is usually indirect and too subtle for isotopic studies at this time.

One exception has already been mentioned above: the gladiators from Ephesus. In this case, there was already evidence suggesting the individuals' occupation: numerous examples of trauma consistent with gladiatorial weapons and simple burial near the stadium. This led investigators to pursue other isotopic evidence, including the presence of strontium and calcium. They calculated the strontium/calcium ratio, which should reflect

---

37. Killgrove, "Identifying Immigrants." Strontium isotopes in the human body are related to the composition of local bedrock and other distinctive geological features. Strontium enters the local water supply through erosion and runoff.

38. Hella Eckardt et al., "Oxygen and Strontium Isotope Evidence for Mobility in Roman Winchester," *JArS* 36 (2009): 2816–25.

the primary source of calcium for an individual, and found that the Sr/Ca ratio was much higher in the suspected gladiators than in the general population. This would be consistent with literary sources that mention an ash drink that was part of a gladiator's regimen (Pliny the Elder, *Nat.* 36.69). So the isotopic evidence confirmed an occupation that was suspected from other evidence.[39]

The military is another occupation that affects one's diet, but again the connection is normally not strong enough to be detected from isotopic analysis without other lines of argument. The burials at Glevum (Gloucestershire, Britain) mentioned above provide an example. Glevum was founded as a Roman fort in the mid-first century CE and became a settlement location for retired veterans late in that same century. The isotopic analysis of skeletal material from first to fifth century burials indicated a different diet for males, and so the known military presence provided a possible explanation that the dietary distinctions were due to the military service of the men.[40] Analysis of burials at York (northern Britain) yielded similar conclusions. In this study, forty-six of eighty individuals in one cemetery had been decapitated. Analysis of carbon, nitrogen, oxygen, and strontium isotopes revealed such diversity of diet that an old theory was disproved, so that the headless burial custom can no longer be explained by similar geographic origins of the deceased. The best explanation now seems to be that the diverse diets of the beheaded individuals can be explained as a function of the military presence—the soldiers who came from many places were brought together in life by the military and in death by a funerary ritual that is not yet well understood.[41]

Thus, stable isotope analysis and diet reconstruction tends to provide secondary evidence for the professions and occupations of individuals.[42] It

---

39. Lösch et al., "Stable Isotope and Trace Element Studies," 13–14.

40. Cheung et al., "New Isotopic Evidence from Gloucestershire." Other studies that focus on diet and mobility tend to confirm this general reconstruction; e.g., Müldner, "Stable Isotopes and Diet."

41. Gundula Müldner, Carolyn Chenery, and Hella Eckardt, "The 'Headless Romans': Multi-Isotope Investigations of an Unusual Burial Ground from Roman Britain," *JArS* 38 (2011): 280–90.

42. Another example is a study that compared skeletal materials from Isola Sacra and from Velia and argued that skeletal signs of external auricular exostosis, location near the sea, and a diet rich in seafood suggested an occupation related to fishing; F. Crowe et al., "Water-Related Occupations and Diet in Two Roman Coastal Communi-

does not normally establish the occupations of individuals without other lines of evidence.

2.6. Burial Contexts and Socioeconomic Status

One unexpected finding in the secondary literature has to do with burial contexts. One would expect that people buried in more expensive tombs with more expensive grave goods would also exhibit signs of having had a more expensive diet in life. But this has only been established at a few sites, three of which I mention here. The Poundbury Camp burials had a good deal of variety in burial contexts, including stone cist graves, wooden coffins, wooden coffins with lead lining, and mausolea. When the diet evidence was plotted according to burial context, there was a clear correlation between better diet and more expensive burials in mausolea and/or lead-lined coffins.[43]

Researchers who examined the Glevum burials found no dietary differences between those buried in coffins and those who were not, nor was there any correlation between diet and amount of grave goods. One interesting difference did emerge, however. The Glevum burials included one mass grave with the remains of seven individuals, perhaps related to an epidemic or other catastrophic event. The individuals in the mass grave had poorer diets than individuals who were inhumed singly, and the authors speculated that the mass grave may have been filled by individuals with lower socioeconomic status.[44]

A recent study on suburban cemeteries near Rome provides some clearer evidence for class-based dietary differences. One of the cemeteries (Casal Bertone) included both a mausoleum and a necropolis with tile burials. In this case the higher $\delta^{13}C$ for 24 individuals from the necropolis suggests they consumed more millet—perceived in antiquity as a lower-status grain—than did the twelve individuals from the mausoleum.[45]

---

ties (Italy, First to Third Century AD): Correlation between Stable Carbon and Nitrogen Isotope Values and Auricular Exostosis Prevalence," *AJPA* 142 (2010): 355–66.

43. Richards et al., "Poundbury Camp," 1250.
44. Cheung et al., "Diet, Social Differentiation and Cultural Change," 69–70.
45. Killgrove and Tykot, "Food for Rome," 29, 36. This isotopic ratio was based on analysis of skeletal apatite (inorganic minerals in the bone). The other $\delta^{13}C$ measurements in this survey are based on collagen (protein in the bone).

A fourth study might support the previous three, not by finding diversity of burial practices in an economically stratified community but rather by noting a unified practice in an economically homogeneous population. The excavations at Vagnari uncovered what appears to be an imperial estate, populated mostly by workers from this locale (as discussed above, six of twenty-three individuals were not from the village, but three of the six could have been born at higher elevations nearby). In this relatively homogenous rural setting, inexpensive roof tile burials with modest grave goods were the norm, either with the tiles forming an inverted *V* over the deceased or with tiles laid flat over the deceased and a funnel for libations. No differences were detected between the burials of locals and those of immigrants.[46]

Other Mediterranean sites, on the other hand, provide no socioeconomic correlations for burial distinctions. The Velia materials from southern Italy manifest no connections between types of burials and the diet of those buried there, but it should be noted that the Velia sample included no high-end mausoleum burials at all.[47] The Leptiminus study identified three types of coffins and three categories of tomb markers in that north African port city but found no clear correlation with diet.[48]

So the economic implications of burial practices clearly require more work since commemoration of the dead involved several other considerations such as ethnicity, kinship, geographic origins, and so on. For example, Killgrove and Tykot point out two difficulties associated with burial in a mausoleum. One complication is that wealthy families often included their slaves and freedpersons in the family mausoleum, which would mitigate the expected signs of a richer diet. A second complication is that in some cases one could secure burial in a mausoleum with a relatively inexpensive *collegium* membership.[49]

---

46. Prowse et al., "Stable Isotope and Mitochondrial DNA," 178, 189.

47. Craig et al., "Site of Velia," 580.

48. Keenleyside et al., "Diet," 58, 60–61. A study of twenty-two individuals in the Christian St. Calixtus Catacomb of Rome from the third to fifth centuries found no dietary differences between those buried in the less expensive loculi and those buried in cubicula; Rutgers et al., "Early Christian Catacombs," 1127–34. That study attempted to reach conclusions about the Christian population but did so with almost no comparative data and without defining crucial terms like *poor* and *poverty*. The study also contains misunderstandings of the secondary literature on early Christianity.

49. Killgrove and Tykot, "Food for Rome," 36. In addition, Alan Cadwallader

2.7. Urban/Rural

One final theme in these studies was the comparison of urban and rural diets. In order to address this issue, the Isola Sacra team compared their results with fourteen burials from a rural salvage excavation in the area. The results from the rural burials fell into two clusters. One cluster yielded dietary findings similar to those from Isola Sacra, while the other cluster produced findings of a lower-quality diet. The reason for the difference in the rural burials is unclear. Were some of the rural inhabitants employed at Isola Sacra and therefore they had a similar diet? Or do the two clusters simply reflect stratification within the rural community?[50]

The study of suburban cemeteries near Rome also found differences along these lines. The investigators concluded that the individuals buried in the cemetery 12 km from the city walls relied more on millet than did the people buried 1.5 km from the walls.[51]

A third study to address urban and rural diets suggests that rural stratification was much narrower than urban stratification. The Gloucestershire study was designed specifically to compare diet evidence from the urban center of Glevum with diet evidence from nearby rural cemeteries. The number of rural burials is greater than the Isola Sacra sample (forty-six individuals rather than fourteen), but the time span is also greater than at Isola Sacra (first through fifth centuries CE rather than second and third centuries). The Gloucestershire study, however, was able to establish that even though rural areas can be distinguished from each other with respect to their diets, these rural diets were still much more uniform and restricted. Both urban and rural areas lived mostly on terrestrial plant resources, but the urban center exhibited slightly elevated $\delta^{13}C$ and $\delta^{15}N$ values, indicating the city's isotopically enriched diet in comparison to its hinterland.

---

noted that the numerous warnings about fines for the reuse of funerary monuments suggest another way in which the remains found in a tomb might not reflect the material resources needed to construct that tomb (personal communication). In some cases, however, careful excavation might be able to detect such reuse.

50. Prowse et al., "Paleodiet Studies," 263–66, 270–71.
51. Killgrove and Tykot, "Food for Rome," 36.

3. Isotopes and Christian Origins

In this paper I have surveyed some recent findings about diet in the Roman world based on stable isotope analysis. In some ways, the findings are not remarkable. They demonstrate that a normal diet in the Roman world consisted mostly of cereals, along with olives, wine, legumes, and vegetables. Meat was a supplement, with tastes leaning toward pork and fish in the Roman period. What is surprising in these studies—to me at least—is that we see a level of radical specificity that allows us to begin to explore questions of inequality related to an individual's regional origins, gender, age, occupation, status, and urbanity.

By way of contrast, it is striking how little importance nutrition and food have been granted in early Christian studies. Dennis's work on dining rituals like the Lord's Supper and studies of associations' meals provides exceptions to this, as do discussions about sacrificial food and Jewish purity laws. These sorts of studies challenged the idealist, nonmaterial orientation of the discipline by relating religion to ritual and food. Stable isotope analysis allows us to take Dennis's concerns further by exploring the material importance of the everyday, nonritual consumption of food for the study of Christian origins. Once we start thinking about this absence of average food in our studies, we see that the study of Christian origins has been more about ideas than about materiality, and more about theology than about the exchanges (of goods, services, and people) that characterize community life. So I conclude by suggesting four avenues for investigation in early Christian studies that might grow out of this kind of work.

First, we could examine redistributions of food in early church rituals. One of the most important was the Lord's Supper or eucharistic meal. In this ritual meal, food played a crucial role in mediating religious health. But the churches included mixed populations, and so we should ask how food access rules played out in terms of material sustenance and social hierarchies. Were dominant inequalities maintained or challenged in this ritual context? Were some factors like gender and slave status maintained, while others such as ethnicity were challenged? Was it harder to break rules about commensality of Jews and gentiles than of men and women? For later periods, we might also consider the possible nutritional consequences of the termination of animal sacrifice. Did the decline of this ubiquitous ritual affect access to protein at various levels of the social hierarchy?

Second, we could examine food charity and the nonritual distribution of food. These often involve moral instruction and evince differing Christian ideologies to explain the responsibility to share food with those who are hungry. For example, Jas 2:14–17 used food charity in an argument with other followers of Jesus over the relation of faith to practice. Didache 13, on the other hand, advocated food charity for prophets as a kind of firstfruits offering to those who served the assemblies with divine oracles. The Shepherd of Hermas (Sim. 5.3.7), however, advocated food charity so that the poor could pray for the wealthy donors (see also Herm. Sim. 2.1–10). Food charity for believing widows provides yet another example. The practice is known from Acts 6, where food redistribution generates a challenge to ethnic hierarchies, and from 1 Tim 5:1–16, where ideologies of family, sexuality, religious practice, gender, and honor are invoked. In all these different Christian ideological contexts food access is a crucial feature of religious practice, but for different reasons.

Third, we could look at the discursive deployment of hunger and the symbolic potential of nourishment in the texts. How does the physical experience of hunger become a tool of religious, social, political, and economic strategy? One avenue into this topic would be to look at the way that foods appear as metaphors in our texts. A quick search of the New Testament and Apostolic Fathers suggests that sheep are a rich resource for metaphorical work, and that bread is almost ubiquitous—not as actual bread that can be eaten but as symbolic bread that becomes food for thought and for action. Fish also appear in a variety of ways, both in text and in early Christian art.[52] But while bread, sheep, and fish appear frequently in our texts, pigs and goats[53] rarely serve as metaphors.

Fourth, we could look at the narrative significance of food and hunger in our literature. A glance at the gospel tradition or the Acts of the Apostles, for example, suggests several points. In the early chapters of Acts, the sharing of food is a sign of new community among the Jerusalem believ-

---

52. Note the appearance of fish in miracle stories (e.g., Mark 6:35–44 // Matt 14:16–21 // Luke 9:12–17 // John 6:8–14; and John 21:1–14, which quickly shifts to a sheep metaphor for the disciples' work), and the use of fishing as a metaphor for the mission of Jesus's disciples that explains both their abandonment of that work and their neglect of their families (Mark 1:16–20 // Matt 4:18–22 // Luke 5:9–11). For a discussion of the fish as a nonnarrative image, see Robin Margaret Jensen, *Understanding Early Christian Art* (New York: Routledge, 2000), 46–59.

53. Matt 25:32–33 is an important exception.

ers. Food supply also has political implications in Acts when the role of Herod Agrippa I as a food exporter becomes a crucial issue in his relations with Tyre and Sidon. This leads, according to the story, to divine honors for Herod and then divine judgment on him for accepting such honors (12:20–23). Or late in the text when Paul and his shipmates are trying to ride out a dangerous storm, the eating of food allows Paul to appear as a leader of his fellow prisoners and even of his captors (27:27–37).

To sum up, the reconstruction of ancient diets through stable isotope analysis does more than give us an idea about what average people normally ate. It allows us to think about ancient social discourses in new ways and with new specificity. A critical engagement with these materials also raises questions about disembodied modern, scholarly discourses on religion and Christian origins. The elucidation of ancient discourses and the interrogation of modern scholarly ones through research on the consumption of food have been crucial aspects of Smith's research agenda, and I hope in these ways we will build on his work.

Bibliography

Chenery, Carolyn, Hella Eckardt, and Gundula Müldner. "Cosmopolitan Catterick? Isotopic Evidence for Population Mobility on Rome's Northern Frontier." *JArS* 38 (2011): 1525–36.

Chenery, Carolyn, Gundula Müldner, Jane Evans, Hella Eckardt, and Mary Lewis. "Strontium and Stable Isotope Evidence for Diet and Mobility in Roman Gloucester, UK." *JArS* 37 (2010): 150–63.

Cheung, Christina, Hannes Schroeder, and Robert E. M. Hedges. "Diet, Social Differentiation and Cultural Change in Roman Britain: New Isotopic Evidence from Gloucestershire." *Archaeology and Anthropological Sciences* 4 (2012): 61–73.

Craig, Oliver E., Marco Biazzo, Tamsin C. O'Connell, Peter Garnsey, Cristina Martinez-Labarga, Roberta Lelli, Loretana Salvadei, et al. "Stable Isotopic Evidence for Diet at the Imperial Roman Coastal Site of Velia (1st and 2nd Centuries AD) in Southern Italy." *AJPA* 139 (2009): 572–83.

Crowe, F., A. Sperduti, Tamsin C. O'Connell, O. E. Craig, K. Kirsanow, Paola Germoni, Roberto Macchiarelli, et al. "Water-Related Occupations and Diet in Two Roman Coastal Communities (Italy, First to Third Century AD): Correlation between Stable Carbon and Nitrogen

Isotope Values and Auricular Exostosis Prevalence." *AJPA* 142 (2010): 355–66.
Cummings, Colleen. "Meat Consumption in Roman Britain: The Evidence from Stable Isotopes." Pages 73–83 in *TRAC 2008: Proceedings of the Eighteenth Annual Theoretical Roman Archaeology Conference, Amsterdam 2008*. Edited by Mark Driessen, Stijn Heeren, Joep Hendriks, Fleur Kemmers, and Ronald Visser. Oxford: Oxbow, 2009.
Eckardt, Hella, Carolyn Chenery, P. Booth, Jane Evans, A. Lamb, and Gundula Müldner. "Oxygen and Strontium Isotope Evidence for Mobility in Roman Winchester." *JArS* 36 (2009): 2816–25.
Fuller, Brian T., B. De Cupere, E. Marinova, W. Van Neer, M. Waelkens, and Michael P. Richards. "Isotopic Reconstruction of Human Diet and Animal Husbandry Practices during the Classical-Hellenistic, Imperial, and Byzantine Periods at Sagalassos, Turkey." *AJPA* 149 (2012): 157–71.
Fuller, Brian T., J. L. Fuller, D. A. Harris, and Robert E. M. Hedges. "Detection of Breastfeeding and Weaning in Modern Human Infants with Carbon and Nitrogen Stable Isotope Ratios." *AJPA* 129 (2006): 279–93.
Jensen, Robin Margaret. *Understanding Early Christian Art*. New York: Routledge, 2000.
Keenleyside, Anne, Henry Schwarcz, Lea Stirling, and Nejib Ben Lazreg. "Stable Isotopic Evidence for Diet in a Roman and Late Roman Population from Leptiminus, Tunisia." *JArS* 36 (2009): 51–63.
Killgrove, Kristina. "Identifying Immigrants to Imperial Rome Using Strontium Isotope Analysis." Pages 157–74 in *Roman Diasporas: Archaeological Approaches to Mobility and Diversity in the Roman Empire*. Edited by Hella Eckhardt. JRASup 78. Portsmouth, RI: Journal of Roman Archaeology, 2010.
Killgrove, Kristina, and Robert H. Tykot. "Food for Rome: A Stable Isotope Investigation of Diet in the Imperial Period (1st–3rd Centuries AD)." *Journal of Anthropological Archaeology* 32 (2013): 28–38.
Kwok, Cynthia S., and Anne Keenleyside. "Stable Isotope Evidence for Infant Feeding Practices in the Greek Colony of Apollonia Pontica." Pages 147–70 in *Archaeodiet in the Greek World*. Edited by Anastasia Papathanasiou, Michael P. Richards, and Sherry C. Fox. HesperiaSup 49. Princeton, NJ: American School of Classical Studies at Athens, 2015.
Lösch, Sandra, Negahnaz Moghaddam, Karl Grossschmidt, Daniele U. Risser, and Fabian Kanz. "Stable Isotope and Trace Element Studies

on Gladiators and Contemporary Romans from Ephesus (Turkey, 2nd and 3rd Ct. AD)—Implications for Differences in Diet." *PLOS ONE* 9.10 (2014): 1–17.

Müldner, Gundula. "Stable Isotopes and Diet: Their Contribution to Romano-British Research." *Antiquity* 87 (2013): 137–49.

Müldner, Gundula, Carolyn Ghenery, and Hella Eckardt. "The 'Headless Romans': Multi-Isotope Investigations of an Unusual Burial Ground from Roman Britain." *JArS* 38 (2011): 280–90.

Nongbri, Brent. *Before Religion: A History of a Modern Concept.* New Haven: Yale University Press, 2013.

Papathanasiou, Anastasia, and Sherry C. Fox. Introduction to *Archaeodiet in the Greek World: Dietary Reconstruction from Stable Isotope Analysis.* Edited by Anastasia Papathanasiou, Michael P. Richards, and Sherry C. Fox. HesperiaSup 49. Princeton, NJ: American School of Classical Studies at Athens, 2015.

Papathanasiou, Anastasia, and Michael P. Richards. "Summary: Patterns in the Carbon and Nitrogen Isotope Data through Time." Pages 195–204 in *Archaeodiet in the Greek World: Dietary Reconstruction from Stable Isotope Analysis.* Edited by Anastasia Papathanasiou, Michael P. Richards, and Sherry C. Fox. HesperiaSup 49. Princeton, NJ: American School of Classical Studies at Athens, 2015.

Prowse, Tracy L., Henry P. Schwarcz, Peter Garnsey, Martin Knyf, Roberto Macchiarelli, and Luca Bondioli. "Isotopic Evidence for Age-Related Immigration to Imperial Rome." *AJPA* 132 (2007): 510–19.

Prowse, Tracy L., Henry P. Schwarcz, Shelley R. Saunders, Roberto Macchiarelli, and Luca Bondioli. "Isotopic Evidence for Age-Related Variation in Diet from Isola Sacra, Italy." *AJPA* 128 (2005): 2–13.

———. "Isotopic Paleodiet Studies of Skeletons from the Imperial Roman-Age Cemetery of Isola Sacra, Rome, Italy." *JArS* 31 (2004): 259–72.

———. "Stable Isotope and Mitochondrial DNA Evidence for Geographic Origins on a Roman Estate at Vagnari (Italy)." Pages 175–97 in *Roman Diasporas: Archaeological Approaches to Mobility and Diversity in the Roman Empire.* Edited by Hella Eckhardt. JRASup 78. Portsmouth, RI: Journal of Roman Archaeology, 2010.

Richards, Michael P., Robert E. M. Hedges, T. I. Molleson, and J. C. Vogel. "Stable Isotope Analysis Reveals Variations in Human Diet at the Poundbury Camp Cemetery Site." *JArS* 25 (1998): 1247–52.

Rutgers, L. V., Mark van Strydonck, Mathieu Boudin, and C. van der Linde.

"Early Christian Catacombs of Ancient Rome: New Insights into the Dietary Habits of Rome's Early Christians." *JArS* 36 (2009): 1127–34.

Scheidel, Walter, and Steven J. Friesen. "The Size of the Economy and the Distribution of Income in the Roman Empire." *JRS* 99 (2009): 61–91.

Schoeninger, Margaret J. "Stable Isotope Studies in Human Evolution." *Evolutionary Anthropology* 4 (1995): 83–98.

Smith, Wilfred Cantwell. *The Meaning and End of Religion.* New York: Harper & Row, 1978.

FOOD CRISES IN CORINTH?
REVISITING THE EVIDENCE AND ITS POSSIBLE
IMPLICATIONS IN READING 1 COR 11:17–34

Ma. Marilou S. Ibita

Some scholars link 1 Corinthians to the famine of 51 CE (and the subsequent food crises) by relating it to 1 Cor 7:26 and connecting it with the Lord's Supper discussed in 1 Cor 11:17–34.[1] Peter Garnsey clarifies that *famine* refers to "a critical shortage of essential foodstuffs leading through hunger to starvation and a substantially increased mortality rate in a community or region" while *food shortage* is "a short-term reduction in the

---

1. See Johann Albert Bengel, *Gnomon Novi Testamenti, in quo ex nativa verborum vi simplicitas, profunditas, concinnitas, salubritas sensuum coelestium indicator*, 5th ed. (London: Williams & Norgate, 1862), 591; Allen B. West, ed., *Latin Inscriptions 1896–1926*, vol. 8.2 of *Corinth: Results of Excavations Conducted by the American School of Classical Studies at Athens* (Cambridge: Harvard University Press, 1931), 73 (hereafter IKorinthWest); James Wiseman, "Corinth and Rome I: 228 B.C.–A.D. 267," *ANRW* 7.1:505, echoes West's conclusion. See also Bruce W. Winter, "The Lord's Supper at Corinth: An Alternative Reconstruction," *RTR* 37 (1978): 81; Winter, "Secular and Christian Responses to Corinthian Famines," *TynBul* 40 (1989): 86–106; Winter, *After Paul Left Corinth: The Influence of Secular Ethics and Change* (Grand Rapids: Eerdmans, 2001), 157, 224–25; Victor Paul Furnish, "Corinth in Paul's Time: What Can Archaeology Tell Us?" *BAR* 15.3 (1988): 19; Bradley B. Blue, "The House Church at Corinth and the Lord's Supper: Famine, Food Supply, and the Present Distress," *CTR* 5 (1991): 235–36; David W. J. Gill, "In Search of the Social Elite in the Corinthian Church," *TynBul* 44 (1993): 332–33. See also James D. G. Dunn, *The Theology of Paul the Apostle* (Edinburgh: T&T Clark, 1998), 610 n. 49; Dunn, *1 Corinthians*, NTG (Sheffield: Sheffield Academic, 1995), 78; Anthony C. Thiselton, *The First Epistle to the Corinthians: A Commentary on the Greek Text*, NIGTC (Grand Rapids: Eerdmans, 2000), 4, 852; Barry N. Danylak, "Tiberius Claudius Dinippus and the Food Shortages in Corinth," *TynBul* 59 (2008): 231–70.

amount of available foodstuffs, as indicated by rising prices, popular discontent, [and] hunger, in the worst cases bordering on starvation."[2] He adds, "The boundary between famine and shortage is indistinct.... In the long run, however, the idea of a spectrum or continuum of food crises holds out more promise than the famine/shortage dichotomy. Each food crisis occupies a place on a continuum leading from mild shortage to disastrous famine."[3] This paper critically reevaluates the evidence regarding the alleged food crises in Corinth and explores their potential implications in understanding 1 Cor 11:17–34.

1. Roman Corinth and Its Food Situation

Some scholars, such as C. K. Barrett and Donald Engels, argue that Roman Corinth is infertile or not agriculturally productive.[4] However, other biblical and archaeological scholars differ. James Wiseman discusses Corinth's economy, including the whole of Corinthia, and notes that agriculture ranks first before trade and manufacture.[5] Guy Sanders describes urban Corinth as well-watered, fertile land, an exporter of natural resources and agricultural produce among other things, as well as flanked by two ports that served as significant entrepôts and emporia of the products shipped by other regions from its ports.[6] Sanders also underlines the possibility

---

2. Peter Garnsey, *Famine and Food Supply in the Graeco-Roman World: Responses to Risk and Crisis* (Cambridge: Cambridge University Press, 1988), 6.

3. Ibid.

4. C. K. Barrett, *A Commentary on the First Epistle to the Corinthians*, BNTC (London: Black, 1968), 1; Donald Engels, *Roman Corinth: An Alternative Model for the Classical City* (Chicago: Chicago University Press, 1990), 27–28. Engels holds that there was no cultivation in urban Corinth "except for a few garden plots" (ibid., 28).

5. See James Wiseman, *The Land of the Ancient Corinthians*, SMA 50 (Göteborg: Aström, 1978), 9, 12–13.

6. See Guy D. R. Sanders, "Urban Corinth: An Introduction," in *Urban Religion in Corinth: Interdisciplinary Approaches*, ed. Daniel N. Schowalter and Steven J. Friesen, HTS 53 (Cambridge: Harvard University Press, 2005), 15; Sanders, "Landlords and Tenants: Sharecroppers and Subsistence Farming in Corinthian Historical Context," in *Corinth in Contrast: Studies in Inequality*, ed. Steven J. Friesen, Sarah A. James, and Daniel N. Schowalter, NovTSup 155 (Leiden: Brill, 2013), 120. Robert L. Scranton, *Ancient Corinth: A Guide to the Excavations*, 6th ed. (Athens: American School of Classical Studies at Athens, 1960), 11, mentions that there were "perhaps a few fields for grain" in Corinth. See also Mogens H. Hansen, *Polis: An Introduction to the Ancient Greek City-State* (Oxford: Oxford University Press, 2006), 93. He explains that the ter-

of Corinth producing more high-value crops than staples of subsistence farming as Corinth evolved and the market grew.[7] Sanders expounds on the recent scholarly discussion regarding the centuriation[8] of Corinthian *ager publicus* and suggests an area of about eight hectares per colonist.[9]

The size of Corinth's population is also important in considering its food situation. Based on land centuration between the late second and mid-first century BCE, Mary Walbank and Sanders propose that the population was about 2,000 to 3,000 household heads, or 7,000 to 10,000 inhabitants in Corinth.[10] Since Corinth was the capital and administrative center of the Roman province of Achaia, the city of about 180 hectares was also important for political, economic, religious, and social reasons to the local people who lived "in the surrounding countryside … often in sizable communities."[11]

Even though these scholars argue that the Corinthian population was considerably smaller than some scholars assume,[12] owing to a series of fac-

---

ritory of a polis includes the surrounding area covered by a day's walk, i.e., about 8–10 km².

7. Sanders, "Landlords," 120.

8. See Marinella Pasquinucci, "Centuriation and Roman Land Surveying (Republic through Empire)," in *Encyclopedia of Global Archaeology*, ed. Claire Smith (New York: Springer, 2014), 1275, http://tinyurl.com/SBL4522p: "*Centuriatio* or *limitatio* was a Roman method of land delimitation and division by means of orthogonal and equidistant *limites* (literally, borders). Depending on the local geomorphology, these were roads and/or ditches and defined mostly square, less frequently rectangular, areas of fixed dimensions named *centuriae*; in many cases, each *centuria* was 200 *iugera* (50.4 ha) wide. Centuriation accompanied Roman colonization and provided the new settlement with productive soil, proper infrastructure (roads, ditches, if necessary bridges), and a cadastral frame for allocating land to colonists."

9. Sanders, "Landlords," 117.

10. See Mary E. Hoskins Walbank, "The Foundation and Planning of Early Roman Corinth," *JRA* 10 (1997): 105. Walbank explains further that the case in Corinthia in 1 BCE can be paralleled to its experience in the early twentieth century CE "in that both were agricultural regions which experienced a sudden influx of population and which had one large centre. This suggests that perhaps we should be thinking of the population of the Corinthia as well below number generally cited, and that in the Roman period it may have always been between 20,000 and 50,000" (ibid., 106). See also Sanders, "Landlords," 118–19.

11. Walbank, "Foundation," 130.

12. Engels, *Roman Corinth*, 28 holds that by the second century CE the population of Corinth and its territory was about 100,000, although he nuances his estimate of the city's population as not exceeding 100,000 depending on what is agriculturally

tors Corinth might still have been prone to food crises. Roman Corinth was a fertile land. However, the increased population due to its being a capital and an administrative center of Achaia (which hosts "sizable communities") as well as the possible decrease in agricultural production of subsistence crops due to their replacement by high-value crops raise the question of food adequacy for its people and visitors. The resulting imbalance between food production/supply and consumption would have been worse when there were natural disasters like famine or other food crises affecting the Mediterranean area.[13] This point brings us to the question of the evidence for the alleged famine when Paul was in contact with the Corinthians.

2. Food Crises in Corinth: The Evidence

For those who argue that food crises are part of the background of Paul's Corinthian correspondence, inscriptions, nonbiblical literary evidence, and allusions in the Pauline corpus serve as evidence.

2.1. Inscriptions

The epigraphic evidence includes twenty-six Corinthian Greek and Latin inscriptions of varying size that speak of a *curator annonae*, but only those dedicated to T. Claudius Dinippus dated under Claudius or Nero are relevant for the present study, as I will discuss below.[14] Based on

---

viable. However, based on water supply he posits 80,000 city dwellers and 20,000 in the rest of the territory (ibid., 84). Gill, "Social Elite," 333, based on city size, argues for a population of about 100,000 in Corinth and its territory, while noting that its size would have required food importation and that a sizeable proportion of the people would have suffered in times of food shortage.

13. Peter Garnsey and Richard Saller, *The Roman Empire: Economy, Society and Culture*, 2nd ed. (London: Bloomsbury, 2014), 124, speak of the endemic food shortages in the Mediterranean region. Garnsey, *Famine*, 227–29 enumerates the causes of food crisis: (1) natural causes (harvest failure, grain shipwreck, epidemic disease that limit farmers, and spoilage of grain stocks through flooding); (2) human error, corruption and irresponsibility; and (3) warfare.

14. The Corinthian inscriptions that mention *curator annonae* (or ἐπιμελητὴς εὐθηνίας) are found in different publications and are collated in Danylak, "Dinippus," 236. For the individual inscriptions, see Benjamin D. Meritt, ed., *Greek Inscriptions 1896–1927*, vol. 8.1 of *Corinth: Results of Excavations Conducted by the American School of Classical Studies at Athens* (Cambridge: Harvard University Press, 1931),

contemporary evidence outside Corinth, a *curator annonae* is a person of wealth, "appointed in times of threatened or actual famine," who used his own resources to address the necessities of the city.[15] The *curator annonae* helps by giving corn to the city, giving money for its purchase, and/or by buying local stocks and selling them at a moderate price.[16] Danylak interprets the large number of Corinthian inscriptions that mention a *curator annonae* as follows:

> The concentration of these inscriptions at Corinth can be accounted for in a number of ways including a greater prestige of the office in Corinth, more surviving records, grain supervision combined with other functions in other cities, etc. But the concentration may also reflect the

---

§76 (hereafter IKorinthMeritt) (Cn Cornelius Pulcher: Trajanic period) and §94 (unknown name: probably third quarter of the second century CE); IKorinthWest §83 (C. Rutillus Fuscus?: Claudian period), §§86, 87, 88, 89 and 90 (T. Claudius Dinippus: Claudian–Neronean periods) as well as §91 (unknown name and period); John H. Kent, ed., *The Inscriptions, 1926–1950*, vol. 8.3 of *Corinth: Results of Excavations Conducted by the American School of Classical Studies at Athens* (Princeton: American School of Classical Studies at Athens, 1966) (hereafter IKorinthKent), contains named Latin inscriptions: §§158, 160 (= IKorinthWest §88) and §162 (T. Claudius Dinippus: Claudian–Neronian periods), §164 (M Antonius Achaicus: Vespasianic period), §170 (Antonius Sospes: Trajanic period), and §177 (L Antonius Priscus: unknown period). There are also some clearly recognizable Greek inscriptions; see IKorinthKent §138 (= IKorinthMeritt §76) and §140 (Cn Cornelius Pulcher: Hadrianic period). IKorinthKent §§142 and 143 are probably also Pulcher's. The name in the mid-second century CE Latin inscription §188 is unclear. One Greek inscription, probably from the third quarter of the second century CE (IKorinthKent §127 = IKorinthMeritt §94) attests to another unknown person. The record in Kent's compilation also includes Latin inscriptions of unknown name and period: IKorinthKent §§169, 227, 234, 235, 236, and 238. For a full discussion of Dinippus's cursus, including his service as *curator annonae* in Corinth during the food shortage in 51 CE, see Danylak, "Dinippus," 236–58.

15. See 1KorinthWest, 73; Geoffrey Rickman, *The Corn Supply of Ancient Rome* (Oxford: Clarendon, 1980), 35; Boudewijn Sirks, *Food for Rome: The Legal Structure of the Transportation and Processing of Supplies for the Imperial Distributions in Rome and Constantinople* (Amsterdam: Gieben, 1991), 10–23. For the various methods of grain management in different places in the Roman Empire, see Paul Erdkamp, *The Grain Market in the Roman Empire: A Social, Political and Economic Study* (Cambridge: Cambridge University Press, 2005), 258–316, esp. 270.

16. See Garnsey and Saller, *Roman Empire*, 124; A. H. M. Jones, *The Greek City: From Alexander to Justinian* (Oxford: Clarendon, 1979), 217–18.

prevalence of food shortages in the city during the first and second centuries.[17]

Seven inscriptions honor Tiberius Claudius Dinippus, who held various offices including that of *curator annonae* in Corinth.[18] Three inscriptions follow clearly the general pattern found in the other inscriptions as shown in West's list: §86 [ANNONAE CVRATORI], §87 [AN], §88 [ANNONA], even if in the fourth, West §90, only the letter *A* of Dinippus's office is readable in the fragment.[19] Three clear Dinippus inscriptions are also found in Kent's list §158 [ANNON], §160 [ANNON], and §162 [ANNONAe curATORI].[20]

Based on archaeological and other research, scholars posit that Dinippus most likely served as *curator annonae* during the famine in 51 CE.[21] Danylak's study of Dinippus's career, particularly as *curator annonae*, suggests that even if he was only named once in this office, his service lasted "for the duration of a significant food crisis in Greece, a period of several years," perhaps as long as five years,[22] making his service contemporaneous with Paul's interaction with the Corinthians. Danylak argues that a prolonged situation of food crisis is supported by the epigraphic evidence recording the overwhelming tribute paid by the ten Corinthian tribes to Dinippus.[23]

Evaluating this evidence, it is clear that there was an office of *curator annonae* in Corinth, but the evidence does not permit a conclusion

---

17. Danylak, "Dinippus," 238 n. 29.
18. Ibid., 242.
19. IKorinthWest, 71-76. In IKorinthWest §89 Dinippus's name is not extant, but it preserves [CVRAT] and is authorized from a local senate's decree.
20. IKorinthKent, 76. Three others follow the general pattern of the Dinippus inscription (§§159, 161, and 163), but the reference to being *curator annonae* did not survive in the fragments.
21. See IKorinthWest, 73; Wiseman, "Corinth and Rome," 505. See also Winter, "Lord's Supper," 81; Winter, "Secular and Christian Responses," 86-106; Winter, *After Paul*, 157, 224-25; Blue, "House Church," 235-36; Gill, "Social Elite," 332-33; Dunn, *Theology*, 610 n. 49; Dunn, *1 Corinthians*, 78. Danylak, "Dinippus," 235-69, considers the epigraphic, literary, and numismatic data and concludes that Corinth suffered an acute famine, most likely in 51 CE, and, according to Dinippus's service as *curator annonae*, it could have lasted up to five years. For more on this topic, see the discussion of the nonbiblical literary evidence below.
22. See Danylak, "Dinippus," 258, 270.
23. See ibid., 270.

that his activities were exactly the same as in Rome and elsewhere in the Roman Empire.[24] Erdkamp speaks of various offices in charge of ensuring food supply in various places and at various times in the Roman Empire.[25] Sanders also cautions against the application of general data (such as economic information) from elsewhere in the Roman Empire to one particular place such as Corinth.[26] Thus, while it is highly likely that Corinth was no different from the rest of the Roman empire, one should question if the *curator annonae* totally replicated identical functions in Corinth and, if so, to what extent Dinippus's help was responsive to the needs of those who lived at or below subsistence level whose hunger problems intensified during the food crises.[27]

2.2. Nonbiblical Literary Evidence

There is nonbiblical literary evidence concerning the food crises during the Claudian era. Tacitus (*Ann.* 12.43), Suetonius (*Claud.* 18.2), and Paulus Orosius (*Hist. adv. Paganos* 7.6.17) speak of the famine in 51 CE that affected Rome and of how Claudius was treated violently by the rioting crowd.[28] According to Tacitus the famine was due to a shortage of corn, while Suetonius writes that it was probably caused by *assiduae sterilitates* (successive bad harvests). Yet the literary contexts of these writings do not mention the same famine affecting Greece. Thus, arguing based on citations from Tacitus and Suetonius, West's claim about a famine in Achaia when Dinippus served as *curator annonae* is hard to validate.[29]

Eusebius wrote about a large famine in *Greece* that a *modius* of grain sold for six *didrachmas*, λιμοῦ κατὰ τὴν Ἑλλάδα γεγονότος μεγάλου, ὁ τοῦ σίτου μόδιος ἐξ διδράχμων ἐπράθη.[30] For Danylak, Eusebius's mention of

---

24. See Garnsey and Saller, *Roman Empire*, 124. See also Jones, *Greek City*, 217–18.
25. Erdkamp, *Grain Market*, 270.
26. See Sanders, "Landlords," 121.
27. See Winter, "Secular and Christian Responses," 100, who notes that Dinippus's activities to address the famine are unknown, but the number of inscriptions suggests the success of his intervention.
28. See also the references in n. 21 above.
29. IKorinthWest, 73: "It is well known that the province of Achaia experienced a severe famine in the reign of Claudius, one that seriously affected Rome also."
30. See Eusebius of Caesarea, *Eusebi chronicorum libri duo*, ed. Alfred Schoene, 2 vols. (Berlin: Weidmann, 1866–1875), 2:152. See also IKorinthWest, 73; Wiseman, "Corinth and Rome," 505; Danylak, "Dinippus," 248.

the very high cost of grain suggests that the food crises could have been prolonged.³¹ However, if Eusebius is referring to the Roman famine in 51, it is not easy to tie it with Tacitus's account, which informs us that "it was only because of the great bounty of the gods and the mildness of the winter that relief was brought to a desperate situation" (*Ann.* 12.43 [Yardley]). Nonetheless, there were other food shortages in the Claudian era around 52–53 CE according to Dio Cassius (*Hist. rom.* 41.10).³² Thus, the famine in 51 CE and the succeeding food shortage around 52–53 CE could be considered collectively as food crises with (probably cumulative) portentous effects.

While this literary evidence suggests widespread food crises in the reign of Claudius, we are faced with a lack of more concrete nonbiblical literary evidence related specifically to Corinth.³³ Peter Garnsey also speaks of "food shortage which affected numerous states in Greece and elsewhere in the 40s and in the 50s" but does not cite Corinth or Achaia as an example.³⁴ Even if Corinth is the capital of Achaia and could have been using its position and resources to get it through any food shortage that was hitting the Mediterranean generally, we have no nonbiblical literary evidence that confirms this suggestion. Thus, the general treatment of food crises in these documents lacks specific reference to Corinth and warns us to qualify any assertion about Corinth's actual experience within the time span of Paul's correspondence with the Corinthians (53–54 CE).³⁵

---

31. See Danylak, "Dinippus," 250, who explains that high food prices could indicate a chronic food shortage, as in the cases of Erythrae, Olbia, and Rev 6:6. He concludes, "Thus not only was the food crisis in Corinth a relatively intense one, it may also have represented a protracted situation."

32. See also Suetonius, *Claud.* 18.1–2, who includes another known food shortage under Claudius's reign in 53 CE.

33. Winter, "Secular and Christian Responses," 90, recognizes Suetonius's lack of a specific place in talking about the Claudian-era food shortages.

34. Garnsey, *Famine*, 261.

35. See Ben Witherington III, *Conflict and Community in Corinth: A Socio-rhetorical Commentary on 1 Corinthians* (Grand Rapids: Eerdmans, 1995), 73, favors "early in 53 or 54"; Barrett, *First Epistle*, 5, opines that it could have been in "the early months of 54, or possibly towards the end of 53." For a discussion of the dating of 1 Corinthians, see Thiselton, *First Corinthians*, 29–32.

2.3 Pauline Allusions?

Do any texts from the Pauline corpus relate to food crises in Corinth?[36] Some scholars proposed that Paul could be referring to the famine at the time of Claudius when he writes about the "present distress" (τὴν ἐνεστῶσαν ἀνάγκην; 1 Cor 7:26).[37] The word ἀνάγκη expresses "a state of distress or trouble, *distress, calamity, pressure,*"[38] a "necessity,"[39] or an "affliction."[40] According to August Strobel, "1 Cor 7:26 gives pointed expression to belief in the *present* (eschatological) time of distress."[41] If the letter was written at the time of the famine, is it possible that Paul's use of ἀνάγκη in this context is an allusion to the famine? However, Paul is not very precise,[42] nor does he explicitly refer to λιμός in 1 Corinthians.[43]

In enumerating the apostolic trials he underwent, Paul writes to the Corinthians ἐν λιμῷ καὶ δίψει, ἐν νηστείαις πολλάκις (2 Cor 11:27).[44] ἐν

---

36. Danylak, "Dinippus," 232: "The letter of 1 Corinthians is replete with vocabulary of 'food', 'eating', 'hungering', 'eating together', 'consumption', and 'dining.'"

37. For those who relate 1 Cor 7:26 to the famine at the time of Claudius, see Bengel, *Gnomon*, 591; Winter, "Secular and Christian Responses," 92–93; Blue, "House Church," 236–37; Thiselton, *First Corinthians*, 573; Danylak, "Dinippus," 233–34. Regarding the question whether τὴν ἐνεστῶσαν ἀνάγκην in 1 Cor 7:26 should be translated as "impending" or "present" crisis/distress, see Gordon D. Fee, *The First Epistle to the Corinthians*, NICNT (Grand Rapids: Eerdmans, 1987), 565, who holds that ἐνεστῶσαν is the perfect participle of ἐνίστημι, which could indicate something the Corinthians were already experiencing. He also refers to the possible relationship of 1 Cor 11:30 with 7:26.

38. BDAG, s.v. "ἀνάγκη."
39. LSJ, s.v. "ἀνάγκη."
40. W. Grundmann, "ἀνάγκη," TDNT 1:346.
41. A. Strobel, "ἀνάγκη," EDNT 1:78.
42. Paul uses ἀνάγκη in the sense of "necessity" in Rom 13:5 and 1 Cor 9:16, and in the sense of "distress" in 1 Thess 3:7.
43. See Garnsey, *Famine*, 18–19, who lists related words in Greek (*limos/limottein, sitodeia, spanis, aporia, endeia,* and *kairos*) and in Latin (*fames, inopia, penuria, caritas, annona* [*cara, gravis*]).
44. The text in 2 Cor 11:27 has been interpreted differently. For example, C. K. Barrett, *A Commentary on the Second Epistle to the Corinthians*, BNTC (London: Black, 1973), 300, relates it to Paul's "abstinence." Margaret E. Thrall, *A Critical and Exegetical Commentary on the Second Epistle to the Corinthians*, 2 vols., ICC (Edinburgh: T&T Clark, 1994–2000), 2:747, focuses on the hardships Paul encountered in his journeys and/or in view of his insistence on refusing maintenance. The catalogues of hardships in Second Corinthians are rhetorical gestures, and it is hard to imagine

λιμῷ is a reference to involuntary hunger, while ἐν νηστείαις pertains to voluntary hunger. When used together with δίψος, λιμός is likely to mean hunger and not famine. Garnsey explains in his study of words pertaining to famine that λιμός refers to a serious, if not life-threatening, lack of food.[45] Paul does not indicate the reason for his hunger. The involuntary nature and the seriousness do not by itself prove a connection with the Corinthian food crises in the recent past. Paul uses λιμός again in Rom 8:35.[46] As part of an enumeration[47] that contains among others θλῖψις and διωγμός, here it is plausible to understand λιμός to mean famine.[48] Since Paul wrote Romans from Corinth, does 8:35 represent some reminiscences of food crises at Corinth?[49] On the basis of the evidence, this is possible but by no means certain.

3. The Alleged Food Crises and 1 Cor 11:17–34

The previous sections have given information regarding food crises in Corinth. The first part demonstrated that Corinth was probably susceptible to food crises due to its geographic, political, economic, and agricultural settings. However, the Dinippus inscriptions, the nonliterary evidence, and the Pauline allusions do not fit perfectly enough with one

---

that every hardship happened historically in the way in which it is told. Nevertheless, even such a rhetorical presentation must be linked to reality in one way or another to be plausible and believable for Paul's addressees. Paul's use of λιμός in 2 Cor 11:27 suggests that it was a reality with which the Corinthians and Paul were familiar.

45. See Garnsey, *Famine*, 19; LSJ, s.v. "λιμός": "hunger, famine."

46. See Joseph A. Fitzmyer, *Romans: A New Translation with Introduction and Commentary*, AB 33 (New York: Doubleday, 1993), 534. Fitzmyer connects Rom 8:35 to the "dangers and troubles of earthly life" without reference to the possibility of Paul referring to the famine in 51 CE. Likewise, Douglas J. Moo, *The Epistle to the Romans*, NICNT (Grand Rapids: Eerdmans, 1996), 543, speaks of the hazards Paul encountered in his apostolic labors but without explicit connection to the famine.

47. For the Pauline "catalogue of hardships," see Robert Hodgson, "Paul the Apostle and First Century Tribulation Lists," *ZNW* 74 (1983): 59–89; John T. Fitzgerald, *Cracks in an Earthen Vessel: An Examination of the Catalogues of Hardships in the Corinthian Correspondence*, SBLDS 99 (Atlanta: Scholars Press, 1988).

48. While most modern versions translate λιμός in Rom 8:35 as famine, BDAG lists it under the meaning "hunger."

49. Concerning the place and date of composition of Romans, see Fitzmyer, *Romans*, 85–88, 755; A. Andrew Das, *Solving the Romans Debate* (Minneapolis: Fortress, 2007), 37–42.

another to clearly support the claim that Corinth was affected by the food crises. This implies that while we cannot be totally certain that Corinth was affected by food crises during the time of Paul's interaction with the Corinthians, at the same time there is no evidence that excludes it and, in fact, it is plausible and even likely. Consequently, it could be asked, how would the interpretation of 1 Cor 11:17–34 be affected if it was assumed that Corinth suffered from the effects of food crises during the time of Paul's Corinthian correspondence? The following section offers an interpretation of the pericope assuming this to be the case.

Garnsey explains that urban dwellers generally were more vulnerable during food crises since they did not have privileged direct access to the land and its resources. Ordinary people's survival and sustenance depended on their horizontal (relatives, friends, neighbors) and vertical (patrons) support groups.[50] Part of their method of coping was to appeal to rich benefactors (euergetists) who (1) had the motive to ensure that the city did not suffer a full-blown famine and (2) had access to both their own food-surplus and the "capacity to secure emergency supplies, through connection, wealth and coercion."[51] Is it possible that this could have been the case in Corinth, too?

Danylak suggests that Dinippus probably responded to the people's immediate needs by procuring an adequate food supply at a reasonable price during the famine of 51 CE and possibly for the prolonged effects of food shortages.[52] However, in the context of the ominous and probably prolonged food crises experienced in Corinth in the 50s, is it possible that Dinippus's generous help was still inadequate for all the Corinthians, including the Christ-believers? This point is related to the limited number of qualified recipients of the grain provision.[53] While the Roman free monthly distribution was given to the "resident, adult, male citizens (about one fifth of the population of the city),"[54] the rest of the population did

---

50. See Peter Garnsey, *Food and Society in Classical Antiquity*, Key Themes in Ancient History (Cambridge: Cambridge University Press, 1999), 41. Contrast, Justin J. Meggitt, *Paul, Poverty and Survival*, SNTW (Edinburgh: T&T Clark, 1998), 166.

51. Garnsey, *Food*, 41. Meggitt, *Paul*, 166–67, points out that they no longer have a sense of civic obligation and responsibility for the poor city dwellers.

52. See Danylak, "Dinippus," 258.

53. See Willem Jongman, "Cura annonae," *DNP* 3 (1997): 234–36.

54. Meggitt, *Paul*, 51; see also Jongman, "Cura annonae," 235; Rickman, *Corn Supply*, 188–90.

not receive it and was, therefore, more vulnerable to hunger and its deadly effects.[55] The five *modii* (about 33 kg) of grain per month could suffice for two persons but would hardly be enough for three.[56] Can we say that the situation in Corinth was comparable to that in Rome, since Corinth was the capital of a Roman province? Who are those who suffered hunger in 1 Cor 11:22 and 34? Was their hunger something that they could remedy on their own, was it related to the chronic hunger suffered by those who live below subsistence level, or was it related to the food crises? Who benefitted from Dinippus's help?

Garnsey points out a vulnerable group in the urban setting that was more exposed to the ill effects of famine. These were the nonslave laborers who did not enjoy the security of the household.[57] Following Garnsey's argument, Blue suggests that these people could be included among those referred to as οἱ μὴ ἔχοντες in 1 Cor 11:22.[58] Considering Steven J. Friesen's "poverty scale" and Bruce W. Longenecker's "economy scale,"[59] it is important to remember this point:

> If Paul's communities took the initiative to care for the poor, and gathered together to share food and drink in corporate dinners and other occasions, it is relatively easy to see what economic attraction such communities would have held for people in ES6 and ES7 [people who live at or below subsistence level] who fell beyond the structures of a household.[60]

---

55. See Meggitt, *Paul*, 51–52: "women, children, slaves, non-citizens, and those citizens only recently domiciled did not receive the grain, and these groups (at the risk of generalization) were already disadvantaged in the struggle for survival."

56. See Jongman, "Cura annonae," 235; Garnsey, *Famine*, 215.

57. Garnsey, *Food*, 45; Garnsey, "Non-slave," 34–47. Following Garnsey, see Blue, "House Church," 233–34; Longenecker, *Remember the Poor*, 54.

58. See Blue, "House Church," 233–34.

59. See Steven J. Friesen, "Poverty in Pauline Studies: Beyond the So-Called New Consensus," *JSNT* 26 (2004): 357. Subsistence level (i.e., the "resources needed to procure enough calories in food to maintain the human body") is between 1,500 and 3,000 calories per day. He locates most of the saints in Corinth at subsistence level (based on to 2 Cor 8:12–15) and some at or below subsistence level (based on 1 Cor 11:22). See also Bruce W. Longenecker, "Socio-economic Profiling of the First Urban Christians," in *After the First Urban Christians: The Social Scientific Study of Pauline Christianity Twenty-Five Years Later*, eds. Todd D. Still and David G. Horrell (New York: T&T Clark, 2009), 36–59. See also Sanders, "Landlords," 117–25.

60. Longenecker, "Socio-Economic," 52. He continues to say that "economic benefit is probably not a *sufficient* explanation for Christianity's attractions among those

Consequently, it is plausible that the vulnerable group of those who were living at subsistence and below subsistence level, including the Christ-believers, would suffer more of the food crises' negative effects and would be less prepared to respond to them. First, they already had a preexisting problem of food insecurity. Second, it is likely that many of them did not qualify to receive the grain dole. Third, they were more vulnerable to the volatile high food prices than others, with their low buying power, unstable wages, limited alternative foodstuffs for urban dwellers, seasonal food price fluctuation, and price volatility.[61] Fourth, the abuses at the Lord's Supper (1 Cor 11:21–22) would have meant that the vulnerable groups who went hungry at the common meal (1 Cor 11:22, 34) would have a reduced possibility of sharing the supper with the rest of the assembly, leading to a worsened physiological and nutritional state.

Garnsey, referring to Galen, explains how food crises could drive people to eat famine foods that were not nutritious compared to the usual provisions and could cause the "progressive dilution and adulteration of the main staple food."[62] The prolonged food crises in Corinth and their effects could have exacerbated the prevailing situations of food inadequacy and malnutrition already suffered by those who lived at or below subsistence level.[63] The resulting, and even the preexisting, malnutrition could have worsened and resulted not only in physiological weakness but also increased one's predisposition to diseases that could eventually cause death, particularly for those living at and below subsistence levels. This condition would have put the poorest Corinthians, including members of the ἐκκλησία τοῦ θεοῦ, at a higher risk of acquiring not only deficiency diseases but also infectious diseases that were a persistent danger

---

in ES6 and ES7 [i.e., subsistence and below subsistence levels], it would nonetheless have been a powerful means of attraction, alongside any other 'non-economic' factors that might be tabled" (the emphasis is Longenecker's).

61. Erdkamp, *Grain Market*, 259–60.

62. Garnsey, *Food*, 36–42, here 40. For examples of famine foods, see Galen, *De sanitate tuenda*; *De alimentorum facultatibus*; *De bonis malisque sucis*; *De victu atenuante*; *De ptisana*, vol. 5.4.2 of *Corpus medicorum Graecorum*, ed. Konrad Koch, Georg Helmreich, Karl Kalbfleisch, and Otto Hartlich (Leipzig: Teubner, 1923), K 523, περὶ βρόμου (241–42); and K 620, αἱ βάλανοι (304–5).

63. Garnsey, *Food*, 61 concludes that malnutrition and morbidity would have affected more women of child-bearing age than men and more urbanites than non-urbanites.

in a port city.⁶⁴ As Garnsey writes, "If malnutrition was already present, infectious diseases were likely to have a significant impact on the sufferer and hasten the decline into acute malnutrition and early death."⁶⁵ Could these negative effects of the food crises that would worsen the preexisting hunger condition of those at or below subsistence levels be behind the physiological symptoms that Paul refers to in 1 Cor 11:30: διὰ τοῦτο ἐν ὑμῖν πολλοὶ ἀσθενεῖς καὶ ἄρρωστοι καὶ κοιμῶνται ἱκανοί?⁶⁶ In light of the prevailing economic condition and the alleged food crises, one can speculate in this direction.⁶⁷

If the food crises are at the background of the writing of First Corinthians, do Paul's commands in 1 Cor 11:33–34 make sense? Can patronage be at play here? Longenecker wonders if first-century benefactors of Christian charity belonged generally to those with "moderate surplus resources" and who are at the "stable near subsistence level," while the beneficiaries belong to those living at and below subsistence levels.⁶⁸ Winter holds that "the well-to-do members of the Corinthian ἐκκλησία would have been expected

---

64. See Jerome Murphy-O'Connor, *Keys to First Corinthians: Revisiting the Major Issues* (Oxford: Oxford University Press, 2009), 228; Engels, *Roman Corinth*, 75–76.

65. Garnsey, *Food*, 37. For further discussion on famine, mortality, and disease, see Peter Garnsey, *Cities, Peasants and Food in Classical Antiquity: Essays in Social and Economic History*, ed. Walter Scheidel (Cambridge: Cambridge University Press, 1998), 280–84. In the COMCAR 2011 lecture on the "Analysis of Human Remains" on 22 August 2011, Sherry C. Fox, Director of Weiner Laboratory at the American School of Classical Studies in Athens, explained that nutritional deficiency can be detected in the teeth of human skeletons. However, to date, there are no skeletal findings nor has any research been conducted on Corinth's first-century CE inhabitants. See also Lynne A. Schepartz, Sherry C. Fox, and Chryssi Bourbou, eds., *New Directions in the Skeletal Biology of Greece*, HesperiaSup 43 (Princeton: American School of Classical Studies at Athens, 2009).

66. For those who favor a spiritual understanding of 11:30, see Ilaria L. E. Ramelli, "Spiritual Weakness, Illness, and Death in 1 Corinthians 11:30," *JBL* 130 (2011): 145–63.

67. See Suzanne Watts Henderson, "'If Anyone Hungers …': An Integrated Reading of 1 Cor 11.17–34," *NTS* 48 (2002): 206–7. Even without reference to the alleged food crises, Henderson comments: "If we take the gravity of the situation to its logical end, a related exegetical move that cannot be developed here would be to construe the judgment of 11.30 (referring to those who are weak, sick, and even dead) as the natural consequence of that hunger" (ibid., 206 n. 42).

68. See Bruce W. Longenecker, "Exposing the Economic Middle: A Revised Economy Scale for the Study of Early Urban Christianity," *JSNT* 31 (2009): 271 and 271 n. 54.

as citizens to make financial contributions, had the *curator annonae* established a corn fund."[69] In contrast, Blue argues that Paul puts forwards "an alternative mechanism within the church to ensure that the economically disadvantaged were taken care of by the church and not the city."[70]

The proposals of Winter and Blue do not have to be mutually exclusive. Paul could be encouraging those who qualify to receive the grain dole and who belong to "moderate surplus resources" and "stable near subsistence" levels, those who would qualify as "haves" in the community. Friesen discusses the "poverty level" in the Pauline assemblies and shows that among those who are in Corinth,[71] Gaius probably belonged in PS4 (moderate surplus), Erastus in PS4 (moderate surplus) or PS5 (stable near subsistence), and Stephanas in PS5 (stable near subsistence). According to Friesen, Phoebe, who lived in nearby Cenchreae and is characterized as προστάτις (not εὐεργέτης; Rom 16:2), most likely belonged in PS5 (stable near subsistence) or possibly in PS4 (moderate surplus). Carolyn Osiek notes that it cannot be ruled out that as προστάτις Phoebe also provided hospitality.[72] Does it include food provision for her own community members and for those in Corinth during the food crises? Is it possible that she could have been one of Paul's unnamed source(s) who told him about the problems at the Corinthians' common meal (1 Cor 11:18), a problem that was not mentioned in the Corinthians' letter to Paul (1 Cor 7:1)? Thus, while it is not very easy to determine to what extent the haves in the community could have helped the have-nots to alleviate the hunger situation, as the main addressees of Paul's critique in this part of the letter, Paul commands the ἐκκλησία to practice sibling-ethics[73] at table. It is char-

---

69. Winter, "Secular and Christian Responses," 106.

70. Blue, "House Church," 238–39.

71. See, Friesen, "Poverty," 348–58, for a discussion of the Christ-believers' poverty or economic level in the Pauline communities, including Corinth—particularly the have-nots in 1 Cor 11:22. See also Ma. Marilou S. Ibita, "Including the Hungry *Adelphoi*: Exploring Pauline Points of View in 1 Corinthians 11:17–34," in *By Bread Alone: The Bible through the Eyes of the Hungry*, ed. Sheila E. McGinn, Lai-Ling Elizabeth Ngan, and Ahida Calderón Pilarski (Minneapolis: Fortress, 2014), 159–84.

72. See Carolyn Osiek, "*Diakonos* and *Prostatis*: Women's Patronage in Early Christianity," *HvTSt* 61 (2005): 365.

73. Reidar Aasgaard, "Role Ethics in Paul: The Significance of the Sibling Role for Paul's Ethical Thinking," *NTS* 48 (2002): 513–30; David G. Horrell, *Solidarity and Difference: A Contemporary Reading of Paul's Ethics*, 2nd ed. (London: Bloomsbury, 2015), 116–26. Although Horrell does not include 1 Cor 11:17–34 in his discussion "A

acterized by everyone, particularly the hungry have-nots, partaking of the same meal at the same time and in the same space where the κυριακὸν δεῖπνον happens.[74] This is a command that is valid with or without the food crises but even more so if there was such a problem.

While none of the foregoing is conclusive in Corinth, there are details in Paul's letters, particularly in 1 Cor 11:17–34, that make more sense when understood in light of the alleged food crises in Corinth and their dire consequences. The vulnerable members living at and below subsistence levels were already nutritionally compromised even without the compounding context of the food crises. Yet with the food crises in the background, is it not likely that this vulnerable group would be more predisposed to hunger and to being weak, ill and in danger of dying due to prolonged malnutrition and its effects (1 Cor 11:22, 30, 34)? With or without the food crises, Sanders's call to shift the archaeological and historical focus to the analysis of human physical remains[75] will provide additional evidence to answer this kind of question. Such a shift could provide more evidence regarding the causes of death of the inhabitants of Corinth when skeletal findings from the first century CE become available and will also provide more information regarding the economic levels of the Corinthians and the Christ-believers among them.

4. Conclusion

This paper briefly revisited and reevaluated the evidence of the alleged food crises that some scholars suggest were behind 1 Corinthians. It considered Roman Corinth's food situation and its population in the first century CE that could predispose Corinth to food crises. The Dinippus inscriptions from Corinth, dated from the Claudio-Neronian era, present him as a *curator annonae*, but it is not easy to determine if his activities exactly replicated the same role as elsewhere in the Roman Empire (since there were various officers who took charge of securing the grain) or to what extent his interventions helped those who lived at or below subsistence level. The nonbiblical literary evidence reflected the situation

---

Community of *Adelphoi*: Identity and Ethos" (ibid., 121–26), I hold that Paul's command in 11:33–34, which starts with ἀδελφοί μου, is a concrete example of what can be called a sibling-ethics.

74. See Ibita, "Including the Hungry *Adelphoi*," 181.
75. Sanders, "Landlords," 124–25.

of food crises in Rome, but even with Eusebius's account, the explicit link to Corinth is hard to establish. The Pauline allusions in the undisputed letters, ἀνάγκη (1 Cor 7:26) and λιμός (2 Cor 11:27; Rom 8:35), may or may not refer to the alleged Corinthian food crises. Thus, it is not possible to firmly establish that the Corinthians, including the members of the ἐκκλησία, and particularly those who live at and below subsistence levels, were suffering the ill-effects of the alleged food crises.

For these reasons, this study opted for an exploratory approach. This means that the paper moved from an assumption that Corinth was suffering the effects of food crises and tested the consequences of this for the interpretation of 1 Cor 11:17-34. The first thing to be noted is that it is possible to interpret 1 Cor 11:17-34 without the presupposition of food crises. There is nothing in the text that cannot be explained without the assumption of food crises. The text does not assume food crises as having affected Corinth; the hunger Paul refers to (11:22, 34) and its physiological manifestations (11:30) can be understood as the chronic malnutrition associated with living at or below subsistence level. The assumption, however, that the Corinthian situation was marked by the ill effects of ongoing food crises would imply that more people were affected by hunger. This would mean that the Corinthian ἐκκλησία was also affected, particularly those who lived at or below the subsistence levels who were deprived of the chance to benefit nutritionally from the common meal due to the abuses at the κυριακὸν δεῖπνον. If the alleged food crises are factored in, Paul's command in 1 Cor 11:33-34 to practice sibling-ethics at table so that the hungry ones (have-nots) partake of the same meal with the rest, at the same time, and at the same place becomes more important and challenging for both the haves and the have-nots.

Bibliography

Aasgaard, Reider. "Role Ethics in Paul: The Significance of the Sibling Role for Paul's Ethical Thinking." *NTS* 48 (2002): 513-30.

Barrett, C. K. *A Commentary on the First Epistle to the Corinthians*. BNTC. London: Black, 1968.

———. *A Commentary on the Second Epistle to the Corinthians*. BNTC. London: Black, 1973.

Bengel, Johann A. *Gnomon Novi Testamenti, in quo ex nativa verborum vi simplicitas, profunditas, concinnitas, salubritas sensuum coelestium indicator.* 5th ed. London: Williams & Norgate, 1862.

Blue, Bradley B. "The House Church at Corinth and the Lord's Supper: Famine, Food Supply, and the Present Distress." *CTR* 5 (1991): 221–39.

Danylak, Barry N. "Tiberius Claudius Dinippus and the Food Shortages in Corinth." *TynBul* 59 (2008): 231–70.

Das, A. Andrew. *Solving the Romans Debate*. Minneapolis: Fortress, 2007.

Dunn, James D. G. *1 Corinthians*. NTG. Sheffield: Sheffield Academic, 1995.

———. *The Theology of Paul the Apostle*. Edinburgh: T&T Clark, 1998.

Engels, Donald W. *Roman Corinth: An Alternative Model for the Classical City*. Chicago: University of Chicago Press, 1990.

Erdkamp, Paul. *The Grain Market in the Roman Empire: A Social, Political and Economic Study*. Cambridge: Cambridge University Press, 2005.

Eusebius of Caesarea. *Eusebi chronicorum libri duo*. Edited by Alfred Schoene. 2 vols. Berlin: Weidmann, 1866–1875.

Fee, Gordon D. *The First Epistle to the Corinthians*. NICNT. Grand Rapids: Eerdmans, 1987.

Fitzgerald, John T. *Cracks in an Earthen Vessel: An Examination of the Catalogues of Hardships in the Corinthian Correspondence*. SBLDS 99. Atlanta: Scholars Press, 1988.

Fitzmyer, Joseph A. *Romans: A New Translation with Introduction and Commentary*. AB 33. New York: Doubleday, 1993.

Friesen, Steven J. "Poverty in Pauline Studies: Beyond the So-Called New Consensus." *JSNT* 26 (2004): 323–61.

Furnish, Victor Paul. "Corinth in Paul's Time: What Can Archaeology Tell Us?" *BAR* 15.3 (1988): 14–27.

Galen. *De sanitate tuenda; De alimentorum facultatibus; De bonis malisque sucis; De victu atenuante; De ptisana*. Vol. 5.4.2 of *Corpus medicorum Graecorum*. Edited by Konrad Koch, Georg Helmreich, Karl Kalbfleisch, and Otto Hartlich. Leipzig: Teubner, 1923.

Garnsey, Peter. *Cities, Peasants and Food in Classical Antiquity: Essays in Social and Economic History*. Edited by Walter Scheidel. Cambridge: Cambridge University Press, 1998.

———. *Famine and Food Supply in the Graeco-Roman World: Responses to Risk and Crisis*. Cambridge: Cambridge University Press, 1988.

———. *Food and Society in Classical Antiquity*. Key Themes in Ancient History. Cambridge: Cambridge University Press, 1999.

Garnsey, Peter, and Richard Saller. *The Roman Empire: Economy, Society and Culture*. 2nd ed. London: Bloomsbury, 2014.

Gill, David W. J. "In Search of the Social Elite in the Corinthian Church." *TynBul* 44 (1993): 323–37.

Hansen, Mogens H. *Polis: An Introduction to the Ancient Greek City-State*. Oxford: Oxford University Press, 2006.

Henderson, Suzanne W. "'If Anyone Hungers ...': An Integrated Reading of 1 Cor 11.17–34." *NTS* 48 (2002): 195–208.

Hodgson, Robert. "Paul the Apostle and First Century Tribulation Lists." *ZNW* 74 (1983): 59–89.

Horrell, David G. *Solidarity and Difference: A Contemporary Reading of Paul's Ethics*. 2nd ed. London: Bloomsbury, 2015.

Ibita, Ma. Marilou S. "Including the Hungry *Adelphoi*: Exploring Pauline Points of View in 1 Corinthians 11:17–34." Pages 159–84 in *By Bread Alone: The Bible through the Eyes of the Hungry*. Edited by Sheila E. McGinn, Lai Ling Elizabeth Ngan, and Ahida Calderón Pilarski. Minneapolis: Fortress, 2014.

Jones, A. H. M. *The Greek City: From Alexander to Justinian*. Oxford: Clarendon, 1979.

Jongman, Willem. "Cura annonae." *DNP* 3 (1997): 233–36.

Kent, John H., ed. *The Inscriptions, 1926–1950*. Vol. 8.3 of *Corinth: Results of Excavations Conducted by the American School of Classical Studies at Athens*. Princeton: American School of Classical Studies at Athens, 1966.

Longenecker, Bruce W. "Exposing the Economic Middle: A Revised Economy Scale for the Study of Early Urban Christianity." *JSNT* 31 (2009): 243–78.

———. "Socio-economic Profiling of the First Urban Christians." Pages 36–59 in *After the First Urban Christians: The Social Scientific Study of Pauline Christianity Twenty-Five Years Later*. Edited by Todd D. Still and David G. Horrell. New York: T&T Clark, 2009.

Meggitt, Justin J. *Paul, Poverty and Survival*. SNTW. Edinburgh: T&T Clark, 1998.

Meritt, Benjamin D., ed. *Greek Inscriptions 1896–1927*. Vol. 8.1 of *Corinth: Results of Excavations Conducted by the American School of Classical Studies at Athens*. Cambridge: American School of Classical Studies at Athens, 1931.

Moo, Douglas J. *The Epistle to the Romans*. NICNT. Grand Rapids: Eerdmans, 1996.

Murphy-O'Connor, Jerome. *Keys to First Corinthians: Revisiting the Major Issues*. Oxford: Oxford University Press, 2009.

Osiek, Carolyn. "*Diakonos* and *Prostatis*: Women's Patronage in Early Christianity." *HvTSt* 61 (2005): 347–70.

Pasquinucci, Marinella. "Centuriation and Roman Land Surveying (Republic through Empire)." Pages 1275–91 in *Encyclopedia of Global Archaeology*. Edited by Claire Smith. New York: Springer, 2014. http://tinyurl.com/SBL4522p.

Ramelli, Ilaria L. E. "Spiritual Weakness, Illness, and Death in 1 Corinthians 11:30." *JBL* 130 (2011): 145–63.

Rickman, Geoffrey. *The Corn Supply of Ancient Rome*. Oxford: Clarendon, 1980.

Sanders, Guy D. R. "Landlords and Tenants: Sharecroppers and Subsistence Farming in Corinthian Historical Context." Pages 104–25 in *Corinth in Contrast: Studies in Inequality*. Edited by Steven J. Friesen, Sarah A. James, and Daniel N. Schowalter. NovTSup 155. Leiden: Brill, 2013.

———. "Urban Corinth: An Introduction." Pages 11–24 in *Urban Religion in Corinth: Interdisciplinary Approaches*. Edited by Daniel N. Schowalter and Steven J. Friesen. HTS 53. Cambridge: Harvard University Press, 2005.

Schepartz, Lynne A, Sherry C. Fox, and Chryssi Bourbou, eds. *New Directions in the Skeletal Biology of Greece*. HesperiaSup 43. Princeton: American School of Classical Studies at Athens, 2009.

Scranton, Robert L. *Ancient Corinth: A Guide to the Excavations*. 6th ed. Athens: American School of Classical Studies at Athens, 1960.

Sirks, Boudewijn. *Food for Rome: The Legal Structure of the Transportation and Processing of Supplies for the Imperial Distributions in Rome and Constantinople*. Amsterdam: Gieben, 1991.

Tacitus. *The Annals: The Reigns of Tiberius, Claudius and Nero*. Translated by J. C. Yardley. Oxford World Classics. Oxford: Oxford University Press, 2008.

Thiselton, Anthony C. *The First Epistle to the Corinthians: A Commentary on the Greek Text*. NIGTC. Grand Rapids: Eerdmans, 2000.

Thrall, Margaret E. *A Critical and Exegetical Commentary on the Second Epistle to the Corinthians*. 2 vols. ICC. Edinburgh: T&T Clark, 1994–2000.

Walbank, Mary E. H. "The Foundation and Planning of Early Roman Corinth." *JRA* 10 (1997): 95–130.

West, Allen B., ed. *Latin Inscriptions 1896–1926*. Vol. 8.2 of *Corinth: Results of Excavations Conducted by the American School of Classical Studies at Athens*. Cambridge: Harvard University Press, 1931.

Winter, Bruce W. *After Paul Left Corinth: The Influence of Secular Ethics and Change.* Grand Rapids: Eerdmans, 2001.

———. "The Lord's Supper at Corinth: An Alternative Reconstruction." *RTR* 37 (1978): 73–82.

———. "Secular and Christian Responses to Corinthian Famines." *TynBul* 40 (1989): 86–106.

Wiseman, James. "Corinth and Rome I: 228 B.C.–A.D. 267." *ANRW* 7.1 (1979): 438–548.

———. *The Land of the Ancient Corinthians.* SMA 50. Göteborg: Aström, 1978.

Witherington, Ben, III. *Conflict and Community in Corinth: A Socio-rhetorical Commentary on 1 Corinthians.* Grand Rapids: Eerdmans, 1995.

Don't Take It Lying Down: Nondining Features of the Omrit Temple Excavations

Daniel N. Schowalter

An essay in honor of Dennis Smith would certainly call for attention to some aspect of dining in the ancient world. Interestingly enough, excavations at the Roman temple complex at Omrit in northern Israel have yielded very little information relating directly to this topic. After nearly twenty years of excavation, no architectural installations have been discovered that can be associated with dining, and a review of artifacts shows nothing specific to dining other than mounds of pottery fragments and several metal skewers.

While a paper on the details of ancient kebab production and consumption would certainly be a worthwhile pursuit (and one that could be tied in with a comprehensive tour of modern Kebab outlets visited by the COMCAR seminars), that investigation will have to wait for another opportunity. In this paper, I would like to consider evidence for several offerings/dedications at Omrit that may or may not be connected to dining but that certainly reveal important insights about ritual practice at this particular location in the eastern Roman Empire in the first century BCE through the fourth century CE.

One of the inscriptions published in *The Roman Temple Complex at Horvat Omrit: An Interim Report* is found on a bevel-cut piece of conglomerate stone (fig. 3.1); it is one of five fragments that appear to belong to the same installation (fig. 3.2).[1] The fragments are all 8 centimeters high, and

---

1. Daniel N. Schowalter, "Small Finds and Inscriptions from Omrit," in *The Roman Temple Complex at Horvat Omrit: An Interim Report*, ed. J. Andrew Overman and Daniel N. Schowalter (Oxford: Archaeopress, 2010), 73–83. The conglomerate

the surviving beveled edges total approximately 0.85 meters in length. One piece features a corner, and it is not clear if the beveled edge continues on the second side. Since none of the pieces join, it is not possible to estimate the size of the entire unit.

Figure 3.1. Inscription on bevel-cut conglomerate stone, from Omrit. All photographs by Daniel N. Schowalter.

Figure 3.2. Fragments of conglomerate stone of the same installation

---

stone comes from a quarry above Kiryat Shmona, a modern town located six kilometers west of Omrit.

The fragmentary inscription includes the Greek letters ΩΝΕΝΣΕΒ, which vary in height between 1.4 and 2 centimeters. The letters are carved in an unsteady hand with very shallow incision into the surface of the conglomerate. This is probably explained by the fragile nature of the stone. The inscribed surface, along with the bevel and the top of the fragment, is finished smooth and polished, while the bottom is flat but otherwise unfinished. There are no signs of cuts or dowel holes on any of the surviving fragments. In its original context, this conglomerate feature must have been in a position where the bottom was not visible.

In the preliminary report, I suggested that these fragments could be part of a tabletop, a shelf, or even a sarcophagus lid. These all continue to be possibilities, but I was mistaken not to include a dining couch as another possible function. As Smith would be quick to remind us, we can be certain that there would have been provision made for dining in the vicinity of the Omrit temple. At this point in the excavations, we do not have evidence of formally defined dining rooms, but it is certain that they existed nearby. The nature of these surviving conglomerate fragments would argue for a couch slab lying on a solid base of some sort or even on a bank of fill, rather than perched on carved legs or on a pedestal.

The fragmentary inscription does not provide enough information to help with identification of the object or its function. The letters ΩΝ may be the ending of a genitive plural noun, a nominative singular present active participle, or a genitive plural relative pronoun or definite article. As suggested in the preliminary report, ΕΝΣΕΒ is a tantalizing set of letters, suggesting that something is being set up in the temple to Augustus (*sebasteion*) or that something is taking place in the games associated with that temple (*sebasteia*), but lacking other evidence, this can only be speculation since the ΣΕΒ could also be associated with the verb σεβάζομαι or a cognate term.

One other inscribed piece of conglomerate has been found since the publication of the material described in the preliminary report. This is a fragment of a rectangular slab bearing the letters ΑΣΙΩΝ on the 4 by 12 centimeter front of the fragment (pl. 3.3).[2] The front and top are finished and polished, while the bottom is flat and hammer dressed. Because this

---

2. A small fragment of a vertical hasta precedes the alpha, which indicates the presence of an eta, iota, mu, nu, or pi.

example is only half the thickness of the previous item, the two pieces cannot have come from the same installation.

Figure 3.3. Partial inscription on a fragment of a rectangular slab

At the same time, both inscribed fragments are cut from the same type of conglomerate stone, and there are apparent similarities in the forms of the letters. The letters in both inscriptions are somewhat shaky and carved with shallow incisions, and the letters on both stones have apices. In terms of common letters, there is a close resemblance between the sigmas, with extended horizontal hastae and apices, although sigma in ΑΣΙΩΝ is more confidently and more deeply carved. The similarities, however, do not extend to the omegas, as the beveled piece features a monumental omega, and the ΑΣΙΩΝ a lunate form.

Because of the thinness and finished quality of the fragment, it seems likely that the ΑΣΙΩΝ piece comes from a tabletop. It is somewhat thinner than the beautiful, unpublished marble tabletop found in the archaeological museum in Chania on Crete. That example from Chania has a very crudely carved inscription on the front edge with a dedication to Asklepios by someone from Kos. Because of the undulating line of the Chania inscription, it may be that it was a secondary addition to the table. At least the ΑΣΙΩΝ inscription from Omrit used grid lines to keep the text straight.

Even if the ΑΣΙΩΝ fragment comes from a table, one must be cautious not to fall into the modern trap of assuming that a table indicates dining. As Smith would remind us, dining took place using couches and small tables (which could be made of stone). Once again, the letters in ΑΣΙΩΝ offer several interesting possibilities for interpretation.³ While the inscription does not provide a clear indication of the function of the inscribed item, the suggestion that it served as some kind of offering table would certainly make sense.

Another rather vivid example of nondining at Omrit has to do with a massive deposit of sacrificial remains that was found to the west of the earliest surviving building from the site, a small (5 by 8 meter) podium temple that we call the Early Shrine (ES).⁴ The deposit is found between the west end of the ES and the eastern side of a frescoed wall that enclosed the ES precinct (fig. 3.4). The deposit covered an area of 5 by 1 by 0.7 meters and consisted of a very dense layer of ash, charcoal, and fragmentary animal bones. The faunal remains have been analyzed by Rachel Hesse and are published in volume two of the final report of the Omrit Temple excavation.⁵ Hesse's findings are significant for a number of reasons.

First of all, the bone fragments come exclusively from victims that were very young (neonate) sheep or goats.⁶ Hesse estimates that there are at least sixty-eight victims represented in this deposit and that the remains

---

3. The most common example of this letter group is the label ΘΑΣΙΩΝ on amphoras for Thasian wine (941 occurrences in the PHI database). Several names with this string appear frequently, including Νικασίων (97 occurrences), Ἐργασίων (53 occurrences), and Πασίων (109 occurrences). Another common association is with the term γυμνασίων (59 occurrences), which could signal a reference to things or people connected to a gymnasium. Support for this reconstruction comes from the fragmentary letter preceding the alpha. Although we have no archaeological evidence for athletic facilities at Omrit, we do have a hint of games in the form of a small marble relief sculpture that appears to represent a togate figure holding up a flag (*mappa*) as if he were starting a race or cheering for his favorite team (Schowalter, "Small Finds," 78–79).

4. Michael C. Nelson, *The Architecture*, vol. 1 of *The Temple Complex at Horvat Omrit*, ed. J. Andrew Overman, Michael C. Nelson, and Daniel Schowalter (Leiden: Brill, 2015), 38–54.

5. Rachel Hesse, "Faunal Remains from the Roman Temple at Omrit," in *Stratigraphy, Artifacts, and Phasing*, vol. 2 of *The Temple Complex at Horvat Omrit*, ed. J. Andrew Overman, Michael C. Nelson, and Daniel N. Schowalter (Leiden: Brill, forthcoming).

6. The young age makes it impossible to distinguish the bones of sheep from those of goats.

Figure 3.4. Omrit Early Shrine, site of deposit of sacrificial remains

were likely placed in this area over a short period of time rather than as a gradual accumulation. She also notes that almost none of the surviving bones have marks of butchering on them, which suggests that these small animals were sacrificed and burned whole as opposed being portioned and consumed as part of ritual dining.

One further notable feature of this deposit is that almost all of the skeletons appear to have been postcranial, meaning that the heads of the victims were removed before burning and possibly displayed or used in some other aspect of the ritual.[7] This layer of sacrificial debris also contained fragments of ostrich egg shells, and it was related to two other deposits that seem to be ritual in nature.

Just above the ash and bone deposit, immediately behind the center of the ES was an assemblage made up of a broken amphora, a terracotta unguentarium, a lamp, and a stone base with a rectangular notch in it (fig. 3.5). It is likely that the amphora was part of a libation ritual, or perhaps

---

7. This possibility is reminiscent of the depiction of bucrania anchoring garlands on altars and other ritual architecture.

it contained oil that was used to fuel the sacrificial fire. The unguentarium needs to be seen in the context of over thirty glass unguentaria that appear to have been deposited around the early shrine at the same time that the sacrificial deposit was laid down. The offering of perfume or pre-

Figure 3.5. Assemblage of finds behind Early Shrine

cious ointment again fits in with this broader ritual activity.[8] The lamp and stone base are probably also connected to some aspect of the ceremony, but it is impossible to know precisely how they might have been involved.

The second area covered by the sacrificial deposit is a small niche that was built into the west enclosure wall of the ES precinct (fig. 3.6).[9] Presumably this niche had a function in ritual activity that took place in the ES courtyard. The fact that it is behind the building would seem to

---

8. Anointing of corpses would have been a regular part of preparation for burial and the burial act. Unguentaria made of both ceramics and glass are a common feature of grave goods. Virginia R. Anderson-Stojanović discusses how the form and composition of ceramic unguentaria can inform us about their function in funerary settings; see her article "The Chronology and Function of Ceramic Unguentaria," *AJA* 91 (1987): 117–21. Penelope M. Allison reviews the evidence to associate unguentaria predominantly with women's funerary remains; see her "Characterizing Roman Artifacts to Investigate Gendered Practices," *AJA* 119 (2015): 111–12.

9. Nelson, *Architecture*, 69.

indicate that a sacred procession around the courtyard was part of the ceremonial activity. We cannot know how the niche functioned during the time when the ES was actively used. Perhaps it held a small statue or was used to make offerings. Its final phase of usage, however, seems to have been immediately before the sacrificial deposit was laid down, since that deposit filled and buried it. In this case, the contents of the niche are very instructive. In addition to nine nails, some of them badly bent, the niche contained fill similar to the sacrificial deposit and three coins. Only one of these coins was readable; it was marked with a counterstrike dating after the year 54 CE.[10]

Figure 3.6. Niche in the west enclosure wall of the Early Shrine

All of the deposits described above seem to have been part of a major event in the life of the temple complex. As described by Michael Nelson in his report on the temple architecture,[11] the foundation for the cella wall of Temple One (T1) shows signs of repair that indicate a major structural failure. In light of this catastrophe, the podium of T1 was completely emptied out, additional support walls were constructed at the west end of the

---

10. Gabriela I. Bijovosky, "Numismatic Evidence from the Temple Excavations," in Overman, Nelson, and Schowalter, *Stratigraphy*.
11. Nelson, *Architecture*, 33–34.

temple, and attempts were made to patch places where joints in the interior podium walls had deteriorated.

During this major repair, the remains of the Early Shrine would have been discovered buried deep in the podium of T1. Since the west end of the ES is built with two chambers under the floor, it would have been easy for the construction workers to assume that they had uncovered the remains of a tomb or other sacred installation. Given that the previous building over this monument had failed in a spectacular way, it is not surprising that great care was given to the physical repair of areas of possible weakness in the structure or that attention was paid to any potential ritual infraction against the spirits represented in the partially preserved ES.

To remedy any potential ritual violation, over thirty unguentaria were deposited with valuable ointment or perfume, at least one amphora of wine was poured as a libation, nails from the structure were placed in a ritual niche along with three coins, and a massive sacrifice of young animals was performed, with the postcranial remains not consumed but rather left behind to ensure that all ritual obligations had been met.[12]

The one datable coin in the niche provides a *terminus post quem* for this event of 54 CE, and given that the date for the completed construction of the final phase of the temple building (Temple Two, abbreviated T2) can be set in the early 80s CE,[13] it makes the most sense to suggest that the major repair of the fallen T1 was actually part of the work associated with the construction of the much enlarged T2. As such, the ritual activities described above would have served in effect as a foundation deposit for that building.[14]

One final aspect of the Omrit Temple complex also relates to the last phase (T2) of the building. In 2007, we first discovered that there was a

---

12. We can assume there would have been sacred dining associated with all of this ritual activity, but it did not involve the young sheep or goat victims.

13. Daniel N. Schowalter, "Inscriptions and Small Finds," in Overman, Nelson, and Schowalter, *Stratigraphy*.

14. Peter Woodward and Anne Woodward discuss coins as part of foundation deposits in Roman Britain ("Dedicating the Town: Urban Foundation Deposits in Roman Britain," *World Archaeology* 36 [2004]: 68–86). The practice extends back to Greek traditions; see Gloria R. Hunt, "Foundation Rituals and the Culture of Building in Ancient Greece" (PhD diss., The University of North Carolina at Chapel Hill, 2006); Paul Jacobsthal, "The Date of the Ephesian Foundation-Deposit," *JHS* 71 (1951): 85–95; and beyond; see Richard S. Ellis, *Foundation Deposits in Ancient Mesopotamia*, YNER 2 (New Haven: Yale University Press, 1968).

niche built into the north parotid wall of T2. The wall on the south side of the front stairway was completely destroyed, but presumably another niche installation would have stood there as well. In addition to the statues, these niches were also equipped with some kind of fountain effect. There are water pipes coming up to the temple just outside the north niche, then a channel runs up to the north niche, down to the back of the third course of the stairway, all the way across the stairs, and up to what would have been the south niche (fig. 3.7). This channel must have housed a pipe that brought water to the southern niche. Thus, in its final phase, T2 included an impressive fountain installation.

Figure 3.7. Channel along the stairway linking north and south niches of the Omrit Temple complex, servicing a fountain installation

Brenda Longfellow has detailed the spread of monumental fountains throughout the Roman provinces starting in the middle of the first century CE.[15] In this case, the installation is not part of a civic display but adorns

---

15. Brenda Longfellow, *Roman Imperialism and Civic Patronage: Form, Meaning, and Ideology in Monumental Fountain Complexes* (New York: Cambridge University Press, 2011).

a temple that stands in a rural setting. Nonetheless, the provision of water at a place like Omrit would have been an essential part of accommodating pilgrims and other visitors to the site.

Excavations so far have revealed many lines of terra cotta piping which would have moved water around the site. There are several potential water sources that would have fed this system. Seasonal streams ran in the valleys to the north and south surrounding the site, and there appear to be springs on the hill located approximately one hundred meters east of the temple. Much more work is needed in terms of excavation and analysis in order to gain a full understanding of how the water system at Omrit functioned, but it is very clear that water was channeled to the front of the temple and used in an ostentatious monumental fountain display.

Fortunately, there is also an inscription that can be associated with the fountain system. The inscription is found on the basalt paving of the temple courtyard, ten meters east of the north niche. It records that a woman, Agrippina, "set it up" for "Echo the Goddess" or "Echo the Daughter."[16] The inscription does not explicitly mention the fountain, but given that the inscription lies directly in front of the niche, with no sign of any installation between the inscription and the niche, it make sense to think that Agrippina set up the fountain system and dedicated it to Echo the nymph.

The inscription includes a date just after 80 CE, which confirms the completion of T2 around that time.[17] If the sacrificial layer and the other foundation deposits were laid down sometime after 54 CE when the ES was discovered in the early stages of emptying the T1 podium in preparation for constructing T2, significant time would have been needed to complete the walls and superstructure of the new building. That construction period would certainly have included numerous additional occasions for sacrifice and ritual dining. The end of construction and the dedication of Agrippina's fountain would have called for more major sacrifice and celebration. Unfortunately, we do not yet have evidence to inform us regarding these events, but thanks to the lessons learned from Smith and others, we know that reclining at table would have been a prominent feature of them. We look forward to future discoveries which will reveal where, when, and how ritual dining took place at Omrit.

---

16. Full publication of the inscription will appear in Schowalter, "Inscriptions and Small Finds."

17. The fountains would have been one of the final details completed on T2.

Bibliography

Allison, Penelope M. "Characterizing Roman Artifacts to Investigate Gendered Practices." *AJA* 119 (2015): 103–23.

Anderson-Stojanović, Virginia R. "The Chronology and Function of Ceramic Unguentaria." *AJA* 91 (1987): 105–22.

Bijovsky, Gabriela I. "Numismatic Evidence from the Temple Excavations." In *Stratigraphy, Artifacts, and Phasing*. Vol. 2 of *The Temple Complex at Horvat Omrit*. Edited by J. Andrew Overman, Michael C. Nelson, and Daniel N. Schowalter. Leiden: Brill, forthcoming.

Ellis, Richard S. *Foundation Deposits in Ancient Mesopotamia*. YNER 2. New Haven: Yale University Press, 1968.

Hesse, Rachel. "Faunal Remains from the Roman Temple at Omrit." In *Stratigraphy, Artifacts, and Phasing*. Vol. 2 of *The Temple Complex at Horvat Omrit*. Edited by J. Andrew Overman, Michael C. Nelson, and Daniel N. Schowalter. Leiden: Brill, forthcoming.

Hunt, Gloria R. "Foundation Rituals and the Culture of Building in Ancient Greece." PhD diss., The University of North Carolina at Chapel Hill, 2006.

Jacobsthal, Paul. "The Date of the Ephesian Foundation-Deposit." *JHS* 71 (1951): 85–95.

Longfellow, Brenda. *Roman Imperialism and Civic Patronage: Form, Meaning, and Ideology in Monumental Fountain Complexes*. Cambridge: Cambridge University Press, 2011.

Nelson, Michael C. *The Architecture*. Vol. 1 of *The Temple Complex at Horvat Omrit*. Edited by J. Andrew Overman, Michael C. Nelson, and Daniel N. Schowalter. Leiden: Brill, 2015.

Overman, J. Andrew, Michael C. Nelson, and Daniel N. Schowalter, eds. *Stratigraphy, Artifacts, and Phasing*. Vol. 2 of *The Temple Complex at Horvat Omrit*. Leiden: Brill, forthcoming.

Schowalter, Daniel N. "Inscriptions and Small Finds." In *Stratigraphy, Artifacts, and Phasing*. Vol. 2 of *The Temple Complex at Horvat Omrit*. Edited by J. Andrew Overman, Michael C. Nelson, and Daniel N. Schowalter. Leiden: Brill, forthcoming.

———. "Small Finds and Inscriptions from Omrit." Pages 73–84 in *The Roman Temple Complex at Horvat Omrit: An Interim Report*. Edited by J. Andrew Overman and Daniel N. Schowalter. Oxford: Archaeopress, 2010.

Woodward, Peter, and Ann Woodward. "Dedicating the Town: Urban Foundation Deposits in Roman Britain." *World Archaeology* 36 (2004): 68–86.

Eating Words in the New Testament

Keith Dyer

We are what we eat, we are told, but it is how we dine that really shapes and is shaped by our culture and religious traditions.[1] Dennis Smith and his colleagues in that most prolific of Society of Biblical Literature Seminars, "Meals in the Greco-Roman World," have explored the customs and implications of communal dining with stunning results. The Smith-Klinghardt paradigm has asserted the pervasive influence of the Greco-Roman banquet across the circum-Mediterranean world as the primary model for all main-meal dining (including Jewish and early Christian meals) in the first century of the Common Era and beyond.[2] The archaeological evidence for this pervasive influence within the dominant elite culture is overwhelming, and the rich and diverse vocabulary for reclining and dining in the

---

1. Our obsessions today with diet, food intolerances, and allergies suggests we are more concerned with our own bodies (eating) than the body corporate (dining) when we eat. One has the strong feeling that Smith agrees more with Plutarch (*Quaest. conv.* 7.1 [697C]): "The Romans ... are fond of quoting a witty and sociable person who said, after a solitary meal, 'I have eaten, but not dined today,' implying that a dinner always requires friendly sociability for seasoning." Quoted in Dennis E. Smith, *From Symposium to Eucharist: The Banquet in the Early Christian World* (Minneapolis: Fortress, 2003), 13. For a helpful reflection on the relationship between faith and food, see Gary Stephen Shogren, "Is the Kingdom of God about Eating and Drinking or Isn't It? (Romans 14:17)," *NovT* 42 (2000): 238–56.

2. See Smith, *Symposium*, for the fullest expression of the paradigm; and Hal E. Taussig, introduction to *Meals in the Early Christian World: Social Formation, Experimentation, and Conflict at the Table*, ed. Dennis E. Smith and Hal E. Taussig (New York: Palgrave Macmillan, 2012), 1–5, for an explanation of the naming of the paradigm. The members and presenters of the SBL Seminar include Andrew McGowan, Susan Marks, Philip Harland, David Balch, Jennifer Glancy, Carolyn Osiek, Kathleen Corley, Richard Ascough, Ellen Aitken, Angela Standhartinger, and many others publishing in this area.

New Testament texts is also consistent with this understanding. But what of that other majority culture, hoi polloi, who were minor clients and slaves of the elite and whose homes (if they had them) had no triclinium, and whose material culture is not usually explored by archaeologists in our time anyway?[3] How might the eating customs of this majority of city dwellers be incorporated into the evidentiary database, and is there textual evidence for suggesting some kind of inverse corollary to the Smith-Klinghardt paradigm?[4]

We should not think that the dominance of the Greco-Roman banquet means a uniformity of meal customs in the first century and beyond.[5] Andrew McGowan has given ample evidence for the diversity of dining practices in the first few centuries of the Christian movement—a diversity that still sits within the norm of the banquet paradigm, though he has shown that every aspect of those traditions (food, location, seating/reclining, meal/drink sequence) may vary in any one instance—and that this also applies to the eucharistic traditions themselves.[6] He argues convincingly that it is not possible to establish on the basis of this diverse evidence any neat linear progression from an *agapē* meal to the eucharist, from a simple meal to more complex ones, from a Lord's Supper to a symbolic sacramental meal; nor do I wish to argue that we can find a progression from early egalitarian meals of the poor and slaves to the more elaborate and hierarchical dining of a rising Christian middle class. Rather—as has been said more than once—"the poor we have with us always," and I seek evidence of this and of ongoing diversity in the language of those New Testament texts

---

3. This is changing insofar as the artifacts used by women and slaves, the toys played with by children, and the display of everyday foods found in shipwrecks and other sealed loci are now featured in many archaeological museums. Nevertheless, the focus on the monumental remains found at the "big end" of town still dominates and shapes our understanding of the past. The lowest classes remain largely invisible.

4. Indeed, the members of the Society of Biblical Literature Seminar have been exploring these same issues in recent years, culminating in the volume of essays cited above and edited by Smith and Taussig, *Meals*.

5. The dating is uncertain, but apparently the different meal posture of the Cretans provoked comment: "Pyrgion, in the third book of his *Cretan Customs*, says that Cretans at the public mess eat together in a sitting posture." See Athenaeus, *Deipn.* 4.143E (Gulick, LCL).

6. See Andrew B. McGowan, *Ascetic Eucharists: Food and Drink in Early Christian Ritual Meals* (Oxford: Clarendon, 1999), especially 89–142, for diversity within early Christian rituals.

that speak about eating, drinking, reclining, and dining. How do slaves, the poor, the day laborers, the itinerant, and nonelite women eat, for example? Apart from the temporary reversals of the Saturnalia and perhaps the occasional wedding feast of a patron or relative, would the lowest half of society ever actually recline to eat?[7] Some may have belonged to funeral clubs or associations and have experienced banquets in those contexts, but it is difficult to see that the majority of slaves, poor widows, and the destitute could ever do this with any regularity. I explore these questions further not to challenge the Smith-Klinghardt paradigm, but to gather more evidence on aspects that Dennis Smith (and others) have already begun to explore.[8]

Given the absence of archaeological evidence for the eating customs of the lower classes and the paucity of textual material from or about them, we need to interrogate what textual evidence we have as best we can for some direction in these areas. We do find occasional references to the social limits of "reclining fellowship." Josephus (*Vita* 222) pleads unsuccessfully with a soldier to sit and dine in the presence of his reclining superiors, and there are other references to wives and children sitting for meals in the presence of the reclining paterfamilias and his male guests.[9] The

---

7. For descriptions of dining behavior during the Saturnalia, see Angela Standhartinger, "The Saturnalia in Greco-Roman Culture," in Smith and Taussig, *Meals*, 179–90; and for different classes of guests at a wedding banquet, see Luke 14:7–11.

8. On the possibility that some slaves might participate in reclining meals in associations, see Richard S. Ascough, "Social and Political Aspects of Greco-Roman Association Meals," in Smith and Taussig, *Meals*, 59–72; and Philip A. Harland, "Banqueting Values in the Associations: Rhetoric and Reality," in Smith and Taussig, *Meals*, 73–86. In the same volume Jennifer Glancy asks not only "Did slaves recline at Christian meals?" but also "Did slaveholders recline at Christian meals?" See Jennifer A. Glancy, "Slaves at Greco-Roman Banquets: A Response," in Smith and Taussig, *Meals*, 205–11. Her answer is a cautious and qualified yes to both questions, but she continues to present clearly the plight of most slaves.

9. Dennis E. Smith, "The Greco-Roman Banquet as a Social Institution," in Smith and Taussig, *Meals*, 25, summarizes the standard Greek custom that "women (respectable women, that is) children, and slaves, if present at a banquet where their betters reclined, were expected to sit" since reclining "was always fundamentally a mark of status." In the Roman period some respectable women began to recline with their husbands. Detailed references to sources can be found in Angela Standhartinger, "Women in Early Christian Meal Gatherings," in Smith and Taussig, *Meals*, 87–108; Ellen Bradshaw Aitken, "Remembering and Remembered Women in Greco-Roman Meals," in Smith and Taussig, *Meals*, 109–22; and Susan Marks, "Present and Absent: Women at Greco-Roman Wedding Meals," in Smith and Taussig, *Meals*, 123–48.

place of slaves at meals is assumed to be serving the food, providing entertainment, and cleaning up; their needs for sustenance are seldom reflected on at all (so Luke 17:7–10).[10] Yet though they are often invisible in the historical records, we know that slaves comprised a large proportion of the population, particularly on the larger estates and in the major cities.[11] This would be especially true of Roman colonies, such as Corinth and Philippi, and around the significant building sites of client rulers, such as the Herodian cities of Caesarea Maritima, Caesarea Philippi, Sepphoris, and Tiberias. The large numbers of slaves in the former cities creates hermeneutical problems for interpreting the Pauline epistles, whereas the early gospel traditions skirt around the latter locations, often ignoring them altogether, and seem to be more familiar with the world of small farmers, fisherman, displaced peasants, women, and day laborers.[12] In either case, the question continues to be asked as to whether such followers of Jesus would ever recline to dine and whether there is any detectable indication of this in the textual traditions of the New Testament. Does the vocabulary used

---

10. Jennifer Glancy expresses their multiple and uncertain roles thus: "more typically, male and female slaves were available to satisfy the varied appetites of (primarily) free male diners." See Glancy, "Slaves at Greco-Roman Banquets," 205. There is always a tension between the textual evidence that we may have for the exceptional inclusion of slaves and the absence of comment on the everyday terrors of the majority of slaves. Glancy has been strong and measured in reminding us of the silent majority.

11. I am persuaded by the attempts of Steven J. Friesen to quantify the proportion of slaves and subsistence day laborers (around 68 percent) in Pauline communities, in "Poverty in Pauline Studies: Beyond the So-Called New Consensus," *JSNT* 26 (2004): 323–61. Even the more conservative estimates of Bruce Longenecker suggest that around 55 percent struggled to exist at the lowest level of society. See Bruce W. Longenecker, "Exposing the Economic Middle: A Revised Economy Scale of the Study of Early Urban Christianity," *JSNT* 31 (2009): 243–78.

12. Jennifer A. Glancy describes the dimensions of the problems for interpreting 1 Cor 6–7 in particular in *Slavery in Early Christianity* (Oxford: Oxford University Press, 2002), 39–70. She asks if Paul is either unaware or insensitive about the presence and plight of slaves among the communities he addresses. I would argue that he is very aware and extremely sensitive; this explains his identification with them as a slave of Christ, his inclusion of slave victims of (ongoing) abuse amongst the "washed and sanctified" (1 Cor 6:11), and his condemnation of abuse within the community (or "body")—but I concede that this is a reading dependent on prior assumptions. On the Gospel traditions, note that the numerous stories about fishermen manage to avoid (ignore?) the Herodian attempts to control and tax the fishing industry by shifting the capital city from Sepphoris to Tiberias (on the lake). In all the stories of crossing "the sea" of Galilee, Tiberias is never mentioned.

in contexts of eating and dining reveal any assumptions about the nature of the meals described? More particularly, why is the wide range of Greek vocabulary for reclining and dining used relatively infrequently in the New Testament traditions when compared with Josephus, for example?[13]

We have to be careful here, because language often lags behind (and sometimes is projected back onto) the realities we are attempting to describe, and especially so when that language is incidental to the main thrust of the narrative. I am struck by how often we use the term *table fellowship* in New Testament scholarship, when the presence of *a* table (singular) is highly unlikely in most meal scenes. There might be multiple small tables beside the reclining couches perhaps, but our images of gospel meal scenes and the language we use to describe them still seem to be shaped more by the Renaissance sensibilities of Leonardo da Vinci's painting of the Last Supper.[14] Smith has shown that the archaeological evidence supports the presence of smaller tables beside the reclining couches in the larger homes and in many associations and clubs around the temples and forums.[15] Yet even he has concluded that "the origin of early Christian meals is not to be found in any one type or originating event but rather in the prevailing custom in the ancient world for groups to gather *at table*."[16] Is it not the reclining to dine that sets the Greco-Roman culture apart

---

13. Statistical comparisons across literary corpora are notoriously fickle (see the attempts in tables 1 and 2 below). Nevertheless, in broad summary, the proportion of eating and drinking vocabulary in Josephus that is associated with reclining and banqueting is around 70 percent; in the gospels, on average, around 30 percent; and in the Pauline corpus, below 7 percent. The distinctive usage of "reclining" verbs is noteworthy: three of the verbs used most frequently in the New Testament for reclining to dine (ἀναπίπτω, ἀνακλίνω, ἀνάκειμαι) occur in Josephus also (the latter some twenty-six times), but *not* in relation to dining. Rather, Josephus makes frequent use of the more formal dining vocabulary: δειπνέω, δεῖπνον, συμπόσιον.

14. Similarly, we speak of "bread and wine" as if the consumption of those items was and is the only way to celebrate the Eucharist. Andrew B. McGowan, "Rethinking Eucharistic Origins," *Pacifica* 23 (2010): 184–85, shows clearly from the historical record that this was not always so. Contemporary mission practice in climates where wheat, corn, and grapes are impossible to grow is to choose elements basic to that culture and context. Celebrating the presence of God with imported elements only has in the past inevitably led to cargo-cult and prosperity theologies.

15. Smith, *Symposium*, 15–17. He goes on to describe how "sitting at table" becomes the dominant motif in later Jewish traditions as represented in the Mishnah (137–38).

16. Ibid., 174, emphasis added.

from the barbarian tribes to the north, rather than the table itself? There are indeed Gospel references to the crumbs from the master's table (Matt 15:27; Mark 7:28) and the rich man's table (Luke 16:21); the hand of the betrayer on the table (Luke 22:21) and "my table in my *basileia*" (Luke 22:30); twice, in Acts, of hospitality (Acts 6:2; 16:34); and Paul's contrast between the "table of the Lord and the table of demons" (1 Cor 10:21)[17]—but nowhere do we find the phrase "recline at table" as such (except in English translations, which often ignore the Greek even further and have "sit at table"). On the other hand, I count ten verbal forms used over fifty times in the New Testament (and many more still in Josephus) to describe the act of reclining to eat[18]—some of which are also used of sickness or death—and so I prefer to use the phrase "reclining fellowship" or "reclining to dine" as a shorthand for the Smith-Klinghardt paradigm, while remaining aware that any one term (table, sitting, reclining) may not accurately reflect the reality it seeks to describe.

While the extended reclining banquet represents the ideal evening meal in first-century Mediterranean cultures, they too had their breakfasts on the run to start the day and their fast-food outlets (the food stalls around the markets) for those lucky enough to afford a midday meal but unable to sit down long enough to eat it. The sage advice of more recent times to "breakfast like a king/queen, lunch like a prince/princess, and dine like a pauper" was reversed in such cultures, but we ought not assume that the lower classes were able to eat three times a day. Poverty and hunger were ever present in the poorer quarters of the cities. For those clients high enough on the social scale to aspire to move even higher, attendance at the banquets of a patron was not only a highly desirable honor in itself but also an opportunity to gain more honor. The complex rules and expectations for reclining and dining were made more complicated by those hosts with the power to flaunt the rules and get away

---

17. Alan Cadwallader has alerted me to the possibility that this contrast evokes the "table/s of the gods" (tables set aside at banquets or in temples) to honor the gods or ancestors. See, for example, Athenaeus, *Deipn.* 4.143F (Gulick, LCL), in the passage describing the "sitting Cretans" (n. 5 above): "There were also chairs reserved for guests, and a third table at the right as one entered the halls, which they called the 'table of Zeus, god of strangers', or 'the strangers' table.'" See also the use of "table of Bel" in *Bel and the Dragon* and the alternating "altar of Baal" / "altar of the Lord" in Judg 6 (LXX).

18. See table 1 below for the details.

with it, and lurid tales of Herodians (Mark 6:14–29!), and Romans who did just that, abound in the histories and popular street mime throughout the empire.[19] How the powerless, poor, and hungry viewed such elite culture and how their own eating and drinking within that wider context was alluded to, ignored, or assumed, is the dimension that I wish to explore. Yet apart from occasional records of exceptional events (such as the Saturnalia), or of those slaves able to afford membership in an association, we are left only with a presumption that the poor are present (in history and in the text) and a suspicion that more slaves are underrepresented and badly treated than we know about.[20] So we can only seek to read these texts in the presence of the impoverished and enslaved and to imagine their response to the stories and language used.[21] That having been said, I will now go on to try to analyze the eating words used in the New Testament to evaluate whether there is any incidental evidence of such sensitivities toward those who serve rather than dine.

Jesus is explicitly invited to recline and dine on a number of occasions in the gospels—with tax collectors (Mark 2:15–17; Matt 9:9–13; Luke 19:5–7) and Pharisees (Luke 7:36–50; 14:1)—though often his disciples

---

19. In the end perhaps it was Herod Antipas's *inability* to flaunt the expectations of his guests that led to the execution of John the Baptist, but the story still bears the marks of a populist send-up of the elite (as does the death of a later Herod in Acts 12:20–23). For accounts of Roman mime and pantomime, sometimes at dinner parties, see Gesine Manuwald, *Roman Republican Theatre* (Cambridge: Cambridge University Press, 2011), and Anthony J. Boyle, *Roman Tragedy* (New York: Routledge, 2006); and for the influence of mime on biblical narrative, see Andrew Simmonds, "Mark's and Matthew's Sub Rosa Message in the Scene of Pilate and the Crowd," *JBL* 131 (2012): 733–54.

20. Martial has an epigram that satirizes one guest handing delicacies to his slave (who was standing behind him) for later sale in the marketplace (*Epig.* 3.23; cf. 2.37). Cicero also has a number of slaves (including his secretary Tiro) standing at the ready to take dictation or to deliver a communication. They are definitely not part of the meal and certainly not reclining—but they are there! See Cicero, *Att.* 14.21.4; cf. 16.2.6 (of a slave, Salvius, reading at a meal).

21. A further body of evidence is being accumulated by those giving attention to the visual exegesis of mosaics and reliefs, some of which depict slaves serving at banquets—often portrayed with diminished stature to convey their lack of social status. On the growing significance of visual exegesis, see, for example, Brigitte Kahl, *Galatians Re-imagined: Reading with the Eyes of the Vanquished* (Minneapolis: Fortress, 2010); and Davina C. Lopez, *Apostle to the Conquered: Reimagining Paul's Mission* (Minneapolis: Fortress, 2008).

seem to disappear from the narrative on those occasions. Jesus appears in these stories as the "trophy guest" in the banqueting rooms of the powerful, while his followers fade from view. Jesus also offers a critique of reclining culture—and the ranking and class distinctions involved—in his wry observations about "taking the lower position" when reclining rather than assuming the best position (Luke 14:7-11), and in his observations on the status of servants, the young, and masters (Luke 22:26-27). Read from a position of solidarity with those who do not recline to dine, these stories take on subversive dimensions—Jesus becomes the champion of the arts of resistance—and provide wonderful examples of mimicry, and even become carnivalesque when the Teacher himself arranges banquets in the wilderness and invites his followers to recline "on the green grass, *symposion* by *symposion*" (Mark 6:39).[22] Such carnivalesque scenes take on tragic tones when the final reclining banquet of Jesus and his circle of friends includes one betrayer. But even this is consistent with the inclusive nature of previous meals in the gospel traditions, where unexpected guests are the norm, women are present, and where, in parable form at least, the invited elite are replaced by those gathered from the streets (Matt 22:1-14).

Arguably, the Pauline traditions also show a similar sensitivity to the eating and drinking of the powerless in the context of the reclining culture of the rich and powerful. Smith begins his analysis of the banquet in the churches of Paul with the assertion that "the only texts in the New Testament that specifically describe early Christian meals" are the account of Paul and Cephas in Antioch (Gal 2:11-14) and the discussion of the Lord's Supper (1 Cor 11:20-27, 33-34a), and he reads both in the light of the *deipnon* traditions.[23] I take his point that the gospel meals, including the last supper, are all pre-Christian meals set in some kind of

---

22. These two instances are the only explicit occurrences of *symposion* in the New Testament, though I agree with Smith that the *symposion* provides the assumed context for many of the Lukan meal scenes in particular (such as the "two cups" at the last supper in Luke 22:15-20). See Walter Brueggemann's engaging interpretation of the wilderness feast in "Food Fight," *WW* 33 (2013): 319-40, and esp. 337-39. For a discussion of the carnivalesque in Mark's account, see Geoff R. Webb, *Mark at the Threshold: Applying Bakhtinian Categories to Markan Characterization* (Leiden: Brill, 2008).

23. Strictly speaking, Paul labels the Corinthian meal as "*not* the Lord's supper/ *deipnon*." McGowan also argues convincingly that we should not assume that this tradition was well known as the "Lord's Supper," since Paul here uses it negatively: "This is *not* the Lord's supper," or "This is *not* the way the Lord dines." McGowan shows that the use of "Lord's Supper" for "Eucharist" or "Communion" is not common in any

Jewish and/or Greco-Roman context, but I would point out that so too are the Pauline accounts, since Paul never once uses the word *Christian*. Even if he was aware of that nomenclature from Antioch (Acts 11:26), he chooses never to use it, and we should not apply it anachronistically to his writings lest we bring with it other baggage from later times. I am not suggesting that Smith does this himself, but that a similar stricture should apply to our discussion of Paul's dining terminology. Just as we are inclined to create idealized scenes of the Lord's Supper as the epitome of "early Christian table fellowship" when "Christians" and a "table" may not even have been present—and possibly not even fellowship at Corinth!—so, too, we can ignore the presence of those who were invisible, who prepared and served the food but had no couch on which to recline. Paul speaks of eating and drinking almost as much as anyone in the New Testament (second only to Luke) but almost never uses the language of reclining to dine (see table 1 below for details). When he does refer explicitly to the "supper" (*deipnon*; twice in 1 Cor 11:20–21) and to "reclining" (only once, in 1 Cor 8:10), it is in the context of the dining problems in the Corinthian community, both in the home and reclining in the temple of an idol. Neither of these terms is used positively. I am not arguing here that therefore Paul was opposed to Greco-Roman banquets as such, nor that reclining to dine seldom occurred in his communities, but rather that in his choice of vocabulary, Paul demonstrates a sensitivity to the majority of the members of his *ekklēsiai* (women, slaves, freedmen and freedwomen, and the poor) who would seldom have the opportunity to recline.

For these reasons, he insists that when the *ekklēsia* is gathering to remember and embody the body and blood of Christ, it does so inclusively and on an equal footing for all participants. What disqualifies the Corinthian way of doing this is not the reclining nor the presence of other food, but the inequality of the sharing—"one is hungry and another is drunk" (1 Cor 11:21)—and thereby they are in danger of "despising the gathering of God and humiliating those having nothing" (1 Cor 11:22). I agree with Smith and others that the pattern of the *deipnon* and *symposion* lies behind this problem in Corinth, such that the food brought by the community is shared unequally—between those in the inner *triclinium* and

---

other early traditions. See Andrew McGowan, "The Myth of the 'Lord's Supper': Paul's Eucharistic Meal Terminology and Its Ancient Reception," *CBQ* 77 (2015): 503–21.

the lower-ranked members left in the courtyard, or those standing behind the recliners and watching, and salivating—or perhaps it was not shared at all.[24] Paul's solution is not to mandate a standard dining procedure but to encourage people to eat at home first if they are hungry (in whatever manner they are accustomed and able to do), before gathering inclusively and sharing equally in giving thanks by a simpler breaking of bread and drinking of wine.[25]

So if, for example, we assume the successful reception of Paul's short letter to Philemon, would Onesimus recline at table with Philemon after his return, or still serve as a slave (albeit as a "brother")? Would they remember the Lord's death together in some simple way but still eat other meals separately? We might wish that Paul could be clearer in his ethical advice (and in 1 Cor 7:21–24 as well), but at least by insisting that the central remembrance of the body and blood of Jesus should be participated in equally (whether as part of a love feast / *agapē* meal, a reformed banquet, or a simple stand-alone celebration), Paul provides a critical focus on "discerning the body" (Christ's, ours, mine) that is not tied to any one cultural dining practice or set of foods.

With one exception, in all the rest of Paul's substantial commentary on eating and drinking—particularly in Rom 14 and 1 Cor 8–11—he consistently uses the most direct vocabulary for eating and drinking and avoids the rich language of reclining and dining used so commonly in Greek lit-

---

24. Smith, *Symposium*, 176–80. Interestingly, he suggests that all worship (as in 1 Cor 14) occurs in this dining setting also, thus requiring those present to sit rather than recline for practical reasons of space. Given that reclining is an expression of status, this would enhance the egalitarian nature of the Corinthian worship even further. I think this could be a possible outcome of Paul's intervention, but the text of Corinthians indicates to me a tension between Paul's understanding of *ekklēsia* and the consequences of the way they are reclining to dine. The Athenaeus reference above (n. 5), suggests that the presence or absence of condiments at the meal could also be used to indicate the relative status of those dining.

25. Again, the elements of bread and wine were eventually standardized, but McGowan gives evidence of the use of water, fish, and other foods in early eucharistic settings. See McGowan, *Ascetic Eucharists*, and McGowan, "Rethinking Eucharistic Origins," 184–85. He also suggests that Paul opts for a simpler solution: Paul's "instruction suggests a preference for a simple common meal practice, perhaps something less than the most desirable banquets in quantity or variety of food and drink, but not necessarily a token meal whose only claim to the word δεῖπνον would be symbolic, or even ironic." See McGowan, "Myth," 507.

erature. In that sole exception, 1 Cor 8:10, Paul warns against reclining in an idol's temple in case someone might be led to actually eat the sacrificial meat in the presence of the idol, which for Paul would be partaking in the "table of demons" (1 Cor 10:21). Many translations use "eating in the temple of an idol" rather than just "reclining" (in 1 Cor 8:10), but Paul's main concern is to protect the weaker one who might be led astray, so both eating and appearing to eat (by reclining) are equally problematic. I think that this concern for the weaker member is consistent with Paul's general avoidance of specific references to reclining culture. He neither assumes it uncritically as the norm nor opposes it, but rather focuses on what is most appropriate for the upbuilding of the weaker members in each specific case that arises.

So is there evidence in the New Testament texts to support a reading from below in solidarity with those who seldom if ever recline to dine? The approach taken here has been to survey these "eating words" in the New Testament traditions (with an analysis of Josephus as a comparison) to find out if the explicit language of reclining/dining/supper/symposium varies as a percentage of the total use of all eating vocabulary in each tradition. The most common terms used for the acts of eating and drinking in general in the New Testament are ἐσθίω and πίνω, which carry no explicit reference to the mode of eating (reclining or sitting at table). There is also a rich vocabulary (at least ten other verbs and several nouns) used to describe the kind of dining referred to in the Smith-Klinghardt paradigm, and the usage of these terms varies widely, as summarized in table 4.1 below. The banqueting language of reclining and dining has then been expressed in table 4.2 as a percentage of the total number of occurrences of eating and drinking language so that direct comparisons can be made between texts of different lengths.

Table 4.1: Overview of Eating and Banqueting Vocabulary[26]

	Paul	Mark	Matthew	Luke	John	Acts	Other	Josephus
ἐσθίω	43	27	24	33	15	7	Heb: 2/1	21
[ἐσθίω and πίνω]	[11]	[–]	[5]	[14]	[1]	[3]	James: 1/0	[2]
πίνω	15	8	15	17	11	3	Rev: 6/3	38
ἀναπίπτω	–	2	1	4	5	–	–	(3)
ἀνακλίνω	–	1	2 (1)	2	–	–	–	(1)
κατακλίνω	–	–	–	5	–	–	–	12 (2)
ἀνάκειμαι	–	2 (1)	5	2	4	–	–	(26)
κατάκειμαι	1	2 (2)	–	2 (1)	– (2)	– (2)	–	10 (6)
συνανάκειμαι	–	2	2	3	–	–	–	–
ἀριστάω	–	–	–	1	2	–	–	2
δειπνέω	1	–	–	2	–	–	Rev: 2	15
δειπνίζω	–	–	–	–	–	–	–	1
δειπνοποιέω	–	–	–	–	–	–	–	4
δεῖπνον	2	2	1	5	4	–	Rev: 2	47
δοχή	–	–	–	2	–	–	–	–
συμπόσιον	–	2	–	–	–	–	–	24
Total reclining/dining	4	13	11	27	15	0	Rev: 4	115
Total eating words	62	48	50	77	41	10	Rev: 13	174

Key: [ ] = not included in totals; ( ) = word not used of reclining to dine (but of sleep, sickness, or death)

---

26. I make no claim to having found the complete list of relevant vocabulary here—the semantic domains are difficult to define and the number of compound verbs is extensive. Nevertheless, a start has been made by making use of Johannes P. Louw and Eugene A. Nida, eds., *Greek-English Lexicon of the New Testament: Based on Semantic Domains* (New York: United Bible Societies, 1988). Using the same extended list of verbs as found in Josephus, I have calculated the percentages of reclining vocabulary at 6.3 percent for the Septuagint, 23.5 percent for the Greek Pseudepigrapha, and 16.7 percent for the Apostolic Fathers. But each corpus may well have used additional terminology that I have not yet located, so these figures are provisional. Nevertheless, they are consistent with the Septuagint reflecting the older Jewish eating customs, a rise in reclining culture in the Greco-Roman period, and the growing critique of reclining culture found in the church fathers.

A survey of a wider body of first-century Greco-Roman literature is clearly needed here for more extensive comparisons, but already the usage of meal terminology in the New Testament is placed in a helpful context. Even Luke's well-known focus on more elaborate meal settings is somewhat limited compared with the diversity of banqueting language in Josephus, for example (see note after table 4.2 below). A rough means of comparison is provided by the percentages in table 4.2.

TABLE 4.2: BANQUETING TERMINOLOGY AS A PERCENTAGE OF ALL EATING VOCABULARY

	Paul	Mark	Matthew	Luke	John	Other	Josephus
Verbs + dining nouns (%)	6.5%	27.1%	22.0%	35.1%	36.6%	Rev: 30.8%	66.1% (79.3%)

Note: For Josephus we could have added the terms ἑστίασις (party/feast; 22 occurrences); ἑστιάω (give a party/feast; 34 occurrences); εὐωχία (feast; 38 occurrences) εὐωχέω (feasting well; 17 occurrences), none of which occur in the New Testament. The new percentage of banqueting vocabulary would then be 79.3 percent.

Of course, there are many factors that might explain the variation in percentages in table 4.2—the genre of the text (narrative, letter, or apocalypse); the dominant cultural location of the author and/or of the readers; the subject matter itself; and the stylistic preferences of the author, for a start. We note the many New Testament texts not even represented in the table because they do not use any of the vocabulary for eating or drinking. Yet the contrast between Paul and Josephus is remarkable. Josephus is ten times more likely to use the specific language of the banquet (reclining/supper/symposium) than is Paul, who only refers to reclining once, to dining once, and to supper twice in the midst of his many discussions about food laws, food offered to idols, eating and drinking, and celebrating the Eucharist. The figures for the gospels are not as surprising—we would expect the more Hellenistic Gospels of Luke and John to use a higher proportion of Greco-Roman eating terminology—but even there a strong undercurrent of dissonance with the assumptions of the dominant reclining culture remains. Jesus is an awkward guest to entertain in Luke's Gospel, even though they keep inviting him and he invariably accepts (Luke 7:36–50; 10:38–42; 11:37–52; 14:1–24; 19:1–27). Then in John, when we expect one last *symposion* of deep liturgical significance to occur, it becomes instead (?) another opportunity to turn the *deipnon* traditions upside down as the host begins to wash feet in the middle of the meal (John 13:1–20).

There is no evidence here for a neat progression or development from Pauline critique to later compromise with the dominant culture, nor from early conformity to later opposition. As Glancy has shown, the Christian critique of the (excesses of) banquet culture waxed and waned in various ways in the succeeding centuries.[27] Whether Paul's letters or the gospel narratives ignore, subvert, mimic, satirize, or simply assume the features of a Greco-Roman banquet, the Smith-Klinghardt paradigm is affirmed, as the *deipnon* still provides the dominant meal tradition within which, and sometimes against which, they must be interpreted. As the table disappears from many meal traditions today and people again recline on couches to eat their meals—but now in front of enormous flat-screens for their entertainment (or in some cases, each with his or her own small screen!)—we may well begin to reflect on where open commensality is still experienced in our community, and whether we can yet "discern the body" as we struggle to remember the host who washes the guests' feet.

It is in the nature of *Festschriften* that some brief personal notes are permitted. In this case the following reflections about Dennis are not gratuitous but are appropriate to the scope of this article. I have had the great pleasure of accompanying Smith on two of the COMCAR expeditions—to Macedonia and to Turkey—and so consequently I have a number of photos of him reclining as if to dine in order to illustrate to our group the location of various dining couches in homes and beside markets and temples. From a shrine to Pan high on Thassos, to Pella, to Pergamon, to Ephesus, and to many places in between, Dennis embodied all that he has written about until it became a standard trope of our travels as we explored countless ruins. But there are other photos, too, of Dennis seated at table with the rest of the group, again embodying the fellowship of the meal as the perfect dinner companion. We are all indebted to him on both counts, as a scholar who lives the truth about which he writes.[28]

Bibliography

Aitken, Ellen Bradshaw. "Remembering and Remembered Women in

---

27. Jennifer A. Glancy, "Temptations of the Table: Christians Respond to Reclining Culture," in Smith and Taussig, *Meals*, 229–38.
28. I am also indebted to the editor, Alan Cadwallader, whose eagle eye and encyclopedic memory have greatly enhanced this essay, and particularly the detail in nn. 5, 17, 20, and 21.

Greco-Roman Meals." Pages 109–22 in *Meals in the Early Christian World: Social Formation, Experimentation, and Conflict at the Table.* Edited by Dennis E. Smith and Hal E. Taussig. New York: Palgrave Macmillan, 2012.

Ascough, Richard S. "Social and Political Aspects of Greco-Roman Association Meals." Pages 59–72 in *Meals in the Early Christian World: Social Formation, Experimentation, and Conflict at the Table.* Edited by Dennis E. Smith and Hal E. Taussig. New York: Palgrave Macmillan, 2012.

Athenaeus. *The Deipnosophists.* Trans. by Charles Burton Gulick. 7 vols. LCL. New York: Putnam's Sons, 1927.

Boyle, Anthony J. *Roman Tragedy.* New York: Routledge, 2006.

Brueggemann, Walter. "Food Fight." *WW* 33 (2013): 319–40.

Friesen, Steven J. "Poverty in Pauline Studies: Beyond the So-Called New Consensus." *JSNT* 26 (2004): 323–61.

Glancy, Jennifer A. *Slavery in Early Christianity.* Oxford: Oxford University Press, 2002.

———. "Slaves at Greco-Roman Banquets: A Response." Pages 205–11 in *Meals in the Early Christian World: Social Formation, Experimentation, and Conflict at the Table.* Edited by Dennis E. Smith and Hal E. Taussig. New York: Palgrave Macmillan, 2012.

———. "Temptations of the Table: Christians Respond to Reclining Culture." Pages 229–38 in *Meals in the Early Christian World: Social Formation, Experimentation, and Conflict at the Table.* Edited by Dennis E. Smith and Hal E. Taussig. New York: Palgrave Macmillan, 2012.

Harland, Philip A. "Banqueting Values in the Associations: Rhetoric and Reality." Pages 73–86 in *Meals in the Early Christian World: Social Formation, Experimentation, and Conflict at the Table.* Edited by Dennis E. Smith and Hal E. Taussig. New York: Palgrave Macmillan, 2012.

Kahl, Brigitte. *Galatians Re-imagined: Reading with the Eyes of the Vanquished.* Minneapolis: Fortress, 2010.

Longenecker, Bruce W. "Exposing the Economic Middle: A Revised Economy Scale of the Study of Early Urban Christianity." *JSNT* 31 (2009): 243–78.

Lopez, Davina C. *Apostle to the Conquered: Reimagining Paul's Mission.* Minneapolis: Fortress, 2008.

Louw, Johannes P., and Eugene A. Nida, eds. *Greek-English Lexicon of the New Testament: Based on Semantic Domains.* New York: United Bible Societies, 1988.

Manuwald, Gesine. *Roman Republican Theatre*. Cambridge: Cambridge University Press, 2011.

Marks, Susan. "Present and Absent: Women at Greco-Roman Wedding Meals." Pages 123–48 in *Meals in the Early Christian World: Social Formation, Experimentation, and Conflict at the Table*. Edited by Dennis E. Smith and Hal E. Taussig. New York: Palgrave Macmillan, 2012.

McGowan, Andrew B. *Ascetic Eucharists: Food and Drink in Early Christian Ritual Meals*. Oxford: Clarendon, 1999.

―――. "The Myth of the 'Lord's Supper': Paul's Eucharistic Meal Terminology and Its Ancient Reception." *CBQ* 77 (2015): 503–21.

―――. "Rethinking Eucharistic Origins." *Pacifica* 23 (2010): 173–91.

Shogren, Gary Steven. "Is the Kingdom of God about Eating and Drinking or Isn't It? (Romans 14:17)." *NovT* 42 (2000): 238–56.

Simmonds, Andrew. "Mark's and Matthew's Sub Rosa Message in the Scene of Pilate and the Crowd." *JBL* 131 (2012): 733–54.

Smith, Dennis E. *From Symposium to Eucharist: The Banquet in the Early Christian World*. Minneapolis: Fortress, 2003.

―――. "The Greco-Roman Banquet as a Social Institution." Pages 23–33 in *Meals in the Early Christian World: Social Formation, Experimentation, and Conflict at the Table*. Edited by Dennis E. Smith and Hal E. Taussig. New York: Palgrave Macmillan, 2012.

Smith, Dennis E., and Hal E. Taussig, eds. *Meals in the Early Christian World: Social Formation, Experimentation, and Conflict at the Table*. New York: Palgrave Macmillan, 2012.

Standhartinger, Angela. "The Saturnalia in Greco-Roman Culture." Pages 179–90 in *Meals in the Early Christian World: Social Formation, Experimentation, and Conflict at the Table*. Edited by Dennis E. Smith and Hal E. Taussig. New York: Palgrave Macmillan, 2012.

―――. "Women in Early Christian Meal Gatherings." Pages 87–108 in *Meals in the Early Christian World: Social Formation, Experimentation, and Conflict at the Table*. Edited by Dennis E. Smith and Hal E. Taussig. New York: Palgrave Macmillan, 2012.

Taussig, Hal E. Introduction to *Meals in the Early Christian World: Social Formation, Experimentation, and Conflict at the Table*. Edited by Dennis E. Smith and Hal E. Taussig. New York: Palgrave Macmillan, 2012.

Webb, Geoff R. *Mark at the Threshold: Applying Bakhtinian Categories to Markan Characterization*. Leiden: Brill, 2008.

Ancient Drinking in Modern Bible Translation

Jorunn Økland

ἡμεῖς δ' οὐδέπω δεδείπναμεν (Athenaeus, *Deipn.* 10.422e)[1]

1. Wining and Dining

In honor of colleague, travel companion, and discussion partner Dennis Smith, I offer this short essay on a topic that should be close to his research interests, because it concerns wining and dining in the ancient world, and that is close to my heart, too, (at least its current installment) because it concerns translation. The topic in question is the translation of terminology relating to drinks, drinking parties, and drinking vessels in (relatively) modern English and Scandinavian translations of the Greek book of Esther.

I will use the Greek book of Esther as an example of how ancient material culture, and in particular material practices of eating, drinking, and feasting, have fared in some modern translations. The example emerges out of my current ongoing work in and for the translation committee of Norwegian Bible Society and their preparation of a new translation of the Apocrypha.[2] As part of the task force submitting the first draft of the new translation of the Greek book of Esther (henceforth ESG) to the translation committee, part of my work was to survey a broader comparative base of texts.

Numerically, most Bible translators in the world today have never traveled to ancient sites with Smith, who is at all times actively imagining what it was like to be eating, drinking, and feasting in an ancient sanctuary or home. Translators are selected on the basis of their knowledge of language, and in some translation societies even on the basis of their

---

1. "We haven't finished dinner yet."
2. The Apocrypha in a new Norwegian translation will appear in 2017 or 2018.

religious faith and call to mission, but never on the basis of their knowledge of material culture. One could argue that for a book collection like the Bible, the material facts on the ground are unimportant, but I will argue that the Bible becomes a much more boring and one-dimensional book when its connections to a particular place, a particular time, and a particular cultural setting are lost. In cultures where the interest in the Bible is on the wane, this is a serious problem. Further, we have concepts only for what we can conceptualize. Without information about the facts on the ground, conceptualizing Esther's challenges in another language becomes difficult.

Susa, the main site of the Esther narrative, as well as the Achaemenid "twin residence,"[3] Persepolis, have been explored and preliminarily excavated since the mid-nineteenth century.[4] The explorers/excavators were looking for items carrying the names of Persian rulers known from Hebrew and Greek historical writings: Darius, Xerxes, or Artaxerxes. The discipline of archaeology has further developed since then, but for our purposes that makes less of a difference. Already early on, the excavations revealed structures of buildings of a scale that makes "palace" a rather modest term. Among other things, King Xerxes is credited for having undertaken the construction of the pretentious Great Hall of Columns,[5] a hall that his successor Artaxerxes had to finish. These spaces and palaces are where the story of Esther is set, and much could be said about how

---

3. With Susa as "une capitale secondaire, probablement la capitale d'hiver" in relation to Persepolis, see François Vallat, *Suse et l'Elam*, Mémoire 1 (Paris: Éditions ADPF, 1980), 4.

4. William. K. Loftus, *Travels and Researches in Chaldaea and Susiana: With an Account of Excavations at Warka, the "Erech" of Nimrod, and Shush, "Shushan the Palace" of Esther, in 1849–1852* (New York: Robert Carter, 1857); Jane Dieulafoy, *À Suse: Journal des fouilles, 1884–1886* (Paris: Librairie Hachette, 1888); Marcel A. Dieulafoy, *L'acropole de Suse: D'après les Fouilles exécutées en 1884, 1885, 1886, sous les auspices du Musée du Louvre*, 4 vols. (Paris: Librairie Hachette, 1890–1892). The couple Jane and Marcel Dieulafoy deserve an article on their own, on another occasion, in a journal of gender studies. The University of Chicago started more systematic excavations in Persepolis in 1931 (according to the foreword, signed 1951, in Erich Friedrich Schmidt, *Structures, Reliefs, Inscriptions*, vol. 1 of *Persepolis*, OIP 68 [Chicago: University of Chicago Press, 1953]).

5. See Jean Perrot, ed., *Le palais de Darius à Suse: Une résidence royale sur la route de Persépolis à Babylone* (Paris: Presses de l'Université Paris-Sorbonne, 2010), 78 and 198–99.

they have fared in translations conducted in parts of the world with other architectural ideals. I will save this much larger topic for a later occasion.

2. The Greek Book of Esther

In much of current translation theory, culture is understood as a product of processes of translation and negotiation, without one stable root or single origin. Translation is one of the primary means by which cultures travel. Therefore in the meeting with new and different worlds, meanings of texts change, and secondarily cultural transformation occurs. Every translation is in this sense a new production.[6] The Greek translation of the Hebrew book of Esther was obviously much more than a translation, and therefore it deserves to be considered as a separate piece of writing. It is expansive in its paraphrases, which are mostly concentrated in six longer additions. The expansions and the translation have turned the book into something else, approximating the way in which the Synoptic Gospels are considered three accounts of the life of Jesus although Matthew and Luke shared some of the same sources: Mark, a sayings source, and possibly others. Where the Hebrew book of Esther is considered the most secular book of the Bible in the sense that the name of God is not even mentioned, the Greek book of Esther was intended to be an "improved" and more pious version, tying the story more clearly to contemporary Jewish religious practices. It adds more theology, but also more local color—as understood from a viewpoint outside the culture described. In some ways, the Greek book of Esther could be described as an orientalizing (and slightly moralizing) court novel, written several hundred years after the events it describes (approximately 100 BCE). Hence all the drinking!

Although the Hebrew *Vorlage* does not dominate the choices made in the Greek text, numerous later translations of the Greek book of Esther have, under the inspiration of a notion of the Hebrew as original, still allowed the Hebrew to overwrite the translation of the Greek in a number of respects. First, this has led nearly to chaos with regard to the chapter

---

6. See, e.g., Lydia H. Liu, ed., *Tokens of Exchange: The Problem of Translation in Global Circulation* (Durham: Duke University Press, 2000); Emily S. Apter, *The Translation Zone: A New Comparative Literature* (Princeton: Princeton University Press, 2006); Sandra Bermann and Michael Wood, eds., *Nation, Language, and the Ethics of Translation* (Princeton: Princeton University Press, 2005).

and verse numbering—which are not original in any case, but belong to the later stages of textual transmission.

Second, the Hebrew Bible included the Hebrew book of Esther only, not Greek Esther. This means that neither the Jewish Publication Society nor many Protestant translation boards include Greek Esther in their translations. The Septuagint included the Greek book of Esther. The Vulgate and its later adaptations into vernacular languages (e.g., the Douay-Rheims surveyed here) include Greek Esther, too, but only the additions that could not be seen as mere translations of the Hebrew: they append them as additional chapters at the end of the Hebrew book of Esther or place them among the other apocryphal books situated between the Old and New Testaments. Versions of the Protestant canon (based on the Hebrew Bible), such as the original King James Version (KJV), have continued this practice of including the "Additions to Esther," but these were removed from the KJV in 1885.

Third, as if this were not enough, translators have also had to negotiate or choose between the two main textual variants of Greek Esther: the L-text or the O-text, of which I will not say much more here, simply referring to the explanation given in De Troyer and Wacker.[7]

Fourth, even when trying to define the narrative time of the story, there are differences between the Hebrew and the Greek text that the translations have had to navigate![8] While the Hebrew book of Esther places the story in the time of King Xerxes (486–465 BCE), the Greek book of Esther places it in the time of his successor, Artaxerxes (465–425 BCE). Josephus (*Jewish Antiquities*) later follows Greek Esther in this respect,[9] but, as Emma Bridges has pointed out, this is the result of a misunder-

---

7. For explanation of the so-called O-text, see Kristin De Troyer and Marie-Theres Wacker, "Esther/Das Buch Ester," in *Genesis bis Makkabäer*, vol. 1 of *Septuaginta Deutsch: Erläuterungen und Kommentare zum griechischen Alten Testament*, ed. Martin Karrer und Wolfgang Kraus (Göttingen: Deutsche Bibelgesellschaft, 2011), 1254–55.

8. See Emma Bridges, *Imagining Xerxes: Ancient Perspectives on a Persian King* (London: Routledge, 2014), 141–42 and 146, and n. 9 below. She chooses to treat "Artaxerxes" as a misunderstanding and reads the king in Greek Esther as Xerxes, as in the Hebrew version.

9. "The Persian king named in the Hebrew text as Ahasuerus has for the last century been positively identified with Xerxes on the basis of Achaemenid inscriptions in which he is named as the Persian equivalent *Xšayāršā*, anglicized via Greek as 'Xerxes.' Prior to the discovery of the Persian texts, however, confusion was caused by the fact

standing. Hence, I shall be following her interpretation, and I consider the king involved as King Xerxes himself.

These complications with regard to deciding which text exactly to translate contribute to the abovementioned chaos when trying to create a general overview of the modern versions of Esther: many find an unsystematic, pragmatic way in the middle, between the variants.

In the Lutheran tradition of the Norwegian Bible Society, among others, both the Hebrew and Greek books of Esther are translated in their totality, with Greek Esther in a separate section of the canon as part of the Old Testament Apocrypha or Deuterocanonical Books. This canonical choice is reminiscent of the choices made by the scribes copying manuscripts in the days before the arrival of print: when in doubt, include both versions![10] But at least this approach acknowledges the two versions as nonidentical.

3. Drinks, Drinking Parties, and Drinking Vessels in the Greek Book of Esther

At this point we will leave behind the distinctions between the Hebrew and Greek accounts of Esther, as well as the various canonical labels and orders of biblical books, in order to focus on Greek Esther only, and especially the way the culture of drinking has been translated in modern versions.

---

that the Greek version of Esther translates Ahasuerus as 'Artaxerxes,' presumably on the basis of the phonetic similarity of the names" (Bridges, *Imagining Xerxes*, 142).

10. For this phenomenon, which they compare with ripples in the water from a pebble cast into a pond, or more aptly (and violently) with earthquakes, see Kurt Aland and Barbara Aland, *The Text of the New Testament: An Introduction to the Critical Editions and to the Theory and Practice of Modern Textual Criticism*, 2nd ed., trans. Erroll F. Rhodes (Grand Rapids: Eerdmans, 1989), 70, 294–96, at 296: "The scribe who already has the (secondary) ending … adds to it the (equally secondary) ending …, sometimes even twice, with less concern for the possibility of repetition than for the danger of losing a part of the text." Compare George Aichele: "The canon of scripture is a hypertextual machine that supports the continual and creative recycling of the Bible. The potential to combine seemingly endless permutations and reconfigurations of the multi-textual collection is one of the great strengths of the biblical canon. The canon opens a semiotic space within which creative interpretation of biblical texts is encouraged." See George Aichele, "Canon, Ideology, and the Emergence of an Imperial Church," in *Canon and Canonicity: The Formation and Use of Scripture*, ed. Einar Thomassen (Copenhagen: Museum Tusculanum, 2010), 45.

3.1. Drinking Parties

Before I move to the analysis and discussion, I will first list the relevant verses under discussion, since Greek Esther is not very well known:[11]

1:3: The king holds a δοχή, literally a "reception" but usually translated "banquet" (NRSV), "feast" (KJV), or similarly. The existing Norwegian translation from 1988 (NO 1988) has *gjestebud*, a familiar term putting the emphasis on the invitees, who are receiving a treat. The Greek L-text has πότος here, which is derived from a root related to drinking (see below).

1:5: After τοῦ γάμου, literally "the wedding," referring back to 1:3, the king gives for all the people present in the citadel of Susa a πότον, a six-day drinking party (NRSV: "banquet"; KJV: "feast"; NO 1988: another *gjestebud*).

1:8: ὁ δὲ πότος οὗτος οὐ κατὰ προκείμενον νόμον ἐγένετο; the drinking party did not follow any preordained law/order (NRSV: "Drinking was by flagons, without restraint"; RSV: "drinking was according to the law, no one was compelled"; NO 1988: something equivalent to "there should be no limitations to the drinking").

1:9: The queen hosts a πότον for the women separately from the male drinking party mentioned in verse 8. Like in 1:5, the translations use "banquet"/"feast"/*gjestebud* respectively.

2:18: The king gave a great, seven-day πότον (RSV and NRSV: "banquet"; KJV: "feast"; NO 1988: *fest*) to his officials, on the occasion of his wedding to Esther and in her honor.

---

11. I have made use of Accordance and Paratext for my surveys and consultations and, where possible, have checked with hard copies, since digital versions licensed by the respective bible societies are often corrected and adjusted compared to the first editions of print versions to which the year of publication refers: *Det gamle testamentes apokryfiske bøker: De deuterokanoniske bøker* (Oslo: Norske Bibelselskap, 1988); *The New Revised Standard Version of the Bible* (New York: National Council of Churches, 1989); I have also consulted *Bibel 2000: Ester enligt den grekiska texten* (Uppsala: Svenska Bibelsällskapet, 2000); David Norton, ed., *The New Cambridge Paragraph Bible, with the Apocrypha: King James Version* (Cambridge: Cambridge University Press, 2005); *The Apocrypha: Revised Standard Version of the Old Testament* (New York: Nelson, 1957); Swift Edgar and Angela M. Kinney, eds., *The Vulgate Bible: Douay-Rheims Translation*, 4 vols. (Cambridge: Harvard University Press, 2010–2013). The citations of the Greek text are taken from the O-text of the Göttingen Septuagint edition: Robert Hanhart, ed., *Esther*, vol. 8.3 of *Septuaginta: Vetus Testamentum Graecum*, 2nd ed. (Göttingen: Vandenhoeck & Ruprecht, 1983).

4:45 [or addition C, Esther's Prayer, v. 17]: In her prayer, Esther refers to the king's συμπόσιον and to the drinking of οἶνον σπονδῶν, translated "I have not honored the king's feast or drunk the wine of libations" (RSV/NRSV); "banquets"; "drink offerings" (Douay-Rheims); "have not greatly esteemed the king's feast … the wine of the drink offerings" (KJV); *drikkelag* and *offervin* ("drinking party" and "wine sacrifices," NO 1988).

5:4: Esther invites the king and Haman to come to her πότον (L-text) or δοχήν (O-text); (RSV/NRSV: "dinner"; NO 1988: *gjestebud*).

5:6: At the πότῳ, the king addresses Esther (RSV/NRSV: "As/While they were drinking wine," and NO 1988 has the equivalent; KJV: "at the banquet of wine").

6:14: His servants come to Haman at home and rush him off to the πότον that Esther has prepared (NRSV: "banquet"; NO 1988: *fest*); the king also attends.

7:1–2: The king and Haman go in to συμπιεῖν, "to drink with" the queen (NRSV); "to feast with" (RSV). Verse 2 includes a reference to what happened on the second day of Esther's small πότος with the king and Haman (RSV/NRSV: "as they were drinking wine"; KJV: "the banquet of wine"; NO 1988 uses *fest* in both verses, with no specific reference to drinking).

7:7: The king leaves the συμποσίου and goes into the garden (NRSV: "feast"; KJV: "banquet of wine") NO 1988: *drikkelag*, "drinking party").

8:16: Among the Jews there was φῶς καὶ εὐφροσύνη (O-text), the L-text has φῶς, πότος, κώθων, "light, drinking party, [and] a drinking vessel"; for the latter, see below. The RSV reads: "gladness and joy, feast and a holiday"; NRSV: "joy and gladness, a banquet and a holiday"; KJV: "light and gladness and joy and honor"; NO 1988 has *jubel og fryd, fest og glede*, meaning as much and as little as the English translations.

As much as the Persian King Xerxes left behind monuments traced by archaeologists, so the fictional monarch in the books of Esther loved throwing parties. In Greek Esther there is a system of various types of parties that replace each other in a given pattern. In the text, at least four terms occur, and they emphasize either the serving of drink, the fellowship in common drinking, the occasion (wedding), or the host (the one who "receives" the guests).

The preferred technical term for "drinking party" is πότος, derived from the root ποτ-, which relates to drinking. It is by far the most frequently used term for any type of festive gathering in ESG (see the list above). In addition, the term συμπόσιον is used twice, in 4:45 and 7:7 (in the L-text also twice, in 1:11 and 7:11—both times as the alternative term for the πότοι already mentioned). De Troyer and Wacker comment that the LXX (and the O-text) tries, to an even greater extent than the MT Hebrew text, to avoid denoting the Jewish feasts with the same terms as used for Persian feasts. Thus, in the case of the Persian feasts, the drinking is emphasized, whereas in descriptions of Jewish feasts towards the end of the book, the emphasis is on gladness and sharing (μετὰ χαρᾶς εὐφροσύνη ESG 8:16; 9:17, 18, 19).[12] It is particularly interesting that there is a difference between the L-text and the O-text on this point, and I will return to this below.

The term πότος is used referring to (at least) six different drinking parties in ESG (1:3, 5, 8; 2:18; 5:4, 6; 6:14; 7:2; 8:16). I have already mentioned the issues involved regarding the last verse (8:16) and will return to this below.

In ESG 1:3, we learn that first, the king throws a large, lavish drinking party/reception/wedding. All three terms are used within a span of three verses to describe the same mega-event; thus on this occasion, at least, they must be more or less synonymous, although they emphasize different aspects of the party: the event lasts for 180 days (!), and the occasion is the celebration of his acquisition of a new batch of brides, as mentioned in 1:5.

When this feast is over, the king extends invitations to a drinking party of a more modest format, lasting for six days only and only including those who were already in the citadel (ESG 1:5). In the previous Norwegian translation of the book, the same term is used both in ESG 1:3 and in 1:5. This makes 1:5 look more like a haplography; anyway it leads to questions of why the king would have two parties immediately following each other. The Greek text, presenting the latter more as a *Nachspiel* to the former, makes much more sense of why two events were required on this occasion. They had different functions in the festive calendar of events.

It is clear from ESG 1:8, which refers to the *Nachspiel*-like drinking party, that drinking parties, too, were highly ritualized. However, on this occasion the rituals were to be abandoned; the king wanted the servants to adjust to the preferences of the participants and to those of the king himself.

We also learn from ESG 1:9 in the same chapter that Queen Vashti also hosted a drinking party for the women. They were not drinking with the men, but in the royal apartments, called the harem.[13] Later (ESG 1:10),

---

12. De Troyer and Wacker, "Esther," 1286.

13. That is, the enclosed royal apartments, not harem in the sense of a group of wives. A large plan of the complicated architecture at Susa, with entrances, separate

ἡδέως γενόμενος ὁ βασιλεύς (RSV/NRSV/KJV: "On the seventh day, when the heart of the king was merry with wine"; Douay-Rheims: "when the king was merry, and after very much drinking was well warmed with wine"; NO 1988 has *godlag*, "in a good temper"), Queen Vashti is supposed to be brought in to the men for all of them to admire her, but she refuses. This must have been part of the ritual of such male drinking parties, at this point called *symposium*, because later on in the story (ESG 4:45 [28]), Queen Esther points out that she has never shown off her glory at the king's *symposia*. Neither has she drunk from the libation offerings.

The third event mentioned (2:18), seems to mirror the previous one: it is a drinking party hosted by the king and lasting seven days to celebrate another royal wedding, that of Esther—still to the same king, though.

In ESG 3:22 (15), there is no mention of a drinking party. But after having issued the decree that all Jews should be exterminated, the king and his deputy Haman start a period of heavy drinking, just the two of them: ἐκωθωνίζοντο. The term κωθωνίζω has the meaning "to make drunk" or, in the passive, as here, "to drink hard." Occasionally English translations have used the term "carouse," indicating a rather drunk group of revelers. The Norwegian translation NO 1988 is in the same vein when it mentions that they "celebrated," and although πότος is *not* the term used here, for once an expression equivalent to "drinking party" is used: *feiret … med et drikkelag*. However, there is nothing merry in the situation. The NRSV/KJV use "sat down to drink," which is better, but too punctiliar to be in accord with the imperfect, rather than aorist, tense of the verb. The *imperfectum* denotes the durative aspect of the drinking. Since the verse also describes the increasing perplexity and confusion in the city, the drinking must have gone on for some time. The Swedish translation (*Bibel 2000*) accurately grasps this, as it indicates that the king and Haman sat drinking together while unrest spread in town. In Norwegian, there exists a more colloquial phrase that overlaps semantically with the Greek, *gå på fylla*, that is, drinking steadily and heavily over an extended period, so that one is constantly inebriated in order to drown one's worries, to revel with friends, or for other reasons. Both apply in the case of the king and Haman. It could be days or even weeks. In English there may be similar colloquial terms that might have been more accurate.

---

exits, passageways with limited access, and guarded posts, can be found in Perrot, *Palais de Darius*, 214, and figs. 211–19. For the women's quarters, see in particular fig. 217.

The next πότοι mentioned, in ESG 5:4 (18) and 5:6; 6:14 and 7:2, respectively, refer to two separate drinking parties or "receptions" (the O-text uses δοχήν in 5:4) hosted by Queen Esther herself, and the invitees are Haman and the king only. This seems to be a small event at which Esther tries to exert her will by giving her guests too much to drink.

On this occasion, too, the main purpose seems to be drinking, since only drink is referred to explicitly. When the king has had something to drink, Esther asks them both to return the day after, and the king agrees.

In ESG 6:14, we learn about that second drinking party. The next verse (7:1) makes clear that the purpose of the gathering is to drink with the queen, and this time the drinking session lasts several days (7:2). As it happens (and as planned by Queen Esther), this drinking session leads to complications that end in disaster (7:1–10): It ends with Haman being killed. Both the L- and the O-text use the term συμπόσιον for variation here, in 7:7 and 7:11, respectively.

The seventh reference to a πότος is found in ESG 8:16, but only in the L-text: it mentions, in addition to the general merriment when the Jews are saved, that they have φῶς, πότος, κώθων—light, a drinking party, and a particular drinking vessel. Theoretically, even the term κώθων in the same verse of the L-text is used in a secondary sense of "drinking bout"—but see under drinking vessels below. I have already mentioned the comment of De Troyer and Wacker on the LXX's attempt to distinguish between Persian and Jewish feasting (the O-text is the main LXX-text). In any case, the emphasis on drinking in the descriptions of Persian court life is not at all reflected in the modern translations, with the effect that the intended contrast of Persian and Jewish feasting practices disappears. The modern translations surveyed consistently choose more neutral terms. Regardless of their other text-critical choices, English translations on this point consistently follow the O-text and omit references to alcohol. Hence there is only "light and gladness" and similar innocuous merriment.

3.2. Drinking Vessels

ESG 1:7 says (NRSV): "Drinks were served in golden goblets, goblets of different kinds, and the royal wine was lavished according to the bounty of the king." The Greek text (and, curiously, only the Norwegian translation among the translations consulted for this piece!) mentions that the drinking vessels were made of gold *and* silver. They are called ποτήρια, which refers to individual goblets. The abundance of drinking vessels in precious materials at the courts of the Achaemenid kings is described by Erich Schmidt in his chapter "Royal Tableware" in volume two of *Persepolis*. The chapter demonstrates that on this point, the ESG is not at all hyperbolic.[14] Regarding the large finds of royal tableware in Persepolis, Schmidt also points out that Xerxes's name is engraved on a range of the vessels in question.[15]

In the same verse, there is also mention of a κυλίκιον, the diminutive of the more familiar κύλιξ, a drinking bowl for sharing. It is ἀνθράκινον (the Norwegian translation says "ruby," but for what reason is unknown) and worth 30,000 talents. Since ἀνθράκινον refers both to coal and to mirrors, it may be a kind of crystalline, precious glass-like bowl. That such translucent materials were in use in the Achaemenid courts is well documented.[16] The English translations consulted are silent with regard to both the material and the economic worth of this precious piece; they just mention that the "goblets" are of different kinds and are diverse. On the basis of the excavation reports and the dizzying lavishness described there, the mention of a κυλίκιον worth 30,000 talents does not appear to be hyperbolic.

In the L-text of ESG 8:16, another drinking vessel is listed, namely, a κώθων. It is left untranslated in all translations of the verse. According to Liddell and Scott, the term denotes a "Laconian drinking-vessel" that was frequently used by soldiers.[17] It is the root term behind the verb discussed above with reference to 3:22, κωθωνίζω, meaning "to make drunk" or "to drink hard." Another derivative of the same root is κωθωνιστής, someone who drinks until he is drunk (see Athenaeus, *Deipn*. 10.433b; see also 10.420e–11). A note to the Athenaeus passage in question explains κώθων as "a wine-flask of some sort" and refers across to book eleven of the same work, where Athenaeus writes that its rim is curved inwards (that is, like on a bottle), and further that one does not see what is inside

---

14. Erich Friedrich Schmidt, *Contents of the Treasury and Other Discoveries*, vol. 2 of *Persepolis*, OIP 69 (Chicago: University of Chicago Press, 2010), 81–89. See esp. 93, where fig. 18 is an attempted reconstruction of a glass chalice, while the main text points out that "the excavators conclude tentatively that the transparent glass was manufactured at Babylon about 600 B.C."

15. Ibid., 81.

16. See n. 14 above; see also Schmidt, *Contents of the Treasury*, 85 (and n. 34): "all Xerxes vessels registered … are said to be made of aragonite." See also p. 91 for an overview of the composition of the tableware, which was made of various types of stone and other materials.

17. LSJ, s.v. κώθων.

it (*Deipn.* 11.483b).¹⁸ A secondary, derived meaning of κώθων is a drinking bout, "carousal"—of the sort in which soldiers sometimes engage—or even "religious banquet," according to the entry in Liddell and Scott.

Exactly why this particular term is chosen in Greek to denote the Persian drinking vessel in question is not clear, but it is found also in preexisting Greek literature indicating Persian drinking vessels, namely, in Xenophon's *Cyropaedia*.¹⁹ There, Xenophon writes about the education of Xerxes's own grandfather, Cyrus: "Furthermore, they bring from home bread for their food, cress for a relish, and for drinking, if any one is thirsty, a cup to draw water from the river" (πιεῖν δέ, ἤν τις κώθωνα; Xenophon, *Cyr.* 1.2.8 [Miller, LCL]).²⁰ Thus, an educated reader of Greek, at least, would know in advance that in Persia, they teach even future kings to drink from the κώθων. However, Davidson has pointed out that educated Greeks of Xenophon's own time would more likely have understood the κώθων as a drinking vessel tailored for excessive consumption of wine, and that is certainly the impression one gets also from reading the larger passage on the topic in Athenaeus.²¹

It is however possible, that κώθων is used in the secondary meaning of drinking bout in this case—but see the earlier reference to De Troyer and Wacker regarding the tendency of the O-text (LXX) not to use the same

---

18. The highly entertaining discussion of the term κώθων and its derivatives continues through 11.484c.

19. Or they may be familiar with the stories Athenaeus retells in book 10 of his *Deipnosophistae* (434), which gives us a lot of information about Western (Greek) perceptions about the Persians, such as the following: "In Persia the king is allowed to get drunk on only one day, when they sacrifice to Mithra.... At only one of the festivals the Persians celebrate, that in honor of Mithra, does the king get drunk and perform the Persian dance. No one else in Asia does this; instead, they all avoid dancing on that day. For the Persians learn to dance in the same way they learn to ride horses, and they believe that the movement this activity involves includes exercise that promotes physical strength." The translation is Olson's; see Athenaeus, *The Learned Banqueters*, trans. S. Douglas Olson, 8 vols., LCL (Cambridge: Harvard University Press, 2006–2012).

20. See also Adam Rabinowitz, "Drinking from the Same Cup: Sparta and Late Archaic Commensality," in *Sparta: Comparative Approaches*, ed. Stephen Hodkinson (Swansea: Classical Press of Wales, 2009), 113–92, at 168 n. 7. Rabinowitz provides a critical evaluation of the argument of James N. Davidson, who, in his *Courtesans and Fishcakes: The Consuming Passions of Classical Athens* (London: HarperCollins, 1997), 63, argues that among Classical Athenian Greeks, this (archaic Lakonian) drinking vessel is associated with excessive and antisocial wine consumption.

21. Davidson, *Courtesans and Fishcakes*, 63.

terms for the drinking parties of the Persians and the much soberer celebrations of the Jews. To give the full quote: "Die LXX scheint es, anders als der MT, zu vermeiden, die jüdische Feste mit den begriffen für die Feste der Perser zu bezeichnen (auch in Kap. 9). Der griech. Terminus κώθων, eigentlich 'Trinkgefäß', findet sich in der LXX überhaupt nur in Est. 8:17 und 3 Makk 3:61."[22] It is clear that the occasion is joyous, but none of the existing translations follow the L-text in this case, and thus they avoid mentioning altogether the Jewish drinking parties in celebration of their victory.

3.3. Drink

In the Greek book of Esther, much is said about the various types of parties and rituals involving drink, as well as the various physical responses to it. Something is also said about the vessels from which the drink is taken. In this perspective, it is striking that very little is said about the drink itself. However, to underscore the argument of this chapter: even less—that is, nothing—is said about the food that we must assume accompanied at least some of the drink at these parties. But we do hear about food being shared at the celebrations of the Jews in the final verses of the book.

From the physical responses described, from our knowledge of ancient practices and rituals, and from the little information that is there, it is clear that wine is the drink being served at the drinking parties. In ESG 1:7, we learn only that for the second drinking party, the six-day event after the big wedding party, οἶνος πολὺς καὶ ἡδύς, "there was much wine, and sweet wine." This was the kind of wine the king himself drank. The Greek book of Esther was clearly written before modern viticulture, so perhaps there was not much more to say? We are informed, both in chapter 1, with reference to Queen Vashti's drinking party, and in chapters 5–7, that the women also were drinking wine.

Conclusion

In this essay I have dealt with the book of Esther in its *Greek* installment and not with the related Hebrew book of Esther, which presents the founding narrative behind the Purim festival. Taking the Greek book on its own terms

---

22. De Troyer and Wacker, "Esther," 1286.

has allowed me to focus on other aspects relating more to Greek drinking culture and on the translation of it into modern Western languages.

Athenaeus's *Deipnosophists*, or *Drinking Companions*, with which the Greek book of Esther shares some resemblance, says in book 10 (433b): "Someone who is eager for wine [οἶνος] is φίλοινος; someone eager to have drinking parties [πότοι] is φιλοπότης; and someone who drinks until he is drunk is a κωθωνιστής." There can be no doubt that the king of Persia was more than usually eager to have drinking parties, and thus he qualified for the term *philopotēs*.[23] It is also clear that on at least one occasion he was drinking until he was drunk, and thus qualified to fit the term *kōthōnistēs*.

For the *author* of the Greek book of Esther, describing the various genres of drinking, ritual drinking, parties, vessels, and their contents was a way of describing the court culture as a whole. For Smith, studying ancient feasts and meal practices has also been a way of approaching ancient culture as a whole and trying to understand it. The day we have a more nuanced understanding of ancient material practices regarding food and drink, and of the ritualized behavior surrounding these basic but scarce necessities, modern Bible translators may become more accurate and may dare to be less worried about translating terminology relating to ancient inebriation.

Bibliography

Aichele, George. "Canon, Ideology, and the Emergence of an Imperial Church." Pages 45–65 in *Canon and Canonicity: The Formation and Use of Scripture*. Edited by Einar Thomassen. Copenhagen: Museum Tusculanum, 2010.

Aland, Kurt, and Barbara Aland. *The Text of the New Testament: An Introduction to the Critical Editions and to the Theory and Practice of Modern Textual Criticism*. 2nd ed. Translated by Erroll F. Rhodes. Grand Rapids: Eerdmans, 1989.

Apter, Emily S. *The Translation Zone: A New Comparative Literature*. Princeton: Princeton University Press, 2006.

Athenaeus. *The Learned Banqueters*. Translated by S. Douglas Olson. 8 vols. LCL. Cambridge: Harvard University Press, 2006–2012.

---

23. Note the mistaken transliteration of this term in the Loeb edition (Athenaeus, *The Learned Banqueters* [Olson, LCL]), 69.

Bermann, Sandra, and Michael Wood, eds. *Nation, Language, and the Ethics of Translation*. Princeton: Princeton University Press, 2005.

Bibel 2000: Ester enligt den grekiska texten. Uppsala: Svenska Bibelsällskapet, 2000.

Bridges, Emma. *Imagining Xerxes: Ancient Perspectives on a Persian King*. London: Routledge, 2014.

Davidson, James N. *Courtesans and Fishcakes: The Consuming Passions of Classical Athens*. London: HarperCollins, 1997.

De Troyer, Kristin, and Marie-Theres Wacker, "Esther/Das Buch Ester." Pages 1253–96 in *Genesis bis Makkabäer*. Vol. 1 of *Septuaginta Deutsch: Erläuterungen und Kommentare zum griechischen Alten Testament*. Edited by Martin Karrer und Wolfgang Kraus. Göttingen: Deutsche Bibelgesellschaft, 2011.

Dieulafoy, Jane. *À Suse: Journal des fouilles, 1884–1886*. Paris: Librairie Hachette, 1888.

Dieulafoy, Marcel A. *L'acropole de Suse: D'après les fouilles exécutées en 1884, 1885, 1886, sous les auspices du Musée du Louvre*. 4 vols. Paris: Hachette, 1890–1892.

Edgar, Swift, and Angela M. Kinney, eds. *The Vulgate Bible: Douay-Rheims Translation*. 4 vols. Cambridge: Harvard University Press, 2010–2013.

Det gamle testamentes apokryfiske bøker: De deuterokanoniske bøker. Oslo: Norske Bibelselskap, 1988.

Hanhart, Robert, ed. *Esther*. Vol. 8.3 of *Septuaginta: Vetus Testamentum Graecum*. 2nd ed. Göttingen: Vandenhoeck & Ruprecht, 1983.

Liu, Lydia H., ed. *Tokens of Exchange: The Problem of Translation in Global Circulation*. Durham: Duke University Press, 2000.

Loftus, William K. *Travels and Researches in Chaldaea and Susiana: With an Account of Excavations at Warka, the "Erech" of Nimrod, and Shush, "Shushan the Palace" of Esther, in 1849–1852*. New York: Robert Carter, 1857.

Norton, David, ed., *The New Cambridge Paragraph Bible, with the Apocrypha: King James Version*. Cambridge: Cambridge University Press, 2005.

Perrot, Jean, ed. *Le palais de Darius à Suse: Une résidence royale sur la route de Persépolis à Babylone*. Paris: Presses de l'Université Paris-Sorbonne, 2010.

Rabinowitz, Adam. "Drinking from the Same Cup: Sparta and Late Archaic Commensality." Pages 113–92 in *Sparta: Comparative Approaches*.

Edited by Stephen Hodkinson. Swansea: Classical Press of Wales, 2009.

Schmidt, Erich Friedrich. *Contents of the Treasury and Other Discoveries.* Vol. 2 of *Persepolis.* OIP 69. Chicago: University of Chicago Press, 2010.

———. *Structures, Reliefs, Inscriptions.* Vol. 1 of *Persepolis.* OIP 68. Chicago: University of Chicago Press, 1953.

Vallat, François. *Suse et l'Elam.* Mémoire 1. Paris: Éditions ADPF, 1980.

Xenophon. *Cyropaedia.* Translated by Walter Miller. 2 vols. LCL. London: Heinemann; New York: Macmillan, 1914.

Making Men in Rev 2–3:
Reading the Seven Messages in the
Bath-Gymnasiums of Asia Minor*

Lynn R. Huber

1. Introduction

Addressed to communities of the faithful living within seven cities in ancient Asia Minor—Ephesus, Smyrna, Pergamon, Thyatira, Sardis, Philadelphia, and Laodikeia—the messages of Rev 2–3 tell of community conflicts and offer images that evoke the realia of the ancient world. The messages are tantalizingly concrete in a book more commonly known for its abstract and fantastic imagery. As a result, Revelation scholars often highlight connections between the messages and the ancient locations to which they refer, using the messages, dictated by the Son of Man, as tools for understanding the lives and identities of Revelation's original audiences. This has occasionally taken a literalistic turn as scholars align textual images with specific archaeological finds or ancient traditions. In contrast, more recent scholars have advocated a more dynamic approach to engaging ancient material cultures in relation to the text, suggesting that both material objects and texts participate in the discursive frameworks in which they are embedded. In this vein, I suggest reading the seven messages of Rev 2–3 in conversation with the bath-gymnasiums of first-century urban Asia Minor, situating these within a larger conversation about

---

* This essay is dedicated to my friend and colleague Dennis Smith, whose love of life and family knows no bounds. I met Dennis by participating in COMCAR, an organization that has contributed greatly to my understanding of the material cultures in which the writings of the New Testament are embedded. I presented the main ideas for this essay as part of the 2013 COMCAR trip to Turkey, and I am appreciative of the feedback I received from other participants.

the construction of masculine gender in the Roman world. In so doing, it is possible to see how the messages participate in imagining a masculine ideal, a victor whose endurance leads to reward in a New Jerusalem.[1]

2. Shifting Our Approach to Revelation and Realia

The messages of Rev 2–3 are often thought of as grounding the book of Revelation in the realities of the ancient world, partly based upon the fact that they are addressed to communities located in cities whose ruins scholars can still visit, see, and experience. In light of this, there is a long tradition of drawing specific connections between these messages and archaeological remains or pieces of material culture.[2] In *The Letters to the Seven Churches*, originally published in 1904, classical archaeologist and New Testament scholar Sir William Ramsay famously paired detailed descriptions of the cities of Revelation, drawing upon ancient texts, archaeological resources, and his own experiences in Turkey, with discussions of the corresponding messages. This approach is based upon his assumption that John "imparts to [the letters] many touches, specially suitable to the individual Churches … showing his intimate knowledge of them all."[3] Ramsay suggests, for instance, that the Son of Man's promise to give the faithful of Smyrna a "crown of life" evokes depictions of a personified Smyrna wearing a mural crown, while he connects the promise of white robes to those in Laodikeia to the wool production for which the city was well known.[4] The detail of Ramsay's associations makes it

---

1. The language of "making men" comes from Maud W. Gleason, *Making Men: Sophists and Self-Presentation in Ancient Rome* (Princeton: Princeton University Press, 1995). I explore some ideas related to this essay in a forthcoming piece, "Gender and Identity in John's Apocalypse," in *The Oxford Handbook of New Testament, Gender, and Sexuality*, ed. Benjamin Dunning (New York: Oxford University Press, forthcoming).

2. Craig R. Koester, "The Message to Laodicea and the Problem of Its Local Context: A Study of the Imagery in Rev 3.14–22," *NTS* 49 (2003): 407–24; Steven J. Friesen, "Revelation, Realia, and Religion: Archaeology in the Interpretation of the Apocalypse," *HTR* 88 (1995): 291–314. See also Robert M. Royalty, "Etched or Sketched? Inscriptions and Erasures in the Messages to Sardis and Philadelphia (Rev. 3.1–13)," *JSNT* 27 (2005): 447–63.

3. William Mitchell Ramsay, *The Letters to the Seven Churches of Asia and Their Place in the Plan of the Apocalypse*, 2nd ed. (Hodder & Stoughton, 1906), 39.

4. Ibid., 275.

easy to understand how some scholars in a field that once aspired to scientific surety would find these connections appealing. In addition, the "local allusions," as Craig Koester calls them, drawn by Ramsay and those who follow in his wake, such as Colin J. Hemer,[5] firmly situate the text within its ancient context, an important thing for those scholars seeking to qualify or complicate popular readings of Revelation as a blueprint for the end times.[6]

Despite the appeal of identifying local allusions, more recent scholars, including Koester and Steven J. Friesen, highlight these types of interpretations as idiosyncratic and historically problematic.[7] Friesen notes that many of these connections reflect accidents of history, as associations are made between the text and those archaeological finds simply available to the New Testament scholar. For example, the connection sometimes drawn between John's reference to "Satan's throne" and the altar of Zeus and Athena in Pergamon (2:13) is most likely due to the altar's availability to European biblical scholars, according to Friesen, since its foundations and friezes "were hauled off and displayed in the Pergamon-Museum in Berlin."[8] Even though this interpretation of 2:13 has grown out of favor with many Revelation scholars, it persists in some sources, especially resources aimed at lay audiences. Thus, despite noting that the reference is disputed, Craig S. Keener offers the "the famous huge throne-like altar of 'Zeus the Savior,' whose sculptures included serpents" as a possible allusion behind John's image.[9] Once an allusion such as this has been drawn, it becomes difficult to dislodge, as it becomes a part of the interpretive tradition surrounding Revelation.

---

5. Colin J. Hemer, *The Letters to the Seven Churches of Asia in Their Local Setting* (Sheffield: Sheffield Academic, 1986).

6. See, for instance, the commentary on Revelation by Grant R. Osborne (*Revelation*, BECNT [Grand Rapids: Baker Academic, 2002]). Osborne discusses his own "conversion" from reading Revelation primarily as a prophetic text describing modern events to reading the text as addressing its historical context as well as having modern relevance. Osborne's commentary, like Ramsay's earlier work, prefaces each message of Rev 2–3 with discussions of the historical situation of each city. These include attention to archaeological and material elements of the cities.

7. Koester, "The Message to Laodicea."

8. Steven J. Friesen, "Satan's Throne, Imperial Cults and the Social Settings of Revelation," *JSNT* 27 (2005): 359.

9. Craig S. Keener, *Revelation: From Biblical Text to Contemporary Life*, NIV Application Commentary, Kindle ed. (Grand Rapids: Zondervan, 2000), 122.

Similarly problematic and persistent is the tendency to assume that metaphors within Revelation's messages are particularly significant within the city named, rather than exploring the more general and, perhaps, mundane reading. For example, the reference to a pillar that cannot be removed from the temple (3:12) is described by Gregory Beale as something that "would have been appreciated by the Philadelphians, since their city suffered from earthquakes more than any of the other cities addressed."[10] However, a number of the cities of Revelation experienced earthquakes, including the earthquake of 17 CE that required massive rebuilding, part of which was funded by Tiberius. Surely, most people in the region could appreciate an image of stability.[11] Another persistent local allusion involves linking the reference to the Laodikeians as being lukewarm and in danger of being vomited out of Christ's mouth (3:16) to assumptions about the city's water being lukewarm. The city's supposedly tepid water is often compared to the water of the nearby Hierapolis, where there are still striking white mineral deposits that can be seen from afar and that are the result of the city's thermal pools. Stories of the bad Laodikeian water abound in modern commentaries on Revelation. Keener, referencing the thermal springs of Hierapolis, implies that the Laodikeians may have found heating the tepid water from their aqueducts a "drudgery" and, therefore, that the reference has something to do with the inhabitants' lack of reliance on Christ.[12] Brian K. Blount takes the local allusion in another direction, drawing upon scholars who suggest that, because Laodikeian water was piped in from Hierapolis, it was medicinal tasting and nauseating. Thus, the water was something people often wanted to spit out.[13] As Koester points out, however, textual and material evidence suggests that Laodikeian water was obtained, like other cities, through an aqueduct supplied by local springs.[14] The water would have been neither more ill-tasting nor more tepid than water from other cities in the area. The problem, however, is bigger than one of misinformation. Rather, as Koester notes, "quests for local allusions often allow the expressions in Revelation

---

10. Gregory K. Beale, *The Book of Revelation: A Commentary on the Greek Text*, NIGTC (Grand Rapids: Eerdmans, 1999), 294.

11. Royalty, "Inscriptions and Erasures," 451.

12. Keener, *Revelation*, 158.

13. Brian K. Blount, *Revelation: A Commentary*, NTL (Louisville: Westminster John Knox, 2009), 80.

14. Koester, "The Message to Laodicea," 410.

to exert too much control over the selection and interpretation of material from other sources.... Archaeological and other ancient materials appear as isolated pieces of evidence that are used without adequate consideration of the broader context from which these materials were taken."[15] The tendency to "fit" an image in Revelation to a particular material object often misses the potential inherent in reading the text in relation to the ancient material world. Rather, as Friesen and Koester argue, material culture helps us appreciate the social structures of the ancient world through which ancient religious discourses were shaped.[16]

While it may seem ironic in an essay titled "Revelation, *Realia*, and Religion," Friesen argues that scholars of Revelation, as well as biblical scholars in general, should attend to the insights of literary theory as they engage the material world of the biblical texts. Friesen challenges the dichotomy drawn between literary texts and material culture, underscoring that both are products of their social contexts, "crafted by humans in particular historical and cultural settings."[17] Archaeological materials are as much in need of interpretation and critical evaluation as are texts and are best understood when considered in the fullness of their milieu. Similarly, archaeologist Rosemary A. Joyce and the coauthors of *The Languages of Archaeology* argue for approaching material culture in terms of storytelling and narrative. Highlighting the interpretive nature of archaeological writing, Joyce explains that even in the field the archaeologist narrativizes the objects and structures around her, determining how individual pieces might fit together, both literally and figuratively.[18] Drawing upon the work of Mikhail Bakhtin, Joyce suggests approaching archaeological writing in terms of the utterance, as dialogical speech act. Jeanne Lopiparo, a contributing author to *The Languages of Archaeology*, extends the idea of the utterance to archaeological objects and artifacts, suggesting that these material objects function as "past utterances."[19] As such, they are

---

15. Ibid., 408. Friesen points to the often unstated political and ideological motivations that undergird these interpretations as well, explaining the imperialistic and Orientalist aspects of Ramsay's work in particular. See Friesen, "Revelation, Realia, and Religion."

16. Friesen, "Revelation, Realia, and Religion," 314.

17. Ibid., 308.

18. Rosemary Joyce, Robert W. Preucel, and Jeanne Lopiparo, *The Languages of Archaeology: Dialogue, Narrative, and Writing*, ed. Rosemary Joyce (Oxford: Wiley-Blackwell, 2002), 10.

19. Ibid., 71.

always embedded within a discursive context, responding to and reflecting past conversations and, more importantly, they always seek a response, whether it is confirmation, critique, or contestation.[20] That is, material finds should be understood as dialogically constructed, embedded within particular conversations that constitute the social framework surrounding them. Among other things, this means that material finds participate in the social construction of meaning, including the construction of gender.[21]

3. Gender and Material Culture

Initial forays into the study of gender and archaeology focused upon uncovering the lives of women from the past, much like early feminist biblical interpretation sought to uncover the lives of women behind and within the texts. For archaeology this involved looking for artifacts believed to reveal the work and lives of women—cosmetic bottles, combs, hairpins, and items related to weaving.[22] Material objects were read as signs pointing to gender and were interpreted as indicators of the presence of women in specific spaces, often reflecting assumptions about ancient gender roles and the division of labor.[23] More recently, archaeologists specializing in the study of gender have begun to advocate for engaging material culture more dynamically. Rather than being part of a fossil record of gender, artifacts and architecture are approached as media of social discourse, communicating gender expectations and shaping the ways in which ancient individuals and groups relate to and engage those expectations. Marie L. S. Sørensen explains, "Gender gains material reality and affects individuals and groups as it becomes acted out and experienced through material culture."[24] It is through the material world that gender becomes realized.

This understanding of gender and material culture pushes the interpreter away from assigning gender to a particular object and toward

---

20. Ibid., 9.

21. The idea that things have "social lives" is often attributed to the volume edited by Arjun Appadurai, *The Social Life of Things: Commodities in Cultural Perspective* (Cambridge: Cambridge University Press, 1988).

22. Marie L. S. Sørensen, "Gender, Things, and Material Culture," in *Handbook of Gender in Archaeology*, ed. Sarah Milledge Nelson (Lanham, MD: AltaMira, 2006), 107.

23. Penelope M. Allison, "Engendering Roman Domestic Space," *British School at Athens Studies* 15 (2007): 347–49.

24. Sorensen, "Gender, Things, and Material Culture," 114.

exploring the multiple ways an object can participate in constructing gender. Penelope M. Allison offers the case of unguentaria, the small glass bottles often found in Roman contexts. With traces of kohl and aromatics found in some, these bottles have been read as indications of feminine gender. Visual and textual associations between women and toilet items similarly suggest the connection. In fact, we easily can imagine feminine gender being constructed in relation to these objects, as the cosmetics and oils that might be held in these delicate remnants of the past could adorn the body in ways that helped ancient individuals conform to expectations associated with elite women's femininity in the Roman context.[25] However, we simply cannot know whether a particular bottle or set of bottles might have been used in concert with gender expectations associated with them or in a way that takes these utterances in a different direction altogether. Further, to assume that these bottles communicate solely in relation to feminine gender conventions is problematic, as they could be interpreted as holding medical remedies, which might be used by women or men. Moreover, Allison notes that these small bottles could contain oils appropriate for an elite male's after-bath massage or for anointing a soldier's military regalia.[26] In these ways, idealized masculine identity could be constructed by interacting with these objects as well. Even if these bottles might be more commonly associated with the construction of feminine gender, this is not something contained in the material object; rather, it is through the interaction between bodies and objects that gender is formed and communicated. As Allison offers, "This material culture is not a passive reflection of society, but is an active agent in the structuring of that society."[27]

The idea that material objects participate in the construction of gender aligns with an understanding of gender and sex as performed, an idea most closely associated with the writings of Judith Butler.[28] In *Gender Trouble*, Butler argues that gender and sex, terms that she resists drawing a stark distinction between, are performed and even created through repeated acts that "congeal over time to produce the appearance of substance, of

---

25. Allison, "Engendering Roman Domestic Space," 346–47.

26. Penelope M. Allison, "Characterizing Roman Artifacts to Investigate Gendered Practices in Contexts without Sexed Bodies," *AJA* 119 (2015): 119–20.

27. Allison, "Engendering Roman Domestic Space," 346.

28. Judith Butler, *Gender Trouble: Feminism and the Subversion of Identity* (New York: Routledge, 1990), 7.

a natural sort of being."²⁹ This does not mean that individuals choose their gender or sex; rather, sex is constructed through the rigid regulatory frameworks of a given culture. In fact, Butler notes, cultures "regularly punish those who fail to do their gender right."³⁰ Thinking about ancient archaeology and material culture in relation to Butler, we can imagine that the spaces and things of the ancient world reflect the assumptions of these frameworks and encourage ancient individuals to act in relation to these frameworks. This is not to say that gender does not change or that it is not transformed. For Butler, gender is malleable and can be transformed through repetition, particularly in communities resignifying gender collectively.³¹ While Butler focuses on drag performance, we might, as suggested below, think about how the writings of the early Jesus movement, including Revelation, promote a resignification of gender.

4. Making Men in the Bath-Gymnasium

Butler's explanation of gender as performed is helpful for understanding ancient Roman perspectives on gender, which generally reflected the idea of a "one-sex" system.³² Ancient experts such as Galen and Soranus maintained that all humans were potentially male, females simply being underdeveloped or imperfect males. Galen famously explains:

> The female is less perfect than the male for one, principal reason because she is colder, for if among animals the warm one is the more active, a colder animal would be less perfect than a warmer. A second reason is one that appears in dissecting.... All the parts, then, that men have, women have too, the difference between them lying in only one thing ... namely, that in women the parts are within [the body], whereas in men they are outside. (Galen, *Usu part.* 14.6–7 [May])³³

---

29. Ibid., 33. Butler challenges the popular distinction between gender as a cultural/social category and sex as a biological reality, arguing instead that gender is the construct through which the sexes are established. See ibid., 6–7.

30. Ibid., 140.

31. Judith Butler, *Undoing Gender* (New York: Routledge, 2004), 216.

32. Thomas Laqueur, *Making Sex: Body and Gender from the Greeks to Freud* (Cambridge: Harvard University Press, 1992), 25–35. See also Colleen Conway, *Behold the Man: Jesus and Greco-Roman Masculinity* (New York: Oxford University Press, 2008), 16–18.

33. See also Soranus, *Gyn.* 3.3.

As a result of this biological understanding of male and female, ancient perspectives on gender can be imagined in terms of a scale on which individuals and groups were placed and along which they could move up, toward being more masculine, or down, toward becoming less masculine. One's place on the scale depended upon a variety of physical, social, and moral factors. In addition to the sex assigned at birth, male or female, an individual's status, slave or free and Roman or non-Roman, contributed to whether one was understood as a man, *vir* in Latin. Given the assumption that everyone was, at least before birth, potentially male, women might be understood as "unmen," along with slaves and non-Roman males.[34]

Although they were important, biological and social factors were not sufficient for making a true man, as certain virtues and activities were also necessary. L. Stephanie Cobb explains, "sex and virtue, it turns out, are so integrally related that a person's sex can be determined by his or her personality and character."[35] Even though there were differences of opinion regarding the virtues central to constituting manhood, among the most commonly cited were moderation, wisdom, justice, and bravery.[36] Possession of these qualities was evident in a man's body, through his appearance, posture, and gait.[37] Moreover, cultivation of these virtues was a constant process, as Cobb notes: "Although anatomically sexed males were closer to the perfect state of masculinity, they, too, had continuously to strive to be men.... They were expected to develop masculine characteristics, but *development* is the key; they could, at any moment, fail at the task and slip down the continuum toward femininity."[38]

One of the primary locations associated with the development and maintenance of ideal masculinity in Roman Asia Minor was the bath-gymnasium. Although Romans in the West viewed the classical Greek gymnasium tradition with suspicion, since exercising in the nude might

---

34. Conway, *Behold the Man*, 15.

35. Cobb notes this primarily in reference to the physiognomist Polemo, but it is applicable to the broader understanding of sex and virtue in the ancient context. See L. Stephanie Cobb, *Dying to Be Men: Gender and Language in Early Christian Texts*, Gender, Theory, and Religion, Kindle ed. (New York: Columbia University Press, 2008), 28.

36. Andrew Wallace-Hadrill, "The Emperor and His Virtues," *Historia* 30 (1981): 298–323.

37. Gleason, *Making Men*, 58–60.

38. Cobb, *Dying to Be Men*, 28, emphasis original.

be erotically charged, it flourished in the East until the third century CE.[39] In the cities of Asia Minor, the Roman bath often was paired with a Greek-style palaestra, a place for exercise and athletics, creating a "bath-gymnasium" complex.[40] These hybrid structures, along with stadiums, theaters, and amphitheaters, were part of a pervasive agonistic culture through which males in Asia Minor established gender, class, and ethnic identities.[41] Pointing to the civic significance of the bath-gymnasium, these sites are found in central urban areas. Ephesus had at least four bath-gymnasium complexes by the second century CE, including the Harbor Baths, which may have been built during the reign of Domitian (ca. 81–96 CE),[42] and Pergamon (fig. 6.1) may have had as many as five during the reign of Tiberius (14–37 CE).[43] Remains of bath-gymnasium complexes also have been found in other cities associated with Revelation, such as Sardis and Laodikeia, as well as other important Asian cities such as Priene, Magnesia, Ankyra, and Miletus.

As in the classical Greek period, during the first century in Asia Minor, the gymnasium was understood as a site primarily for the formation of young men. While women did use the public baths and there may have been mixed-gender bathing, girls were not the primary clientele for gymnasium training, as they were typically being prepared for marriage at the same age young boys were entering the *ephebeia*.[44] Although the age

---

39. Zahra Newby, *Greek Athletics in the Roman World: Victory and Virtue* (Oxford: Oxford University Press, 2005), 230–31; Jason König, *Athletics and Literature in the Roman Empire* (Cambridge: Cambridge University Press, 2005), 47. For a discussion of the decline of the agonistic culture and the gymnasium, see Sofie Remijsen, *The End of Greek Athletics in Late Antiquity* (Cambridge: Cambridge University Press, 2015), 88.

40. Fikret K. Yegül, *Bathing in the Roman World* (New York: Cambridge University Press, 2009), 155.

41. Onno van Nijf, "Local Heroes: Athletics, Festivals and Elite Self-Fashioning in the Roman East," in *Being Greek under Rome: Cultural Identity, the Second Sophistic and the Development of Empire*, ed. Simon Goldhill (Cambridge: Cambridge University Press, 2001), 306–34.

42. Newby, *Greek Athletics*, 229–31.

43. E. Norman Gardiner, *Athletics in the Ancient World* (Mineola, NY: Dover, 2002), 79.

44. Yegül, *Bathing in the Roman World*, 156. For information on mixed gender bathing, see Roy Bowen Ward, "Women in Roman Baths," *HTR* 85 (1992): 125–47. Bain notes that there are some games that included contests for girls, and there is some evidence that girls may have been allowed into the gymnasium; see Katherine Bain,

Figure 6.1. Overlooking the palaestra of a bath-gymnasium complex, often labeled the "Upper Gymnasium," in Pergamon. All photographs by Lynn R. Huber.

of entrance varied, *epheboi* were generally teenage boys from the elite and more middle-class families of Asia Minor[45] who became part of the bath-gymnasium in order to continue their educations after studying grammar and literature.[46] While a teen might only be part of the *ephebeia* for a year or two, with a financial contribution he could continue training within the bath-gymnasium as one of the *neoi*, a class of young men in their twenties.[47] In some settings, such as in Pergamon, different age groups may have used different bath-gymnasium complexes for their training. Entrance into these spaces was a first step toward achieving manhood. An inscribed stele

---

Women's Socioeconomic Status and Religious Leadership in Asia Minor in the First Two Centuries C.E. (Minneapolis: Fortress, 2014), 31. However, Caldwell suggests that exercise was recommended for girls and young women primarily as a recourse for the problem of females' excessive moisture. See Lauren Caldwell, *Roman Girlhood and the Fashioning of Femininity*, Kindle ed. (Cambridge: Cambridge University Press, 2014), 87.

45. Onno van Nijf notes that in Roman Asia Minor there seem to have been traders and craftsman who participated in gymnasium culture, even though it was primarily intended for cultivating the identities of elite males. See van Nijf, "Local Heroes," 325.

46. Christian Laes and Johan Strubbe, *Youth in the Roman Empire: The Young and the Restless Years?* Kindle ed. (Cambridge: Cambridge University Press, 2014), 70.

47. Ibid., 71–72; König, *Athletics and Literature*, 47–48.

from Beroia, Macedonia (compare fig. 6.2), references those not allowed to participate in the activities of the gymnasium, including slaves, freedmen, prostitutes, and those who are drunk or insane.[48] These are the people for whom ideal masculinity was not an option.

Figure 6.2. The top of an inscribed stele from Amphipolis, Greece, displaying reliefs of characteristic features valued at a gymnasium—all linked, in this context, with male prowess: the *lekythos* (oil jug), the victor's laurel, the taenia, the victor's palm, the strigil, and the *sphaera* (ball). Like the regulations at Beroia mentioned in the text, this stele is inscribed with ephebic laws, governing everything from the checking of performance and appearance to regulating behavior outside the gymnasium.

Whether devoted to training *epheboi* or *neoi*, the bath-gymnasium was a site designed for the production of virtuous and disciplined young men. Intellectual subjects, such as literature, mathematics, and rhetoric, might be offered in these places, but the primary focus was on physical

---

48. Loukretia Gounaropoulou and Miltiades B. Hatzopoulos, *Epigraphes Katō Makedonias (metaxy tou Vermiou orous kai tou Axiou potamou)* (Athens: Ypourgeío Politismoú, 1998) (EKM 1. Beroia), §1B, ll. 27–29. See David Potter, *The Victor's Crown: A History of Ancient Sport from Homer to Byzantium* (Oxford: Oxford University Press, 2011), 132; Roger S. Bagnall and Peter Derow, *The Hellenistic Period: Historical Sources in Translation* (New York: Wiley & Sons, 2008), 78.

exercise.[49] A telling funerary inscription, in the form of a dialogue with the passerby, found in Hadriani, Asia Minor, highlights this. After giving his name, Cladus, and age, thirteen, the dialogue continues, "'So you did not like the Muses then?'—Not quite. They did not love me very much, but Hermes cared a great deal for me. For in wrestling contests I often received the praiseworthy garland."[50] Athletics were valued most by young Cladus and, it seems, to many others in this context, for it was through athletic training that males acquired the virtues that constituted them as men. Sports such as boxing and racing developed endurance, an important quality in a man, and other activities cultivated discipline, physical harmony, and moderation.[51] In a eulogy to a deceased boxer named Melancomas, Dio Chrysostom gushes:

> He therefore, recognizing that, of all the activities conducive to courage, athletics is at once the most honourable and the most laborious, chose that. Indeed, for the soldier's career no opportunity existed, and the training also is less severe. And I for my part would venture to say that it is inferior also in that there is scope for courage alone in warfare, whereas athletics at one and the same time produce manliness, physical strength, and self-control. (*Or.* 29.9 [Cohoon, LCL])

It is through the training of the body in athletics that one develops the qualities necessary to become an ideal man.

One way the bath-gymnasium participated in the formation of masculine identities was through the articulation and enforcement of gymnasiarchic laws. These laws regulated the administration of the complex as well as the behaviors and bodies of the *epheboi*. The stele in Beroia provides an example of the content typical of these laws, listing guidelines for electing the *gymnasiarch* (the head of the gymnasium), financing supplies such as olive oil and firewood, and training various age groups.[52] The gymnasiarchic laws, moreover, articulated a set of standards by which the

---

49. Laes and Strubbe, *Youth in the Roman Empire*, 71–73, 110–15.

50. IHadrianoi 77; this late Hellenistic or early Roman inscription is translated in ibid., 115.

51. Newby, *Greek Athletics*, 151–54; Laes and Strubbe, *Youth in the Roman Empire*, 75.

52. For an English translation of this law, see Bagnall and Derow, *The Hellenistic Period*, 78. The Greek inscription can be found at the Packard Humanities Institute Inscription Database, http://tinyurl.com/SBL4522q.

epheboi were to be assessed. Among other things, the laws emphasize the importance of the *epheboi* acting out of obedience and with honor (e.g., not cheating, competing fairly, not giving up one's victory). Guidelines for punishing both misbehaving boys and employees (e.g., trainers) are also noted. Pointing to the importance of these laws and of the *gymnasiarch* for instilling a sense of discipline among the bath-gymnasium clientele, an inscription in Pergamon honors a *gymnasiarch*, Agais, who "rigidly devoted himself to the cause of just behaviour at the gymnasium."[53] These laws were public, according to the Beroia inscription, so that "the young men will feel a greater sense of shame and be more obedient to their leader."[54] In other words, these laws were intended to create, in the sense of Michel Foucault, an internalized gaze regulating the actions, identity, and gender performance of the young men attending the bath-gymnasium.[55]

Additionally, the ideals of the ephebic laws were made visible for *epheboi* through the honorific portraits and statues strategically placed throughout the bath-gymnasiums. In his study of these popular portraits, John Ma notes that statues of donors and gymnasium leaders, such as the *gymnasiarch*, were placed in areas, especially closed rooms, where they were most likely to be seen by the young men frequenting the gymnasium for training:

> At first sight, the reason for the location of statues in closed rooms might seem practical, to avoid taking up spaces reserved for violent physical movement. Yet the main effect of locating honorific portraits "indoors" was to impose the presence of benefactors, at bottlenecks in the circulation of persons, in spaces where gatherings and activities occurred, or within spaces specifically designed to create an encounter with the image of the benefactor and heighten the image's impact.[56]

Young men frequenting the gymnasium would come face to face with representations of men, and sometimes women,[57] whom they should emulate

---

53. *MDAIA* 1908.379–81.2, as quoted in Laes and Strubbe, *Youth in the Roman Empire*, 74.

54. Bagnall and Derow, *Hellenistic Period*, 78.

55. Michel Foucault, *Discipline and Punish: The Birth of the Prison* (New York: Random House, 1995).

56. John Ma, *Statues and Cities: Honorific Portraits and Civic Identity in the Hellenistic World* (Oxford: Oxford University Press, 2013), 87.

57. The reconstruction of the major bath-gymnasium complex at Sardis, for

on account of their honor or generosity.[58] The people of Pergamon in this way honored Mithridates son of Menodotos, a significant benefactor to the city in general, with a statue in the gymnasium,[59] and the bath-gymnasium of Vedius in Ephesus included two portrait statues of Publius Vedius Antoninus, who was the primary donor for the complex.[60] As Ma explains, "exemplarity leads to social reproduction."[61]

In addition to the portraits of donors and virtuous citizens, the statuary of the baths often included representations of deities, especially Asclepius and Hygeia (both of whom were associated with health), members of the imperial family, Greek athletes and mythological characters such as heroes or others who overcame in physical struggles.[62] The virtues that were to be instilled through the discipline of gymnastic training were physically and visually manifest in the very structure and decoration of the bath-gymnasium.

Even though we can imagine particular individuals and groups, such as the slaves attending young men in the baths or gymnasium (fig. 6.3), responding to the gendered utterances of the bath-gymnasium in diverse ways, the masculinist gender ideology of these places rings loud and clear. These are places for constructing and claiming a male identity. When visiting the overgrown ruins of the gymnasium in Priene, this is quite evident (fig. 6.4), as one can see abundant—over seven hundred, in fact—examples of topoi graffiti written by young men proclaiming their presence at the gymnasium: "Apollonios was here!" "Menandros was here!" "Theophilos was here!"[63]

---

instance, was financed in part by two notable local women, Claudia Antonia Sabina and Flavia Pollitta; see Fikret K. Yegül, *The Bath-Gymnasium Complex at Sardis* (Cambridge: Harvard University Press, 1986), 166.

58. Newby, *Greek Athletics*, 240.
59. *IGRR* 4.1682; Ma, *Statues and Cities*, 90.
60. Newby, *Greek Athletics*, 240.
61. Ma, *Statues and Cities*, 299.
62. Newby, *Greek Athletics*, 232–35.
63. Claire Taylor, "Graffiti and the Epigraphic Habit: Creating Communities and Writing Alternate Histories in Classical Attica," in *Ancient Graffiti in Context*, ed. Jennifer Baird and Claire Taylor (New York: Routledge, 2010), 134–35 n. 31. For the actual inscriptions, see Friedrich Hiller von Gaertringen et al., *Inschriften von Priene* (Berlin: Reimer, 1908), 313. This type of graffiti is not unique to the bath-gymnasium, and it is found in other locations where one might want to claim a civic identity, such as the tetrastoon at Aphrodisias. See Luke Lavan, Ellen Swift, and Toon Putzeys, "Material

Figure 6.3. A fourth-century CE mosaic of a slave tending to an athlete, from the private gymnasium at the Villa Romana del Casale, Sicily, Italy

Figure 6.4. Topoi graffiti in the gymnasium at Priene, Turkey

Furthermore, the gendered discourses that occurred in and through the ancient bath-gymnasium, discourses about how to be a true man, spilled

---

Spatiality in Late Antiquity: Sources, Approaches and Field Methods," in *Objects in Context, Objects in Use: Material Spatiality in Late Antiquity*, ed. Luke Lavan, Ellen Swift, and Toon Putzeys (Leiden: Brill, 2008), 14–15.

out of the walls of these monumental spaces and into the agoras, streets, and other civic spaces of the cities of Asia Minor. Monuments and inscriptions documented the victories of those who participated in the numerous festivals and games held throughout the region, including those sponsored by the Council of Asia and by significant urban centers, such as Smyrna, Pergamon, and Ephesus.[64] It is not enough to win, but one must be recognized as victor, according to van Nijf: "the large number of agonistic inscriptions throughout Asia Minor suggests that athletic victory was one of the most powerful and widespread images around."[65] Funerary altars and sarcophagi could similarly communicate a man's virtue through the visual depiction of the important prizes he had won during his lifetime, including crowns, wreathes, palm branches, and even moneybags (fig. 6.5).[66]

Depictions of the athlete and the athletic training of the bath-gymnasium within this context are cast mostly in a positive light, although there

Figure 6.5. Sarcophagus of Lucius Septimius Theronides depicting prize crowns, dated to the third century CE, from Patara, Turkey. Now held in the Antalya Archaeological Museum, Antalya, Turkey.

---

64. Remijsen, *End of Greek Athletics*, 72–73.
65. Van Nijf, "Local Heroes", 324.
66. Katherine M. D. Dunbabin, "The Victorious Charioteer on Mosaics and Related Monuments," *AJA* 86 (1982): 65–89; Gregory M. Stevenson, "Conceptual Background to Golden Crown Imagery in the Apocalypse of John (4:4, 10; 14:14)," *JBL* 114 (1995): 257–72.

were some who had different estimations of the value of athletics. Negative opinions ranged from humorous depictions of athletes as a sort of dumb jock to concerns that rewards of athleticism, including glory and wealth, might lead one to neglect the intellectual life. So Galen warned:

> The only thing I am afraid of is the activity of the athletes, in case it deceives any one of our young men into preferring it to a genuine art, through offering, as it does, bodily strength and popular fame and daily public payments from the elders of our cities, and honors equal to those given to outstanding citizens. (Galen, *Protr.* 9)[67]

Even though there was concern that the athletic training of the gymnasium might overshadow intellectual matters, König notes that athletics still functioned as a metaphor for philosophical training and the cultivation of virtue.[68] Epictetus, the first-century Stoic philosopher, wrote: "It was for this purpose [living a tranquil life] that you used to practice exercise; for this purpose were used the halteres (weights), the dust, the young men as antagonists" (*Diatr.* 4.4 [Long, BCL]). In this way, the realia of the gymnasium were part of constructing the ideal Stoic man. Similarly, the author of Hebrews calls his audience to envision themselves as spiritual athletes, writing, "with endurance [ὑπομονή], let us run the race [ἀγών] that is set before us" (Heb 12:1).[69] The image of the athlete and the training of the gymnasium would also be appropriated by the authors of early Christian martyrologies as well, portraying their subjects as athletes engaged in training and in contests, receiving crowns and prizes as awards for their victories (e.g., 4 Macc 6:1–12; Mart. Pol. 17).[70] Thus, the image of the athlete and the training of the gymnasium were productive tools for

---

67. As quoted by König, *Athletics and Literature*, 2.
68. Ibid., 133.
69. For a discussion of the range of meaning for (ἀγών), which has connotations of contest and struggle, see ibid., 35. The translation is that of the author.
70. Martyrologies also employ the image of the gladiator to characterize Christian virtue. The figure of the gladiator in the Roman world is complex, as gladiators were typically of low social status. However, gladiators were sometimes understood as paragons of masculine virtue, given their courage and their willingness to die. Thus, the image of the gladiator could be deployed as an image of ideal masculinity in a way similar to the athlete. For the purposes of this essay, however, I am focusing primarily on the athlete. For a discussion of the complex masculinity of the gladiator, see Cobb, *Dying to Be Men*, 46–54.

ancient authors thinking through issues of identity and what it meant to be virtuous.

Even though John does not employ an explicit image of the athlete, aspects of the messages in Rev 2–3 evoke the ways masculinity was constructed in the bath-gymnasium. This does not involve making direct connections, even though there are a few possible allusions to those material worlds. Rather, following the lead of Joyce and Lopiparo, I want to approach these places as part of a discourse about ideal masculinity, utterances to which Revelation's author responds. In the following, we examine the messages of Revelation in light of some of what we know about the material world of the bath-gymnasium.

5. Reading Revelation's Messages in the Bath-Gymnasium

Dictated to John by "one like a Son of Man" and evoking the authority of an imperial dispatch,[71] the seven messages of Rev 2–3 stand out from the rest of the narrative. While this has led some scholars to ponder whether the letters were an addition or even circulated independently from one another,[72] this has been dismissed based not only on a lack of manuscript evidence but also on the basis of the number seven intentionally evoking wholeness or completeness. Thus, while ostensibly addressing local issues, as highlighted by Ramsay (see above), the messages would be heard by all the communities. These messages, therefore, are both particular and universal in their scope, and taken together they present to their audiences a shared identity.

Each of these messages follows a highly structured pattern, beginning with a command to John to write to an association or community (ἐκκλησία) of the faithful within a particular city.[73] These commands are

---

71. While they are often called the "seven letters," these messages from the Son of Man to the communities do not follow the model of an ancient letter; instead, they bear more similarity to prophetic speeches and to imperial edicts. See David E. Aune, *Revelation*, WBC 52A–C (Dallas: Word, 1998), 124–29.

72. For a discussion of some of the different composition theories of Revelation, see Elisabeth Schüssler Fiorenza, "The Composition and Structure of Revelation," in *The Book of Revelation: Justice and Judgment* (Minneapolis: Fortress, 1998), 159–80.

73. Many versions of Revelation translate ἐκκλησία as "church." This popular translation is misleading for a couple of reasons. First, it might imply a more formal organization than would have existed at the time. Second, it might suggest a church building or a physical space, although at the time Revelation was written, the followers

followed by evocative descriptions of the ultimate author, the Son of Man. The content of each message is introduced with the phrase "I know" (οἶδα), which leads to either praise or criticism of the community's behavior. For instance, to the community at Sardis the Son of Man announces, "I know [οἶδα] your works; you have the name of being alive, but you are dead" (3:1; NRSV) and to Philadelphia, "I know [οἶδα] your works. Look, I have set before you an open door, which no one is able to shut" (3:8; NRSV). Finally, each message concludes with an exhortation, "Let anyone who has an ear hear what the spirit says to the communities [ταῖς ἐκκλησίαις],"[74] and a promise of a reward to ὁ νικῶν, "the victor."[75]

While scholars often focus on what these letters reveal about the current situations of the communities, including the conflicts happening within the associations and in relation to others,[76] one of the functions of these letters is to shape the audience's identity.[77] Repeatedly, the Son of Man tells his audiences that he *knows* their actions and attitudes, their trials and temptations. This ability to know even the innermost conflicts within the communities is facilitated by the fact that the Son of Man, a reference to the risen Christ, is surrounded by seven lampstands that happen to be the seven communities (Rev 1:12, 20; 2:1). According to Revelation's visionary logic, the Son of Man stands among the communities observing and, presumably, evaluating all that they do. Referencing Foucault's theorizing about the panopticon, the prison system in which a central guard tower gives the impression of continual surveillance, Harry O. Maier notes the disciplinary function of Christ's gaze in Revelation. This is far from passive observation; rather, the gaze serves to instill a sense of obedience within the members of the audience—Christ knows whether the communities have

---

of Jesus were likely meeting in domestic spaces. Thus, I prefer to use the language of "association" or "community."

74. Elisabeth Schüssler Fiorenza observes that the reference to the communities or churches at the end of this phrase points to the fact that the messages address the communities as a whole. See Schüssler Fiorenza, "Composition and Structure," 165.

75. The messages vary on whether the promise to the victor comes before or after the final exhortation. The first three letters reference the victor last.

76. Paul Brooks Duff, *Who Rides the Beast? Prophetic Rivalry and the Rhetoric of Crisis in the Churches of the Apocalypse* (Oxford: Oxford University Press, 2001), 31–47; Friesen, "Satan's Throne," 352–56.

77. This is in line with DeSilva's treatment of Rev 2–3 as part of the text's use of honor discourse. See David A. DeSilva, "Honor Discourse and the Rhetorical Strategy of the Apocalypse of John," *JSNT* 71 (1998): 79–110.

been faithful and he will know how they respond to the commands made in the text.[78] The reprimands and instances of praise are designed to change or to reinforce current behavior within the communities.[79] In this way, these messages serve as part of John's effort at shaping and controlling the communal identity of his audience. We might also compare the one like a Son of Man to the *gymnasiarch*, who was the chief administrator of the ancient bath-gymnasium and who monitored the behavior of *epheboi* inside and outside of its walls. Extending this metaphor further, we might imagine that Revelation's author intends these messages, like the gymnasiarchic inscription in Beroia, to be internalized by the text's audience members.

Heard seven times over, "the victor" stands out as the idealized masculine identity to which the audience is called. English translations of Revelation vary in their translation of ὁ νικῶν, often rendering it as "he who overcomes" (NIV, KJV, NASB) or "he who conquers" (NRSV). Translated in these ways, νικάω suggests a military action, as Stephen Moore notes,[80] or a metaphorical type of overcoming. Blount highlights the latter meaning, writing, "To conquer is to witness resistantly. Such conquest, however, does not mean that the believer 'wins.' Jesus, after all, was executed because of the revelation he proclaimed.... Conquest does, however, mean that ultimately the believer will, like Christ, through the very act of witnessing, overwhelm the bestial forces of draconian Rome."[81] Reading Revelation in the context of Asia Minor's bath-gymnasium complexes suggests, however, that we hear John's references to ὁ νικῶν as echoing references to the victors of the games and contests associated with these important sites. Inscriptions and honorific statues referencing these victories filled the public places of urban Asia Minor. Van Nijf describes

---

78. Harry O. Maier, "Staging the Gaze: Early Christian Apocalypses and Narrative Self-Representation," *HTR* 90 (1997): 131–54.

79. As David DeSilva notes, the messages are a blend of rhetorical strategies that are both deliberative, seeking to change behavior, and epideictic, praising or censuring current behavior. See David A. DeSilva, "Out of Our Minds?: Appeals to Reason (Logos) in the Seven Oracles of Revelation 2–3," *JSNT* 31 (2008): 123–55.

80. Moore does not explicitly reference the use of νικάω in the seven messages, but explains in reference to other uses of the term in Revelation that its militaristic meaning is "unmistakable." See Stephen D. Moore, *God's Beauty Parlor: And Other Queer Spaces in and around the Bible* (Stanford, CA: Stanford University Press, 2001), 184–85.

81. Blount, *Revelation*, 52. Gregory K. Beale similarly highlights the ironic nature of the "conquering" implied in νικάω. See Beale, *Book of Revelation*, 269–72.

one location, explaining, "There was no escape: wherever you went in Termessos you were confronted with the powerful image of the victorious youth."[82] This image of the victor does, of course, suggest military conquest as well, for the roots of the athletic training of the gymnasium emerged out of military training.[83] Furthermore, this training was not only about developing physical strength; rather, it was arguably more about becoming a virtuous man.

As explained above, athletic training was not only about developing physical strength; rather, it was closely associated with becoming a virtuous *man*, and one of the virtues closely associated with athletics was the ability to endure hardship or to hold fast during a trial.[84] Dio Chrysostom, again, lauds the endurance or hard work (πονέω) of the boxer Melancomas, who was able to fight for a whole day, and even in the heat, noting that this characteristic is worth more than any of his prizes (*Or.* 29.10–11). Endurance is a characteristic of the victor, including the victor imagined in Revelation. Even though other virtues are referenced in Rev 2–3, including love, faith, service (2:19), and purity (3:3), the importance of endurance predominates. Specifically, the term "endurance" or "patient endurance" (ὑπομονή), as it is translated in the NRSV, is mentioned twice in reference to Ephesus. In this message, it is combined with an acknowledgement of the community's toil or suffering (κόπος): "I know your works, your toil and your patient endurance.... I also know that you are enduring patiently and bearing up for the sake of my name, and that you have not grown weary" (3:2–3). Endurance is also ascribed to Thyatira and Philadelphia.[85] Likewise, the Son of Man praises the ability of the community in Pergamon to "hold fast" to Christ's name in the midst of distress (2:13), and some of the people of Thyatira are to hold fast in light of problematic teachings in the community (2:25). The Son of Man also encourages those communities who need to develop an ability to endure. Smyrna, he warns,

---

82. Van Nijf, "Local Heroes," 324.

83. Although the expectations around military service and training had shifted during the Roman imperial period, the militaristic aspect of gymnasium training continued. See König, *Athletics and Literature*, 47.

84. N. Clayton Croy, *Endurance in Suffering: Hebrews 12:1–13 in Its Rhetorical, Religious, and Philosophical Context* (Cambridge: Cambridge University Press, 2005), 64–65; Newby, *Greek Athletics*, 151–54; Remijsen, *The End of Greek Athletics*, 269–70.

85. Endurance is a theme throughout Revelation. See 1:9; 2:2, 3, 19; 3:10; 13:10; and 14:12.

is about to undergo testing, so they should not fear suffering (2:10). Since those in Laodikeia are lukewarm, seemingly lacking conviction,[86] the Son of Man threatens to come and "discipline" (παιδεύω) them, clearly evoking the training or *paideia* of the bath-gymnasium.

The victories associated with the ancient bath-gymnasium were traditionally accompanied by prizes, including crowns or wreathes, palm branches, vases, and even money. The victors in Revelation's messages are similarly rewarded with prizes, some of which parallel those typically associated with the games. Most notable, for instance, is the crown or wreath (στέφανος) of life promised to the victor in Smyrna, which evokes a common reward for athletes.[87] The victors in Philadelphia have apparently already won this prize, as they are instructed not to let anyone seize their crown or wreath (3:11). In a clever play on the tradition of memorializing victory through inscription, the Son of Man promises the victors in the community at Philadelphia that they will become a pillar inscribed with the names of God, Christ, and the New Jerusalem.[88] Other prizes or awards promised by the Son of Man include permission to eat from the tree of life (2:7), freedom from the "second death" (2:11), a white stone with a new name (2:17), authority over the nations and the morning star (2:26-28), being clothed in white robes (3:5), and the chance to sit on God's throne (3:21). While some of these are quite different from the traditional prizes awarded athletes, the topic of prize-winning evokes the agonistic culture of ancient Asia Minor in which athletes receive rewards for their success.[89]

The differences between the prizes awarded to the victors of ancient Asia Minor and the victors envisioned by John in Rev 2-3 points to the primary way that this text constructs masculinity in response to the material utterances surrounding it. As commentators note, many of the rewards promised in the messages to the communities are items of eschatological import, foreshadowing the community's life as the New Jerusalem.[90] The promise made to the victors in Laodikeia, that they will share the throne with God, points to the time when those who have been faithful to the

---

86. Blount describes the community as lacking "zeal" (*Revelation*, 82).
87. Stevenson, "Conceptual Background," 258-59.
88. Royalty, "Inscriptions and Erasures," 454.
89. Although Revelation does not use the term πρόκειμαι ("to set before"), which is Croy's focus, the discussion of prize imagery here is helpful for understanding how widespread the imagery is (Croy, *Endurance in Suffering*, 66-67).
90. For example, Schüssler Fiorenza, "Composition and Structure," 165.

Lamb will be resurrected so that they can reign with Christ (20:4–6); the new name inscribed on the white stone given to the victors in Pergamon suggests the new names worn by those who follow the Lamb (14:1; 22:4); and the tree of life promised to those in Ephesus grows in the New Jerusalem described at the conclusion of John's vision (22:2). Moreover, the white robes promised to the victors in Sardis (3:5) will appear again when they are given to those souls under the heavenly altar who have been slaughtered for the Word of God (6:9) and to the 144,000 who have "come out of the great ordeal" (7:13–14). In this way, some of the rewards promised by the Son of Man suggest that endurance is demonstrated by holding fast and remaining faithful even to the point of death (14:12–13). Ironically, being the victor entails what many might understand as being conquered (e.g., 13:7).[91]

Returning to the idea that the remains of archaeological and material cultures are utterances seeking a response, in the messages of Rev 2–3 we hear echoes of the conversations about ideal masculinity conveyed in and through the bath-gymnasiums of Roman Asia. Repeated references to "the victor," along with specific descriptions of the rewards given to those who endure, evoke the agonistic culture fostered in these important civic spaces and suggests the possibility that Revelation imagines audience members whose identities are shaped in relation to these monumental buildings. Revelation's voicing of these discourses, moreover, highlights the importance of endurance, a virtue also valorized among athletes. In this way, the Son of Man's appeals to those who would be victors parallel the discipline voiced by the *gymnasiarch* and the gymnasiarchic laws. Like those laws, calls to endure, hold fast, and to remain faithful are ideally internalized by "the one who reads aloud and … those who hear" the messages dictated to John (1:3). While we might note that the messages of Revelation do not seem to envision a physical contest or battle, as noted above, others in Revelation's context employ these images metaphorically. John is in keeping with those Stoics and other early Christian authors who will use athletic imagery to envision a life of virtue. Eventually, however, early Christian authors will be more explicit in resignifying the gendered performances shaped by the agonistic culture of the Roman world, as they begin to use

---

91. Beale, *Book of Revelation*, 269.

the imagery to interpret the deaths of those killed for their faith.[92] In Revelation, however, we only see the beginnings of this shift in discourse.

Finally, while it is easy to understand the impulse among many to ground the text of Revelation in the seeming surety of the material world, we know the physical remains of the past are as much in need of narrativizing as the textual and discursive. The "stones and bones" of Asia Minor can help us envision Revelation's milieu; however, this requires a move away from drawing connections to possible local allusions and toward using the material world to help us imagine the social, cultural, and religious discourses with which the text converses.

Bibliography

Allison, Penelope M. "Characterizing Roman Artifacts to Investigate Gendered Practices in Contexts without Sexed Bodies." *AJA* 119 (2015): 103–23.

———. "Engendering Roman Domestic Space." *British School at Athens Studies* 15 (2007): 343–50.

Appadurai, Arjun, ed. *The Social Life of Things: Commodities in Cultural Perspective*. Cambridge: Cambridge University Press, 1988.

Aune, David E. *Revelation*. 3 vols. WBC 52A–C. Dallas: Word, 1998.

Bagnall, Roger S., and Peter Derow. *The Hellenistic Period: Historical Sources in Translation*. New York: Wiley & Sons, 2008.

Bain, Katherine. *Women's Socioeconomic Status and Religious Leadership in Asia Minor in the First Two Centuries C.E.* Minneapolis: Fortress, 2014.

Beale, Gregory K. *The Book of Revelation: A Commentary on the Greek Text*. NIGTC. Grand Rapids: Eerdmans, 1999.

Blount, Brian K. *Revelation: A Commentary*. Louisville: Westminster John Knox, 2009.

Butler, Judith. *Gender Trouble: Feminism and the Subversion of Identity*. New York: Routledge, 1990.

———. *Undoing Gender*. New York: Routledge, 2004.

Caldwell, Lauren. *Roman Girlhood and the Fashioning of Femininity*. Kindle ed. Cambridge: Cambridge University Press, 2014.

---

92. Cobb, *Dying to Be Men*.

Cobb, L. Stephanie. *Dying to Be Men: Gender and Language in Early Christian Texts*. Kindle ed. Gender, Theory, and Religion. New York: Columbia University Press, 2008.

Conway, Colleen. *Behold the Man: Jesus and Greco-Roman Masculinity*. New York: Oxford University Press, 2008.

Croy, N. Clayton. *Endurance in Suffering: Hebrews 12:1–13 in Its Rhetorical, Religious, and Philosophical Context*. Cambridge: Cambridge University Press, 2005.

DeSilva, David A. "Honor Discourse and the Rhetorical Strategy of the Apocalypse of John." *JSNT* 71 (1998): 79–110.

———. "Out of Our Minds?: Appeals to Reason (Logos) in the Seven Oracles of Revelation 2–3." *JNST* 31 (2008): 123–55.

Dio Chrysostom. *Discourses*. Translated by J. W. Cohoon. 5 vols. LCL. New York: Putnam's Sons, 1932–1951.

Duff, Paul Brooks. *Who Rides the Beast? Prophetic Rivalry and the Rhetoric of Crisis in the Churches of the Apocalypse*. Oxford: Oxford University Press, 2001.

Dunbabin, Katherine M. D. "The Victorious Charioteer on Mosaics and Related Monuments." *AJA* 86 (1982): 65–89.

Epictetus. *The Discourses of Epictetus: With the Encheiridion and Fragments*. Translated by George Long. BCL. London: Bell, 1877.

Foucault, Michel. *Discipline and Punish: The Birth of the Prison*. New York: Random House, 1995.

Friesen, Steven J. "Revelation, Realia, and Religion: Archaeology in the Interpretation of the Apocalypse." *HTR* 88 (1995): 291–314.

———. "Satan's Throne, Imperial Cults and the Social Settings of Revelation." *JSNT* 27 (2005): 351–73.

Gaertringen, Hiller von, Carl Johann Fredrich, Hans Theodor Anton von Prott, Hans Schrader, Theodor Wiegand, Hermann Winnefeld, and Königliche Museen zu Berlin. *Inschriften von Priene*. Berlin: Reimer, 1908.

Galen. *Galen on the Usefulness of the Parts of the Body*. Translated by Margaret Tallmadge May. Cornell Publications in the History of Science. Ithaca, NY: Cornell University Press, 1968.

Gardiner, E. Norman. *Athletics in the Ancient World*. Mineola, NY: Dover, 2002.

Gleason, Maud W. *Making Men: Sophists and Self-Presentation in Ancient Rome*. Princeton: Princeton University Press, 1995.

Gounaropoulou, Loukretia, and Miltiades B. Hatzopoulos. *Epigraphes Katō Makedonias (metaxy tou Vermiou orous kai tou Axiou potamou).* Athens: Ypourgeío Politismoú, 1998.

Hemer, Colin J. *The Letters to the Seven Churches of Asia in Their Local Setting.* Sheffield: Sheffield Academic, 1986.

Huber, Lynn R. "Revelation." In *The Oxford Handbook of New Testament, Gender, and Sexuality.* Edited by Benjamin Dunning. New York: Oxford University Press, forthcoming.

Joyce, Rosemary, Robert W. Preucel, and Jeanne Lopiparo. *The Languages of Archaeology: Dialogue, Narrative, and Writing.* Edited by Rosemary Joyce. Oxford: Wiley-Blackwell, 2002.

Keener, Craig S. *Revelation: From Biblical Text to Contemporary Life.* NIV Application Commentary. Kindle ed. Grand Rapids: Zondervan, 2000.

Koester, Craig R. "The Message to Laodicea and the Problem of Its Local Context: A Study of the Imagery in Rev 3.14–22." *NTS* 49 (2003): 407–24.

König, Jason. *Athletics and Literature in the Roman Empire.* Cambridge: Cambridge University Press, 2005.

Laes, Christian, and Johan Strubbe. *Youth in the Roman Empire: The Young and the Restless Years?* Kindle ed. Cambridge: Cambridge University Press, 2014.

Laqueur, Thomas. *Making Sex: Body and Gender from the Greeks to Freud.* Cambridge: Harvard University Press, 1992.

Lavan, Luke, Ellen Swift, and Toon Putzeys. "Material Spatiality in Late Antiquity: Sources, Approaches and Field Methods." Pages 1–42 in *Objects in Context, Objects in Use: Material Spatiality in Late Antiquity.* Edited by Luke Lavan, Ellen Swift, and Toon Putzeys. Leiden: Brill, 2008.

Ma, John. *Statues and Cities: Honorific Portraits and Civic Identity in the Hellenistic World.* Oxford: Oxford University Press, 2013.

Maier, Harry O. "Staging the Gaze: Early Christian Apocalypses and Narrative Self-Representation." *HTR* 90 (1997): 131–54.

Moore, Stephen D. *God's Beauty Parlor: And Other Queer Spaces in and around the Bible.* Stanford, CA: Stanford University Press, 2001.

Newby, Zahra. *Greek Athletics in the Roman World: Victory and Virtue.* Oxford: Oxford University Press, 2005.

Nijf, Onno van. "Local Heroes: Athletics, Festivals and Elite Self-Fashioning in the Roman East." Pages 306–34 in *Being Greek under Rome:*

Cultural Identity, the Second Sophistic and the Development of Empire. Edited by Simon Goldhill. Cambridge: Cambridge University Press, 2001.

Osborne, Grant R. *Revelation*. BECNT. Grand Rapids: Baker Academic, 2002.

Potter, David. *The Victor's Crown: A History of Ancient Sport from Homer to Byzantium*. Oxford: Oxford University Press, 2011.

Ramsay, William Mitchell. *The Letters to the Seven Churches of Asia and Their Place in the Plan of the Apocalypse*. 2nd ed. London: Hodder & Stoughton, 1906.

Remijsen, Sofie. *The End of Greek Athletics in Late Antiquity*. Cambridge: Cambridge University Press, 2015.

Royalty, Robert M. "Etched or Sketched? Inscriptions and Erasures in the Messages to Sardis and Philadelphia (Rev. 3.1–13)." *JSNT* 27 (2005): 447–63.

Schüssler Fiorenza, Elisabeth. "The Composition and Structure of Revelation." Pages 159–80 in *The Book of Revelation: Justice and Judgment*. Minneapolis: Fortress, 1998.

Soranus. *Gynecology*. Translated by Oswei Temkin. Baltimore: Johns Hopkins Press, 1956.

Sørensen, Marie L. S. "Gender, Things, and Material Culture." Pages 105–35 in *Handbook of Gender in Archaeology*. Edited by Sarah Milledge Nelson. Lanham, MD: AltaMira, 2006.

Stevenson, Gregory M. "Conceptual Background to Golden Crown Imagery in the Apocalypse of John (4:4, 10; 14:14)." *JBL* 114 (1995): 257–72.

Taylor, Claire. "Graffiti and the Epigraphic Habit: Creating Communities and Writing Alternate Histories in Classical Attica." Pages 115–35 in *Ancient Graffiti in Context*. Edited by Jennifer Baird and Claire Taylor. New York: Routledge, 2010.

Wallace-Hadrill, Andrew. "The Emperor and His Virtues." *Historia* 30 (1981): 298–323.

Ward, Roy Bowen. "Women in Roman Baths." *HTR* 85 (1992): 125–47.

Yegül, Fikret K. *The Bath-Gymnasium Complex at Sardis*. Cambridge: Harvard University Press, 1986.

———. *Bathing in the Roman World*. New York: Cambridge University Press, 2009.

At the Origins of Christian Apologetic Literature: The Politics of Patronage in Hadrianic Athens*

William Rutherford

226th Olympiad. 9th year of Hadrian. (a) Hadrian, after his initiation into the sacred rites of Eleusis, made numerous gifts to the Athenians. (b) Quadratus, a disciple of the apostles, and Aristides of Athens, our philosopher, gave to Hadrian some works composed in favor of the Christian religion. (Eusebius, *Chronicon* [Jerome's Latin version])

The Christian historiographic tradition exemplified in the epigraph above identifies the beginnings of Christian apologetic literature with the activity of Quadratus and Aristides, who ostensibly directed written compositions to the emperor Hadrian in defense of the Christian faith. Despite discrepancies in the historiographic testimonies, Eusebius and Jerome cooperate in advancing an account of Christian defense literature that locates its beginnings in an auspicious space and time. Christian apologies directed to the Roman emperor began to be produced on the occasion of Hadrian's visit to the city of Athens in the eighth or ninth year of his reign (124/125 or 125/126 CE), during which time Hadrian was initiated into the Eleusinian mysteries and lavished public largess on the city.[1]

---

* I wish to congratulate Dennis Smith, whom I had the privilege of first meeting in Athens in June, 2011, on his retirement and to thank Alan Cadwallader for the invitation to participate in this project.

1. Eusebius, *Chron.*, ad ann. Hadr. 8 [Arm.] = 124/125 CE; ad ann. Hadr. 9 [Lat.] = 125/126 CE); cf. Eusebius, *Hist. eccl.* 4.3; Jerome, *Vir. ill.* 20; *Ep.* 70.4 (*Ad Magnum*). The emperor visited Athens in 124/125, in 128/129, and in 131/132 CE; cf. Simone Follet, *Athènes au II*^{e} *et au III*^{e} *siècle: Études chronologiques et prosopographiques* (Paris:

Eusebius's *Chronicon* fails to explain why an imperial visit to Athens should correspond with the first writings of Christian apology. Yet by juxtaposing Hadrian's activities at Athens with the writing of Aristides "of Athens," the text does encourage its readers to view the emperor's patronage to Athens and Eleusis as more than an occasion for apologetic writing. It insinuates that Hadrian's ritual initiation at Eleusis and his favors to Athens served to stimulate the writing of Christian defense literature. If so, the ancient writers of sacred history challenge us to search for the origins of Christian apologetic literature in a place we do not normally look. The *Chronicon* makes no mention of literary precursors in the venerable tradition of Jewish apologetic literature, of textual borrowings from early Christian literature, or of the use of traditional mythic tropes from hellenistic literature or cultural memes prominent in the Second Sophistic. Instead, it recalls a way of seeing—native to ancient audiences, foreign to modern ones—in which the emperor's ritual acts and material donations in the cities of the empire constructed webs of meaning by which residents could situate themselves, their cities, and their local traditions in relation to other cities and to the capital of the empire. What did Emperor Hadrian's benefactions to Athens communicate? Can an urban imperial script or scripts be reclaimed and correlated as a meaningful intertext for the earliest apologies, so that they might be read with renewed sensitivity to the semiotics of Hadrian's patronage to Athens?

In the case of Hadrian, the possibility of reclaiming an urban imperial intertext is redolent. Not since the time of Augustus had so many cities of the Roman Empire experienced such a boon of imperial munificence and personal attention as they did under Hadrian. In a monumental study of Hadrian's interactions with municipalities across the empire, Mary Boatwright describes the emperor as possessed of a "city-based vision of the Roman world."[2] She identifies some 210 marks of Hadrian's favor bestowed on more than 130 cities across East and West. Among the many cities he patronized, Hadrian lavished particular attention on Athens, establishing it in 131/132 as the headquarters of a newly formed league of Greek cities known as the Panhellenion.[3] As part of his so-called Panhellenic program,

---

Belles Lettres, 1976), 107–16. Unless noted otherwise, all dates refer to the Common Era and all translations are mine.

2. Mary T. Boatwright, *Hadrian and the Cities of the Roman Empire* (Princeton: Princeton University Press, 2003), 144.

3. Hadrian's munificence to Athens is documented by Boatwright, *Hadrian*,

the emperor added several new sizeable constructions to the cityscape of Athens, including the Olympieion or Temple of Olympian Zeus, the (still unlocated) Panhellenion sanctuary, a Temple (ναός) of Hera and Zeus Panhellenios, the Pantheon basilica, and the so-called Library of Hadrian (Dio Cassius, *Hist. rom.* 69.16.1-2; Pausanias, *Descr.* 1.18.6-9).[4] In the Olympieion, Hadrian was assimilated to Zeus Olympios and honored with the epithet Hadrian Olympios, with cities across the Greek-speaking world celebrating the emperor by raising altars to him (Pausanius, *Descr.* 1.18.6).[5] In the Panhellenion sanctuary he was assimilated to Zeus Panhellenios and worshiped alone (i.e., not as *synnaos*).[6] Yet well before the completion of the Panhellenic program, the emperor had commissioned engineering works and other buildings, renovated the city's ancestral laws, and reinvigorated its artistic and cultural institutions, and the evidence suggests that his special relationship to Athens was perceptible to his contemporaries by the time Quadratus and Aristides are thought to have written their apologies in 124/125.

This essay investigates the two Hadrianic activities mentioned in the *Chronicon* in connection with Hadrian's stay at Athens in 124/125—

144-57; John Day, *An Economic History of Athens under Roman Domination* (New York: Columbia University Press, 1942), 183-251; Follet, *Athènes*, 107-35; Daniel J. Geagan, *The Athenian Constitution after Sulla*, HesperiaSup 12 (Princeton: American School of Classical Studies at Athens, 1967), passim; and Paul Graindor, *Athènes sous Hadrien* (Cairo: Boulac, 1934). Surveys include Daniel J. Geagan, "Roman Athens, Some Aspects of Life and Culture I: 86 B.C.-A.D. 267," *ANRW* 7.1:389-99; J. H. Oliver, "Roman Emperors and Athens," *Historia* 30 (1981): 419; and T. Leslie Shear Jr., "Athens: From City-State to Provincial Town," *Hesperia* 50 (1981): 372-74.

4. Dietrich Willers, *Hadrians panhellenisches Programm: Archäologische Beiträge zur Neugestaltung Athens durch Hadrian*, BHAK 16 (Basel: Vereinigung der Freunde antiker Kunst, 1990); A. J. Spawforth and S. Walker, "The World of the Panhellenion, I: Athens and Eleusis," *JRS* 75 (1985): 78-104; Boatwright, *Hadrian*; and Boatwright, "Further Thoughts on Hadrianic Athens," *Hesperia* 52 (1983): 173-76. C. P. Jones, "The Panhellenion," *Chiron* 26 (1996): 29-35, shows that the Panhellenion sanctuary is not to be confused with Pausanias's Temple of Hera and Zeus Panhellenios. He argues that the Greeks formally requested the building of the Panhellenion sanctum in Hadrian's honor soon after the Olympieion was completed. Hadrian ratified and regulated the project (see *Hist. rom.* 69.16.2: τόν τε σηκὸν ... οἰκοδομήσασθαι τοῖς Ἕλλησιν ἐπέτρεψε).

5. Anna S. Benjamin, "The Altars of Hadrian in Athens and Hadrian's Panhellenic Program," *Hesperia* 32 (1963): 57-86; William E. Metcalf, "Hadrian, Iovis Olympius," *Mnemosyne* 27 (1974): 59-66.

6. Jones, "Panhellenion," 34-35.

Hadrian's religious performances and his public acts of munificence. Among the former are included the emperor's initiation into the Eleusinian Mysteries and his presidency of the city Dionysia. Among the latter must be included his building donations and his legacy of legal and financial reforms. I argue that Hadrian's early benefactions to Athens reveal a discourse rooted in the emperor's dual Roman and Athenian citizenship. The bulk of the essay is concerned with recovering prominent aspects of that discourse. In the conclusion I offer some preliminary suggestions for how the discourse of Hadrianic patronage may be brought into conversation with the *Apology* of Aristides.[7]

1. Early Hadrianic Patronage to Athens (111–125 CE)

From a young age, Hadrian's natural disposition (*ingenium*) for Hellenica was evident to his Roman contemporaries, who playfully, and perhaps at times mockingly, teased him as a "Greekling" (*Graeculus*) (Hist. Aug., Hadr. 1.5; Pseudo-Aurelius Victor, *Epit. Caes.* 14.2).[8] Numerous ancient authors record his famous affection for the city of Athens.[9] Hadrian's formal political ties with Athens began in 111 CE, when the Athenian citizens honored him with the city's preeminent annual public magistracy, the eponymous archonship, so designated because the Athenian year was named for its officeholder.[10] In practice, emperors and their kin conducted honorary municipal magistracies in absentia, delegating quotidian responsibilities to a magistrate known as a *praefectus*, appointed from the local population to govern in their stead.[11] Hadrian almost certainly followed prevailing

---

7. Quadratus survives in one citation (Eusebius, *Hist. eccl.* 4.3), while Aristides's *Apology* appears in four textual traditions representing three distinct recensions. For discussion, see Bernard Pouderon and Marie-Joseph Pierre, eds., *Aristide: Apologie*, SC 470 (Paris: Cerf, 2003), 107–72; and William Rutherford, "Reinscribing the Jews: The Story of Aristides' *Apology* 2.2–4 and 14.1b–15.2," *HTR* 106 (2013): 61–91.

8. Ronald Syme, "Hadrian as Philhellene: Neglected Aspects," in *Roman Papers*, ed. Anthony Birley (Oxford: Clarendon, 1988), 5:546–62.

9. Cited passim; see Boatwright, *Hadrian*, 20–26; and Willers, *Programm*, 35–36.

10. Follet, *Athènes*, 507; *IG* 2.2024, 3286; Hist. Aug., Hadr. 19.1; Hist. Aug., Gall. 11.3–4; Dio Cassius, *Hist. rom.* 69.16.1 (chronologically ambiguous). Hadrian held at least eighteen honorary magistracies in thirteen cities, including Sparta and Delphi (Boatwright, *Hadrian*, 63–64; cf. Hist. Aug., Hadr. 19.1).

11. W. Dittenberger, "Kaiser Hadrians erste Anwesenheit in Athen," *Hermes* 7 (1873): 224–29; Boatwright, *Hadrian*, 57–72; and Follet, *Athènes*, 29.

practice; consequently, the archonship involved little from him administratively, while it greatly honored Athens. The Athenians also offered their newest archon honorary citizenship. Hadrian accepted the offer and opted to be enrolled in the tribe Besa.[12]

Hadrian's earliest interactions with Athens reflect the patronage politics of the era. The Athenian offer of a magistracy and citizenship was as much an expression of Athenian pride in their civic traditions as it was an attempt to ingratiate themselves with a member of the imperial family. Hadrian's acceptance of the honors was not compulsory. He specifically elected to identify with the city, its institutions, and its traditions. His choice showcased his philhellenism and presaged the friendship and benefaction the Athenians could anticipate if he were ever to assume the throne. In celebration of his eponymous archonship, the Athenians feted Hadrian with an honorary commemorative portrait. Its pentelic marble pedestal, recovered in the Theater of Dionysos, bears a bilingual dedicatory inscription that lists in seven Latin lines the course of public offices (*cursus honorum*) held by P. Aelius Hadrianus through his consulship of 108 CE.[13] Three Greek lines identify Hadrian as archon and list as donors the Council of the Areopagus, the Council of the Six Hundred, and the people of Athens.[14] In Hadrian, the city had an honorary citizen and a powerful Roman friend. Hadrian had already established himself as a philhellenic Roman patron to Athens, before he ever assumed the throne.

The reflorescence of Athens under Hadrianic patronage began in earnest when Hadrian became emperor in 117 CE.[15] At that time, the Athenians

---

12. James H. Oliver, "Athenian Citizenship of Roman Emperors," *Hesperia* 20 (1951): 346–49.

13. *IG* 2.3286. Paul Graindor, *Athénes de Tibère à Trajan* (Cairo: Imprimerie Misr, 1931), 26–27 (commentary) and fig. 3 (photograph). Early firsthand descriptions of its location appear in A. S. Rousopoulos, "Τὰ ἐκ τοῦ Διονυσιακοῦ Θεάτρου" ["The Precincts of the Theater of Dionysos"], *ArchEph* (1862): 153–54, and Wilhelm Vischer, "Die Entdeckungen im Theater des Dionysos zu Athen," *Neues Schweizerisches Museum* 3 (1863): 62.

14. Lines 8–10: ἡ ἐξ Ἀρείου πάγου βουλὴ καὶ ἡ τῶν ἑξακοσίων καὶ ὁ δῆμος ὁ Ἀθηναίων τὸν ἄρχοντα ἑαυτῶν Ἀδριανόν. This is the official title of the government of the Athenian polis in the Roman period (Geagan, *Constitution*, 62, 140–45).

15. Pausanias, *Descr.* 1.20.7: Ἀθῆναι ... αὖθις Ἀδριανοῦ βασιλεύοντος ἤνθησαν. Vanessa A. Champion-Smith, "Pausanias in Athens: An Archeological Commentary on the Agora of Athens" (PhD diss., University College London, 1998), 12–13 and passim, attributes Pausanias's predilection for Hadrian to the emperor's philhellenism.

sent an embassy headed by a young Herodes Atticus (Philostratus, *Vit. soph.* 2.1 [§565]). We may presume that among other things they wished to congratulate the new emperor personally and to offer honorary decrees for him to refuse or to accept.[16] In the interval between his accession to the throne and his arrival at Athens in late 124 CE, the Athenians sought Hadrian's continued patronage on at least two occasions. They asked him to carry out reforms to their civic constitution, and the Epicurean school sought changes to their own succession process.[17] In both cases, the emperor responded favorably and went further to initiate his first building projects at Athens, with a renovation of the Via Sacra. The early flourish of activity was punctuated with further legal and financial reforms, new construction projects, and at least two public religious spectacles during Hadrian's visit to Athens in 124/125 CE. These are discussed below.

1.1. Constitutional Reforms (121/122–125 CE)

According to Aristotle, the first rudimentary Athenian law code was composed by Draco in the late seventh century BCE and was repealed in the early sixth century by Solon, who nevertheless preserved the Draconian homicide laws. Solon introduced an Athenian Council of Four Hundred (Plutarch, *Sol.* 19.1). Less than a century later, Cleisthenes overhauled the system of tribal representation in the Council, establishing a new system of ten tribes in which tribal affiliation was determined by one's deme of residence. The 139 demes of Attica were organized into thirty groups, or *trittyes*, by geographical region—ten from the city, ten from inland, and ten from the coastland. Each tribe comprised three *trittyes*, one from each region, and was represented in the Athenian Council by fifty members. The Cleisthenic system would undergo periodic reform (in 307/306, 224/223, and 201/200 BCE), yet would remain "an extremely stable and regular system" for over seven centuries.[18] And Hadrian would add his name to the venerable list of those who reformed the Athenian constitution.

---

16. Paul J. Alexander, "Letters and Speeches of the Emperor Hadrian," *HSCP* 49 (1938): 142–44, discusses congratulatory embassies.

17. Constitution: see below. Epicureans: attested in a series of letters dating 121–122 CE. For bibliography, see Follet, *Athénes*, 22 n. 4. Hadrian also wrote a letter dated February–March 125 CE to the Epicureans; see James H. Oliver, "An Inscription Concerning the Epicurean School at Athens," *TAPA* 69 (1938): 494–99 and pl. 1.

18. John S. Traill, *The Political Organization of Attica: A Study of the Demes, Trit-

The Athenians had been conducting legal reforms since 119/120 CE. A series of Delian inscriptions dated 119/120 to 125/126 CE describes M. Annius Pythodorus as "lawgiver" (νομοθέτης), suggesting that an office of "judicial overseer" (νομοθεσία) existed at Roman Athens during Hadrian's reign.[19] If lawgiver is not merely an honorific, then Pythodorus was involved in the official oversight and revision of common laws at Athens and may have explored legal precedents in Draco, Solon, and Cleisthenes in preparation for constitutional reforms. In 121/122 the Athenians asked the emperor to reform their constitution.[20] Whatever official tasks Pythodorus undertook, the scope of his activities did not match the sweeping character of the reforms Hadrian carried out sometime between 121/122 and the end of his Athenian visit in 125 CE.[21] While there is much we do not know about the constitutional reforms, the surviving evidence allows us to surmise that their chief aspects survive.[22] They influenced the civic, religious, and financial institutions of Athens and have left a clear imprint in historical documents.[23]

---

tyes, and Phylai, and Their Representation in the Athenian Council, HesperiaSup 14 (Princeton: American School of Classical Studies at Athens, 1975), xiii.

19. IDelos 5.2535-37; Geagan, *Constitution*, 122–23, surveys the "faint traces" of an office of νομοθεσία. Graindor, *Athènes*, 32 n. 1; and Boatwright, *Hadrian*, 91 n. 39, treat νομοθέτης as a title; as does Anastasios P. Christophilopoulos, "Ἡ νομοθετικὴ λειτουργία εἰς τὰς Ἑλληνικὰς πόλεις" ["The Legislative Liturgy in Greek Cities"], *Athēna* 69 (1967): 24–30, nos. 28–29. Hadrian is designated "lawgiver" in inscriptions from Megara, Thespiae, and Cyrene (for references, see Christophilopoulos, "λειτουργία," 24 nn. 2–4), and in Sib. Or. 12.173–74.

20. James H. Oliver, "Philosophers and Procurators, Relatives of the Aemilius Juncus of *Vita Commodi* 4,11," *Hesperia* 36 (1967): 50 n. 18; Follet, *Athénes*, 116–25.

21. Follet, *Athénes*, 116–21, notes judiciously that "même s'il est encore impossible d'en fixer la date" (116), the literary texts raise the possibility of major reforms between 121/122 and 125 CE.

22. So Willers, *Programm*, 9.

23. Follet, *Athénes*, 121–25; Geagan, *Constitution*, 68; Oliver, "Athens of Hadrian," 131. According to Dio Cassius, *Hist. rom.* 69.16.2, Hadrian "introduced many other laws," among which may be included a "lease/farm (?) tax." If we read Dio Cassius chronologically (a precarious task), then Hadrian introduced further laws in 131/132, probably independent from the earlier constitutional reforms. Compare Daniel J. Geagan, "A Decree of the Council of the Areopagus," *Hesperia* 42 (1973): 352–57 and plates 63–64; Geagan, *Athenian Constitution*, 121–22.

1.1.1. Reform of Political Organs and Offices

Hadrian reorganized the system of tribal representation in the Athenian Council. In 200 BCE, the number of tribes represented in the council had been altered to twelve, with Ptolemeis and Attalis added in honor of foreign sovereigns, and the council brought to 600 members. In 121/122 or 124/125 CE, Hadrian reduced the number of councilmen from 600 to the Cleisthenic 500 and added a thirteenth tribe named Hadrianis.[24] Antony Raubitschek has shown that the council actually amounted to 520 members at this time to accommodate thirteen tribes.[25] The creation of Hadrianis further involved the distribution of Attic demes from the existing tribes into the new tribe. In so doing, the emperor restructured a bouleutic arrangement that was more than 300 years old and had weathered even the sack of Sulla in 86 BCE. A change in the number of prytanies necessarily accompanied the reorganization of the council.[26] As for other offices, Hadrian does not seem to have reformed the old archonships, though he may have lowered the minimum age for assuming an archonship.[27] It is uncertain whether the emperor modified the organization of the ephebate, since the ephebic catalogues from his reign are summary or incomplete.

1.1.2. Financial Reforms

Some of Hadrian's reforms safeguarded the supply of essential commodities for Athens and Eleusis. This is certainly the case with his famous Oil Law, which secured for the Athenian state the right to purchase oil from

---

24. Antony E. Raubitschek, "Note on the Post-Hadrianic Boule," in Γέρας Ἀντωνίου Κεραμοπούλλου, ed. A. D. Keramopoullos, EPHMS.PT 9 (Athens: Society of Macedonian Studies, 1953), 242–55, has shown that the events were contemporaneous. The Council of Five Hundred is first attested with certainty in a letter from Hadrian (IG 2.1102) dated to 132 CE (or 129?), though it may be mentioned in a dedication made prior to the suffect consulship of L. Aemilius Juncus in 127 (IG 2.4210). Hadrianis is probably attested in 141/142 (IG 2.1764B) and is certainly attested in 142/143 (IG 2.2049). James A. Notopoulos, "The Date of the Creation of Hadrianis," TAPA 77 (1946): 53–56, argues for a date of 126/127 for the creation of Hadrianis. Follet, Athènes, 119–23 and 364, roundly critiques this suggestion and places the creation of Hadrianis in 121/122 or 124/125 CE.

25. Raubitschek, "Note."

26. Geagan, Constitution, 95–96.

27. Oliver, "Philosophers and Procurators," 53–56; Follet, Athènes, 13.

the annual yield of olive crops in Attica.[28] The law required cultivators of oil to deliver a third of their yields to state officials who were responsible for buying oil for public use.[29] Those who leased properties on the lands of Claudius Hipparchus, which the Roman *fiscus* had confiscated, were obligated to deliver an eighth of their oil stores. Payment was calculated in proportion to the total amount of oil harvested and had to be remitted at the beginning of the harvest.[30] The person making the deposit—whether landowner, cultivator, or middleman—was required to give sworn statement identifying himself as the seller and declaring the harvest size and the name of the slave or freedman who produced it.[31] Anyone selling oil to an exporter had to declare the amount sold, name the buyer, and identify the location of the ship's anchorage;[32] and exporters had to declare the quantity of oil being shipped and the names of the suppliers.[33] The Oil Law required all declarations to be presented to the city treasurers and the herald of the Boule and to be ratified by signature.[34] It imposed stiff penalties on any who tried to circumvent it.

The Oil Law showcased the emperor as supreme benefactor. It secured for the city an adequate supply of the oil required for civic functions, including the operation of the gymnasia and the celebration of rites in the Dionysia and the Eleusinian Mysteries.[35] The law also displayed Hadrian's concern for civic virtues in marketplace transactions. It protected oil producers against rate fixing and thereby provided them with

---

28. *IG* 2.1100. The law is expressly labeled as belonging to Hadrian's legal code: κε(φάλαιον) νό(μου) θε(ιοτάτου) Ἀδριανοῦ. For discussion, see Graindor, *Hadrien*, 74–79; and Day, *Economic History*, 189–92.

29. Lines 2–14.

30. Lines 6–9.

31. Lines 15–21.

32. Lines 21–23.

33. Lines 41–42.

34. Lines 11–15: πρὸ[ς τοὺς ταμίας κα]ὶ τὸν κήρυκα δύο ... ἰδόντες ὑπογραφήν; lines 66–67: ο[ἱ] ἀργυροταμίαι.

35. In a monumental study of benefaction in Asia Minor, Arjan Zuiderhoek identified oil as "one of the most popular types of goods distributed by benefactors" to the benefit of the whole citizen body and whose distribution pattern indicates "a broad 'renaissance' of gymnasial culture in the eastern provinces during the high Empire (*The Politics of Munificence in the Roman Empire: Citizens, Elites and Benefactors in Asia Minor* (Cambridge: Cambridge University Press, 2009), 89–92; cf. fig. 5.5 and table 5.1.

an equitable market. The law was not intended to be punitive or coercive. By mandating a system of recorded transactions between suppliers and exporters, the law sought to limit the profits of middlemen. It established a system of cross-references between suppliers and exporters by which the state could ensure transactions. In years when the state's annual quota of oil was exceeded, "owing to a fulsome olive crop," the oil collectors (οἱ ἐλαιῶναι) and treasurers (ἀργυροταμίαι) were required to issue a rebate to oil cultivators.[36]

Another likely chapter in Hadrian's law code regulated the sale of fish at Eleusis.[37] The price of fish was subject to inflation from increased demand during festival times when the rolls of visitors swelled (Philostratus, *Vit. Apoll.* 4.17), and the Fish Law attempted to alleviate supply shortages by diverting the sale of fish from the Piraeus to Eleusis at the time of the Mysteries. The law was prominently displayed in front of the Deigma at the Piraeus, where it proclaimed an exemption from the standard two obol tax (ἡ διοβελία) for fishermen who sell their catch at Eleusis. The inflation of fish prices was exacerbated by the multiplication of middlemen. To circumvent artificial inflation, only the fisherman and the original buyer were given by law the right to sell fish. "When there are three parties," the law announced, "the selling of the same goods raises prices."[38] The Fish Law confirmed the pattern of imperial concern for securing essential commodities at Athens. It further secured supplies for the celebration of civic functions, including rites at Eleusis.

Hadrian's financial reforms probably involved substantially more than the Oil Law and Fish Law. James Oliver produced evidence suggesting that Hadrian considerably restructured the city's public finances by creating a new agency of the public treasury and new offices of treasurer to administer it.[39] An inscription found in the Athenian Agora and dating to the reign of Commodus or Marcus Aurelius records a list of public

---

36. Lines 59–68.

37. *IG* 2.1103. Graindor, *Hadrien*, 127–29; Day, *Economic History*, 192–93; Adolf Wilhelm, "Inschriften aus Erythrai und Chios," *JÖAI* 12 (1909): 146–48; Boatwright, *Hadrian*, 90–91.

38. Lines 10–12: τὸ δὲ καὶ τρίτους ὠνητὰς γεινομένους τῶν αὐτῶν ὠνίων με[τὰ] πιπράσκειν ἐπιτείνει τὰς τειμάς.

39. James H. Oliver, "The Athens of Hadrian," in *Les empereurs romains d'Espagne*, Colloques internationaux du Centre national de la recherche scientifique, Sciences humaines (Paris: Centre national de la recherche scientifique, 1965), 123–33.

and private contributions given for an occasion no longer recorded.[40] The inscription states that the city of Athens made a payment of 278 denarii from the public Opisthodomos and of 302 from the Sacred Diataxis.[41] The contributions, assessed in denarii rather than Attic drachmas, were not intended for the Athenian state but represent annual payments to the Roman *fiscus* by titleholders and others for use of the estates of Hipparchus, which the Roman *fiscus* had confiscated and later leased to Athenians. The pairing of the Opisthodomos and Sacred Diataxis attests the presence of *two* financial agencies in Athens in the last few decades of the second century. An Athenian department of sacred finances (i.e., Sacred Diataxis) is attested from the end of the first century BCE, when it was administered by a single treasurer,[42] but this inscription is the first recovered that formulates the Opisthodomos as a financial agency for administering city funds in Roman times. From this evidence, Oliver argued that it was Hadrian who established the Opisthodomos, "an Athenian public treasury reformed with Roman methods of accounting and operation and with some prescribed service for the emperor, a service protecting the polis as well as the fiscus."[43] Further, the Opisthodomos is simply the Athenian counterpart for the public loan office, or *kalendarium*, managed in the West by *curatores kalendarii* and in the East by treasury officers (ἀργυροταμίαι).[44] The identification is salient, since the Oil Law makes reference to "treasurers" who collected debts owed the city.[45] The presence of ἀργυροταμίαι in the Oil Law and in another Hadrianic-era inscription suggests Oliver's interpretation is accurate.

---

40. *SEG* 19.172; Benjamin D. Meritt, "Greek Inscriptions," *Hesperia* 29 (1960): 29–32, no. 37 and pl. 8.

41. Lines 17–18: καὶ ἃ ἡ πόλις ἐκ τοῦ ὀ[π]ισθοδόμου vacat *ΣΟΗ | καὶ ἀπὸ ἱερᾶς διατάξεω[ς] vacat *ΤΒ. The term ὀπισθόδομος also appears in lines 2, 4, and 15, where it indicates, according to Meritt, "private banks, treasure boxes, strong-boxes perhaps, in which small savings were kept" ("Inscriptions," 32). Oliver, "Athens," argues more convincingly that the transactions represent contributions of real estate (cf. line 5: τὸ χω[ρίο]ν) and that the term ὀπισθόδομος consistently refers to a state financial agency.

42. *IG* 2.3503: τ[α]μίαν τῆς ἱερᾶς διατάξεως; cf. James H. Oliver, *The Sacred Gerousia*, HesperiaSup 6 (Athens: American School of Classical Studies at Athens, 1941), 133–34.

43. Oliver, "Athens," 129.

44. Pierre Paris, "Inscriptions d'Élatée," *BCH* 10 (1886): 372–74, no. 11.

45. On *argyrotamiai*, see *IG* 2.1104, line 8, dated to 117–38 CE.

1.1.3. Legal Enforcement and Judicial Appeals

The constitutional reforms were outfitted with state enforcement mechanisms and procedures for appeals. The Oil and Fish Laws defined procedures by which penalties were assessed and appeals adjudicated. Under the Oil Law, the Athenian Council decided cases involving less than fifty amphorae; the Ekklesia made determinations in cases exceeding fifty amphorae. If a person appealed to the emperor or to a proconsul, the Ekklesia was to appoint public advocates (οἱ σύνδικοι).[46] Violators of the Fish Law were referred to the Areopagus. Treasury officers (ἀργυροταμίαι) were created under the Opisthodomos to collect debts owed the city. Hadrian introduced "a regular and modernized procedure in the case of delay or default by those who have entered into a government contract."[47]

Hadrian further restructured the judicial appeals process in Attica and beyond. An inscription from Mistra, which Oliver dates to Hadrian's reign, sets guidelines for determining which cases were excluded from appeal to the emperor: "I forbid any disputes which are for less than nine hundred denarii and [which] will not involve a trial, or a pre-judicial ruling in a capital case, or civil rights to be appealed to me."[48] For a case that met the appeals criteria, local civic boards known as *synedria* (συνέδρια) were to vet the case for legitimacy to decide if it should reach an audience with the emperor.[49] Hadrian thereby solidified the role of *synedria* in Athens, the effects of which continued to be felt in post-Hadrianic times.[50]

The constitutional reforms reveal Hadrian's efforts to inscribe himself into a venerable lineage of Athenian lawgivers. He invoked a Cleisthenic archetype and wrote himself into a central political institution by addition of an eponymous tribe, Hadrianis. They also show the emperor's concern for the modernization (i.e., Romanization) of aspects of the city's economy, and his concern to provide resources for the regular functioning of the city's festivals, its religious cults (including those of Eleusis), and its gym-

---

46. *IG* 2.1100, lines 46–56.
47. Oliver, "Athens," 130.
48. *IG* 5.1.21, col. II, lines 5–9.
49. So James H. Oliver, "Hadrian's Reform of the Appeal Procedure in Greece," *Hesperia* 39 (1970): 332–36. On the appeals system, see Oliver, *Marcus Aurelius: Aspects of Civic and Cultural Policy in the East*, HesperiaSup 13 (Princeton: American School of Classical Studies at Athens, 1970), 1–42.
50. Geagan, *Constitution*, 36–38.

nasia. Any attempt to recover a discourse of Hadrian's early patronage at Athens must account for the image of Hadrian as lawgiver, his archaizing appeal to the Greek past, and his patronage of the city's religious, cultural, and political institutions.

1.2. Building Donations and Subventions (121/122–125 CE)

Between 117 and 125 CE, Hadrian sponsored at least six building projects at Athens and two rare subventions. Before his visit to Athens, Hadrian arranged for the renovation of the Via Sacra between Athens and Eleusis, along which initiates (μύσται) would process to celebrate the Mysteries. He had a bridge built over the river Cephisus to ease traffic to Eleusis and a system of stone dikes for the Ilissos to restrain flood waters.[51] The engineering projects were completed between 122 and 123/124 CE.[52] In view of Hadrian's famous predilection for the Mysteries (see below), the renovation of the Via Sacra monumentalized his personal and imperial affirmation and adoption of a sacred Athenian rite. The project also served commercial traffic between Athens and Eleusis and displayed the emperor's concern for the material welfare of Athens. Hadrian's care to provide material resources to Athens is also evidenced in his efforts to construct an aqueduct, which at the time of his death remained incomplete.[53]

Two imperial subventions possibly given during the first visit also showcase Hadrian's concern for material provision at Athens (Dio Cassius, *Hist. rom.* 69.16.2).[54] Hadrian granted Athens a portion of the island of Cephallenia and its associated tax revenues,[55] and he provided the city with an ancestral grain dole, that is, an imperially funded annual grain

---

51. Graindor, *Athénes*, 250–51.
52. Eusebius, *Chron.*, ad ann. Hadr. 7 (Lat.) = 123/124; ad ann. Hadr. 5 [Arm.] = 121/122 CE): Cefisus fluuius Eleusinam inundauit, quem Hadrianus ponte coniungens Athenis hiemem exegit; see Willers, *Programm*, 13.
53. *ILS* 1.337; Shawna Leigh, "The 'Reservoir' of Hadrian in Athens," *JRA* 10 (1997): 279–90; Graindor, *Athénes*, 251–52; Willers, *Programm*, 13.
54. The placement of these subventions in the first trip is compatible with one way of reading Dio Cassius; cf. Follet, *Athénes*, 115. Spawforth and Walker, "Panhellenion," 90, date the annual grain endowment to the creation of the Panhellenion in 131/132 CE.
55. *IG* 2.3301; Dio Cassius incorrectly claims Hadrian granted the entire island; cf. Day, *Economic History*, 188.

supply. These gifts were exceptionally rare Hadrianic endowments, and they conspicuously indicate Hadrian's special favor for Athens.[56]

During his stay in Athens, Hadrian also initiated construction on the Olympieion, the massive Temple of Olympian Zeus.[57] The foundations of the Olympieion had been laid over six hundred years earlier by the Peisistratids, and, despite the attempts of the Hellenistic king Antiochus Epiphanes and later Roman client kings to complete it, the seemingly interminable project was at last brought to completion in 131/132 under Hadrianic sponsorship. The finished Olympieion integrated the archaic Greek plan with a Roman-style *temenos*. Its dedication marked the beginning of the Panhellenion, a league for which the temple would serve an integral role.[58] The Panhellenion brought together at least twenty-eight cities, mainly in Achaia and Asia, who claimed Greek pedigree, whether real or fabricated. The league fulfilled a variety of functions—religious, cultural, and political—but its primary raisons d'être seem to have been to honor the Roman imperial house and to revive a sense of shared Greek cultural heritage and prestige among Greek municipalities and Greek colonies, preeminent among which was Athens.[59] The Panhellenion "elevated and rewarded 'Greekness' and looked to the past for self-definition. The past, however, embraced legendary history and more recent interactions with Rome and the emperor, and 'Greekness' seems to have been as much cultural as strictly ancestral."[60] By initiating construction on the Olympieion, Hadrian signaled that he was already making plans to embellish the Athenian cityscape and to establish Athens as the capital of his Panhellenic vision.

---

56. Boatwright, *Hadrian*, 83–88, discusses the rarity of Hadrianic land grants and settlements. Athens shared the distinction of an annual grain dole only with Rome, though Hadrian offered to Ephesus and Tralles *temporary* grants to purchase Egyptian grain (Boatwright, *Hadrian*, 92–94); cf. Zuiderhoek, *Politics of Munificence*, 32 n. 26.

57. A. Kokkos, "Ἀδριάνεια ἔργα εἰς τὰς Ἀθήνας" ["Hadrianic Works in Athens"], *Archaiologikon Deltion* 25 (1970): 150–73. Hist. Aug., Hadr. 13.6: Denique cum post Africam Romam redisset, statim ad orientem profectus per Athenas iter fecit atque opera, quae apud Athenienses coeperat, dedicavit, ut Iovis Olympii aedem et aram sibi. Mention of the journey to Africa (128 CE) indicates that Hadrian had initiated the temple constructions during the first journey and dedicated them on his second or third journey.

58. See nn. 4–5 above. Willers, *Programm*, 36: the Temple "einen besonderen Rang in seiner (= Hadrians) Baupolitik für Athen einnahm."

59. Spawforth and Walker, "Panhellenion"; Boatwright, *Hadrian*, 147–57.

60. Boatwright, *Hadrian*, 150.

Hadrian's donation of a gymnasium south of the city and endowment for its maintenance indicate that he was also seeking to revive Athenian cultural institutions at this time.[61] Construction on three other edifices, the so-called Library of Hadrian, the Temple (ναός) of Hera and Zeus Panhellenios, and the Panhellenion, may also have begun during the first visit, though this is highly uncertain.[62]

Early Hadrianic constructions and subventions highlight the emperor's concern for the provision of material resources, protection against natural disaster, embellishment and renovation of the Athenian cityscape, the revival of the city's cultural institutions and heritage, and the flourishing of ancient Greek cults under Roman imperial sponsorship. By 125 CE, the construction program and the changing cityscape it brought evoked the imposing power, presence, and patronage of the Roman emperor and his identification with the glorious Greek past.

1.3. Religious Spectacles (February–March 125 CE)

Hadrian's constitutional reforms left their traces on public offices, and the new makeup of the Council was immediately perceptible to council members. Festival goers would have sensed the influence of the Oil and Fish Laws, and the renovation of the Via Sacra. Many Athenians might have speculated as to whether Hadrian would be able to complete the Olympieion. For the common Athenian, however, it was likely the spectacular nature of Hadrian's religious performances that attracted most immediate attention. The sources record two public religious displays during the emperor's first visit to Athens. Both punctuated the end of his stay in the city.

In 125 CE, Hadrian was initiated into the Lesser Mysteries at Eleusis during the prescribed month, Anthesterion (February–March) (Eusebius,

---

61. *IG* 2.1102, 3620; cf. *SEG* 3.111; Pausanias *Descr.* 1.18.9; Willers, 14. The project, possibly a renovation of the ancient Cynosarges gymnasium, was only completed in 131/132 CE. For evidence on the endowment, see Paul Graindor, "Inscriptions attiques d'époque impériale," *BCH* 38 (1914): 396–401; and Graindor, *Hadrien*, 45–47.

62. On the identification of the library with Pausanius's "hundred pillars of Phrygian marble" (*Descr.* 1.18.9), see Willers, *Programm*, 14–21. Follet notes a possible reading of *Historiae romanae* and Historia Augusta in which construction of the Panhellenion sanctuary would have begun during Hadrian's first trip to Athens. Christopher Jones offers an alternate view; see supra, n. 4.

Chron., ad ann. Hadr. 9 [Lat.]).[63] In the Lesser Mysteries, celebrants underwent a purification ritual at the banks of the Ilissos near Athens. We know almost nothing for certain about the details of the purification rituals, yet the emperor of Rome himself would have joined the ranks of other prospective celebrants to become an initiate (μύστης) into the famous Mysteries. Hadrian's celebration of the Lesser Mysteries would have been a mark of distinction for Athens.

In March of 125, Hadrian served as "director of the games" (ἀγωνοθέτης) for the Greater Dionysia.[64] According to Dio Cassius, Hadrian fulfilled his *agonothesia* in exemplary fashion. In a spectacular display of identification with his Athenian citizenship, he donned Athenian ethnic costume, setting aside the Roman toga in favor of the Greek *chitōn*. At the Dionysia, Hadrian also sported a short beard, an atypical feature for a reigning emperor and one which conspicuously distinguished him from his clean-shaven predecessor. Hadrian's biographer explained the peculiar practice as an effort to cover facial blemishes (Hist. Aug., Hadr. 26.1).[65] This may be correct, but another interpretation seems equally likely and offers a more comprehensive explanation of the practice. Paul Zanker has argued that the emperor adopted a "cultivated beard" to assimilate himself to the "classical face" of a sophisticated intellectual elite and to commemorate the notion of a classical Greek past.[66] Hadrian publicized the beard as imperial iconography in his official portraits. His facial hair expressed in terms of Greek physiognomy the emperor's authorization of a growing Roman interest in classical Greek culture. In sum, Hadrian's adoption of outward indicia of Greek identity evidences not only his concern for the office of

---

63. Paul Foucart, "Les empereurs romains initiés aux mystères d'Éleusis," *RevPhil* 17 (1893): 200, incorrectly claims Hadrian was initiated into the Lesser Mysteries in March 125 CE and into the Greater Mysteries in September of the same year. This is rendered impossible by an imperial letter to the Delphians dated August–September 125, written from his villa on the Tiber (cited Follet, *Athénes*, 108).

64. Hist. Aug., Hadr. 13.1: *pro agonotheta resedit*; Hist. rom. 69.16.1: τά τε Διονύσια … ἐν τῇ ἐσθῆτι τῇ ἐπιχωρίῳ λαμπρῶς ἐπετέλησε. The emperor did not celebrate the Dionysia during his archonship in 111/112 CE, as some suggest (*pace* Geagan, *Constitution*, 6, 9; Geagan, "Roman Athens," 389), since Hadrian almost certainly held his archonship *in absentia*.

65. Promissa barba, ut uulnera quae in facie naturalia erant tegeret.

66. Paul Zanker, *The Mask of Socrates: The Image of the Intellectual in Antiquity* (Berkeley: University of California Press, 1995), 198–233; challenged by Caroline Vout, "Hadrian, Hellenism, and the Social History of Art," *Arion* 18 (2010): 55–78.

agōnothetēs but also his personal pride in identifying with the Athenian citizenry and his emulation of the Greek past.

2. A Discourse of Patronage in Hadrianic Athens?

Hadrian's early patronage to Athens comprised a patchwork of engineering works, temple foundations, legislative reforms, restructuring and creation of civic institutions, gifts of grain and tax revenues, a new system of philosophical succession for the Epicurean school, and more. The list is impressive and would grow significantly in the coming years, when Hadrian would twice more visit Athens. What did this patchwork of imperial benefactions to Athens communicate?

In a letter dated 125/126 CE, Avidius Quietus, then governor of Asia, described Hadrian as "having combined justice with benevolence" in his interactions with the cities of the empire.[67] This ancient testimony certainly suits the character of Hadrian's early Athenian benefactions. Whether maintaining civic and imperial infrastructure, providing material grants, protecting supplies of indigenous resources, preserving and renovating civic institutions, securing the equitable administration of justice and appeals, or celebrating local religious rites and customs, the emperor disclosed a predilection for mixing order and justice with his generosities. Athens represents one instance among many of Hadrian's just and benevolent patronage.

Dietrich Willers sees in Hadrian's Athenian donations a policy of imperial unification (*Reichseinigungspolitik*) that began in the capital and reverberated into the provinces.[68] Hadrian's Panhellenic program, centered at Athens, sought to unify the Greek East under the auspices of Roman patronage. As the seat of the Panhellenion, Athens assumed a central role in the emperor's program of uniting Roman West with Greek East. Boatwright particularly emphasizes Hadrian's role as patron to cities

---

67. SEG 54.1275: μείξας τῷ φιλανθρώπῳ τὸ δίκαιον.

68. Willers, *Panhellenism*, 7–8 and 12: "Am Ende des Weges soll als Ergebnis deutlich werden, dass Hadrian die Stadt Athen schliesslich dazu ausersehen hatte, nicht nur kulturell-geistiges Zentrum der griechischen Welt zu sein, sondern auch als politischer Vorort des Ostens diese Reichshälfte an den lateinischen Westen anzubinden." Compare Benjamin, "Altars," 47: "Hadrian's willingness to accept divine honors and his encouragement of Panhellenism have, among many complex motives, the common purpose of the consolidation of the empire."

across the empire. Hadrian, she argues, sought to fortify the system of imperial patronage that joined local municipal elites to the capital in networks of friendship and reciprocity—"a much less costly way to achieve the empire's cohesion and cooperation throughout Italy and the provinces than the display and use of state violence."[69] Boatwright identifies a Hadrianic program of urban Romanization, by which Hadrian staged a display of Roman power and beneficence without homogenizing or standardizing local populations. Hadrian's patronage politics integrated the emperor into local traditions and thereby reintegrated local municipal cults into the empire. While Willers and Boatwright are careful not to reduce each of Hadrian's benefactions to a single narrative, they do emphasize Hadrian in his capacity as "father of the fatherland" (*pater patriae*), the great benefactor of the empire.

The interpretations of Willers and Boatwright are certainly accurate. Yet several features of Hadrian's munificence suggest that his benefactions to Athens are not entirely exhausted by their assessments. Consider the following peculiarities:

1. From 111 to 112 CE, Hadrian held dual citizenship at Rome and Athens. Acceptance of the Athenian franchise was hardly perfunctory. While the grant of Roman citizenship had extended to Athens under the Claudian and Flavian dynasties,[70] a longstanding Roman taboo against dual citizenship meant that very few Roman elite accepted Athenian citizenship. Hadrian was only the second important Westerner and the first Roman senator ever to do so.[71] Hadrian's acceptance of the Athenians' offer signaled his distinct favor for the city and his enthusiasm to identify with all aspects of the city's life.

---

69. Boatwright, *Hadrian*, 206. In Boatwright's construal, Romanization is no one-way street in which Rome transmits and enforces its norms to the provinces. The new Romanization allows for Greek traditions and acculturating forces at the local level within a Roman imperial framework. Compare Boatwright, "Further Thoughts."

70. Daniel J. Geagan, "The Great Catalogue from the Eleusinion at Athens," *ZPE* 33 (1979): 93–115; G. M. Woloch, "Roman and Athenian Citizenship at Athens, A.D. 96-161," *Historia* 20 (1971): 744–50.

71. The first attested case is the *eques* Q. Trebellius Rufus of Toulouse, and the first emperor was Commodus (James H. Oliver, "Civic Status in Roman Athens: Cicero, *Pro Balbo* 12.30," *GRBS* 22 [1981]: 83–88). Pomponius Atticus and Marcus Porcius Cato resided in Athens, yet neither accepted citizenship (Edward W. Bodnar, "Marcus Porcius Cato," *Hesperia* 31 [1962]: 393–95). The first emperor to accept the franchise was Commodus.

2. Among the cities in the empire, only Rome and Athens benefitted from an imperially funded grain dole.[72]

3. Hadrian's grant to Athens of land and revenues from Cephallenia was one of only six (or possibly eight) recorded grants of territory or of territorial disputes that he was personally involved in deciding. Five of these are in Achaia. The singularity of these gifts "reflects the importance Hadrian accorded [to Athens and Sparta] as he cultivated the glorious Greek past and encouraged the Panhellenion."[73]

4. Hadrian restructured a longstanding tribal arrangement in the Athenian Council, at once restoring the number of councilmen to the Cleisthenic five hundred and adding his own eponymous tribe Hadrianis in the seventh and central position.

5. Several of his known constitutional reforms lavish special attention on Athens. The Oil Law and Fish Law demonstrate the emperor's "unusually high level" of personal involvement in Athenian civic life.[74] Other surviving rescripts indicate that Hadrian's normal practice was to relegate civic disputes to local authorities or appointees from Rome, yet the Athenian Oil Decree twice names Hadrian as arbiter of disputes.

6. During his second trip to Athens, Hadrian would become the only Roman emperor since Augustus to have been inducted into the Lesser Mysteries and to have achieved the epopty—the most advanced stage of initiation—in the Greater Mysteries at Eleusis.[75] He would later have the distinction of transferring the Eleusinian rites to Rome.[76]

7. Hadrian personally presided at the Dionysia in 125 CE in native Athenian clothing.

These features suggest that Hadrian sought to craft a distinctive display of patronage at Athens. While the emperor's patronage is correctly described as "Romanization" or a "policy of imperial unification," the distinctive elements enumerated above disclose a personal affection for

---

72. See above, n. 56.

73. Boatwright, *Hadrian*, 83–88, citing 84.

74. Boatwright, *Hadrian*, 91.

75. Dietmar Kienast, "Hadrian, Augustus und die eleusinischen Mysterien," *JNG* 10 (1959–60): 61–69, studies the coins minted on the occasion of Hadrian's celebration of the epopty in 129 CE. The coins feature Augustus on the obverse and Hadrian on the reverse.

76. Claudius's attempts to do so had been unsuccessful; Suetonius, *Claud.* 25: *Sacra Eleusinia etiam transferre ex Attica Romam conatus est.*

Athens not fully realized in the analyses of either Willers or Boatwright. In the next section, I supplement their interpretations to account for some of these distinctive features of Hadrian's patronage.

3. Princeps Civitatis, Princeps Atheniensium

I propose that the whole assemblage of Hadrian's early donations to Athens may be interpreted in light of his spectacular display at the Dionysia, where he showcased his dual status as citizen of Rome and Athens in one final public performance. Dio Cassius, commenting on the performative nature of Hadrian's *agōnothesia*, notes that the emperor demonstrated his affection for the city in splendid fashion (λαμπρῶς) (*Hist. rom.* 69.16.1). During his presidency of the Dionysia, Emperor Hadrian exchanged the royal purple for local Athenian attire. The gesture did not mask the might of Rome behind the cultural nobility and particularity of Greek costume. Instead, it capitalized on the semiotics of civic belonging. To dress as an Athenian citizen was to identify with Athens and its institutions. The change of wardrobe celebrated Hadrian's Athenian citizenship,[77] but it was his identity as the empire's "first citizen" (*princeps civitatis*), or preeminent benefactor, that imbued the gesture with its fullest significance. In the culminating act of his Athenian visit, the empire's first citizen performed a public liturgy as the "first citizen of Athens" (*princeps Atheniensis*). Hadrian thus embodied in his person and dress his Roman and Athenian citizenships. By homology, the performance enacted the unification of the Latin West and Greek East in his very person. By invoking the semantics of dual citizenship, Hadrian could offer a public performance of his *Reichseinigungspolitik* and could thereby intimate Athens as a "second capital of the empire."[78]

A discourse of dual citizenship is also perceptible in Hadrian's legal reforms, which bear the stamp of his archaizing tendencies and his desire for civic renewal in the empire. The Athenian legal reforms represent Hadrian's effort to have himself inscribed into the venerable Athenian past. When he reduced the council to five hundred members and altered the tribal arrangement, Hadrian emulated the Athenian legislator Cleis-

---

[77]. Geagan understood this point, since he gave this reason for reading Cassius Dio's description as referring to a Hadrianic presidency of the Dionysia during his archonship ("Roman Athens," 392).

[78]. Oliver, "Roman Emperors," 419.

thenes. When he legislated the sale and trade of oil, he imitated Solon (Plutarch, *Sol.* 24.1). The imitative character of the legal reforms was not lost on ancient authors, who contended that Hadrian styled himself in the vein of the classical Athenian legislators Draco, Solon, Cleisthenes, "and others."[79] Further, when Hadrian added the eponymous thirteenth tribe Hadrianis in the seventh and central position of the official tribal order, he placed a self-commemorative institution at the very heart of the city's governmental functioning. His eponymous tribe now joined the ten original Greek tribes and the two additional foreign tribes, Ptolemais, named for the Egyptian king Ptolemy Euergetes, and Attalis, named for Attalus of Pergamon, which had been added in 200 BCE. The patronage of Athens's preeminent citizen was now commemorated in the city's political institutions.

The legal reforms also evoke Hadrian's concerns as emperor for civic renewal across his empire. According to his biographer, an oracle had portended that the young Hadrian would become a Roman emperor, "whose laws will establish the city [of Rome] anew."[80] The citation describes Hadrian's legislative activity as a mode of civic renovation and reconstitution of the capital city. Without doubt, Hadrian's "unusual concern" for the laws of Athens also evokes this motif.[81] He renovated existing civic institutions, financial agencies, and judicial appeals procedures, and he created new civic agencies, such as the Opisthodomos and the tribe Hadrianis, which integrated Roman power at the heart of the Athenian political and economic structure. In Hadrian, the city of Athens had a citizen-patron with the power and authority as Roman emperor to act as legislator and to reconstitute and renovate the city's laws for a new era of Roman imperial

---

79. Eusebius, *Chron.*, ad ann. Hadr. 6 (Lat.): Hadrianus Atheniensibus leges petentibus ex Draconis et Solonis reliquorumque libris iura composuit; George Syncellus, *Ecloga Chronographica*, 659.9: ὁ αὐτὸς Ἀθηναίοις ἀξιώσασιν ἐκ τῶν Δράκοντος καὶ Σόλωνος νόμους ἐπισυνέταξε; Dio Cassius, *Hist. rom.* 69.16.2: ἐνομοθέτησε δὲ ἄλλα τε πολλά; cf. *IG* 2.1075, lines 3–5. According to Pausanias, *Descr.* 1.29.6, Cleisthenes was the legislator thought at the time of Hadrian to have invented the tribes. See E. Ruschenbusch, "Πάτριος πολιτεία: Theseus, Drakon, Solon und Kleisthenes in Publizistik und Geschichtsschreibung des 5. und 4. Jahrhunderts v. Chr.," *Historia* 7 (1958): 389–424.

80. Hist. Aug., Hadr. 2.8, interpreting Virgil, *Aen.* 6.808–12 (of Numa) as a Hadrianic reference.

81. Boatwright, *Hadrian*, 91–92.

rule. Through his legislative acts, the Roman emperor would be celebrated as "restorer" of the city.[82]

A narrative of dual citizenship also appears in Hadrian's sponsorships of the ancient religious rites associated with neighboring Eleusis. His renovation of the Via Sacra, provision of oil and fish resources for Eleusis, and initiation into the Lesser Mysteries demonstrate a peculiar respect for the ancient and venerable Eleusinian rites. They reveal Hadrian's desire to write himself into their sacred history. At the same time, his initiation into the Mysteries may well have been an attempt to emulate Augustus. In Athens, Hadrian's sponsorship of the Temple of Olympian Zeus reinvigorated a longstanding Greek construction project under Roman imperial sponsorship. Once built, the Olympieion would monumentalize the Greek past and would become a site of imperial cult in a Roman-style *temenos*. Hadrian sought the flourishing of ancient Greek cults under Roman imperial sponsorship.

Hadrian's early patronage to Athens seems deeply intertwined with the notion of his dual Athenian and Roman citizenship. As first citizen of Athens, he identified with the Athenian past, the city's ancient religious rites, its ancestral law code, and its civic institutions. He sought to revive the city's former glory, positioning himself as a new citizen-founder of Athens. He undertook this local project in view of imperial realities. As first citizen of the empire, he introduced considerable resources to fortify the city and its public, religious, and cultural institutions and to tether the Greek East to the Roman capital. Hadrian's early munificence offered a fiercely local integration of the Athenian past and the imperial framework of the Roman present. It also signaled his intentions to restore the city to a place of cultural preeminence among the municipalities of the East. The integration of the empire is the story of the emperor's own dual citizenship writ large.

---

82. The Roman mint issued a series of Hadrianic coins whose legend reads "to the Restorer of Achaia" (*Restitutori Achaiae*). Henry Cohen, *Description historique des monnaies frappées sous l'Empire romain communément appelées médailles impériales*, 2nd ed., 8 vols. (Paris: Rollin & Feuardent, 1880–92), 2:209, nos. 1214–20; Harold Mattingly and Edward A. Sydenham, *Vespasian to Hadrian*, vol. 2 of *The Roman Imperial Coinage* (London: Spink & Son, 1926), 377, no. 321; 463, nos. 938–39; Joseph H. von Eckhel, *De Moneta Romanorum*, vol. 6.2, of *Doctrina numorum veterum*, 2nd. ed. (Vienna: Camesina, 1828), 487–88.

4. The Intertextuality of Hadrianic Patronage

In the introduction of this essay, I suggested that Eusebius's *Chronicon* implies that Hadrian's early favors to Athens served as a stimulus for the writing of early Christian apology, particularly the *Apology* of Aristides of Athens. If this reading is correct, then the politics of Hadrian's Athenian patronage presumably served as an intertext for Aristides's *Apology*. In conclusion, I wish to sketch in very preliminary fashion some connections between the discourse of Hadrianic patronage and the argument of Aristides's *Apology*.

Recent research on the text of Aristides's *Apology* has shown it to be a work of political theology rooted in a cosmopolitan philosophy, in which the natural universe is construed as a city operating in accord with the divine monarchy.[83] Subsidiary to the cosmopolitan philosophy is a cultural discourse. In *Apology*, culture is a means of educating individuals to know the true God and to live as excellent philosopher-citizens in this world in harmony with the God who made the natural universe. *Apology* divides the world of humanity into four "cultural kinships" (γένη)—barbarians, Greeks, Jews, and Christians—and differentiates each group according to their knowledge (or lack thereof) of God. Each kinship was founded by a philosopher-legislator who constituted the mythic systems and laws that operate in the respective cultures. The founder of each culture transmitted an ethic and ritual system to the kin group. The constitutional figures thus represent the ultimate patrons and benefactors of their cultural heritages.

This summary of *Apology*'s argument reveals how notions of citizenship, cultural kinship, benefaction, legislation, mythopoesis, religious rites, and archaic traditions are constitutive to the text's major argument. Do these themes represent simply a chance correlation with the politics of patronage in Hadrianic Athens, with its emphasis on citizenship and civic belonging, benefaction, legislative reform, religious sponsorships, and cultural kinships? Or does the thematic overlap represent a program of causation or imitation? It seems at least possible that Aristides wrote his *Apology* in response to the politics of patronage in Hadrianic Athens. To answer the question with greater certainty, however, more research is required. One

---

83. For the argument, see William Rutherford, "Citizenship among Jews and Christians: Civic Discourse in the *Apology* of Aristides," in *Papers Presented at the Sixteenth International Conference on Patristic Studies Held in Oxford, 2011*, ed. Markus Vinzent, StPatr 65 (Leuven: Peeters, 2013), 3–26.

would like to know, for example, how Hadrian's project of civic patronage at Athens was received by the Athenians themselves. I plan to explore elsewhere Athenian responses to Hadrian's early patronage politics and to correlate the material context and reception of Hadrianic benefaction to Athens more closely with the argument of Aristides's *Apology*.

BIBLIOGRAPHY

Alexander, Paul J. "Letters and Speeches of the Emperor Hadrian." *HSCP* 49 (1938): 141–77.

Benjamin, Anna S. "The Altars of Hadrian in Athens and Hadrian's Panhellenic Program." *Hesperia* 32 (1963): 57–86.

Boatwright, Mary T. "Further Thoughts on Hadrianic Athens." *Hesperia* 52 (1983): 173–76.

———. *Hadrian and the Cities of the Roman Empire*. Princeton: Princeton University Press, 2003.

Bodnar, Edward W. "Marcus Porcius Cato." *Hesperia* 31 (1962): 393–95.

Champion-Smith, Vanessa A. "Pausanias in Athens: An Archeological Commentary on the Agora of Athens." PhD diss., University College London, 1998.

Christophilopoulos, Anastasios P. "'Η νομοθετική λειτουργία εἰς τὰς Ἑλληνικὰς πόλεις" ["The Legislative Liturgy in Greek Cities"]. *Athēna* 69 (1967): 17–53.

Cohen, Henry. *Description historique des monnaies frappées sous l'Empire romain communément appelées médailles impériales*. 2nd ed. 8 vols. Paris: Rollin & Feuardent, 1880–92.

Day, John. *An Economic History of Athens Under Roman Domination*. New York: Columbia University Press, 1942.

Dittenberger, W. "Kaiser Hadrians erste Anwesenheit in Athen." *Hermes* 7 (1873): 213–29.

Eckhel, Joseph H. von. *De Moneta Romanorum*. Volume 6.2 of *Doctrina numorum veterum*. 2nd ed. Vienna: Camesina, 1828.

Follet, Simone. *Athènes au IIe et au IIIe siècle: Études chronologiques et prosopographiques*. Paris: Les Belles Lettres, 1976.

Foucart, Paul. "Les empereurs romains initiés aux mystères d'Éleusis." *RevPhil* 17 (1893): 197–207.

Geagan, Daniel J. *The Athenian Constitution after Sulla*. HesperiaSup 12. Princeton: American School of Classical Studies at Athens, 1967.

———. "A Decree of the Council of the Areopagus." *Hesperia* 42 (1973): 352–57.

———. "The Great Catalogue from the Eleusinion at Athens." *ZPE* 33 (1979): 93–115.

———. "Roman Athens, Some Aspects of Life and Culture I: 86 B.C.–A.D. 267." *ANRW* 7.1:371–437.

Graindor, Paul. *Athènes de Tibère à Trajan*. Cairo: Imprimerie Misr, 1931.

———. *Athènes sous Hadrien*. Cairo: Boulac, 1934.

———. "Inscriptions attiques d'époque impériale." *BCH* 38 (1914): 351–443.

Jones, C. P. "The Panhellenion." *Chiron* 26 (1996): 29–56.

Kienast, Dietmar. "Hadrian, Augustus und die eleusinischen Mysterien." *JNG* 10 (1959–1960): 61–69.

Kokkos, A. "Ἁδριάνεια ἔργα εἰς τὰς Ἀθήνας" ["Hadrianic Works in Athens"]. *Archaiologikon Deltion* 25 (1970): 150–73.

Leigh, Shawna. "The 'Reservoir' of Hadrian in Athens." *JRA* 10 (1997): 279–90.

Mattingly, Harold, and Edward A. Sydenham. *Vespasian to Hadrian*. Volume 2 of *The Roman Imperial Coinage*. London: Spink & Son, 1926.

Meritt, Benjamin D. "Greek Inscriptions." *Hesperia* 29 (1960): 1–77.

Metcalf, W. E. "Hadrian, Iovis Olympius." *Mnemosyne* 27 (1974): 59–66.

Notopoulos, James A. "The Date of the Creation of Hadrianis." *TAPA* 77 (1946): 53–56.

Oliver, James H. "Athenian Citizenship of Roman Emperors." *Hesperia* 20 (1951): 346–49.

———. "The Athens of Hadrian." Pages 123–33 in *Les empereurs romains d'Espagne*. Colloques internationaux du Centre national de la recherche scientifique, Sciences humaines. Paris: Centre national de la recherche scientifique, 1965.

———. "Civic Status in Roman Athens: Cicero, *Pro Balbo* 12.30." *GRBS* 22 (1981): 83–88.

———. "Hadrian's Reform of the Appeal Procedure in Greece." *Hesperia* 39 (1970): 332–36.

———. "An Inscription Concerning the Epicurean School at Athens." *TAPA* 69 (1938): 494–99.

———. *Marcus Aurelius: Aspects of Civic and Cultural Policy in the East*. HesperiaSup 13. Princeton: American School of Classical Studies at Athens, 1970.

——. "Philosophers and Procurators, Relatives of the Aemilius Juncus of *Vita Commodi* 4,11." *Hesperia* 36 (1967): 42–56.

——. "Roman Emperors and Athens." *Historia* 30 (1981): 412–23.

——. *The Sacred Gerousia*. HesperiaSup 6. Athens: American School of Classical Studies at Athens, 1941.

Paris, Pierre. "Inscriptions d'Élatée." *BCH* 10 (1886): 356–85.

Pouderon, Bernard, and Marie-Joseph Pierre, eds. *Aristide: Apologie*. SC 470. Paris: Cerf, 2003.

Raubitschek, Antony E. "Note on the Post-Hadrianic Boule." Pages 242–55 in Γέρας Ἀντωνίου Κεραμοπούλλου. Edited by A. D. Keramopoullos. EPHMS.PT 9. Athens: Society of Macedonian Studies, 1953.

Rousopoulos, A. S. "Τὰ ἐκ τοῦ Διονυσιακοῦ Θεάτρου" ["The Precincts of the Theater of Dionysos"]. *ArchEph* (1862): 153–84.

Ruschenbusch, E. "Πάτριος πολιτεία: Theseus, Drakon, Solon und Kleisthenes in Publizistik und Geschichtsschreibung des 5. und 4. Jahrhunderts v. Chr." *Historia* 7 (1958): 389–424.

Rutherford, William. "Citizenship among Jews and Christians: Civic Discourse in the *Apology* of Aristides." Pages 3–26 in *Papers Presented at the Sixteenth International Conference on Patristic Studies Held in Oxford, 2011*. Edited by Markus Vinzent. StPatr 65. Leuven: Peeters, 2013.

——. "Reinscribing the Jews: The Story of Aristides' *Apology* 2.2–4 and 14.1b–15.2." *HTR* 106 (2013): 61–91.

Shear, T. Leslie, Jr. "Athens: From City-State to Provincial Town." *Hesperia* 50 (1981): 356–77.

Spawforth, A. J., and Susan Walker. "The World of the Panhellenion, I: Athens and Eleusis." *JRS* 75 (1985): 78–104.

Syme, Ronald. "Hadrian as Philhellene: Neglected Aspects." Pages 546–62 in vol. 5 of *Roman Papers*. Edited by Anthony Birley. Oxford: Clarendon, 1988.

Syncellus, George. *Ecloga Chronographica*. Edited by Alden A. Mosshammer. BSGRT. Leipzig: Teubner, 2012.

Traill, John S. *The Political Organization of Attica: A Study of the Demes, Trittyes, and Phylai, and Their Representation in the Athenian Council*. HesperiaSup 14. Princeton: American School of Classical Studies at Athens, 1975.

Vischer, Wilhelm. "Die Entdeckungen im Theater des Dionysos zu Athen." *Neues Schweizerisches Museum* 3 (1863): 35–77.

Vout, Caroline. "Hadrian, Hellenism, and the Social History of Art." *Arion* 18 (2010): 55–78.
Wilhelm, Adolf. "Inschriften aus Erythrai und Chios." *JÖAI* 12 (1909): 126–50.
Willers, Dietrich. *Hadrians panhellenisches Programm: Archäologische Beiträge zur Neugestaltung Athens durch Hadrian*. BHAK 16. Basel: Vereinigung der Freunde antiker Kunst, 1990.
Woloch, G. M. "Roman and Athenian Citizenship at Athens, A.D. 96–161." *Historia* 20 (1971): 744–50.
Zanker, Paul. *The Mask of Socrates: The Image of the Intellectual in Antiquity*. Berkeley: University of California Press, 1995.
Zuiderhoek, Arjan. *The Politics of Munificence in the Roman Empire: Citizens, Elites and Benefactors in Asia Minor*. Cambridge: Cambridge University Press, 2009.

One Grave, Two Women, One Man: Complicating Family Life at Colossae*

Alan H. Cadwallader

1. Introduction

When Plato recommended that the inscription on an epitaph should be no more than four lines, he had a large vision of the regulation of funerals as a reinforcement of the shaping and education of the populace—hence they were to be "heroic lines" (ἡρωικῶν στίχων).[1] Moreover, graves themselves were to be modest. It seems that his successors took his words to heart—there are three or four epitaphs that are said to have adorned Plato's grave: one is two lines long, another four, and another five; so at least to that extent, by and large, his injunction was observed.[2] Elsewhere, such circumspection was known more by its contravention than by its observance,

---

* I acknowledge with gratitude the critical insights on this essay generously provided by Angela Standhartinger. We both join in thanking Dennis for his friendship, his scholarship, and his own gentle criticism of our ideas over the years.

1. χῶμα δὲ μὴ χοῦν ὑψηλότερον πέντε ἀνδρῶν ἔργον, ἐν πένθ' ἡμέραις ἀποτελούμενον· λίθινα δὲ ἐπιστήματα μὴ μεῖζω ποιεῖν ἤ.ὅσα δέχεσθαι τῶν τοῦ τετελευτηκότος ἐγκώμια βίου μὴ πλείω τεττάρων ἡρωικῶν στίχων. "[The citizens] are not to pile up a burial mound higher than five men can achieve in five days; neither shall they make tombstones larger than is necessary to contain four heroic lines of celebration of the life of the departed" (Plato, *Leg.* 12.958e). All translations are mine unless noted otherwise. See also Marcus Folch, *The City and the Stage: Performance, Genre, and Gender in Plato's Laws* (Oxford: Oxford University Press, 2015), 177. Folch suggested that Plato was operating from foundational constitutions that incorporated funerary restrictions, citing Cicero, *Leg.* 2.63. The evidence harnessed by Robert Garland is supportive; see Garland, "The Well-Ordered Corpse: An Investigation into the Motives behind Greek Funerary Legislation," *Bulletin of the Institute of Classical Studies* 36 (1989): 1–15.

2. See L. Tarán, "Plato's Alleged Epitaph," *GRBS* 25 (1984): 63–82.

especially in Hellenistic and Roman Asia. What is constant, however, is the recognition that the necropolis was understood not as a sanitary disposal location but as a theological/philosophical statement and/or a mimetic reinforcement of civic values.[3] "Care in death is consistent with care in life," commented Sarah Pomeroy.[4] The position of the necropolis complemented this intent; as John Pearce noted, "the location of the dead can be as significant in terms of cultural identity as the form of burial."[5] The eminent examples of these two aspects are the mausoleum of Diogenes at Oinoanda that was adorned with Epicurean philosophy and the circular heroon of Hierokles that was installed by city decree in the main street at Stratonikeia.[6] But Colossae, like neighboring Hierapolis, appears to have ensured that travelers from west and east would enter the city in full view of the dead, or rather of the monuments, reliefs, and inscribed testimonies that were prepared for or by them, sometimes before they died. Some of the epitaphs from Colossae, as elsewhere, dispense greetings to those who pass by.[7]

---

3. Folch, *City and the Stage*, 178: "The limitations on the size of the tomb and on the length of the inscriptions form part of a larger project to create an economy in which monetary value follows philosophical value."

4. Sarah B. Pomeroy, *Families in Classical and Hellenistic Greece: Representations and Realities* (Oxford: Clarendon; NY: Oxford University Press, 1997), 120.

5. John Pearce, "Burial and Ethnicity," in *Burial, Society and Context in the Roman World*, ed. John Pearce, Martin Millett, and Manuela Struck (Oxford: Oxbow, 2000), 179. Again, Plato's recommendation that graves be positioned on infertile land (*Leg.* 12.958d) was inconsistently followed.

6. On the mausoleum of Diogenes at Oinoanda, see A. S. Hall, N. P. Milner, and J. J. Coulton, "The Mausoleum of Licinnia Flavilla and Flavianus Diogenes of Oinoanda: Epigraphy and Architecture," *AnSt* 46 (1996): 111–43. Pieces of the mausoleum inscription continue to be found and assembled. See also Jürgen Hammerstaedt and Martin F. Smith, "Diogenes of Oinoanda: The Discoveries of 2011 (NF 191–205, and Additions to NF 127 and 130)," *EA* 44 (2011): 79–114, with the bibliography there cited. Note also the online Oinoanda project of the Deutsches Archäologisches Institut, "Oinoanda und die größte Inschrift der antiken Welt," http://tinyurl.com/SBL4522t. On the circular heroon of Hierokles, see B. Söğüt, "Stratonikeia 2008 Yılı Çalışmaları," *Kazı Sonuçları Toplantısı* 4 (2010): 272–74. On the intramural burials, see C. Berns, "The Tomb as a Node of Public Representation," in *Le mort dans la ville: Pratiques, contextes et impacts des inhumations intra-muros en Anatolie, du début de l'Age du Bronze à l'époque romaine; 2èmes rencontres d'archéologie de l'IFEA*, ed. Olivier Henry (Istanbul: Ege yayınları, 2013), 231–42.

7. For example *MAMA* 6.47 (= Ritti §113). See further below.

These remains are not monochrome in display. They fall on a spectrum of grave types and epigraphical memorialization, precisely because of the variegated ethnocultural influences in Asia.[8] Moreover, they were more than memorialization of the dead. They memorialized, mirrored, and reinforced the values of the group and society that took responsibility for the internment. "Cemeteries are, in essence, repositories of biographical narratives and social memory, giving them highly affective potential in the overall landscape."[9] Rome itself has sometimes been portrayed as promoting a nuclear family model, and to some extent this is reflected in the reliefs and inscriptions of epitaphs.[10] But the recent work by Peter Thonemann on households and families that can be extracted from funerary artefacts, inscriptions, and reliefs has highlighted the gap between Roman preference and the diversity of colonized expression.[11]

As this chapter will endeavor to show, the family structures and values held and/or displayed in the Colossian necropolis were also not monochrome. They indicate not only a spectrum of types but also, by their very public presence before locals and visitors, an acceptance of such diversity in Colossian society. There is, as Jean-Pierre Vernant so incisively put it, a "politics of death that every social group must institute and administer in continuity according to its own rules if it is to establish itself with its own

---

8. R. Strelan, "The Languages of the Lycus Valley," in *Colossae in Space and Time: Linking to an Ancient City*, ed. Alan H. Cadwallader and Michael Trainor, NTOA 94 (Göttingen: Vandenhoeck & Ruprecht, 2011), 77–103; Gregory Kantor, "Law in Roman Phrygia: Rules and Jurisdictions," in *Roman Phrygia: Culture and Society*, ed. Peter Thonemann, Greek Culture in the Roman World (Cambridge: Cambridge University Press, 2013), 157. Note especially Sarah H. Cormack, *The Space of Death in Roman Asia Minor*, Wiener Forschungen zur Archäologie 6 (Vienna: Phoibos, 2004).

9. D. Krsmanovic and W. Anderson, "Paths of the Dead: Interpreting Funerary Practice at Roman-Period Pessinus, Central Anatolia," *Melbourne Historical Journal* 40 (2012): 75.

10. Peter Thonemann, "Households and Families in Roman Phrygia," in Thonemann, *Roman Phrygia*, 125.

11. To date, no evidence of the Roman republican and early imperial preference for cremation has been found at Colossae, even if the distinction between Roman cremation and Greek inhumation does not fit all instances. See Sven Ahrens, "'Whether by Decay or Fire Consumed…': Cremation in Hellenistic and Roman Asia Minor," in *Death and Changing Rituals: Function and Meaning in Ancient Funerary Practices*, ed. J. Rasmus Brandt, Håkon Ingvaldsen, and Marina Prusac, Studies in Funerary Archaeology 7 (Oxford: Oxbow, 2015), 185–222.

specific features and have its own structures and goals over time."[12] But what is apparent is that "every social group" might be as small as a married couple and sometimes as large as the city itself, and in such a span, no monolithic set of values operates. Coexistence, competition, and change seem to be able to held within the larger polity,[13] even when that polity may have its own agendas running. There *are* limits on diversity signaled, in part by the fines and imprecations for disturbance of the grave and for an illegitimate addition of an unknown corpse among those authorized to be embraced by the grave. These are clearly in evidence at Colossae, even if, to date, we have no extant regulatory provisions governing the city's funerary arrangements.

I wish to explore the indications of family and household at Colossae that are yielded through the epigraphy and reliefs of funerary stones and monuments.

2. Methodological Considerations

From the outset, it must be acknowledged that there are considerable methodological problems that constrain the observations that can be made:

1. The overall epigraphic inventory from Colossae is quite small. To date there are only twenty-eight published inscriptions, if one includes two from other places (Smyrna and Boubon) mentioning a Colossian ethnic.[14] Two more will be added in this essay by the kind permission of Professor Dr. Ender Varinlioğlu. Two grave-stones—a stele and a sarcophagus—have been damaged and no longer hold their inscribed section.[15] One inscrip-

---

12. Jean-Pierre Vernant, introduction to *La mort, les morts dans les sociétés anciennes*, ed. Gherardo Gnoli and Jean-Pierre Vernant (Cambridge: Cambridge University Press; Paris: Maison des sciences de l'homme, 1982), 7.

13. See Christine M. Thomas, "Placing the Dead: Funerary Practice and Social Stratification in the Early Roman Period in Corinth and Ephesos," in *Urban Religion in Roman Corinth: Interdisciplinary Approaches*, ed. Daniel N. Schowalter and Steven J. Friesen, HTS 53 (Cambridge: Harvard University Press, 2005), 281–304; Katharine Derderian, *Leaving Words to Remember: Greek Mourning and the Advent of Literacy*, MnemosyneSup 209 (Leiden: Brill, 2001), 69–70.

14. ISmyrna 1.440; IBoubon 102.

15. *MAMA* 6.50; 6.51a, b. See further, Alan H. Cadwallader, "Revisiting Calder on Colossae," *AnSt* 56 (2006): 106, 109. Kelp takes the presence of an "Asiatic sarcophagus" as an indication of a "big city"; see Ute Kelp, "Grave Monuments and Local Identities in Roman Phrygia," in Thonemann, *Roman Phrygia*, 84.

tion I have not been able to verify in its published or curated origins.¹⁶ The same applies to one which gained a reference but no publication.¹⁷ Two or three more have been removed from consideration even though either publication or museum information (misleadingly) attributes the items to Colossae or is ambiguous about attribution.¹⁸

2. Of the total, twelve are funerary, to which three or four further inscriptions or part thereof may be added that indicate a deceased male about whom something can be learned of his family.¹⁹ This has the danger of promoting a jaundiced view of the evidence for Colossae generally. It needs to be recognized that the expansive necropolis of Colossae still

---

16. J. Demargne, "Monuments figurés et inscriptions de Crète," *BCH* 24 (1900): 239 §2: Τύχη πρωτογ(ένης) Κολοσσαί(ων), followed by P. G. P. Meyboom, *The Nile Mosaic of Palestrina: Early Evidence of Egyptian Religion in Italy*, RGRW 121 (Leiden: Brill, 1995), 210 n. 37. The situation has changed since this was written.

17. W. H. Mare, "Archeological Prospects at Colossae," *PNEAS* 7 (1976): 39–59. Note also that Robert Wood reported what was probably a milestone near Laodikeia on the road to Hierapolis that appears to have mentioned Colossae; see Wood, journals, vol. 6, fol. 67, Institute of Classical Studies Library (Joint Library of the Hellenic and Roman Societies), University of London. See also Lampakis, infra, n. 34. Georg Weber implied that he saw many *bōmoi* with epitaphs inscribed on them, but his published reports gave only a few: "Der unterirdische Lauf des Lykos bei Kolossai," *MDAIA* 16 (1891): 198.

18. Ernst Pfuhl and Hans Möbius, *Textband und Tafelband*, vol. 2.1–2 of *Die Ostgriechischen Grabreliefs* (Mainz: von Zabern, 1979), §§236, 1607, 1634, 1665b, 1920, 1973, 2005. All of these were originally published as in the environs of Attouda (with some allowance for Trapezopolis in the case of §1973), and there is no reason to change this assignment, even though Pfuhl-Möbius blurs this to the region between Attouda and Colossae. At least one (§1920) has been mislabeled as from Colossae at the Basmahane Museum in İzmir. Pfuhl-Möbius's annotation for the original publication of this inscription is also incorrect; it should read: A. E. Kontoleon, "Variétés," *BCH* 11 (1887): 297 §2.

19. *CIG* 3.3955 should probably be rejected as funerary, in spite of Boeckh's judgment—see below. The further inscriptions include: *MAMA* 6.42, the provision of a monument and bequest for annual stephanation; *MAMA* 6.39 (= Ritti §59), an honor as "hero" for Crispinus; a rosette preceding the name Μῆνας (Alan H. Cadwallader, "Honouring the Repairer of the Baths: A New Inscription from Kolossai," *Antichthon* 46 [2012]: 150–83, inscription line 23), the only one in a list of thirty names (though some lines have been damaged so that the beginnings are missing for nine lines), likely to indicate death given the frequent use of rosettes on grave monuments. Sometimes, because of the fragmentary nature of the surviving inscription, there is difficulty in deciding whether the inscription is an actual epitaph or a memorial monument, as in *MAMA* 6.46 (epitaph/memorial for Damokrates).

retains significant visible remains, unlike the biconical *höyük* ("mound") across the Çürüksu (Lycus) River immediately to the south. In recent times this part of the site has delivered the most returns, more or less in situ to their original foundation. When William Buckler and William Calder spent a half day at the site of Colossae in May 1933, their recorded entries, both published and, in one case, unpublished, all concerned funerary *bōmoi*,[20] that is, large, heavy altar-shaped stones carved from a single block. My own publications from Colossae carry the same bias, with only one nonfunerary inscription found at the site—on a pedestal dispatched into the river.[21]

3. The surviving inscriptions need to be set into more expansive burial practices, ranging across a longer period of history. The funerary and related inscriptions are circumscribed by a two-hundred-year span, or by three centuries at most. The tumuli at Colossae and possibly some of the Phrygian-style cliff tombs predate the surviving inscribed remains by two hundred or more years.[22] No doorstones for tumuli or rock tombs, which presumably held at least symbolic reliefs, are known.[23]

4. The concentration of burial monuments in this paper (viz., *bōmoi*) presupposes a certain general class of subscribers. The florid Asiatic-style garland sarcophagus of Dokimeion marble known from Colossae[24] indicates the wealthy elite, "classes for whom a sarcophagus ... required a significant outlay, thought and financial and practical planning"[25] and

---

20. *MAMA* 6.44 (still, as at 2015, extant in the necropolis), 45 (not extant to my knowledge). See Cadwallader, "Revisiting Calder," 108.

21. Alan H. Cadwallader, "Two New Inscriptions, a Correction and a Confirmed Sighting from Colossae," *EA* 40 (2007): 109–18.

22. See H. Yıldız, "Denizli Müzesi Müdürlüğü Lycos Vadisi Çalışmaları," *Müze Kurtarma Kazıları Semineri* 9 (1999): 247–62; Cadwallader, *Fragments of Colossae: Sifting through the Traces* (Hindmarsh: ATF, 2015), 155–79. The tumulus has an ancient Greek pedigree; see Homer, *Il.* 14.675.

23. See Kelp, "Grave Monuments," 70–71.

24. *MAMA* 6.51a and b. Since the publication of *MAMA* 6, a third section of the broken longitudinal side has been discovered, making one complete wall of the sarcophagus. See H. Yıldız and C. Şimşek, "Sarcofagi a Ghirlande dall Necropoli di Laodicea al Lykos," in *Ricerche archeologiche turche nella valle del Lykos*, ed. Francesco D'Andria and Francesca Silvestrelli, Archeologia e storia (Università degli studi di Lecce, Scuola di specializzazione in archeologia classica e medioevale) 6 (Galatina, Lecce: Congedo, 2000), 108–12, 134 (pl.).

25. See R. R. R. Smith, "Sarcophagi and Roman Citizenship," in *New Research on the City and Its Monuments*, vol. 4 of *Aphrodisias Papers*, ed. C. Ratté and R. R.

an unmarked, multicorpse location, as yet unknown from Colossae, points to the other end of the internment market.[26] Accordingly, circumspection about social status, rank, and wealth must act as a control on deductions that, here, are largely focused on a particular material production financed by and large by a particular socioeconomic capacity. A *chamosorion* in a dedicated and constructed plot with slab and carved, inscribed *bōmos*, even if intended for more than one occupant, involved no small outlay. Nonetheless, our knowledge of the cost of such items—and therefore a clue to who patronized them—is sparse.[27] According to Richard Duncan-Jones, there are fewer than ninety-one known prices for tombstones in Italy for the Roman imperial period, fifty-one for Africa.[28] These however cover a huge range in types of monument and price. The most expensive in Africa amounts to more than eighty thousand sestercii; in Italy, to more than five hundred thousand sestercii.[29] The second most common burial cost in Italy was two thousand sestercii.[30] This is significant because this roughly matches the fines for disturbance given on three imperial-period funerary *bōmoi* from Colossae, that is, five hundred denarii, a figure that might be correlated to the cost of all the preparations for burial, given that, elsewhere, such penalties rose according to general inflationary pressures.[31] A comparison with a footsoldier's pay at

---

Smith, JRASup 70 (Portsmouth, RI: Journal of Roman Archaeology, 2008), 349. Smith recognizes that there is a range of quality and design in sarcophagi. See also Ben Russell, *The Economics of the Roman Stone Trade*, Oxford Studies on the Roman Economy (Oxford: Oxford University Press, 2013), 256–60.

26. The so-called potter's fields. See John Bodel, "Dealing with the Dead: Undertakers, Executioners and Potter's Fields in Ancient Rome," in *Death and Disease in the Ancient City*, ed. Valerie M. Hope and Eireann Marshall (London: Routledge, 2000), 128–35.

27. On the evidence from the papyri, see, for example, P.Oslo 3.130; *SB* 18.13176; *SPP* 22.56.

28. Richard Duncan-Jones, *The Economy of the Roman Empire: Quantitative Studies*, 2nd ed. (Cambridge: Cambridge University Press, 1982), 127.

29. Africa: *CIL* 8.21; Italy: *CIL* 10.5624.

30. Duncan-Jones, *Economy*, 127. He found ten instances of costed monuments in Italy of two thousand sesterces. However, there were eleven instances of monuments at twenty thousand sesterces and yet only five instances of those at three thousand sesterces. This would suggest that the contingencies of survival have affected the figures. He reckoned that the standard cost was twenty thousand sesterces.

31. *MAMA* 6.43; *IGRR* 4.871. See Cadwallader, "Revisiting Calder," 109. Charlotte Roueché, *Aphrodisias in Late Antiquity: The Late Roman and Byzantine Inscrip-

the turn of the second century (that is, about three hundred denarii per annum) gives some perspective on who might afford the outlay involved in these monuments for the dead, even allowing for potential overreach by some households.

5. The movement of stones away from the site of Colossae is well attested.[32] Colossae was a major quarry for the village of Honaz, now three kilometers to the south of the *höyük*—Buckler and Calder found a number of inscriptions in gardens, on walls, and on fences in the small town, just as others had before them.[33] The medieval fortress built on the rise of Honazdağ (ancient Mount Cadmus) has clearly incorporated previously-carved stones such as blocks, drums, and even a column from the site, though to date no inscriptions have been found there.[34] It has also been suspected that the construction of the Ak Khan caravanserai, in 1253–1254, relied to some extent on materials carted from Colossae about 10 kilometers away, even though Laodikeia is closer.[35] A number of fragmen-

---

tions; Including Texts from the Excavations at Aphrodisias Conducted by Kenan T. Erim, JRSMS 5 (London: Society for the Promotion of Roman Studies, 1989), 195; John H. M. Strubbe, *Arai Epitymbioi: Imprecations against Desecrators of the Grave in the Greek Epitaphs of Asia Minor*, IK 52 (Bonn: Habelt, 1997), 74, 75, 88.

32. The movement of ancient stones around Anatolia has long been the subject of comment. See Peter Thonemann and F. Ertuğrul, "The Carminii of Attouda," *EA* 38 (2005): 76 n. 2.

33. *MAMA* 6.38–42, 47–50. Ernst Renan's discovery of the famous honorific for an anonymous office holder (*IGRR* 4.870) occurred at the western end of the village of Honaz in the Greek church between the nave and the iconostasis, according to Waddington's reading of Renan's 1865 notes (LBW 3.1693b). Following the repatriation of Turks and Greeks in 1923, the church became a still-operational (carpeted) mosque (Cadwallader, *Fragments of Colossae*, 16, 19, 198). Robert asserts that Buckler and Calder did not find it in 1933, but this presumes that they looked for it and knew where to look; see Louis Robert, "Les Inscriptions," in *Laodicée du Lycos: Le nymphée; Campagnes 1961–1963*, ed. J. des Gagniers et al. (Quebec: Université Laval, 1969), 269. See also Francis V. J. Arundell, *A Visit to the Seven Churches of Asia: With an Excursion into Pisidia* (London: Rodwell, 1828), 97.

34. The nationalist archaeologist George Lampakis reported seeing an ancient inscription as part of a grave in the Moslem cemetery on the rise of the fortress; see Lampakis, Οἱ ἑπτὰ ἀστέρες τῆς Ἀποκαλύψεως [The Seven Stars of the Apocalypse] (Athens: 1909), 452. See generally Cadwallader, *Fragments of Colossae*, 97–109.

35. For a detailed overview of the Ak Khan, see M. Kutlu "Seljuk Caravanserais in the Vicinity of Denizli: Han-Abad (Çardakhan) and Akhan" (MA thesis, Bilkent University, 2009), 40–63, plus prerestoration photographs on pp. 95–109. A briefer coverage is to be found in Kurt Erdmann and Hanna Erdmann, *Das anatolische Kara-*

tary inscriptions from the Greco-Roman and early Byzantine periods are to be found in the walls and grounds.³⁶ Significantly for my concerns, the inscribed epitaphs with reliefs have never been reported as found at the necropolis. This indicates that the stelae are not only easier to remove than the heavy, functionally-weighted *bōmoi*³⁷ but they are, likely, more attrac-

---

vansaray des 13. Jahrhunderts, 3 vols., Istanbuler Forschungen 21, 31 (Berlin: Mann, 1961–1976), 2:161–62. On the distance to Colossae, see Richard Pococke, *A Description of the East: And Some Other Countries* (London: Bowyer, 1745), 78; Richard Chandler, *Travels in Asia Minor and Greece: Or, An Account of a Tour Made at the Expense of the Society of Dilettanti*, 3rd ed., 2 vols. (London: Booker & Priestly, 1817), 240 (repeating Pococke's general mention of "some ancient ruin," but in the context of traveling to Colossae). On the distance to Laodikeia, see Friedrich P. T. Sarre, *Reise in Kleinasien, Sommer 1895: Forschungen zur seldjukischen Kunst und Geographie des Landes* (Berlin: Reimer, 1896), 11. Sarre simply deduced that the closest site (Laodikeia, approximately two kilometers away) was the origin, a reasonable factor but ignoring other influences such as waterways, the ongoing use of Colossae as a quarry, local cooperation, and perhaps most significantly, the attitudes of the Seljuks themselves. They had recently inherited both Laodikeia and Colossae (1205 CE) only to have Colossae (Chonai) returned to Byzantine control in 1257 (George Akropolites, *History* 69 [ed. Macrides]) for barely a few years (Theodore Skoutariotes, *Synopsis Chronike* 531.8–9 [ed. Heisenberg]). One can readily see damaged if not denuded goods being the result of these exchanges, just as one can view the building of such a majestic khan in such a contested period and place, as a profound statement of control and presence, not only hospitality for Seljuk traders (*pace* Peter Thonemann, *The Maeander Valley: A Historical Geography from Antiquity to Byzantium* [Cambridge: Cambridge University Press, 2011], 127).

36. For example, one column base, lying in the northeast garden, has one of the familiar types of crudely styled inscription asserting Christian ownership, ΚΕ ΑCΙΝΟΥ, here in the form of a prayer/petition. See also Ahmet Ali Bayhan, "Ak Han (Goncalı Hanı)," in *Anadolu Selçuklu Dönemi Kervansarayları*, ed. Hakkı Acun, Kütüphaneler ve Yayımlar Genel Müdürlüğü Sanat Eserleri Dizisi (Ankara: Kültür ve Turizm Bakanlığı, 2007), 301. Another, more carefully chiseled, inscribed stone is placed upside down in the west wall, containing the fragment ΙΚΑΣΟΙ | ΕΙΣΑΝΑ. Later Arabic inscriptions are also to be found at the khan, such as on the inner and outer capstones of the doorway arch; see Kutlu, "Seljuk Caravanserais in the Vicinity of Denizli," 43–44.

37. Note, however, Georg Weber, "Inschriften aus Sued-Phrygien," *MDAIA* 18 (1893): 206 §3, reported (by Weber) as having been removed from Colossae and installed outside the stationmaster's residence at the Appa railway station. It was photographed by Gertrude Bell in 1907; see Bell, diary, 25 April 1907, photograph F 210, Gertrude Bell Archive, Newcastle University Library; mentioned also as a tourist attraction in Charles William Wilson, *Handbook for Travellers in Asia Minor, Transcaucasia, Persia, etc.* (London: Murray, 1895), 104. A second exception might be *CIG*

tive to the interests of new homes (including museums) than the *bōmoi*. All the *bōmoi* that I have seen and/or that have been published are aniconic (apart from occasional motifs such as bosses, cones, and thunderbolts carved at the side of a *bōmos* or in its pediment). The single exception is in the gardens of a Honaz café; it is so weathered, however, that no part of an inscription remains.

6. Calder's notes of his visit to the necropolis, published and unpublished, report a number of "recently smashed" stones, so destruction as well as spoliation, "conversion,"[38] and private appropriation have had a deleterious effect on the evidence that is available for interpretation.

7. The passing of time has sometimes meant also the passing of the stones from previously known locations, and all that remains is the published record, which can be incomplete.

8. There is always a gap between how much can be asserted of a society or a household on the basis of epitaphs, partly because of the hold of convention (though as we shall see, this is not necessarily monolithic) and partly because other factors and evidence can skew the results.

9. Comparison with evidence from other sites can be important as a means of noticing common and distinctive features. The *bōmoi*, for example, are a funerary type shared with Eumeneia—that is, reaching beyond the Lycus Valley; the stelae reliefs are quite similar to those at Attouda and Laodikeia—that is, within the Lycus Valley.

10. One of the critical checks on the contents of a grave expressed in an epitaph is, of course, the bones within. To date, no intact graves have been recorded, and the only contents are a few items—sherds, perfume bottle fragments, an alabaster vessel—recovered from the organized excavations of some of the tumuli at Colossae.[39]

3.3955, but Arundell's transcription is barbaric: "*certa via nihil restitui potest nisi* vs 3 καὶ ἡ γύνη αὐτοῦ," said Boeckh. But he then proceeded to suggest that it was a sepulcher on the basis of the title, which would seem to require καὶ τῆς γυναικὸς αὐτοῦ. Arundell's opening line could be reconstructed as ὁ δῆμος as easily as τὸ μνημεῖον. Arundell recorded it at Honaz, which also probably argues against a funerary bōmos.

38. *MAMA* 6.45; William Calder, 1933 Notebook, 53 §203, in MS 3286/4/"Bundle of Three Notebooks," Calder Archives, University of Aberdeen Special Libraries. Arundell reported a Greek mason reshaping a beautiful frieze taken from Laodikeia into a "Turkish tombstone" and "splitting the finest sculptured marbles" (*Seven Churches*, 157–58).

39. See Yıldız, "Denizli Müzesi Müdürlüğü Lycos Vadisi Çalışmaları," noted above; summarized in Cadwallader, *Fragments of Colossae*, 163–66.

Figure 8.1a (left). Funerary (?) *bōmos* with relief, Honaz. The style of the *bōmos* is virtually identical to those populating the Colossae necropolis, though higher than most. The figures in the panel are worn but appear to be holding hands, right to left and wearing chitons. *Bōmoi* of this design do not figure in Pfuhl and Möbius's catalogue. The closest relief design to this is §2104, though the clothing is far more elaborate. The design is paralleled in many Phrygian votive stelae; see Thomas Drew-Bear, Christine M. Thomas, and Melek Yıldızturan, *Phrygian Votive Steles* (Ankara: Ministry of Culture, 1999); and Thomas Drew-Bear et al., *Ben Anadolu'da doğdum / I Was Born in Anatolia / Je suis né en Anatolie*, Tugay Anadolu Kültür-Sanat ve Arkeoloji Müzesi Yayınları 1 (Kütahya: Tugay Anadolu Kültür Sanat ve Arkeoloji Müzesi, 2007). There may be an object between the figures below their joined hands, perhaps an altar. If so, then the *bōmos* might be closer to its meaning of an altar.

Dimensions: height: 1.6 m (the plinth is set into the pavement so the overall height is likely about 1.62 m; some intact *bōmoi* at the necropolis measure up to 1.9 m high); plinth: 0.83 m^2; base: 0.60 m x 0.17 m; shaft: 0.40 m x 0.46 m; pediment: 0.52 m x 0.52 m.

Figure 8.1b (right). Closeup of relief with two (?) standing figures, molding, boss in pediment.

Unless otherwise indicated, all photographs by Alan H. Cadwallader.

Accordingly, what is offered in this paper must be seen as impressionistic rather than exhaustive.[40] Even so, without requiring such impressions to provide any definitive results for the mainstream Colossian population, the analysis can offer some indication of what *was* present in the population and what *was* acceptable to display publically, without requiring such to be the dominant or majority practice or values.

3. New Inscriptions

Both inscriptions, published here for the first time, were found within 20 meters of the bank of chamosoria visible on the northern rise of the necropolis basin. The first new inscription is the most simple, complete epitaph discovered to date at Colossae, four lines of text on a standard but broken *bōmos*.[41] Thus it fulfills Plato's length if not the call for heroic inspiration![42]

The inscription transcribed as laid out is:

1. ΕΠΙΚΤΗΤΟΣ
2.   ΚΑΙ
3.   ΑΡΙΣΤΗ ΓΥ
4.   ΝΗ ΑΥΤΟΥ

All together, the inscription reads:

Ἐπίκτητος καὶ Ἀρίστη γυνή αὐτοῦ

Epictetus and his wife Ariste

---

40. So Thonemann, "Households and Families," 124–25, for whom the small number of "extended family" tombs were yet significant for social reconstruction.

41. It is more basic than the standardized epitaphs from Thrace, which at least add a farewell greeting (χαίρετε) and sometimes a brief genealogy (*CIRB* 266, 372, 400, 443; cf. *SEG* 15.416; IKyzikos 324). I remain always grateful to that magnanimous scholar, Professor Ender Varinlioğlu, for his kind permission to publish these inscriptions of Colossae.

42. Compare the honorific monument to the boxer "Kastor" that bears a five-line epigram (J. G. C. Anderson, "A Summer in Phrygia: II," *JHS* 18 [1898]: 90 §26, as corrected by Reinhold Merkelbach and Josef Stauber, *Steinepigramme aus dem griechischen Osten*, 6 vols. [Stuttgart: Teubner; Munich: Saur, 1998–2015], 1.02.15.01). At the very least, it demonstrates that such "heroic lines" were possible.

Figures 8.2a (left) and 8.2b (right). The funerary *bōmos* of Epictetos and Ariste, with detail of inscription. Letters: 0.05 m (initial E and A), 0.04 m (remainder); evenly spaced; serifs; four-bar sigma, broken-bar alpha. Words on each line are centered; Bomos: shaft: 0.48 m²; pediment base: 0.64 m²; Date: First to second century CE (based on letter shapes, absence of Roman citizenship, and similarity to other *bōmoi* designs with epitaphs)

Unlike most other epitaphs from Colossae, there is no genealogy for husband or wife and no mention of children.[43] Unlike a number of epitaphs, there is no greeting to passersby: τοῖς παραδίταις χαίρειν.[44] Unlike some, there is no mention of a penalty (or imprecation) for disturbance or mention of memorialization, as in the familiar form χάριν/ἕνεκα μνίας.[45] There is another example from Colossae of a husband and wife alone—

---

43. Compare Weber, "Inschriften," 206 §3; Cadwallader, "Two New Inscriptions," 109–11 §1.

44. Cadwallader, "Two New Inscriptions," 110 §1; cf. the simple χαίρειν in *MAMA* 6.44. There appears to be both a phonological and at times a spelling interchange between χαίρειν and χαριν (μνίας), indicating that the greeting and the call to memory are evoked together, the one calling the other to mind.

45. This pronouncement is found in *CIG* 3.4380k³ = IBoubon 102, used of the Colossian woman named Aphias buried in the region of Boubon. The phrase is not as yet attested on epitaphs from Colossae itself; see PfuhlMöbius §1920.

Karpon and Tatas—but the grave is carefully protected against disruption by express statement (βούλομαι μηδένα ἕτερον κηδευθῆναι) reinforced by a penalty invoking the oversight/authority of the ταμεῖον, the civic treasury.[46]

The husband's name is common, but the wife's name far less so.[47] Both names are value laden, "newly acquired/a bonus" for Ἐπίκτητος; "beautiful/best" for Ἀρίστη. This family is constituted solely by the husband and wife, with no reference to preceding or succeeding generations. Who took responsibility for the funerary arrangements is unknown, though one suspects this was organized by the couple before death (as is explicitly stated in another Colossian epitaph).[48] We are dealing here with an absence of evidence, and this requires care in interpretation. After all, slaves are rarely mentioned in epitaphs apart from those that they themselves have erected.[49]

The simplicity of the epitaph reinforces the functionality of a *bōmos*—that is, a single heavy stone carved to sit neatly into a shallow-recessed section of the slab that covers the chamosorion (in-ground sarcophagus).

However, the functionality of the *bōmos* is combined with sacredness—indicated by the mimesis of a temple with its pediment and stylized acroteria.[50] Roman law explicitly assigned sacredness to the place of the

Figure 8.3a (left). Chamosorion half-sealing slab (left) has a recess in which the bōmos sits and a rabbet edging to enable a second section to lock onto it. The slab measures 1.67 m x 1.42 m with the recess 1.15 m x 0.95 m. Figure 8.3b (right). The chamosorion grave (right) shows a half section of the slab in position.

---

46. *IGRR* 4.871; cf. Weber, "Inschriften," 206 §3; *MAMA* 6.43 (= Ritti §167); Cadwallader, "Revisiting Calder," 108.

47. Ἐπίκτητος: 432 examples in *LGPN* online; Ἀρίστη: twenty-eight examples.

48. ζῶσειν *MAMA* 6.43; cf. *MAMA* 6.306.

49. But see *MAMA* 4.114; cf. *MAMA* 4.27; *SEG* 28.1154; *MAMA* 6.276.

50. See further Cadwallader, *Fragments of Colossae*, 157–59; Kelp, "Grave Monuments," 82.

ONE GRAVE, TWO WOMEN, ONE MAN

Figure 8.4 (left). The sketch by Georg Weber ("Der unterirdische Lauf," 198) of the undamaged *bōmos*, measuring 1.28 m high and 0.58 m across the plinth and almost certainly (given the lettering included) of Dion the leatherworker. At right, figure 8.5, is the same *bōmos* today.

buried deceased; Plato actually uses the word *bōmos* in his discussion of funerary monuments—an altar to the chthonic gods.[51]

The second new inscription complicates the picture of family life at Colossae considerably. Again the inscription occurs on an aniconic *bōmos* (see figs. 8.6a and 8.6b below). The inscription transcribed as laid out is:

1. ΤΟ ΜΝΗΜΕΙΟΝ
2. ΑΥ ΜΕΝΙΑΝΔΡΟΥ
3. Β ΤΟΥ ΕΡΜΟΓΕΝΟΥ
4. Κ ΑΥ ΖΗΝΩΝΙΔΟΣ
5. ΤΗΣ ΓΥΝΑΙΚΟΣ
6. ΑΥΤΟΥ ΕΝ Ω ΚΗ
7. ΔΕΥΘΗΣΕΙΤΑΙ
8. ΚΑΙ ΙΕΙΚΕΣ ΔΙΟΥ
9. ΓΥΝΗ ΖΗΝΩΝΟΣ

All together, the inscription reads:

---

51. Dig. 7.4 (Ulpianus); cf. 7.2 pref. (Aristo), 7.2.5, 7.2.9. Plato, *Leg* 12.959d. Admittedly, Plato's point is to compare the soulless corpse with an altar whose significance resides not in itself but in the gods to whom it is set up. However, the correlation establishes the aptness of the connection between a *bōmos* and a grave.

Figures 8.6a and 8.6b. The *bōmos* for Meniandros, Zenonis, and Hieikis (?), with detail of the funerary inscription. Letters: 0.03 m; serifs; four-bar sigma, broken-bar alpha, curvilinear omega, ligatures (l.1 MNH; l.4 HN; l.9 NH and HM), puncts (l.2 after AY; l.3 after B; l.4 after K [?], after AY), possible insert of upsilon in omicron at end of l.2; Phonology: l.7 EI for E; l.8 E for I; Date: late second to early third CE (based on letter styles, use of puncts, plus and minus Roman citizenship formulae).

The absence of M. before Aurelius might indicate the sometimes haphazard indications of Roman citizenship following the *Constitutio Antoniniana* of 212/214 CE (e.g., *IGRR* 4.871; cf. *BGU* 2.655; *P.Oxy.* 12.1458), though status displays would err to its inclusion; see J. G. Keenan, "The Names Flavius and Aurelius as Status Designations in Later Roman Egypt," *ZPE* 11 (1973): 42 n. 41. The absence of the gentilicum for Hieikis, Dios, and Zenon (even allowing for the dictations of space) means that a late second century date cannot be ruled out (cf. also *MAMA* 6.42). Such variations in the indication of Colossian and Roman citizenship are also apparent on Colossian coin legends of the second century.

τὸ μνημεῖον Αὐ(ρηλίου) Μενιάνδρου Β τοῦ Ἑρμογένου κ(αὶ)
Αὐ(ρηλίας) Ζηνωνίδος τῆς γυναικὸς αὐτοῦ ἐν ᾧ κηδευθήσεται καὶ
Ἰεικές(?) Δίου γυνὴ Ζήνωνος

The tomb of Aurelius Meniandros son of Meniandros, grandson of Hermogenes; also of Aurelia Zenonis, his wife; in which grave is also to be buried Hieikis (?) daughter of Dios, wife of Zenon.

In this epitaph, genealogies are important, as are the marriage lines. This is extremely familiar at Colossae, with genealogies sometimes extending beyond the father and grandfather.[52] Two names are unusual: Meniandros for its form (compared to the usual Menandros); Hieikis is unique and, given slight abrasion at this point on the stone, a little uncertain.[53] Colossae has previously yielded unattested names.[54]

Most unusual, however, is the presence of two wives in Meniandros's grave, even though the epitaph is concerned to demonstrate that the second named wife, Hieikis, is honorably embedded, listing both her father and her husband, Zenon. The clue, I think, lies in the name of Meniandros's wife, Zenonis. It is evident from Greek and Roman naming practices that siblings often were given variants of the same name, sometimes as variants of the father's name, though this is not the case here. A close parallel is found in another inscription from Colossae—the memorial that the brothers Apollonios and Apollonides erected for their father, Damokrates.[55] On this basis, Hieikis's husband, Zenon, was the brother of Zenonis, the wife of Meniandros. What became of Zenon is unknown, though it appears reasonable to assume either death or desertion. In favor of death is the fact that he is named on the stone; in favor of desertion is the fact that Hieikis is not buried with her husband. Convention preserves her honor by having her husband named, but a lack of provision for her

---

52. See Cadwallader, "Honouring the Repairer," 150–83.

53. For Meniandros: While the stone is abraded at this letter, there is clear space for a letter between Μεν- and -ανδρος as well as a serif and partial vertical to indicate a letter. Compare Μενιάδας: *IG* 12.3.581/1437; and Μενίας: *TAM* 3.703; Μηνιάς: *IG* 2.12113. For Hieikis: Compare Ιεικοκουλα in ILipara 422; Ἐπιείκης: *SEG* 38.935; *IG* 2.2245; and personified Ἐπιείκεια in Plutarch, *Caes.* 57).

54. Tryphonionos, Skeparnos, Anot-, Mokeas (Cadwallader, "Honouring the Repairer," 150); Tryphion (IBoubon 102), Eugenetoriane (coin: Hans von Aulock, *Münzen und Städte Phrygiens*, 2 vols. [Tübingen: Wasmuth, 1980–1987], 2:548).

55. *MAMA* 6.46.

is evident, whether or not Zenon might have died afar off from disease, disaster, or military engagement.

The future κηδευθήσειται (for κηδευθήσεται) suggests that at least Meniandros, if not Zenonis, has predeceased Hieikis. Considerable concern is indicated for her proper care, presumably in the absence of any children or wider family prepared to take the responsibility. It may indicate that Hieikis received at least part of an inheritance from Meniandros.[56] So, it appears likely that, as in death, so in life, Hieikis was taken into Meniandros's household, after whatever happened with Zenon. In this sense the designation of the grave as τὸ μνημεῖον (as distinct from θήκη, σῆμα, σορός, τάφος, τύμβος, τύμβευμα, and even μνῆμα)[57] is not only a call to memorialization, but becomes itself a little household, just as the household was a little civic society—recognized, walled, grouped, protected, resistant to intruders, and so on. It thus preserves, albeit in a managed balance of remembering and forgetting, the place of the deceased in the narrative and landscape of the city.[58] Sometimes an epitaph's self-referentiality brings in the sacredness of both memory and household by naming the stone, a *bōmos*.[59] There is no such funerary example of the term *bōmos* at Colossae, but the pedestal and statue monument to Korymbos, the repairer of the baths at Colossae, is also called a *bōmos*, suggesting either a debasement of the currency of the word or a heightened sense of the sacred in life.[60] This *bōmos* not only reinforces the memory; it also reinforces the values of the household, in this case the care for a bereft relative, just as, elsewhere, graves might be opened to receive close friends.[61]

---

56. Cf. Thonemann, "Households and Families," 134.

57. See *MAMA* 6.45; Cadwallader, "Two New Inscriptions," 109 §1. See also Jadwiga Kubínska, *Les monuments funéraires dans les inscriptions grecques de l'Asie Mineure*, Travaux du Centre d'archéologie méditerranéenne de l'Académie polonaise des sciences 5 (Warsaw: PNW, 1968), who sees a regional indicator in the use of different terminology.

58. So Krsmanovic and Anderson, "Paths of the Dead," 76–80.

59. For example, *SEG* 28.1125; *AltHierapolis* 64, 103; *TAM* 4.109. See also above, n. 1 and Plato, *Leg.* 12.959d.

60. Cadwallader, "Honouring the Repairer," inscription line 5. On the expansion of the application of the word *bōmos*, see J. J. Coulton, "Pedestals as 'Altars' in Roman Asia Minor," *AnSt* 55 (2005): 127–57.

61. So *Dig.* 7.2.6; *CBP* 385 §§231, 232, 236; *SEG* 28.1125; *IGRR* 4.731; *MAMA* 4.343.

Thonemann notes that at Apameia children were interred with their parents only if they were minors; thereafter they had responsibility for their own graves. At the same time, he observes that funerary inscriptions in the Upper Tembris valley often emphasized extended family relations,[62] as here with Meniandros's epitaph. While there is no mention of children in Meniandros's epitaph, this is not always the case at Colossae. The *bōmos* epitaph of Markos, son of Rufus, for example, explicitly states that it is for himself and his son Dionyseios.[63] No wife/mother is mentioned; one wonders whether the warning about interment of anyone else (for which a penalty of five hundred denarii was to be paid to the φίσκος, the Roman treasury office) might have had someone specific in mind!

4. Funerary Monuments and Relationship Structures

Thus far, from the limited evidence of aniconic *bōmoi*, the household structures indicated have been quite varied. A full assembly of the household structures and other elements in all the few funerary inscriptions we have from Colossae[64] does not disturb this initial impression. In fact, there is at least one and possibly three inscriptions that altogether removes blood or legal family ties and responsibilities from the picture and shifts them elsewhere—to associations. The clearest example is that of οἱ ἑταῖροι, "the society of friends," possibly a religious association, who sponsored the erection of the epitaphal relief for Glykon.[65] But it is likely that Dion

---

62. Thonemann, "Households and Families" 124–26.
63. *MAMA* 6.43; cf. Weber, "Inschriften aus Sued-Phrygien," 18.206 §3; Cadwallader, "Two New Inscriptions," 109 §1.
64. See the appendix.
65. *MAMA* 6.47. The formal style of the funerary dedication is very similar to *MAMA* 4.299; 9.86; *SEG* 32.1169, 1170 (also οἱ θιασεῖται), 1185; 35.1337; *EAD* 30.143 (different word order); Philip A. Harland, "Funerary Honors by Companions for Glykon (I–II CE)," on Associations in the Greco-Roman World: An Expanding Collection of Inscriptions, Papyri, and Other Sources in Translation, http://tinyurl.com/SBL4522r, takes the name as that of a woman, translating it as "the companions honoured Glykona." However, normally the privileged person in such reliefs is at the right for the viewer, as also the clothing and gesture of the man. It is likely the Doric accusative of Γλύκων: note *AltHierapolis* 269, and especially *SEG* 40.1241 where the accusative υἱόν occurs in apposition to the name Γλύκωναν. Γλύκωνα also occurs as an accusative. Buckler and Calder are mistaken in suggesting that it is a Jewish association (citing *OGIS* 573)—so Louis Robert, "Bulletin épigraphique," *REG* 52 (1939): 392.

the leatherworker also received his *bōmos*-closed burial from an association, given that, although there is a genealogy (Αππας), no other relative, nor his own initiative, is mentioned.⁶⁶ The leather trade is known elsewhere to be supported by associations.⁶⁷ Ulrich Huttner has suggested that the συνγενικὸν νεώτερον that set up a funerary stele for another Colossian, Tatianos, may have been a phratry acting similarly to an association.⁶⁸ Roman law, perhaps even the Twelve Tables, recognized Greek associations, noting specific functions that included religious banquets and burial provision (βωμοτάφοι).⁶⁹

A concentration on the written jaundices the picture of how such public portrayals are to be interpreted, so it is fitting that we now incorporate the nonverbal communication more fully.⁷⁰ This is where the even fewer, but all the more significant, reliefs associated with inscriptions need to enter the analysis. One in particular, that just mentioned, is particularly striking because of an apparent tension between the relief and the inscription—the funerary stele of Tatianos. The inscription transcribed as laid out is:

ΣΥΝΓΕΝΙΚΟΝ ΝΕΙΩΤΕΡΟΝ
ΤΑΤΙΑΝΩ Β' ΑΡΤΟΥ⁷¹

The term οἱ ἑταῖροι is expressly recognized as the Greek designation of associations: Dig. 47.22.4 (Gaius).

66. See *MAMA* 6.44; cf. *SEG* 53.293. I have followed *LGPN* in providing no diacritical marks here, indicating a probable epichoric name (see *LGPN* IV, ix–x and V, xv–xvi).

67. See Philip A. Harland, *Associations, Synagogues and Congregations: Claiming a Place in Ancient Mediterranean Society* (Minneapolis: Fortress, 2003), 39–40. Note however that the specific terminology used in the Colossian epitaph (διφθεροπύς for διφθεροποιός) is, to my knowledge, singular. The implied specialization in the term may indicate a maker of parchment; cf. Cadwallader, "Two New Inscriptions," 111–12.

68. *MAMA* 6.48 = Ritti §73 = PfuhlMöbius §1974. Ulrich Huttner, *Early Christianity in the Lycus Valley*, Early Christianity in Asia Minor 1 (Leiden: Brill, 2013), 31; similarly Tullia Ritti's comment in Ritti, *Museo Archeologico di Denizli-Hierapolis: Catalogo delle iscrizioni greche e latine; Distretto di Denizli*, Pubblicazioni del Dipartimento di discipline storiche 25 (Naples: Liguori, 2008), 170; cf. *SEG* 50.528.

69. Dig. 47.22.4 (Gaius); see Ilias Arnaoutoglou, *Ancient Greek Laws: A Sourcebook* (London: Routledge, 1998), 37, §34, and commentary.

70. It should be recalled that the *bōmoi* themselves were not merely functional.

71. My tracing in the photo, which is from William Hepburn Buckler and William Moir Calder, *Monuments and Documents from Phrygia and Caria*, vol. 6 of *Monumenta Asiae Minoris Antiqua* (Manchester: Manchester University Press, 1939).

ONE GRAVE, TWO WOMEN, ONE MAN

Figure 8.7. The grave stele for Tatianos. Letters: 0.015 m to 0.025 m crudely formed; occasional serifs; lunate sigma and epsilon; curvilinear omega with underbar; Phonology: συνγενικόν for συγγενικόν; Ionic spelling (?) νειώτερος for νεώτερος; second century CE

All together, the inscription reads:

Συνγενικὸν νειώτερον Τατιανῷ Β′ Ἄρτου

The younger kin-group (set this up) for Tatianos son of Tatianos grandson of Artos.[72]

The difficulties begin with the interpretation of συνγενικόν. Informally, it suggests a wider spread of relatives beyond the immediate bloodlines or marriage lines of a family and also distinct from friendship.[73] Sometimes the distinction is made between one's συγγενεία and one's ἴδιοι, that is, wife and children.[74] Clear assignment to one or other category is probably not to be found, so one wonders how Hieikis would be designated. Certainly

---

72. Buckler and Calder thought the name read as Βάρτος. However, both PfuhlMöbius §1974 and Robert, "Bulletin épigraphique," *REG* 92 (1979): 415 suggested the reading adopted here, even though Ἄρτος is rare (one instance in *LGPN* online). No examples of Βάρτος are to be found in *LGPN* or *PHI*, though there is a Βίαρτος in *IGBR* 3.2.1690. If one accepts this reading, then the -ιανος ending, which traditionally indicated a (Roman-style) patronymic, has lost that significance. See Thomas Corsten, "Names in -ιανος in Asia Minor: A Preliminary Study," in *Onomatologos: Studies in Greek Personal Names Presented to Elaine Matthews*, ed. R. W. V. Catling and F. Marchand (Oxford: Oxbow, 2010), 456–63.

73. Isaeus, *Or.* 8.33; Aristotle, *Eth. nic.* 1161b; Plutarch, *Frat. amor.* 8 [481F].

74. *SGO* 2.16.31.91 (but see *IG* 4.1.678); cf. IBoubon §102: ἰδία qualifying γυνή, a reasonably common accent (cf. *MAMA* 7.404, 507). On the distinction of friends and relatives generally, see Louis Robert, Jeanne Robert, and Mario Segre, *Hellenica: Recueil d'épigraphie de numismatique et d'antiquitiés grecques*, 13 vols. (Limoges: Bontemps, 1940–1948), 11–12:210.

Roman law required that in the absence of children or other designated heirs, some member of a kinship group was required to take responsibility for proper burial.[75] Perhaps Hieikis, who apparently survived at least Meniandros, assumed this responsibility. After all, Greek law, which was less amenable to the Roman development of patronage, allowed male or female relatives to fulfill the necessary obligations.[76] Buckler and Calder listed συνγενικόν as a sepulchral term, suggesting perhaps that this might be intended to be a (type of) family plot—probably unlikely here, though the appropriated use of the grave by relatives is not unknown.[77] At Laodikeia the term designates the group responsible *for* the burial,[78] though usually the word is anarthrous and unqualified. The qualifier νεώτερον may be quasi-technical, as was sometimes used of *paides* and *ephebes* to designate a distinct subgroup.[79]

Be that as it may, the real difficulty comes with taking what has been learned from the inscription itself and engaging it in the context of the relief of the stele (or indeed the reverse). There are two cautions that need to guide analysis. Firstly, the inheritance of the modern period of archaeology has unwarrantedly privileged written remains (the literary bias), usually on a hierarchical gradation of scripture, classical text, inscription, papyri, and "leftovers" (ostraka, graffiti, etc). Where a relief coexists with some inscriptional remains, students of the past have tended to interpret the sculptured section within the confines of the writing.[80] Secondly, there has been an assumption that the relief is specific to the one memorialized (the particularity bias). Just as funerary texts are dominated by conventional phrases, so also funerary reliefs and monuments followed standardized formulae and symbolism.[81] Even though a mason's yard might offer a

---

75. Dig. 7.12.4; cf. 7.4, 7.6.

76. Stephen C. Todd, *The Shape of Athenian Law* (Oxford: Clarendon, 1993), 207.

77. As in *TAM* 4.231, 283; *TAM* 2.46. See M. Ricl, "Greek Inscriptions in the Museum of Tire (Turkey)," *Dialogues d'histoire ancienne* 35 (2009): 188; cf. *SEG* 28.840.

78. *MAMA* 6.24; cf. *MAMA* 8.237.

79. *MAMA* 6.74 (an honorific that includes νεώτερος as an office along with στεφανηφόρος in the list of credentials); cf. *GIBM* 905; *SEG* 16.653; *CIJ* 755 (of an association of "younger" Jews); Luke 22:26. Whether the νεώτεροι were simply the same as the νέοι requires further investigation. Aphrodisias certainly had a place (τόπος) marked for the νεώτεροι on a seat of the Odeion (*ALA* 180i).

80. See the critical comments of John Boardman, "Classical Archaeology: Whence and Whither?" *Antiquity* 62 (1988): 795–97.

81. Of course, the symbolism might be multivalent. This is the particular criti-

range of offerings from which to choose, it was resolutely finite (for both economic and social reasons). There are considerable variations even, say, in the vast collection of Pfuhl and Möbius, and some fine tuning of features was executed, but the thematics are considerably restricted. Nevertheless, for those responsible for the burial, if not for the deceased, the symbolism meant *something*.[82]

These observations become relevant for the analysis of the stele relief here. The weathering and damage of the sculpture aside, the display is commonplace. The funerary *klinē* (banquet scene) is one of the most prolific monumental representations of/for the dead. Here a couple are together reclining, probably evocative of husband and wife if the observations of size given above are correct. A seated child frames the scene, each drawing attention to the laid-out food, but instead of the ubiquitous, anticipating hound below the dining table, there appears to be a goose—a slightly more specialized element in the frame.[83]

While the funerary banquet scene has been variously interpreted, my concern in this context is that there is no naming of wife or children in the inscription, just as there is no mention of a wife or sister in the Glykon epitaph previously mentioned.[84] Indeed, Tatianos is likely not to have had

---

cism of the PfuhlMöbius collation by Tomasz Wujeski, *Anatolian Sepulchral Stelae in Roman Times*, Seria Historia sztuki 21 (Poznán: Uniwersytet im. Adama Mickiewicza w Poznaniu, 1991).

82. The specifics of the *klinē*-formation could come under legislative oversight as well as, occasionally, mention in the epitaphal inscription itself—suggesting that considerable meaning was attached to the display. See Elizabeth P. Baughan, *Couched in Death:* Klinai *and Identity in Anatolia and Beyond*, Wisconsin Studies in Classics (Madison: University of Wisconsin Press, 2013).

83. Buckler and Calder describe it as a "bird"; Pfuhl-Möbius as a "Vogel." I am indebted to Angela Standhartinger for the designation of "goose," which best seems to fit the enlarged wings and craning neck. There is nothing parallel to this feature in Pfuhl-Möbius, though the closest in general arrangement is §1973 (from Attouda, following William Mitchell Ramsay, *The Cities and Bishoprics of Phrygia: Being an Essay of the Local History of Phrygia from the Earliest Times to the Turkish Conquest*, 2 vols. [Oxford: Clarendon, 1897], 181–82 §69) but here, under the table, is a sheep and a dog! Strikingly, this stele also has a Συγγενικόν taking responsibility.

84. The distinctive clothing and headdress of the figure on the left may suggest a priestess—perhaps, given the net evocation in the robe's texture, a priestess of Cybele. On Cybele and the dream net, see John R. Clarke, *Art in the Lives of Ordinary Romans: Visual Representation and Non-Elite Viewers in Italy, 100 B.C.–A.D. 315* (Berkeley: University of California Press, 2003), 90–91.

them, given the role of the συγγενικὸν νεώτερον. This raises a suite of questions seeking an explanation: Is the scene reflective of the thwarted hopes and aspirations of Tatianos? Were Tatianos and/or his relatives expressing their adherence to a social convention that they recognized as dominant, either among their immediate peers or superiors, or as perceived to be imperially backed? Or was it simply that the mason's yard had a shortage, and the most familiar type was all that was left? The bird under the table tends to thwart this last conjecture. In any case, what it conveyed was the predominant type of funerary stele in Asia Minor, albeit a type that had a variety of elements sometimes added, such as slaves, cupbearers, and even horses peering through windows. This type privileged a reclining paterfamilias, sometimes with wife reclining with him, sometimes in the female or child's seated position.[85] The relief reinforces accepted conventions not only promoted by various Greek and Roman commentators but reinforced as part of imperial policy.[86] So, regardless of the intent and practice of Tatianos, what is conveyed within the range of values conceivable in the early to high imperial periods is an acceptance of the dominant values. However, and this is crucial, Tatianos was quite able to convey his nondominant household connections through the inscription attached to the dominant nuclear Roman family. In this sense, Tatianos is of a piece with the other epitaphs, iconic and aniconic, that we currently have from Colossae—one more instance of the variegated scene of households and differentiated family structures. Variety is the norm and, given the expense that appears to have been connected with the majority of the grave contexts bearing the epitaphs, a variety that runs into the wealthier sections of Colossian society, if not into the elite. Some fall closer to the dominant model, some are further away; all are held within the necropolis at Colossae, a necropolis that was not only viewed by passersby but, if Colossae had viewing benches as we know from other necropoleis, able to be absorbed in a more reflective manner by inhabitants of and visitors to the city. One would expect that variety to diversify further the lower down the socioeconomic scale one went. As Thonemann has observed for Acmo-

---

85. For the latter, see *MAMA* 6.50 (damaged stele relief with no surviving inscription).

86. See, for example, Horace, *Carm.* 3.6; Velleius Paterculus, *Hist.* 2.103.5; Arius Didymus *apud* Stobaeus 2.7.26.

neia, Eumeneia, and Apameia, "restrictive 'nuclear' burial customs did not fully reflect the reality of family and other affective relations."[87]

5. Implications for the Interpretation of the Letter to the Colossians

After all this, we turn to a semiliterary text connected with this context. When the letter to the Colossians seeks to set out family structures as if they are the Roman nuclear norm, one is entitled to wonder how many within the audience actually saw themselves fitting the paradigm. Was a Tatianos-type within the group identifying as Christians happy to salute the paradigm in a passing fashion but to continue in his apparently single lifestyle, just like Paul (1 Cor 7:7)? What of the grandparents at least implied by the genealogies in some of the epitaphs, even if not explicitly included in the burial plot? What of the apparent care extended to the widowed or deserted Hieikis? Just how many household structures in some or other connection with the early Christian presence in Colossae even came close to the paradigmatic form presumed in the letter? One must be wary of assuming that relationships correlate transparently to households or to burial plots, but they can be suggestive. If we take the letter to Philemon as written into a Colossian context, it is striking that neither husband, wife, nor biological children are mentioned, even if some commentators, following some ancient subscripts, like to assume a happily-married couple in Philemon and Apphia, with Archippos one of those close friends brought into the circle, if not their son[88]—thus showing the success of

---

87. Thonemann, "Households and Families," 127.

88. I am aware of the robust, perceptive argument for a Roman/Italian context for Philemon recently mounted by Vicky Balabanski, "Where Is Philemon? The Case for a Logical Fallacy in the Correlation of the Data in Philemon and Colossians 1.1–2; 4.7–18," *JSNT* 38 (2015): 1–20. I am unable to agree with her while yet concurring that there are considerable problems in using Colossians and Philemon to ratchet one another's provenance at the same time as acknowledging the pseudonymity of Colossians (so also Huttner, *Early Christianity*, 81, 110–12). Detailed engagement cannot detain us here, but I note that her assertion that there is no evidence to tie Philemon to Asia falters at the name "Apphia," a ubiquitous epichoric-come-*lallname* that is virtually unknown in the West. See Phlm 10 for a metaphorical use of the word "child" (τέχνον). Some scribes turned Onesimus into Apphia's slave (L, 326, 1241), thereby exonerating Philemon (and perhaps suggesting some Potiphar-type association?). See R. McL. Wilson, *A Critical and Exegetical Commentary on Colossians and Philemon*,

the promotion of the Roman nuclear model. The mention of Nympha as the head of a household (Col 4:15) likewise fails to conform to the paradigmatic structure, however her position be explained.[89] The relationship between Barnabas and Mark implied in the final greetings (ἀνεψιός; 4:10) is closer to Tatianos's relationship with his younger kin group than to the nuclear paradigm.[90] Finally, the accent on "brothers" (ἀδελφός/οί; 4:7, 9, 15), especially in conjunction with ministers, slaves, soldiers, and workers (4:7, 10–12) is more akin to the association of friends or even leatherworkers that we have met in the Colossian epitaphs.[91]

Given that none of the people mentioned in Colossians—all of whom are given a variety of relational connections—are factored according to the relationships outlined in the household code, one wonders therefore what function the code has, not merely in the letter itself but among the recipients to whom the letter is addressed. This is not the place to review the manifold suggestions that have been made. But what has been established from the review of the evidence that we have of the considerable variety of household structures obliquely signaled in the funerary inscriptions from Colossae is that none of the epitaphs fits the form implied in the code in the letter. They are, as Margaret MacDonald finds for Nympha, "largely

---

ICC (London: T&T Clark, 2005), 319–20, 333–34. Wilson, with a number of modern commentators, slides back into a family unit even though acknowledging that nothing in the text actually supports it; contrast Roy R. Jeal, *Exploring Philemon: Freedom, Brotherhood, and Partnership in the New Society*, RRA 2 (Atlanta: SBL Press, 2015), 40.

89. Margaret Y. MacDonald, "Can Nympha Rule This House? The Role of Domesticity in Colossians," in *Rhetoric and Reality in Early Christianities*, ed. Willi Braun (Waterloo, ON: Wilfred Laurier University Press, 2005), 99–120. I note that there remain some who take the name as the masculine Νυμφᾶς. If this were the case, then that household might be claimed as potentially closer to the paradigm. See E. A. Judge, *The First Christians in the Roman World: Augustan and New Testament Essays*, ed. James R. Harrison, WUNT 229 (Tübingen: Mohr Siebeck, 2008), 544 (reprinted from a 1961 essay); J. M. Petersen, "House Churches in Rome," *VC* 23 (1969): 265; John D. Zizioulas, *Eucharist, Bishop, Church: The Unity of the Church in the Divine Eucharist and the Bishop during the First Three Centuries* (Brookline, MA: Holy Orthodox Press, 2001), 90–91.

90. ἀνεψιός and συγγενής are often treated as synonyms (along with ἔκγονος and cognates) in honorific metaphors; see *IGRR* 4.617; IPerge 1.317; IArykanda 67. Hagiographical traditions such as in the fifth-century Acts of Barnabas have Mark fulfilling kin obligations by burying the martyr Barnabas on Cyprus—along with a copy of Matthew's Gospel copied by Mark's own hand!

91. Compare *IG* 10.2.1.824; *CIRB* 1283; IKilikiaBM 2.201b.

exempt from the impact of the restrictions."[92] If these epitaphs are in any way a reasonable sample of Colossian society—as Thonemann suggests of Phrygia as a whole—then perhaps the code not only had little to do with the membership of the Colossian congregation but also had entirely, and "prudently," as McDonald observes, another audience, fictive or otherwise, in view.[93] Some Christian groups were far from alone in this posturing for outside observance, as Angela Standhartinger has shown from the teaching of street philosophers and from a striking inscription positioned outside a probably mistrusted mystery-cult center in Philadelphia.[94] These dynamics are about positioning in relation to those who run the ideological powerhouse[95] and demonstrate that the Colossian household code is far from unique either in its form or in its purpose. Nor is it emblematic of a monochrome Christian response.[96] I do not think that we need to surrender a specific Colossian address for the New Testament letter.[97] But it does suggest that some of the negotiations of the unfolding Roman imperial realities were not joined by the Jesus-followers in regard to a generally conforming Colossian society but rather *as part of that society* in regard to a growing Roman influence on that society's affairs. Given that the author of the letter (Epaphras?) brings a perspective from outside that society (Col 2:1), the awareness of imperial realities is likely to be highly charged. The Romanization of Colossian society (and of the church within it?) is, however, another question for another discussion, one which, I am sure, Dennis Smith would be only too eager to join!

---

92. MacDonald, "Nympha," 115.

93. Ibid. See also David L. Balch, *Let Wives Be Submissive: The Domestic Code in 1 Peter*, SBLMS 6 (Chico, CA: Scholars Press, 1981), 80, 118–21; Balch, "Household Codes," in *Greco-Roman Literature and the New Testament: Selected Forms and Genres*, ed. David E. Aune (Atlanta: Scholars Press, 1988), 35.

94. Angela Standhartinger, "The Origin and Intention of the Household Code in the Letter to the Colossians," *JSNT* 79 (2000): 117–30. See *SIG* 2.985.

95. See Alan H. Cadwallader, "The Struggle for Paul in the Context of Empire: Mark as a Deutero-Pauline Text," in *Two Authors at the Beginning of Christianity*, part 1 of *Paul and Mark: Comparative Essays*, ed. Oda Wischmeyer, David C. Sim, and Ian J. Elmer, BZNW 198 (Berlin: de Gruyter, 2014), 557–87.

96. This does not discount particular Christian twists; see Standhartinger, "Household Code," 123–25.

97. *Pace* Standhartinger, *Studien zur Entstehungsgeschichte und Intention des Kolosserbriefs*, NovTSup 94 (Leiden: Brill, 1999), 10–16; Standhartinger, "Colossians and the Pauline School," *NTS* 50 (2004): 582–88.

Appendix: Epitaphs and Memorials from Colossae

The following table presents the various elements of the inscribed epitaphs from Colossae, plus extant epitaphs of Colossian citizens buried elsewhere. Dating assigned by editors and/or AHC by naming practices (cf. Roman citizen, letter styles, comparative penalty size).

Key: f. father, s. son, h. husband, w. wife, d. daughter, b. brother, gf. grandfather, il. in-law

Catalogue	Type	Relief	Deceased	Genealogy
MAMA 6.43	bōmos	x (boss)	Μᾶρκος s. Διονύσειος	f. Ῥοῦπος
MAMA 6.44	bōmos	x (boss)	Δίων	f. Απτας
MAMA 6.45	bōmos	x	Τρόφιμος w. Διογένεια (?)	f. Πρόβος gf. Δίων
MAMA 6.47	Facade	√	Γλύκων	x
MAMA 6.48	Stele	√	Τατιανός	f. Τατιανός gf. Ἄρτος
CIG 3.3955 (!)	(unlikely)	?	w. (?)	?
"Revisiting Calder," 114	bōmos	x?	Δάτυος?	f. Ζήνων
IGRR 6.871	bōmos	x	Κάρπων w. Τάτας	x
"Inschriften aus Sued-Phrygien," 206.3	bōmos	x (boss)	Διονύσιος w. Τάτα d. Ἰρήνη	f. Ἀγγελικός
"Two New Inscriptions," 109.1	bōmos	x	Κάρπος w. Εὐθηνία s. Ἀρτεμιδώρος	x

ONE GRAVE, TWO WOMEN, ONE MAN 185

Descriptors	Memorialis'n	Greet.	Penalty	Provision	Date
x	τὸ μνημεῖον	x	500 denarii to fiskus	ζῶσειν	C1-2
διφθεροπύς	x	√	x	Association?	C2
x	τὸ μνημεῖον	x	?	x	C1-2
x	x	√	x	οἱ ἑταῖροι	C2
x	x	x	x	συνγενικὸν νεώτερον	C2 (Ritti C2-3)
?	?	?	?	?	?
?	τὸ μνημεῖον?	?	?	?	?
>212 Roman Citizenship	τὸ μνημεῖον	x	500 denarii to tameion	x	C3
x	τὸ μνημεῖον (on pediment horizontal)	x	1000 denarii to fiskus	x	C1
x	τὸ μνημεῖον	√	x	x	C1

Catalogue	Type	Relief	Deceased	Genealogy
"Revisiting Calder," 109	bōmos	?	?	?
new 1	bōmos	x	Ἐπίκτητος w. Ἀρίστη	x
new 2	bōmos	x	Μενιάνδρος w. Ζηνωνίς il. Ἰεικίς (?)	f. Μενιάνδρος gf. Ἑρμογένης
CIG 3.4380k³	Pedestal (small)	x	Ἄφιας	h. Ἑρμᾶς f. Τρύφιων
ISmyrna 440	Plaque	x	Διόδοτος	x
MAMA 6.39	Plaque	?	Κρισπεῖνος	f. Πάπιος
MAMA 6.42	Pedestal	?	Ἡρακλέon	m. Ἀμμιανή f. Καρπίων gf. Τρύφων
MAMA 6.46?	fragment	?	Δαμοκράτης	s. Ἀπολλώνιος b. s. Ἀπολλωνίδης

Descriptors	Memorialis'n	Greet.	Penalty	Provision	Date
?	?	?	500 denarii to fiskus	?	C1 (?)
x	x	x	x	x	C1-2
Roman C'ship f². Δίος h. Ζήνων	τὸ μνημεῖον	x	x	For sister-in-law	C2-3
τῇ ἰδίᾳ γυναικί Κολοσσηνῇ	μνήμης ἕνεκα	x	x	h. Ἑρμᾶς	?
Κολοσηνός φιλόλογος	προνοοῦντος τοῦ μνημείου	x	x	Ἀττίνας τοῦ Ἀττίνου	C2
Roman C'ship ἥρως	ἡ βουλὴ καὶ ὁ δῆμος ἐτείμησεν	x	x	f. ἐπιμεληθέντος Ἐπαφροδείτου	C1
ἥρως	annual stephanation	x	x	m.500 denarii f. monument	C3
πάτηρ ἀδελποί	√	x	x	διαθήκη	C1 BCE– C1(?)

Bibliography

Ahrens, Sven. "'Whether by Decay or Fire Consumed...': Cremation in Hellenistic and Roman Asia Minor." Pages 185–222 in *Death and Changing Rituals: Function and Meaning in Ancient Funerary Practices*. Edited by J. Rasmus Brandt, Håkon Roland, and Marina Prusac. Studies in Funerary Archaeology 7. Oxford: Oxbow, 2015.

Akropolites, George. *The History*. Edited and translated by Ruth Macrides. Oxford Studies in Byzantium. Oxford: Oxford University Press, 2007.

Anderson, J. G. C. "A Summer in Phrygia: II," *JHS* 18 (1898): 81–128, 340–44.

Arnaoutoglou, Ilias. *Ancient Greek Laws: A Sourcebook*. London: Routledge, 1998.

Arundell, Francis V. J. *A Visit to the Seven Churches of Asia: With an Excursion into Pisidia*. London: Rodwell, 1828.

Aulock, Hans von. *Münzen und Städte Phrygiens*. 2 vols. Tübingen: Wasmuth, 1980–1987.

Balabanski, Vicky. "Where Is Philemon? The Case for a Logical Fallacy in the Correlation of the Data in Philemon and Colossians 1.1-2; 4.7-18." *JSNT* 38 (2015): 1–20.

Balch, David L. "Household Codes." Pages 25–50 in *Greco-Roman Literature and the New Testament: Selected Forms and Genres*. Edited by David E. Aune. Sources of Biblical Study 21. Atlanta: Scholars Press, 1988.

———. *Let Wives Be Submissive: The Domestic Code in 1 Peter*. SBLMS 6. Chico, CA: Scholars Press, 1981.

Baughan, Elizabeth P. *Couched in Death:* Klinai *and Identity in Anatolia and Beyond*. Wisconsin Studies in Classics. Madison: University of Wisconsin Press, 2013.

Bayhan, Ahmet Ali. "Ak Han (Goncalı Hanı)." Pages 287–303 in *Anadolu Selçuklu Dönemi Kervansarayları*. Edited by Hakkı Acun. Kütüphaneler ve Yayımlar Genel Müdürlüğü Sanat Eserleri Dizisi. Ankara: Kültür ve Turizm Bakanlığı, 2007.

Bell, Gertrude. Diary. Gertrude Bell Archive. Newcastle University Library.

Berns, C. "The Tomb as a Node of Public Representation." Pages 231–42 in *Le mort dans la ville: Pratiques, contextes et impacts des inhumations intra-muros en Anatolie, du début de l'Age du Bronze à l'époque romaine; 2èmes rencontres d'archéologie de l'IFEA*. Edited by Olivier Henry. Istanbul: Ege yayınları, 2013.

Boardman, John. "Classical Archaeology: Whence and Whither?" *Antiquity* 62 (1988): 795–97.
Bodel, John. "Dealing with the Dead: Undertakers, Executioners and Potter's Fields in Ancient Rome." Pages 128–35 in *Death and Disease in the Ancient City*. Edited by Valerie M. Hope and Eireann Marshall. London: Routledge, 2000.
Cadwallader, Alan H. *Fragments of Colossae: Sifting through the Traces*. Hindmarsh: ATF, 2015.
———. "Honouring the Repairer of the Baths: A New Inscription from Kolossai." *Antichthon* 46 (2012): 150–83.
———. "Revisiting Calder on Colossae." *AnSt* 56 (2006): 103–11.
———. "The Struggle for Paul in the Context of Empire: Mark as a Deutero-Pauline Text." Pages 557–87 in *Two Authors at the Beginning of Christianity*. Part 1 of *Paul and Mark: Comparative Essays*. Edited by Oda Wischmeyer, David C. Sim, and Ian J. Elmer. BZNW 198. Berlin: de Gruyter, 2014.
———. "Two New Inscriptions, a Correction and a Confirmed Sighting from Colossae." *EA* 40 (2007): 109–18.
Calder, William. Notebooks. Calder Archives. University of Aberdeen Special Libraries.
Chandler, Richard. *Travels in Asia Minor and Greece: Or, An Account of a Tour Made at the Expense of the Society of Dilettanti*. 3rd ed. 2 vols. London: Booker & Priestly, 1817.
Clarke, John R. *Art in the Lives of Ordinary Romans: Visual Representation and Non-elite Viewers in Italy, 100 B.C.–A.D. 315*. Berkeley: University of California Press, 2003.
Cormack, Sarah H. *The Space of Death in Roman Asia Minor*. Wiener Forschungen zur Archäologie 6. Vienna: Phoibos, 2004.
Corsten, Thomas. "Names in -ιανος in Asia Minor: A Preliminary Study." Pages 456–63 in *Onomatologos: Studies in Greek Personal Names Presented to Elaine Matthews*. Edited by R. W. V. Catling and F. Marchand. Oxford: Oxbow, 2010.
Coulton, J. J. "Pedestals as 'Altars' in Roman Asia Minor." *AnSt* 55 (2005): 127–57.
Demargne, J. "Monuments figurés et inscriptions de Crète." *BCH* 24 (1900): 222–46.
Derderian, Katharine. *Leaving Words to Remember: Greek Mourning and the Advent of Literacy*. MnemosyneSup 209. Leiden: Brill, 2001.

Deutsches Archäologisches Institut. "Oinoanda und die größte Inschrift der antiken Welt." http://tinyurl.com/SBL4522t.

Drew-Bear, Thomas, Feza Demirkök, Esra S. Dönmez, and Metin Türktüzün. *Ben Anadolu'da doğdum / I Was Born in Anatolia / Je suis né en Anatolie*. Tugay Anadolu Kültür-Sanat ve Arkeoloji Müzesi Yayınları 1. Kütahya: Tugay Anadolu Kültür-Sanat ve Arkeoloji Müzesi, 2007.

Drew-Bear, Thomas, Christine M. Thomas, and Melek Yıldızturan. *Phrygian Votive Steles*. Ankara: Ministry of Culture, 1999.

Duncan-Jones, Richard. *The Economy of the Roman Empire: Quantitative Studies*. 2nd ed. Cambridge: Cambridge University Press, 1982.

Erdmann, Kurt, and Hanna Erdmann. *Das anatolische Karavansaray des 13. Jahrhunderts*. 3 vols. Istanbuler Forschungen 21, 31. Berlin: Mann, 1961–1976.

Folch, Marcus. *The City and the Stage: Performance, Genre, and Gender in Plato's Laws*. Oxford: Oxford University Press, 2015.

Garland, Robert. "The Well-Ordered Corpse: An Investigation into the Motives behind Greek Funerary Legislation." *Bulletin of the Institute of Classical Studies* 36 (1989): 1–15.

Hall, A. S., N. P. Milner and J. J. Coulton. "The Mausoleum of Licinnia Flavilla and Flavianus Diogenes of Oinoanda: Epigraphy and Architecture." *AnSt* 46 (1996): 111–43.

Hammerstaedt, Jürgen, and Martin F. Smith, "Diogenes of Oinoanda: The Discoveries of 2011 (NF 191–205, and Additions to NF 127 and 130)." *EA* 44 (2011): 79–114.

Harland, Philip A. *Associations, Synagogues and Congregations: Claiming a Place in Ancient Mediterranean Society*. Minneapolis: Fortress, 2003.

———. "Funerary Honors by Companions for Glykon (I–II CE)." Associations in the Greco-Roman World: An Expanding Collection of Inscriptions, Papyri, and Other Sources in Translation. http://tinyurl.com/SBL4522r.

Heisenberg, August, and Peter Wirth. *Georgii Acropolitae Opera: Synopsis Chronike*. 2nd ed. Bibliotheca scriptorum Graecorum et Romanorum Teubneriana. Stuttgart: Teubner, 1978.

Huttner, Ulrich. *Early Christianity in the Lycus Valley*. Early Christianity in Asia Minor 1. Leiden: Brill, 2013.

Jeal, Roy R. *Exploring Philemon: Freedom, Brotherhood, and Partnership in the New Society*. RRA 2. Atlanta: SBL Press, 2015.

Judge, E. A. *The First Christians in the Roman World: Augustan and New Testament Essays*. Edited by James R. Harrison. WUNT 229. Tübingen: Mohr Siebeck, 2008.

Kantor, Georgy. "Law in Roman Phrygia: Rules and Jurisdictions." Pages 143–67 in *Roman Phrygia: Culture and Society*. Edited by Peter Thonemann. Greek Culture in the Roman World. Cambridge: Cambridge University Press, 2013.

Keenan, J. G. "The Names Flavius and Aurelius as Status Designations in Later Roman Egypt." *ZPE* 11 (1973): 33–63.

Kelp, Ute. "Grave Monuments and Local Identities in Roman Phrygia." Pages 70–94 in *Roman Phrygia: Culture and Society*. Edited by Peter Thonemann. Greek Culture in the Roman World. Cambridge: Cambridge University Press, 2013.

Kontoleon, A. E. "Variétés," *BCH* 11 (1887): 296–301.

Krsmanovic, D., and W. Anderson, "Paths of the Dead: Interpreting Funerary Practice at Roman-Period Pessinus, Central Anatolia." *Melbourne Historical Journal* 40 (2012): 58–87.

Kubínska, Jadwiga. *Les monuments funéraires dans les inscriptions grecques de l'Asie Mineure*. Travaux du Centre d'archéologie méditerranéenne de l'Académie polonaise des sciences 5. Warsaw: PWN, 1968.

Kutlu, M. "Seljuk Caravanserais in the Vicinity of Denizli: Han-Abad (Çardakhan) and Akhan." MA thesis, Bilkent University, 2009.

Lampakis, George. Οἱ ἑπτὰ ἀστέρες τῆς Ἀποκαλύψεως [The Seven Stars of the Apocalypse]. Athens: 1909.

MacDonald, Margaret Y. "Can Nympha Rule This House? The Role of Domesticity in Colossians." Pages 99–120 in *Rhetoric and Reality in Early Christianities*. Edited by Willi Braun. Studies in Christianity and Judaism 16. Waterloo, ON: Wilfred Laurier University Press, 2005.

Mare, W. H. "Archeological Prospects at Colossae." *PNEAS* 7 (1976): 39–59.

Merkelbach, Reinhold, and Josef Stauber. *Steinepigramme aus dem griechischen Osten*. 6 vols. Stuttgart: Teubner; Munich: Saur, 1998–2015.

Meyboom, P. G. P. *The Nile Mosaic of Palestrina: Early Evidence of Egyptian Religion in Italy*. RGRW 121. Leiden: Brill, 1995.

Pearce, John. "Burial and Ethnicity." Page 179 in *Burial, Society and Context in the Roman World*. Edited by John Pearce, Martin Millett, and Manuela Struck. Oxford: Oxbow, 2000.

Petersen, J. M. "House Churches in Rome." *VC* 23 (1969): 264–72.

Pfuhl, Ernst, and Hans Möbius. *Textband und Tafelband.* Vol. 2.1–2 of *Die Ostgriechischen Grabreliefs.* Mainz: von Zabern, 1979.

Pococke, Richard. *A Description of the East: And Some Other Countries.* London: Bowyer, 1745.

Pomeroy, Sarah B. *Families in Classical and Hellenistic Greece: Representations and Realities.* Oxford: Clarendon; New York: Oxford University Press, 1997.

Ramsay, William Mitchell. *The Cities and Bishoprics of Phrygia: Being an Essay of the Local History of Phrygia from the Earliest Times to the Turkish Conquest.* 2 vols. Oxford: Clarendon, 1897.

Ricl, M. "Greek Inscriptions in the Museum of Tire (Turkey)." *Dialogues d'histoire ancienne* 35 (2009): 186–89.

Ritti, Tullia. *Museo Archeologico di Denizli-Hierapolis: Catalogo delle iscrizioni greche e latine; Distretto di Denizli.* Pubblicazioni del Dipartimento di discipline storiche 25. Naples: Liguori, 2008.

Robert, Louis. "Bulletin épigraphique." *REG* 52 (1939): 445–538.

———. "Bulletin épigraphique." *REG* 92 (1939): 413–541.

———. "Les Inscriptions." Pages 247–389 in *Laodicée du Lycos: Le nymphée; Campagnes 1961–1963.* Edited by J. des Gagniers, P. Devambez, L. Kahl, and R. Ginouves. Quebec: Université Laval, 1969.

Robert, Louis, Jeanne Robert, and Mario Segre. *Hellenica: Recueil d'épigraphie de numismatique et d'antiquitiés grecques.* 13 vols. Limoges: Bontemps, 1940–1948.

Roueché, Charlotte. *Aphrodisias in Late Antiquity: The Late Roman and Byzantine Inscriptions; Including Texts from the Excavations at Aphrodisias Conducted by Kenan T. Erim.* JRSMS 5. London: Society for the Promotion of Roman Studies, 1989.

Russell, Ben. *The Economics of the Roman Stone Trade.* Oxford Studies on the Roman Economy. Oxford: Oxford University Press, 2013.

Sarre, Friedrich P. T. *Reise in Kleinasien, Sommer 1895: Forschungen zur seldjukischen Kunst und Geographie des Landes.* Berlin: Reimer, 1896.

Smith, R. R. R. "Sarcophagi and Roman Citizenship." Pages 347–94 in *New Research on the City and Its Monuments.* Vol. 4 of *Aphrodisias Papers.* Edited by Christopher Ratté and R. R. R. Smith. JRASup 70. Portsmouth, RI: Journal of Roman Archaeology, 2008.

Söğüt, B. "Stratonikeia 2008 Yılı Çalışmaları." *Kazı Sonuçları Toplantısı* 4 (2010): 263–86.

Standhartinger, Angela. "Colossians and the Pauline School." *NTS* 50 (2004): 572–93.

———. "The Origin and Intention of the Household Code in the Letter to the Colossians." *JSNT* 79 (2000): 117–30.

———. *Studien zur Entstehungsgeschichte und Intention des Kolosserbriefes.* NovTSup 94. Leiden: Brill, 1999.

Strelan, R. "The Languages of the Lycus Valley." Pages 77–103 in *Colossae in Space and Time: Linking to an Ancient City.* Edited by Alan H. Cadwallader and Michael Trainor. NTOA 94. Göttingen: Vandenhoeck & Ruprecht, 2011.

Strubbe, Johan H. M. *Arai Epitymbioi: Imprecations against Desecrators of the Grave in the Greek Epitaphs of Asia Minor.* IK 52. Bonn: Habelt, 1997.

Tarán, L. "Plato's Alleged Epitaph." *GRBS* 25 (1984): 63–82.

Thomas, Christine M. "Placing the Dead: Funerary Practice and Social Stratification in the Early Roman Period in Corinth and Ephesos." Pages 281–304 in *Urban Religion in Roman Corinth: Interdisciplinary Approaches.* Edited by Daniel N. Schowalter and Steven J. Friesen. HTS 53. Cambridge: Harvard University Press, 2005.

Thonemann, Peter. "Households and Families in Roman Phrygia." Pages 124–42 in *Roman Phrygia: Culture and Society.* Edited by Peter Thonemann. Greek Culture in the Roman World. Cambridge: Cambridge University Press, 2013.

———. *The Maeander Valley: A Historical Geography from Antiquity to Byzantium.* Cambridge: Cambridge University Press, 2011.

Thonemann, Peter, and F. Ertuğrul, "The Carminii of Attouda." *EA* 38 (2005): 75–85.

Todd, Stephen C. *The Shape of Athenian Law.* Oxford: Clarendon, 1993.

Vernant, Jean-Pierre. Introduction to *La mort, les morts dans les sociétés anciennes.* Edited by Gherardo Gnoli and Jean-Pierre Vernant. Cambridge: Cambridge University Press; Paris: Maison des sciences de l'homme, 1982.

Weber, Georg. "Inschriften aus Sued-Phrygien." *MDAIA* 18 (1893): 206–7.

———. "Der unterirdische Lauf des Lykos bei Kolossai." *MDAIA* 16 (1891): 194–99.

Wilson, Charles William. *Handbook for Travellers in Asia Minor, Transcaucasia, Persia, etc.* London: Murray, 1895.

Wilson, R. McL. *A Critical and Exegetical Commentary on Colossians and Philemon.* ICC. London: T&T Clark, 2005.

Wood, Robert. Journals. Institute of Classical Studies Library (Joint Library of the Hellenic and Roman Societies), University of London.

Wujeski, Tomasz. *Anatolian Sepulchral Stelae in Roman Times.* Seria Historia sztuki 21. Poznán: Uniwersytet im. Adama Mickiewicza w Poznaniu, 1991.
Yıldız, H. "Denizli Müzesi Müdürlüğü Lycos Vadisi Çalışmaları." *Müze Kurtarma Kazıları Semineri* 9 (1999): 247–62.
Yıldız, H. and C. Şimşek, "Sarcofagi a Ghirlande dall Necropoli di Laodicea al Lykos." Pages 99–165 in *Ricerche archeologiche turche nella valle del Lykos.* Edited by Francesco D'Andria and Francesca Silvestrelli. Archeologia e storia (Università degli studi di Lecce, Scuola di specializzazione in archeologia classica e medioevale) 6. Galatina, Lecce: Congedo, 2000.
Zizioulas, John D. *Eucharist, Bishop, Church: The Unity of the Church in the Divine Eucharist and the Bishop during the First Three Centuries.* Brookline, MA: Holy Cross Orthodox Press, 2001.

The Corinthian ΚΑΙΝΑΙ ΚΤΙΣΕΙΣ? Second Corinthians 5:17 and the Roman Refoundation of Corinth

Dominika Kurek-Chomycz and Reimund Bieringer

Introduction

ὥστε εἴ τις ἐν Χριστῷ, καινὴ κτίσις· τὰ ἀρχαῖα παρῆλθεν, ἰδοὺ γέγονεν καινά.[1] These Pauline words were originally addressed to the Corinthians in the middle of the first century CE, in what was possibly Paul's fourth letter to this community, even though only two of them have been passed down to us. Second Corinthians 5:17, and especially Paul's elliptical reference to καινὴ κτίσις, usually translated as "new creation" or "new creature," opened up a wide range of interpretive options for commentators throughout the centuries. Modern scholars tend to neutralize it by focusing on the Jewish background of the idea, implying thereby a significant amount of continuity between Paul and Judaism. Early Christian writers, by contrast, often invoked the notion of new creation to emphasize the tension between continuity in the history of humankind begun with the first creation and discontinuity brought about by the second Adam, that is, by the incarnation and Christ's resurrection. They thus appropriated the idea of new creation as an ingenious device which allowed them to retain tradition (the Old Testament idea of creation and the continuity

---

1. This is the reading accepted by the majority of interpreters and attested in witnesses such as P46 ℵ B C D* F G 048, 0243, 629, 1175, 1739. The elliptical syntax, which is open to different interpretations, is likely to have been the reason for various attempts to "correct" the verse in the process of copying, resulting in two other readings attested in textual tradition: ἰδοὺ γέγονεν τὰ πάντα καινά (6, 33, 81, 365, 614, 630, 1241, 1505, 1881 *pm*) and ἰδοὺ γέγονεν καινὰ τὰ πάντα (D² K L P Ψ 104, 326, 945, 2464 *pm*).

between the Creator God of the Jewish Scriptures and the New Testament Father of Jesus) and to claim the antiquity of their beliefs, while at the same time rejecting traditional (that is, Jewish) interpretations and asserting the validity of (their own) new interpretations. The focus of our contribution, however, is not the text's *Wirkungsgeschichte*, significant as it may be, but rather a suggestion as to how 2 Cor 5:17 may have been read and understood in the context of first-century Corinth as a Roman refoundation of the ancient Hellenic city. It is not our contention that this verse was *intended* by Paul as a polemic against the Roman ideology present in manifold ways in first-century Corinth. We do suggest, however, that 2 Cor 5:17 can be regarded as part of Paul's project, to borrow Peter Oakes's term, of "re-mapping the universe,"[2] analogous to that which we may observe in the Letter to the Philippians (note especially the notion of the heavenly πολίτευμα in Phil 3:20).

We begin with (1) a brief overview of how the Pauline term καινὴ κτίσις in 2 Cor 5:17 has been interpreted in recent scholarship. Next (2) we discuss the use of the verb κτίζω and its cognates in both biblical and extrabiblical Greek.[3] The meaning prevalent in extrabiblical literary and inscriptional evidence, that of a foundation of a city, brings us to the third, and longest, section of the present paper, in which (3) we focus on first century Corinth as a Roman new creation—not *ex nihilo*, but in both continuity *and* discontinuity with the city's Greek past. We then (4), finally, return to 2 Corinthians, in order to show how both the immediate and a broader context of 2 Cor 5:17 could strengthen the reading of this verse against the background of the situation in first-century Roman Corinth. In this section, we focus especially on the reference to the βῆμα of Christ in 2 Cor 5:10, demonstrating how material evidence can throw unexpected

---

2. Compare Peter Oakes, "Re-mapping the Universe: Paul and the Emperor in 1 Thessalonians and Philippians," *JSNT* 27 (2005): 301–22.

3. This distinction is purely functional in that it refers to the various corpora of texts where these terms are attested. It is not intended to imply that "biblical Greek" or "Jewish Greek" is a language distinct from Hellenistic Greek, as was sometimes asserted in the past. See G. H. R. Horsley, "The Fiction of 'Jewish Greek,'" in *Linguistic Essays*, vol. 5 of *New Documents Illustrating Early Christianity*, ed. G. H. R. Horsley (North Ryde, NSW: Ancient History Documentary Research Centre, Macquarie University, 1989), 5–40. A helpful collection of the classic contributions to the debate concerning the status of biblical Greek, albeit with a focus on the New Testament, is provided in Stanley E. Porter, ed., *The Language of the New Testament: Classic Essays*, JSNTSup 60 (Sheffield: JSOT Press, 1991).

insights on how this verse may have resonated among the Corinthians. We also consider whether there is anything in 2 Cor 5:17 or its context that would make impossible or discourage our interpretation. We end with a few concluding reflections.

1. The Interpretation of 2 Cor 5:17 in Recent Biblical Scholarship

The term καινὴ κτίσις appears only twice in the Pauline letters; besides 2 Cor 5:17, Paul refers to it also in Gal 6:15: οὔτε γὰρ περιτομή τί ἐστιν οὔτε ἀκροβυστία ἀλλὰ καινὴ κτίσις. Other New Testament references to new or renewed creation / new humanity are all later, and none of them contains exactly the same formulation.

There is a broad consensus among interpreters that the background of the Pauline notion of καινὴ κτίσις is to be sought in Jewish literature. Of particular importance in this regard are the Deutero-Isaiah references to newness, and, in spite of the absence of exact verbal parallels, Paul's dependence on Isa 43:18–19 is quite plausible in view of other allusions to Isaiah. The connection between Isa 43:18–19 or other Isaiah passages and 2 Cor 5:17 will recur in ancient Christian writings, most remarkably in Tertullian's *Adversus Marcionem*, which ascribes Paul's words to the prophet (*Marc.* 1.20.4).

At the same time, the notion of newness in other prophetic writings, especially in Jeremiah and Ezekiel, and, on the other hand, the disparaging tone of Qohelet need to be kept in mind when exploring the background of the concept. The concept of new creation, and even the phrase itself, appears also in some other Jewish writings.[4] Even though it is unclear with which of these Paul may have been familiar, we can reasonably assume that the concept was known in the late Second Temple Jewish period, and thus the idea of new creation could well have been part of Paul's overarching narrative of God's dealing with the world.

In addition to the background of the expression, among other points that scholars have debated is the more specific denotation of the term, that is, how exactly καινὴ κτίσις should be understood. Since the phrase is

---

4. The phrase occurs in 1 En. 72:1 and Jub. 4:26 (cf. also Jub. 1:29), yet the relevant parts of these books are only extant in Ethiopic. For the concept, but not the exact wording, see also, for example, Wis 19:6 and LAB 3.10. In Paul's own letters, the only other occurrence is in Gal 6:15.

elliptical, the missing elements are variously supplemented in translations, which also include certain exegetical decisions. One major interpretive option, supported by Moyer Hubbard in his monograph,[5] is to understand the phrase anthropologically: "if someone is in Christ, he/she is a new creation/creature." Another possibility, endorsed, among others, by Peter Stuhlmacher,[6] is to interpret the concept cosmologically. This could be rendered in translation as "if someone is in Christ, there is a new (act) of creation." In a more recent contribution to the discussion, T. Ryan Jackson argues that "Paul's conception of new creation has both anthropological as well cosmological dimensions."[7] Finally, according to Mark D. Owens, new creation in Gal 6:15 and 2 Cor 5:17 is to be understood along anthropological, cosmological, and ecclesiological lines.[8]

These differences in the understanding of the scope of the concept notwithstanding, the majority of scholars believe that, at least in the Christian context, Paul was the first to use the phrase. There are also authors, Ulrich Mell in particular, who have suggested that it is a pre-Pauline formula, derived from the community in Antioch, where unrestricted table fellowship was practiced. The formula allegedly would have been developed in polemics with the Jewish concept of the eschatological new creation in order to stress its present significance.[9] There is, however, no evidence for this; we only know that its earliest attestation is in Paul's letters.

2. The Term κτιζω and Its Cognates in Biblical and Extrabiblical Greek

The reasons why exegetes have traditionally focused on the Jewish background of the expression and why the term κτίσις is, as a rule, translated

---

5. Moyer V. Hubbard, *New Creation in Paul's Letters and Thought*, SNTS MS 119 (Cambridge: Cambridge University Press, 2002).

6. Peter Stuhlmacher, "Erwägungen zum ontologischen Charakter der καινὴ κτίσις bei Paulus," *EvT* 27 (1967): 1–35.

7. T. Ryan Jackson, *New Creation in Paul's Letters: A Study of the Historical and Social Setting of a Pauline Concept*, WUNT 2/272 (Tübingen: Mohr Siebeck, 2010), 173.

8. Mark D. Owens, *As It Was in the Beginning: An Intertextual Analysis of New Creation in Galatians, 2 Corinthians, and Ephesians* (Eugene, OR: Pickwick, 2015), 73–87 and 105–9.

9. See Ulrich Mell, *Neue Schöpfung: Eine traditionsgeschichtliche und exegetische Studie zu einem soteriologischen Grundsatz paulinischer Theologie*, BZNW 56 (Berlin: de Gruyter, 1989), 298–303.

as "creation" or "creature" are understandable. It is not our intention to question the appropriateness of translations such as "new creation," but to point out that the term could have other connotations.

In the Septuagint, κτίζω and cognate nouns were employed to denote the creative activity of God and its result, even though this did not exclude the normal Greek usage (see below).[10] The two Hebrew verbs that κτίζω served mainly to translate were ברא and קנה, but occasionally also other Hebrew verbs were thus rendered. More importantly, in the Hebrew Bible there seems to be a distinction made between ברא, denoting God's activity that results in something completely new and dependent solely on God for its coming into existence, and עשה, "to make." The latter can refer to various kinds of activities, and, as opposed to ברא, it is not limited to acts performed by God. When used of God's activity, עשה tends to be employed in reference to God's work on a material that already exists (see Gen 1:7). This distinction appears to have been disregarded by the Septuagint translator(s) of the creation account in Gen 1, who chose to render both ברא and עשה with the same common Greek verb ποιέω. The verb κτίζω and its cognates are absent not only from the creation narratives but also from the translated historical books (Joshua, Judges, 1–4 Kingdoms, 1–2 Chronicles, Ezra, Nehemiah). In Genesis, the verb occurs only twice—in chapter 14 (vv. 19 and 22). Except for the single occurrence of the noun ὁ κτίστης in 2 Kgdms 22:32 (LXX), all the substantives derived from κτίζω, namely, κτίσις (creation), κτίστης (creator), and κτίσμα (creature), in the Septuagint occur only in deuterocanonical books.

In the Pauline letters, κτισ- terms are especially prominent in Romans. Paul's usage seems to be in line with the prevalence in the Septuagint, including the biblical notion of God the Creator, ὁ κτίσας (the substantive κτίστης does not occur in the Pauline letters). Given that Greek was the language spoken by the majority of Paul's addressees, it must not be

---

10. For a helpful overview of the use of κτίζω and cognate nouns, both in the LXX and in other Greek literature, as well as in inscriptions and papyri, see Eberhard Bons and Anna Passoni Dell'Acqua, "A Sample Article: κτίζω, κτίσις, κτίσμα, κτίστης," in *Septuagint Vocabulary: Pre-History, Usage, Reception*, ed. Jan Joosten and Eberhard Bons, SCS 58 (Atlanta: Society of Biblical Literature, 2011), 173–87. See also Eberhard Bons, "Le verbe κτίζω comme terme technique de la création dans la Septante et dans le Nouveau Testament," in *Voces Biblicae: Septuagint Greek and Its Significance for the New Testament*, ed. Jan Joosten and Peter J. Tomson, CBET 49 (Leuven: Peeters, 2007), 1–15.

taken for granted that they would all be familiar with the Septuagint usage. In extrabiblical Greek, beginning with Homer's epics, there is evidence for the use of κτίζω that was to prevail in later Greek literature. Throughout the centuries, the verb and cognate nouns are employed particularly frequently in reference to the establishment, or foundation, of cities, especially the mythical foundation attributed to a divinity or a hero, the κτίστης.[11] This usage is well attested also in inscriptions roughly contemporary with Paul's letters.[12]

In this context the verb is best rendered as "to found," while the English equivalent of the noun κτίσις would be "foundation," in the active sense of the word or in the abstract sense, among others in reference to the foundation of *the* city, Rome. The phrase ἀπὸ κτίσεως Ῥώμης could be used as the Greek equivalent of the Latin expression *ab urbe condita*.[13] Indeed, the semantic domain of the Latin verb *condo, -ere*, and its cognates to a large

---

11. See Bons and Passoni Dell'Acqua, "κτίζω." Compare also Gregory P. Fewster, *Creation Language in Romans 8: A Study in Monosemy*, Linguistic Biblical Studies 8 (Leiden: Brill, 2013), who analyses the lexeme κτίσις in Rom 8 and in Hellenistic Greek by employing "a corpus-driven model of Systemic Functional Monosemy." As he observes, "The first and most common collocates that have significant semantic content (i.e., not a preposition, etc.) are the lexemes πόλεων and πόλεως (of city/cities). In these cases κτίσις is used in terms of the creation or founding of a city" (105). He acknowledges the following: "while the κτίζω-family has a non-divine antecedent, it often operates as part of a formative mythos. For Greco-Roman authors, creation language is part of the recounting and interpretation of a narrative that is considered at least somewhat formative to that society." Even in stating this, Fewster's lack of appreciation for the significance of foundation narratives shines through. He then even more problematically poses a disjunction between, to use his terms, "Greco-Roman authors," on the one hand, and "Jewish and Christian" authors, on the other, associating the former with the "founding of the cities" and the latter with "creation in theological discourse." The confusing and debatable disjunction notwithstanding, apart from a few exceptions he fails to notice the instances where "founding of the cities" is mentioned in Jewish or Christian literature. While his analysis may at first sight seem rigorous and objective, it is difficult not to perceive a certain theological agenda driving this project.

12. See, for example, *SEG* 37.526—an honorific inscription from Nikopolis dated to the first half of the first century, for Dikaia, daughter of Demaretos, referred to as the "first priestess of Artemis after the foundation of the city" (μετὰ τὴν τῆς πόλεως κτίσιν).

13. See Theophilus, *Autol.* 3.27: ὀλυμπιάδι ἑξηκοστῇ καὶ δευτέρᾳ, γίνεται ὁ καιρὸς ἀπὸ κτίσεως Ῥώμης ἔτη σκ'. Notably, the translator in the *Ante-Nicene Fathers* series renders the text as follows: "in the 62d Olympiad, this date falls 220 A.U.C." See also the

extent overlaps with that of κτίζω. In addition to the establishment of cities or other inhabited entities, in first century Greek literary and epigraphic evidence, the verb κτίζω and the substantive κτίσις are also attested, likewise in line with earlier usage, to denote the institution of festivals and games, and the establishment of public buildings and structures such as temples, theatres, streets, city walls, baths, and so on.

This meaning of κτίζω in reference to the foundation of cities is also present in the Septuagint. First Esdras shows that the term could occur in the same writing with the sense "to found (a city)" and "to create (the world)."[14] Similarly, in later Christian literature the classical Greek usage continues to be well attested alongside the references to the divine act of creation and its result. To return to the first century, however, it is of interest to note that the only place where the phrase καινὴ κτίσις is used in a first-century writing outside the New Testament, albeit in the plural, καιναὶ κτίσεις, is Flavius Josephus's reference to new Jewish settlements in *Ant.* 18.373. Flavius Josephus, in whose writings the substantive κτίσις occurs about fifteen times, most of the time also uses it in the sense "foundation"/"establishment" (but cf. *B.J.* 4.533). Philo of Alexandria employs the term only once, in *Mos.* 2.51, but the context is also noteworthy. He observes that Moses did not wish to begin his writings with the foundation of a city made with human hands (πόλεώς τε χειροποιήτου κτίσις), as it was below the dignity of the laws (κατὰ τὴν ἀξίαν τῶν νόμων). This is a possible reference to Livy's renowned *Ab urbe condita*, but also a polemical allusion to the foundation legends of which various Greek and Roman cities were proud. Instead, Philo continues, Moses narrated the genesis of the Great City, deeming that the laws were the image most resembling the constitution of the world (τοὺς νόμους ἐμφερεστάτην εἰκόνα τῆς τοῦ κόσμου πολιτείας ἡγησάμενος εἶναι). This shows that in the mind of a first-century Jewish author there was no disjunction between the mean-

---

repeated use of the verb κτίζω in reference to the founding of Rome in Plutarch's *Romulus*, including the genitive absolute construction in *Rom.* 13.1: κτισθείσης τῆς πόλεως.

14. Compare 1 Esd 4:53 (καὶ πᾶσιν τοῖς προσβαίνουσιν ἀπὸ τῆς Βαβυλωνίας <u>κτίσαι τὴν πόλιν</u> ὑπάρχειν τὴν ἐλευθερίαν αὐτοῖς τε καὶ τοῖς τέκνοις αὐτῶν καὶ πᾶσι τοῖς ἱερεῦσι τοῖς προσβαίνουσιν; rendered in NETS as follows: "and that all who would come from Babylonia to found the city should have their freedom, both they and their children and all the priests who would come") with 1 Esd 6:12 (οἱ δὲ ἀπεκρίθησαν ἡμῖν λέγοντες ἡμεῖς ἐσμεν παῖδες τοῦ κυρίου <u>τοῦ κτίσαντος τὸν οὐρανὸν καὶ τὴν γῆν</u>; NETS: "But they answered us, 'We are the servants of the Lord who created heaven and earth'").

ing "to found" (a city) and "to create" (the world). At the same time, Philo's text exemplifies how the term could be used in a polemical context, in an attempt to demonstrate the superiority of Jewish over against Greek and Roman ways of conceiving of history.

3. First Century Corinth as a Roman New Creation

We may presume that Paul's Corinthian addressees knew, better than we do today, the content of Paul's message about καινὴ κτίσις, which still remains elusive for us. Especially if Paul spent as much time in Corinth as Luke tells us that he did (see Acts 18—but even if one does not regard the Lukan account as reliable, Paul's own letters testify to a close relationship between Paul and the Corinthians), it is likely that the Corinthians would have been acquainted with the narrative that underlies Paul's theological reflection. This is also the narrative that he must have made more explicit in the course of his proclamation in Corinth: the story of God the Creator who in Jesus Christ, faithful to his promises expressed in the prophetic writings, was creating the world anew. At the same time, they lived in a city which was a—relatively—new Roman foundation. The ancient city of Corinth, completely destroyed by the Romans in 146 BCE, was then refounded as a Roman colony by—at least officially—Julius Caesar in 44 BCE. In spite of the fact that the place was most likely not completely deserted in the interim period, there is virtually no evidence of civic continuity between the two Corinths. In addition to Paul's story, the Corinthians were constantly confronted with the Roman narrative about their native city, which they could encounter expressed in manifold ways in the streets, temples, and other public spaces in Corinth. In spite of our limited knowledge about first-century Corinth, archaeological excavations unambiguously suggest that this was a story of a Roman colony, with the Greek past appropriated and transformed by the Roman colonizers to serve their own ends. We may note that this story differs to a significant extent from the story that Pausanias will tell in the second century in book 2 of his *Description of Greece*, the story of the Greek Corinth and its continuity, deliberately playing down the Roman character of the refounded city. A good many historians and archaeologists take Pausanias's version of the story for granted, as if it were a photographic representation of reality, which even modern guidebooks are not.

Whether intended by Paul or not, in spite of the limitations of our knowledge about Paul's original audience, what we know about first-century Roman Corinth, based not only on literary but also on material evidence, throws light on how 2 Cor 5:17 may have resonated among the Corinthians when the letter was read to them, possibly in the autumn of the year 54 CE.[15]

Roman Corinth was a Roman colony, and thus a new Roman creation, καινὴ κτίσις or κτίσμα. While the term κτίσις is often used in the abstract sense or in reference to the act of founding, κτίσμα as a rule denotes the material result. We note in this context an interesting inscription from another Roman colony. In a third century inscription from Philippi, a foreigner claims to have been ordered by a δαίμων to die in the famous land of the city founded by Philip and Augustus:

Δαίμων δέ μ' ἐκέλευσε θανεῖν κλυτῆς ἐπὶ γαίης
κτίσματος Φιλίπποιο καὶ Αὐγούστου βασιλῆος[16]

The inscription attests that (1) it was possible for a city to have two founders, κτίσται, and (2) that the memory of the founding figures would have survived throughout the centuries. In addition, it is also important to note that the act of "foundation," κτίσις, by no means needs to refer to creation *ex nihilo*, which it does not mean either in the Septuagint or in the New Testament. Philip of Macedon was the person after whom the city was named, even though it had existed earlier; Augustus was the one with whose name the foundation of Philippi as a Roman colony was associated. At least based on a preliminary review, no comparable inscription has been

---

15. Giving any absolute date in reference to Paul's letters is always fraught with difficulties and to a significant extent remains guesswork. In the case of 2 Corinthians, the additional complication is associated with the disputes about the letter's unity and integrity. In what follows we assume the unity of 2 Corinthians, but even if there had been several separate letters sent to Corinth, this would not substantially affect our argument. With regard to Paul's chronology, for a balanced discussion, see Loveday Alexander, "Chronology of Paul," in *Dictionary of Paul and His Letters*, ed. Gerald F. Hawthorne, Ralph P. Martin, and Daniel G. Reid (Downers Grove, IL: InterVarsity Press, 1993), 115–23. It must be noted that Alexander shares the general scholarly optimism concerning the precision with which the Gallio inscription allows us to date Paul's encounter with Gallio. For a cautionary note, see Dixon Slingerland, "Acts 18:1–18, the Gallio Inscription, and Absolute Pauline Chronology," *JBL* 110 (1991): 439–49.

16. For the text of the inscription, commentary, and bibliography, see Peter Pilhofer, *Katalog der Inschriften von Philippi*, vol. 2 of *Philippi*, WUNT 119 (Tübingen: Mohr Siebeck, 2000), 301–4.

found in Corinth—although we need to remember that for Corinth the number of inscriptions excavated is rather limited, and that especially for the earlier period they are almost exclusively in Latin. This would change only in subsequent centuries.

The term κτίστης, initially used in reference to gods or heroes, mythical "founders" of cities, did not necessarily imply the original founder and is attested in its use in connection with benefaction throughout the Roman East, even prior to the imperial period. It is well known that in the Roman East there are numerous inscriptions honoring the emperor Hadrian as a κτίστης, often coupled with εὐεργέτης and σωτήρ, yet the use of these titles goes back to a much earlier period. The title κτίστης was also used for Alexander the Great. In the Roman context, already in the first century BCE, at the end of the Republican period, Pompey the Great was honoured in Mytilene as "benefactor, savior, and founder" (εὐεργέτης, σωτὴρ καὶ κτίστης).[17]

In Corinth there is a fourth-century inscription honouring Flavius Hermogenes, proconsul of Achaia between 353 and 358 CE, who is referred to as εὐεργέτης (benefactor) and κτίστης τοῦ λι[μένος], κτίστης of the harbor, "for the improvements he made at the Corinthian harbor of Lechaion."[18] Lechaion obviously existed many centuries before Flavius Hermogenes made improvements in it. Thus he was surely not its original "founder," yet this use of the noun is consistent with the use of the noun in the Roman imperial context.

In assessing possible associations the Corinthians would have made with regard to Roman Corinth as a καινὴ κτίσις, two points need to be kept in mind—and in balance. Roman Corinth was a Roman colony, founded and most likely laid out according to standard procedures for a Roman colony.[19] In the middle of the first century, Corinth still remained to some

---

17. See, for example, *SEG* 3:693; *IG* 12.2.141, 163, 165. Interestingly, in one of these inscriptions (*IG* 12.2.163), not only Pompey but also his client and friend, Theophanes, is honored as "savior, benefactor, and second founder of the fatherland" (Θεοφάνη τῷ σωτῆρι καὶ εὐεργέτᾳ καὶ κτίστᾳ δευτέρῳ τᾶς πάτριδος). Translations are those of the authors unless noted otherwise.

18. IKorinthKent 503: Φλάβιον Ἑρμ[ο]γένην | τὸν λαμ(πρότατον) ἀνθύπατον | ἡ βουλὴ καὶ ὁ δῆμος ὁ Κορινθίων | τὸν εὐεργέτην καὶ κτίστην τοῦ λι[μένος] ἀνέθηκαν.

19. See especially Mary E. Hoskins Walbank, "The Foundation and Planning of Early Roman Corinth," *JRA* 10 (1997): 95–130. Note the recent criticisms of the idea that there was a standard procedure in this regard, but this pertains mostly to the republican era. Compare Edward Bispham, "*Coloniam deducere*: How Roman Was

extent a construction site, its spatial design involving a carefully calculated program of display of imperial propaganda. Not only literary, but also epigraphic, sculptural, numismatic, and other material evidence can help us envisage the narrative inherent in the landscape of *Colonia Laus Iulia Corinthiensis*, designed constantly to remind the inhabitants and visitors alike of Corinth's new rulers. At the same time, the Roman foundation of Corinth was a refoundation of a famous ancient Hellenic city, and Romans were well aware of its illustrious past. While asserting their power, Romans presented the new order as both new *and* ancient, grounded in the past, and thus worthy of respect. They did this inter alia by reusing ancient Greek cultic sites, and in this way co-opting the tradition of pre-Roman Corinth for their own ends. When we speak about Romans in the Corinthian context, it is important to note that the emperor was not directly involved in the decisions concerning the everyday functioning of the colony. These decisions were made by the local administration, and thus the enthusiasm of the ruling elite for the imperial family—as evidenced, for example, on coins—is a result of a much more complex and subtle process than a straightforward imperial ruling would have been.

Even though the importance of the Roman imperial context for the understanding of the New Testament, and of the Pauline letters in particular, has been emphasized, especially in the scholarship of the last decade, only in one of the most recent monographs devoted to καινὴ κτίσις (in 2010) has the Roman Empire been mentioned as a context in which Paul's words would have been received by his addressees. While the authors of the two earlier monographs on the subject limited themselves to the Jewish background of the Pauline notion of καινὴ κτίσις, T. Ryan Jackson includes a discussion of Roman imperial ideology, noting especially the importance of the image of the Augustan period as the paradisiacal Golden Age of happiness—the time of cosmic transformation—as propagated by various media, including both literary sources such as Virgil's famous Fourth Eclogue and monuments such as the well-known *Ara Pacis*, the altar of Augustan peace.[20]

Roman Colonization during the Middle Republic?," in *Greek and Roman Colonization: Origins, Ideologies and Interactions*, ed. Guy Bradley and John-Paul Wilson (Swansea: Classical Press of Wales, 2006), 73–160.

20. Jackson, *New Creation*, 60–80. Owens, *As It Was in the Beginning*, 14–42 and 43–67, only considers biblical (especially Isaian) and Second Temple Judaism texts as potential parallels. The title of another recent contribution, an unpublished doctoral dissertation by Sejong Chun, "Paul's New Creation: Vision for a New World and

However, he only very briefly comments on the specific Corinthian situation, limiting his remarks mostly to the imperial cult, through which "the ideology of *Romanitas* was communicated most blatantly."[21] Yet as Price reminds us, "there was no such thing as 'the imperial cult,' and in some important contexts, imitation of the transformed system of Augustan Rome was of far greater significance than direct worship of the emperor."[22]

The comment of Aulus Gellius (*Noct. att.* 16.13.8–9) that Roman colonies were "small copies and representations of Rome" (*effigies parvae simulacraque*) is often repeated in this context. Indeed, colonies mirrored various institutions of the city of Rome, and colonial charters constituted a means through which Romans could impose their culture, manners, and morality; but what is more, to quote James Walters, "Roman officials had even devised foundation rituals for colonies that echoed the mythical foundation of Rome: auspices were taken, and the founder ploughed a furrow around the site to mark the *pomerium*."[23]

As a Roman κτίσις, *Colonia Laus Iulia Corinthiensis* must have had its founder, κτίστης. The mythical founder of Greek Corinth was Corinthus.[24] But what about Roman Corinth? Even if Julius Caesar planned it, modern historians suggest that his plans were not realized before March 44 BCE. Support for the hypothesis that the colony was officially founded only after March 44, as Mary Walbank notes, is found in a detailed study of

---

Community in the Midst of Empires" (PhD diss., Vanderbilt University, 2012), could imply that the author engages with the Roman imperial context at more length. The author's focus, however, is on a contextual reading that would be "most beneficial for the Korean immigrant churches." As far as we can see, his work does not contribute in a substantial way to our understanding of the Roman context of the Pauline notion of new creation.

21. Jackson, *New Creation*, 68.

22. S. R. F. Price, "The Place of Religion: Rome in the Early Empire," in *The Augustan Empire, 43 B.C.–A.D. 69*, vol. 10 of *The Cambridge Ancient History*, ed. Alan K. Bowman, Edward Champlin, and Andrew Lintott, 2nd ed. (Cambridge: Cambridge University Press, 1996), 841.

23. James C. Walters, "Civic Identity in Roman Corinth and Its Impact on Early Christians," in *Urban Religion in Roman Corinth: Interdisciplinary Approaches*, ed. Daniel N. Schowalter and Steven J. Friesen, HTS 53 (Cambridge: Harvard University Press, 2005), 401.

24. Interestingly, in an inscription from the Greek period, dated to 341 BCE, Corinthus is referred to as κτιστήρ (IKorinthKent 23).

duovirate coinage by Michel Amandry.[25] Ancient historians tend to attribute the foundation to Augustus, but it is possible that actually the settlement and implementation of Julius Caesar's plans were Anthony's doing. Yet as a result of his *damnatio memoriae* in 30 BCE, the memory of this was erased, and apparently in the case of Anthony's colonial foundations, Augustus "took credit for his fellow triumvirs' foundations as well."[26]

Eventually it is thus these two figures, Caesar and Augustus, who came to be associated with the foundation of Roman Corinth. This connection was reflected in the most representative part of the city, the forum, where three new temples were built, all of them small "jewel temples," promoting cults closely linked to the emperor and to Rome: temple D, dedicated to Tyche/Fortuna; temple G, to Clarian Apollo, progenitor of Augustus, thus to celebrate the cult of Augustus; temple F, to Venus Genetrix, mother of the Roman colony and of the Roman nation—all three cults with close ties to *gens Iulia* and to Rome. As for the last of these temples, it has been suggested that it was built in direct imitation of the Temple of Venus Genetrix, dedicated by Julius Caesar in 46 BCE and completed by Augustus.

The cult of Julius Caesar himself is also attested in Corinth in a fragmentary inscription that reads divo iul[io] caesari,[27] dated either in the late Republic or in the very early Empire, suggesting that Caesar was worshiped in this Roman colony from very early on. As Walbank notes, "That the Corinthians regarded Julius Caesar as the founder of their colony … is made clear by the foundation coin issue, dated to 44–43 B.C., which has the laureate head of Caesar and the exceptionally full ethnic LAUS IULII CORINT—*Colonia Laus Iulia Corinthensis*—on the obverse."[28] Walbank also draws attention to yet another, much later issue of coins—dated by Amandry to 32/33 or 33/34 CE—on which a hexastyle temple is represented, usually inscribed with the words gent(i) or GENT(is) iuli(ae) on the architrave. No such inscription to Gens Iulia is found among the provincial coinages, and Walbank suggests that these Tiberian coins were an anniversary issue commemorating the original dedication of the temple

---

25. Walbank, "Foundation," 98; the study she refers to is Michel Amandry, *Le monnayage des duovirs corinthiens*, BCHSup 15 (Paris: de Boccard, 1988).

26. Walbank, "Foundation," 98.

27. Mary E. Hoskins Walbank, "Evidence for the Imperial Cult in Julio-Claudian Corinth," in *Subject and Ruler: The Cult of the Ruling Power in Classical Antiquity*, ed. Alastair Small, JRASup 17 (Ann Arbor, MI: Journal of Roman Archaeology, 1996), 201.

28. Ibid., 201.

soon after the foundation of the colony. These coins were likely still in circulation when Paul arrived in Corinth in the year 49. This particular coin issue, primarily meant to keep alive the memory of the dedication of a temple devoted to the gens of the original founder of the colony and thus also to keep alive the memory of the act of foundation as such, is typical of the Roman preoccupation with anniversaries.[29]

It would be wrong to think that the idea was necessarily imposed by the central authority, however. We need to remember that those directly responsible for the ongoing re-creation of Corinth were mostly members of the Corinthian elite, eager to serve and to please the emperor, but at the same time interested in promoting their own city as distinct from other colonies. In this way the Pauline notion of καινὴ κτίσις could be viewed by the members of the Corinthian community not only as a challenge to Roman rule in general, but more specifically as an alternative to the civic identity propagated in Roman Corinth. The decisions concerning both the architectural design and other visual elements, which affected the experiences of inhabitants and visitors alike, rested with the local authorities. Their enthusiasm for the imperial family is well evidenced not only on coins but also in sculptures representing members of the imperial family densely populating another new building of particular public significance, the Julian basilica.

As has often been observed, as a typical colony—Rome "in miniature"—*Colonia Laus Iulia Corinthiensis* also should have had its Capitolium, a temple dedicated to the main Roman deities, the Capitoline triad (Jupiter, Juno, and Minerva). To date, however, there is no consensus among scholars as to where the Corinthian Capitolium could have been located. While some identify it with temple E, commonly known as the Temple of Octavia, based on one possible way of reading Pausanias, this is by no means certain.[30]

---

29. Compare Walbank, "Evidence," 204, who further adds that "the year A.D. 33/34 was a significant one in the Roman calendar. It was the 20th anniversary of the death of Augustus and the accession of Tiberius. It also commemorated the two most important dates in the reign of Augustus, namely the 60th anniversary of the *respublica restituta* in 27 B.C. and the 50th anniversary of the *ludi seculares* of 17 B.C. It was the kind of multiple anniversary that was dear to the Romans and it was widely observed both at Rome and on provincial coinages. The Corinthians were ... peculiarly attentive to the Julio-Claudians in this regard, faithfully recording events in the political and domestic life of the imperial family ... on the civic coinage."

30. See Nancy Bookidis, "Religion in Corinth: 146 B.C.E. to 100 C.E.," in Schow-

Whether imperial cult was the most blatant way of communicating the ideology, we must not forget that the Roman refoundation of ancient Corinth involved a broad range of means of communication, and, most importantly, it involved the tension between newness and the Roman appropriation of the Greek past of the city. In this respect two elements may be mentioned. While Roman colonists brought some new cults, they also reused four of the well-known ancient Greek cultic sites: the Sanctuary of Aphrodite on top of Acrocorinth, the Sanctuary of Demeter and Kore on the northern slope of Acrocorinth, the Temple of Apollo off the Forum, and the Sanctuary of Asklepios near the northern city wall.[31] Yet rather than viewing it simply as an attempt to enhance the value of the Greek past, we can interpret the choice of the authorities to reuse the ancient cultic sites as an attempt to appropriate the memory of this past in asserting their own power.

A second element is the revival of the Isthmian games under Roman rule. Athletics often tend to be presented as a particularly strong marker of Greek identity, and the Greek character of the inscriptions about the Isthmian games seems to confirm this. However, as the Dutch historian Onno van Nijf has convincingly argued:

> The Greek festive culture of the Roman period was appropriated to serve the needs both of the local elites, and of the central authorities in Rome. It mobilized the resources of a glorious Greek past enabling urban elites

---

alter and Friesen, *Urban Religion in Roman Corinth*, 141–64, who lists both the supporters of the identification of this temple as a Capitolium (155) and those who "assume that Pausanias is essentially right, but associate the temple with the imperial cult" (156).

31. Bookidis, "Religion in Corinth," 151–64, provides a lucid overview. See also Christine M. Thomas, "Greek Heritage in Roman Corinth and Ephesos: Hybrid Identities and Strategies of Display in the Material Record of Traditional Mediterranean Religions," in *Corinth in Context: Comparative Studies on Religion and Society*, ed. Steven J. Friesen, Daniel N. Schowalter, and James C. Walters, NovTSup 134 (Leiden: Brill, 2010), 117–47. As Thomas notes, while "Corinth shows an interesting mix of continuity and discontinuity in its religious sites between the Classical-Hellenistic periods and its Roman colonization" (119), there is much evidence for discontinuity even in the case of the reuse of the ancient Greek sites. With regard to cultic practice, Thomas observes, "Instead of 'refoundation,' which suggests cultic continuity, a more accurate term might be 'revival' or 'renewal,' which would parallel the renewals of long-forgotten cults and priesthoods in the city of Rome by Augustus during the same period, renewals which often involved significant changes" (123).

to display their social superiority in several ways. But at the same time it was clearly focused on Rome and the emperor, who ultimately underwrote the hierarchical world view of which it was an expression. Festivals were in many ways an invented tradition that effectively blurred the boundaries between Greek and Roman."[32]

This is an important caveat for those who are tempted to see in the Isthmian games—which are often mentioned in commentaries in the context of Paul's athletic metaphor in 1 Cor 9:24–27—an assertion of Greek identity and a straightforward continuation of the illustrious tradition of one of the four crown games of the Greek period. Ultimately even the Isthmian athletic games were a Roman reinvention, or restoration, a καινὴ κτίσις, of a Greek tradition.

4. Back to 2 Cor 5:17 and Its Surrounding Context

Let us now return to the text of 2 Cor 5. The inferential particle ὥστε ("so that") in verses 16 and 17 refers back to verses 14–15. Verse 16 describes Paul's change of perspective, due to what he expressed in verse 14ab, while verse 17 is more directly connected with verses 14c–15. All these verses, however, are tightly interconnected: the main thrust seems to be that the consequence of the Christ event (Christ's death and resurrection) is a radically altered perception. We suggest that, as the Corinthians were listening to Paul's words, they were also challenged to question the way in which their own perception was shaped by the surrounding context. We first note a couple of other elements in chapter 5 that the Corinthians would have heard first and foremost as a metaphor of which the source domain was in the political sphere. Some scholars have suggested that the terminology of reconciliation, in particular the verb καταλλάσσω and the noun καταλλαγή, belong mainly to the political (diplomatic) context,[33] and Paul's

---

32. Onno van Nijf, "Local Heroes: Athletics, Festivals and Elite Self-Fashioning in the Roman East," in *Being Greek under Rome: Cultural Identity, the Second Sophistic and the Development of Empire*, ed. Simon Goldhill (Cambridge: Cambridge University Press, 2001), 334.

33. See, for instance, Cilliers Breytenbach, *Versöhnung: Eine Studie zur paulinischen Soteriologie*, WMANT 60 (Neukirchen-Vluyn: Neukirchener Verlag, 1989), 80: "Wir kommen zu dem *Schluß*, daß die Verwendung der Versöhnungsterminologie bei Paulus eine Übertragung einer ursprünglich diplomatischen Vorstellung auf das Verhältnis Gott—Mensch bzw. Gott—Apostel ist."

use of these terms in 2 Corinthians is quite innovative. It will later be taken over in Romans and become part of the standard theological vocabulary of Christianity.³⁴ The political connotation is even more evident when in 5:20 Paul presents himself as an ambassador for Christ. As often noted by commentators, "the verb πρεσβεύω and the noun πρεσβευτής are found in inscriptions in connection with the legates of the Emperor." ³⁵

In a broader context of the letter, the imagery of the triumph in 2 Cor 2:14 is the clearest example of a metaphor evoking an imperial context (whether it was intended in a polemical sense or not). As suggested recently by Christoph Heilig, it could perhaps allude even more particularly to one specific triumph that took place during Paul's lifetime, namely that celebrated by Emperor Claudius in 44 CE, following his British campaign.³⁶

While in 2 Cor 2:14 the Corinthians would have been likely to hear an allusion to the Roman institution of triumph, implying obviously that the one celebrating the triumph was God, not the Roman emperor, we would like to suggest that in 2 Cor 5 we encounter a reference that would have been more evocative of the *local* Corinthian context. The reference to the βῆμα τοῦ Χριστοῦ in 5:10 would have made the Corinthians recall the architectural design of their own, continuously refurbished city. The term βῆμα was significant *not* because this is where the author of Acts situates Paul's appearance before Gallio in Acts 18:12–17. The historicity

---

34. Reimund Bieringer, "Verzoening met God in 2 Korintiërs 5,18–21: Een voorbeeld van paulinische theologie in wording," *Collationes* 39 (2009): 21–30.

35. Margaret E. Thrall, *Commentary on 2 Corinthians I–VII*, vol. 1 of *The Second Epistle to the Corinthians*, ICC (Edinburgh: T&T Clark, 1994), 436; see also the monograph of Anthony Bash, *Ambassadors for Christ: An Exploration of Ambassadorial Language in the New Testament*, WUNT 2/92 (Tübingen: Mohr Siebeck, 1997), 88: "explicit ambassadorial language."

36. See Christoph Heilig, *Paul's Triumph: Reassessing 2 Corinthians 2:14 in Its Literary and Historical Context*, BiTS 27 (Leuven: Peeters, 2016), 129–36. Compare also Heilig's evaluation of the various previously suggested attempts to understand the imagery. Among the more influential in recent decades has been Paul Duff's article, in which he argued that 2 Cor 2:14 is to be understood against the backdrop of religious epiphany processions such as the one described in Apuleius, *Met.* 11 (see Paul Brooks Duff, "Metaphor, Motif, and Meaning: The Rhetorical Strategy behind the Image 'Led in Triumph' in 2 Corinthians 2:14," *CBQ* 53 [1991]: 79–92). Yet the verb θριαμβεύω is sufficiently attested in Greek literature to warrant the conclusion that in whatever metaphorical sense it may have been used, in the first century it would most naturally be taken as referring to a celebration of the Roman triumph.

and accuracy of this text is debatable; thus to suggest that the Corinthians may have thought of this event when hearing the reference to the βῆμα in 2 Cor 5:10 is rather speculative. It is far more important to observe that the βῆμα was one of the focal elements of civic life, conveniently located "near the administrative offices at the east end of the South Stoa, and an ideal place to address a large crowd."[37] This is where formal announcements were made by Roman officials, where orations were delivered, and where tribunals took place. Possibly also, the "meetings of the *comitia*, at which city officials were elected, took place in the open forum in the vicinity of the *rostra*."[38] The Latin term *rostra* is used in two first-century inscriptions, cut on different elements of the structure, with "an elaborate, marble superstructure with benches in the corners and piers which formed a triple entrance from the rear."[39] Notably, yet another inscription has been found, dated to the first part of the second century CE, which includes a part of a rescript of a decree, issued probably by the governor of Achaia, allowing a certain Priscus to erect a building at Isthmia. The text is in Greek, but it is followed by a Latin addition underneath (very fragmentary), explaining when the decree was issued and where it was publicly read: *pro rostris lecta*.[40]

To those familiar with the architecture of ancient Rome, the term *rostra* would bring to mind the famous speakers' platform on the Forum Romanum, or rather two of them: the old republican rostra, decorated with the prows (*rostra*) of the ships commemorating the victory over Antiates in 338 BCE and restored in 42 BCE as part of the program of the triumvirs' alleged "restoration of the republic," and the second, erected by Augustus, opposite, in the temple of deified Caesar. The new rostra, this time decorated with the prows of Egyptian ships captured after Octavian's victory over Mark Anthony in the Battle of Actium (September of 31 BCE), as Paul Zanker comments, "consciously set up a comparison between a vic-

---

37. Walbank, "Foundation," 121.
38. Ibid.
39. Ibid.; for the inscriptions, see IKorinthKent 157 and 322. When commenting on the latter, Kent observes that there is sufficient "epigraphical evidence to support the following statements: (1) the large rectangular structure in the center of the Roman Forum (Agora) at Corinth was indeed the Bema, (2) this structure was known officially as the Rostra, and (3) its marble revetments date from the first half of the first century after Christ, probably from the second quarter of the century" (IKorinth 129).
40. IKorinthKent 306.

tory in civil war and a historic naval victory of the old Republic."[41] Based on the scattered remains, archaeologists have concluded that, as Robert Scranton puts it, "the arrangements are strikingly similar to those of the Rostra in Rome."[42]

There is no question that the structure was a focal point of the Corinthian forum, and while it is debated at which point specific elements of the βῆμα, or rather rostra, were added, scholars tend to agree that it was completed by the middle of the first century,[43] thus not long before Paul arrived there. Not only was the structure impressive, but it is also likely that the unusual square base in its vicinity is the *locus gromae*, the base on which the *groma*, the principal Roman surveying instrument, was originally set up when the urban grid was being laid out—an integral part of the colonial foundation procedure—accompanied by a specific ritual. This would therefore be the place where the act of the foundation of the colony, its κτίσις, was particularly remembered, while the never-ending additions to the city's landscape witnessed to its continuous renewal. Paul's reference to the βῆμα of Christ would remind the Corinthians of their own rostra/βῆμα, and the subsequent reference to καινὴ κτίσις in verse 17 would have triggered a nexus of associations related to their own experiences of the city.

Assuming the possibility, maybe even the probability that the original Corinthian addressees would have interpreted καινὴ κτίσις in 2 Cor 5:17a as new creation in light of the metaphor of the new foundation of a city, we now need to reread 2 Cor 5:14–21, especially the immediate context of 5:17, in order to examine whether there is anything in the text that would make impossible or discourage such an interpretation, and, on the other hand, we need to search for aspects in the text that would support such an interpretation. The most immediate test of the hypothesis concerns τὰ ἀρχαῖα παρῆλθεν, ἰδοὺ γέγονεν καινά in 5:17b. These two paratactic clauses,

---

41. Paul Zanker, *The Power of Images in the Age of Augustus*, trans. Alan Shapiro, Jerome Lectures 16 (Ann Arbor: University of Michigan Press, 1990), 81.

42. Robert L. Scranton, *Monuments in the Lower Agora and North of the Archaic Temple*, vol. 1.3 of *Corinth: Results of Excavations Conducted by the American School of Classical Studies at Athens* (Princeton: American School of Classical Studies at Athens, 1951), 128.

43. Compare Scranton's suggestion: "Possibly the construction of the Bema marked the return of the city, in A.D. 44, after its capital had been replenished, to its dignity as capital of Achaea, when the need of a place for public, official oratory would have been marked" (ibid., 130).

which are antithetical (τὰ ἀρχαῖα versus καινά; παρῆλθεν versus γέγονεν) and chiastic (abcb´a´), explain the meaning of the adjective καινή in the expression καινὴ κτίσις. A καινὴ κτίσις has become necessary since the ἀρχαῖα κτίσις has passed away; it has come to its end. The καινὴ κτίσις is explained with the words γέγονεν καινά, that is, "new things have come into being."[44] If it is correct that καινὴ κτίσις borrows its metaphorical strength from the foundation of a new city, then 5:17b, if it continues along the lines of the same metaphor, would need to be read as speaking about the destruction of the old city and the founding of a new one. Looking at the language of 5:17b, such an interpretation does not immediately impose itself, but it is not impossible either. The verb παρέρχομαι is used in the Bible of something that passes away in the sense of coming to an end (as, e.g., God's anger in Isa 26:20 or a storm in Isa 28:15). The meaning of the verb γίνομαι is so general that it can hardly be used as evidence in one way or another.

Many interpreters are convinced that in 5:17b Paul heavily relies on Isa 43:18–19 (LXX)[45]: (v. 18) μὴ μνημονεύετε τὰ πρῶτα καὶ τὰ ἀρχαῖα μὴ συλλογίζεσθε (v. 19) ἰδοὺ ποιῶ καινὰ ἃ νῦν ἀνατελεῖ καὶ γνώσεσθε αὐτὰ καὶ ποιήσω ἐν τῇ ἐρήμῳ ὁδὸν καὶ ἐν τῇ ἀνύδρῳ ποταμούς.[46] This is the only biblical text besides 2 Cor 5:17 where the adjectives ἀρχαῖος and καινός occur together (and in antithesis) including the same use or disuse of the definite article (τὰ ἀρχαῖα and καινά). In Isa 43:19 (LXX) ἰδοὺ ποιῶ καινὰ is explained with the metaphors of making a road in the desert and of making a river in the dry land. In this light, it may not be so unusual to explain ἰδοὺ γέγονεν καινά by means of the new foundation of a formerly destroyed city.[47]

---

44. See Victor Paul Furnish, *II Corinthians: A New Translation with Introduction and Commentary*, AB 32A (Garden City, NY: Doubleday, 1984), 316, who favors the translation: "new things have come to be" rather than "they are become new." So also Murray J. Harris, *The Second Epistle to the Corinthians: A Commentary on the Greek Text*, NIGTC (Grand Rapids: Eerdmans; Milton Keynes: Paternoster, 2005), 434. Compare *Stuttgarter Neues Testament: Einheitsübersetzung mit Kommentar und Erklärungen*, 5th ed. (Stuttgart: Katholisches Bibelwerk, 2010): "Neues ist geworden."

45. See Harris, *Second Epistle*, 433: "in terminology (but not in content)."

46. NETS: "Do not remember the former things or consider the things of old. Look, I am doing new things that will now spring forth, and you will know them, and I will make a way in the wilderness and rivers in the dry land."

47. Note also Isa 54:16–17a (LXX), which differs remarkably from the MT: (v. 16) ἰδοὺ ἐγὼ κτίζω σε οὐχ ὡς χαλκεὺς φυσῶν ἄνθρακας καὶ ἐκφέρων σκεῦος εἰς ἔργον ἐγὼ δὲ ἔκτισά σε οὐκ εἰς ἀπώλειαν φθεῖραι (v. 17) πᾶν σκεῦος φθαρτόν (NETS: "See, I create you,

In fact, that latter idea is also rather common in Isaiah, for whom the rebuilding of ruined cities is a prevalent idea of the newness that the return from the exile encompasses. The most relevant text is found in Isa 61:4: καὶ οἰκοδομήσουσιν ἐρήμους αἰωνίας ἐξηρημωμένας πρότερον ἐξαναστήσουσιν καὶ καινιοῦσιν πόλεις ἐρήμους ἐξηρημωμένας εἰς γενεάς.[48] Here οἰκοδομήσουσιν ἐρήμους αἰωνίας and καινιοῦσιν πόλεις ἐρήμους are more or less synonymous parallels. There is an antithetical parallel between old and new (αἰωνίας vs. καινιοῦσιν) as well as a parallel between building up and renewing (οἰκοδομήσουσιν and καινιοῦσιν). If we compare the building up of desert places and the renewing of desert cities with 2 Cor 5:17b, it is clear that Isa 61:4 does not speak of the old as having come to its end, as Paul is saying in 2 Cor 5:17b: τὰ ἀρχαῖα παρῆλθεν. The old is rather being rebuilt and renewed; it has not passed away. This could, however, be due to a need in Isaiah (we do not perceive any differences in this regard in the Hebrew and the Greek texts) to stress the continuity. Paul, on the other hand, seems to be opting for a radical discontinuity. Different terminology is used for the old (αἰώνιος versus ἀρχαῖος) in Isa 61:4 and in 2 Cor 5:17, which might mirror the difference between continuity and discontinuity. For the new, both texts use cognate terminology (καινιοῦσιν and καινά). There is a remarkable verse in Jdt 16:14 in which creation and building activity are closely related to each other: σοὶ δουλευσάτω πᾶσα ἡ κτίσις σου ὅτι εἶπας καὶ ἐγενήθησαν ἀπέστειλας τὸ πνεῦμά σου καὶ ᾠκοδόμησεν καὶ οὐκ ἔστιν ὃς ἀντιστήσεται τῇ φωνῇ σου.[49] But admittedly, comparable texts are not found in Isaiah.

---

not as a smith who blows the coals and produces a vessel for work. But I have created you not for destruction, to ruin every perishable vessel.") On the one hand, God's creative activity is compared to but also contrasted with that of a blacksmith; on the other, the combination of the Lord as the subject, κτίζω as a predicate, and Jerusalem as implied direct object suggests that God is here envisaged as Jerusalem's founder, evoking the mythical founders that all the important Greek cities used to boast of.

48. NETS: "They shall build the desolate places of old; they shall raise up the former devastated places; they shall renew the desolate cities, places devastated for generations."

49. NETS: "Let your entire creation be subject to you; for you spoke, and they came into being. You sent your spirit, and it built them up, and there is no one who will withstand your voice."

5. Concluding Reflections

One of the central aspects of 2 Cor 5 seems to be that the consequence of the Christ event (Christ's death and resurrection) is a radically altered perception. By considering the canonical Second Letter to the Corinthians at the intersection of Paul's story and the story of Corinth as a Roman refoundation, we may envisage the Corinthians who, while listening to Paul's words, were also invited to question the way in which their own perceptions were shaped by the surrounding context.

In this paper we have argued that the members of the Corinthian community were likely to understand it as a challenge to the ideology underlying the Roman new creation of the ancient Hellenic city, offering an alternative model to the way this ongoing re-creation of Corinth was being put into practice. It would be farfetched to claim that when Paul referred to God or Jesus using the titles that would have also been used for the emperor, we each time need to add "Caesar is not."[50] However, in the specific context of the communities that he was addressing, we cannot be sure that his addressees would not have added this in their minds. Real καινὴ κτίσις is a result of the peace of Christ and of divine reconciliation, not of *pax Augusta* and *securitas Augusti*. To paraphrase the famous saying by Adolf Deissmann,[51] it must not be supposed that the Corinthian believers went through their city, *Colonia Laus Iulia Corinthensis*, blindfolded.

---

50. Compare the title of the volume edited by Scot McKnight and Joseph B. Modica, *Jesus Is Lord, Caesar Is Not: Evaluating Empire in New Testament Studies* (Downers Grove, IL: InterVarsity Press Academic, 2013). Andy Crouch, in the foreword to that volume, makes a helpful distinction between saying "Caesar is not [Lord]," and *not saying* "Caesar is Lord." To say "Jesus is Lord," as he notes, based on New Testament evidence, only seems to entail the latter (McKnight and Modica, *Jesus Is Lord*, 13). The title of the book itself is an allusion to N. T. Wright's (and other supporters' of anti-imperial readings of Paul) assertion that whenever Paul says "Jesus is Lord," he implies "Caesar is not." Among N. T. Wright's numerous publications, see especially N. T. Wright, "Paul's Gospel and Caesar's Empire," in *Paul and Politics: Ekklesia, Israel, Imperium, Interpretation; Essays in Honor of Krister Stendahl*, ed. Richard A. Horsley (Harrisburg, PA: Trinity Press International, 2000), 160–83. For the most insightful critical response to Wright's perspective, see John M. G. Barclay, "Why the Roman Empire Was Insignificant to Paul," in Barclay, *Pauline Churches and Diaspora Jews*, WUNT 275 (Tübingen: Mohr Siebeck, 2011), 363–87.

51. Adolf Deissmann, *Light from the Ancient East: The New Testament Illustrated by Recently Discovered Texts of the Graeco-Roman World*, trans. Lionel R. M. Strachan (London: Hodder & Stoughton, 1910), 344: "It must not be supposed that St. Paul and

Deissmann's list of Greek terms that recur in the New Testament and that are evocative of Roman imperial ideology included terms such as θεός, θεοῦ υἱός/*divi filius*, θεῖος, κύριος, κυριακός, σωτήρ, εὐαγγέλιον, παρουσία, and ἐπιφάνεια.[52] Taking into account the references to Pompey (and others) as εὐεργέτης and σωτήρ καὶ κτίστης as well as all the later inscriptions honoring emperors as founders, adding at least the term κτίστης to this list could be justified. In spite of the way this has been later interpreted, Deissmann himself made it clear that an overlap with the Roman usage need not imply genealogical relation. The origin of the Christian use, as he rightly noted, was, in most cases, based on the Septuagint. The same is true for κτίσις.

As we hope to have shown, however, our reading of 2 Corinthians in the Corinthian context is not based merely on an overlap in terminology, but rather constitutes an attempt to take seriously into account what we know about the city in which Paul's addressees lived and in which Paul, too, for a long time resided.

Bibliography

Alexander, Loveday. "Chronology of Paul." Pages 115–23 in *Dictionary of Paul and His Letters*. Edited by Gerald F. Hawthorne, Ralph P. Martin, and Daniel G. Reid. Downers Grove, IL: InterVarsity Press, 1993.

Amandry, Michel. *Le monnayage des duovirs corinthiens*. BCHSup 15. Paris: de Boccard, 1988.

Barclay, John M. G. *Pauline Churches and Diaspora Jews*. WUNT 275. Tübingen: Mohr Siebeck, 2011.

Bash, Anthony. *Ambassadors for Christ. An Exploration of Ambassadorial Language in the New Testament*. WUNT 2/92. Tübingen: Mohr Siebeck, 1997.

Bieringer, Reimund. "Verzoening met God in 2 Korintiërs 5,18–21: Een voorbeeld van paulinische theologie in wording." *Collationes* 39 (2009): 21–30.

Bispham, Edward. "*Coloniam deducere*: How Roman Was Roman Colonization during the Middle Republic?" Pages 73–160 in *Greek and Roman Colonization: Origins, Ideologies and Interactions*. Edited by

---

his fellow-believers went through the world blindfolded, unaffected by what was then moving the minds of men in great cities."

52. Deissmann, *Light*, esp. 347–78.

Guy Bradley and John-Paul Wilson. Swansea: Classical Press of Wales, 2006.

Bons, Eberhard. "Le verbe κτίζω comme terme technique de la création dans la Septante et dans le Nouveau Testament." Pages 1–15 in *Voces Biblicae: Septuagint Greek and Its Significance for the New Testament.* Edited by Jan Joosten and Peter J. Tomson. CBET 49. Leuven: Peeters, 2007.

Bons, Eberhard, and Anna Passoni Dell'Acqua. "A Sample Article: κτίζω, κτίσις, κτίσμα, κτίστης." Pages 173–87 in *Septuagint Vocabulary: Prehistory, Usage, Reception.* Edited by Jan Joosten and Eberhard Bons. SCS 58. Atlanta: Society of Biblical Literature, 2011.

Bookidis, Nancy. "Religion in Corinth: 146 B.C.E. to 100 C.E." Pages 141–64 in *Urban Religion in Roman Corinth: Interdisciplinary Approaches.* Edited by Daniel N. Schowalter and Steven J. Friesen. HTS 53. Cambridge: Harvard University Press, 2005.

Breytenbach, Cilliers. *Versöhnung: Eine Studie zur paulinischen Soteriologie.* WMANT 60. Neukirchen-Vluyn: Neukirchener Verlag, 1989.

Chun, Sejong. "Paul's New Creation: Vision for a New World and Community in the Midst of Empires." PhD diss., Vanderbilt University, 2012.

Crouch, Andy. Foreword to *Jesus Is Lord, Caesar Is Not: Evaluating Empire in New Testament Studies.* Edited by Scot McKnight and Joseph B. Modica. Downers Grove, IL: InterVarsity Press Academic, 2013.

Deissmann, Adolf. *Light from the Ancient East: The New Testament Illustrated by Recently Discovered Texts of the Graeco-Roman World.* Translated by Lionel R. M. Strachan. London: Hodder & Stoughton, 1910.

Duff, Paul Brooks. "Metaphor, Motif, and Meaning: The Rhetorical Strategy behind the Image 'Led in Triumph' in 2 Corinthians 2:14." *CBQ* 53 (1991): 79–92.

Fewster, Gregory P. *Creation Language in Romans 8: A Study in Monosemy.* Linguistic Biblical Studies 8. Leiden: Brill, 2013.

Furnish, Victor Paul. *II Corinthians: A New Translation with Introduction and Commentary.* AB 32A. Garden City, NY: Doubleday, 1984.

Harris, Murray J. *The Second Epistle to the Corinthians: A Commentary on the Greek Text.* NIGTC. Grand Rapids: Eerdmans; Milton Keynes: Paternoster, 2005.

Heilig, Christoph. *Paul's Triumph: Reassessing 2 Corinthians 2:14 in Its Literary and Historical Context.* BiTS 27. Leuven: Peeters, 2016.

Horsley, G. H. R. "The Fiction of 'Jewish Greek.'" Pages 5–40 in *Linguistic Essays.* Vol. 5 of *New Documents Illustrating Early Christianity.* Edited by G. H. R. Horsley. North Ryde, NSW: Ancient History Documentary Research Centre, Macquarie University, 1989.

Hubbard, Moyer V. *New Creation in Paul's Letters and Thought.* SNTSMS 119. Cambridge: Cambridge University Press, 2002.

Jackson, T. Ryan. *New Creation in Paul's Letters: A Study of the Historical and Social Setting of a Pauline Concept.* WUNT 2/272. Tübingen: Mohr Siebeck, 2010.

McKnight, Scot, and Joseph B. Modica, eds. *Jesus Is Lord, Caesar Is Not: Evaluating Empire in New Testament Studies.* Downers Grove, IL: InterVarsity Press Academic, 2013.

Mell, Ulrich. *Neue Schöpfung: Eine traditionsgeschichtliche und exegetische Studie zu einem soteriologischen Grundsatz paulinischer Theologie.* BZNW 56. Berlin: de Gruyter, 1989.

Nijf, Onno van. "Local Heroes: Athletics, Festivals and Elite Self-Fashioning in the Roman East." Pages 306–34 in *Being Greek under Rome: Cultural Identity, the Second Sophistic and the Development of Empire.* Edited by Simon Goldhill. Cambridge: Cambridge University Press, 2001.

Oakes, Peter. "Re-mapping the Universe: Paul and the Emperor in 1 Thessalonians and Philippians." *JSNT* 27 (2005): 301–22.

Owens, Mark D. *As It Was in the Beginning: An Intertextual Analysis of New Creation in Galatians, 2 Corinthians, and Ephesians.* Eugene, OR: Pickwick, 2015.

Pilhofer, Peter. *Katalog der Inschriften von Philippi.* Vol. 2 of *Philippi.* WUNT 119. Tübingen: Mohr Siebeck, 2000.

Porter, Stanley E., ed. *The Language of the New Testament: Classic Essays.* JSNTSup 60. Sheffield: JSOT Press, 1991.

Price, S. R. F. "The Place of Religion: Rome in the Early Empire." Pages 812–47 in *The Augustan Empire, 43 B.C.–A.D. 69.* Vol. 10 of *The Cambridge Ancient History.* Edited by Alan K. Bowman, Edward Champlin, and Andrew Lintott. 2nd ed. Cambridge: Cambridge University Press, 1996.

Scranton, Robert L. *Monuments in the Lower Agora and North of the Archaic Temple.* Vol. 1.3 of *Corinth: Results of Excavations Conducted by the American School of Classical Studies at Athens.* Princeton: American School of Classical Studies at Athens, 1951.

Slingerland, Dixon. "Acts 18:1–18, the Gallio Inscription, and Absolute Pauline Chronology." *JBL* 110 (1991): 439–49.

Stuhlmacher, Peter. "Erwägungen zum ontologischen Charakter der καινή κτίσις bei Paulus." *EvT* 27 (1967): 1–35.

Thomas, Christine M. "Greek Heritage in Roman Corinth and Ephesos: Hybrid Identities and Strategies of Display in the Material Record of Traditional Mediterranean Religions." Pages 117–47 in *Corinth in Context: Comparative Studies on Religion and Society*. Edited by Steven J. Friesen, Daniel N. Schowalter, and James C. Walters. NovTSup 134. Leiden: Brill, 2010.

Thrall, Margaret E. *Commentary on 2 Corinthians 1–7*. Vol. 1 of *The Second Epistle to the Corinthians*. ICC. Edinburgh: T&T Clark, 1994.

Walbank, Mary E. Hoskins. "Evidence for the Imperial Cult in Julio-Claudian Corinth." Pages 201–14 in *Subject and Ruler: The Cult of the Ruling Power in Classical Antiquity*. Edited by Alastair Small. JRASup 17. Ann Arbor, MI: Journal of Roman Archaeology, 1996.

———. "The Foundation and Planning of Early Roman Corinth." *JRA* 10 (1997): 95–130.

Walters, James C. "Civic Identity in Roman Corinth and Its Impact on Early Christians." Pages 397–417 in *Urban Religion in Roman Corinth: Interdisciplinary Approaches*. Edited by Daniel N. Schowalter and Steven J. Friesen. HTS 53. Cambridge: Harvard University Press, 2005.

Wright, N. T. "Paul's Gospel and Caesar's Empire." Pages 160–83 in *Paul and Politics: Ekklesia, Israel, Imperium, Interpretation; Essays in Honor of Krister Stendahl*. Edited by Richard A. Horsley. Harrisburg, PA: Trinity Press International, 2000.

Zanker, Paul. *The Power of Images in the Age of Augustus*. Translated by Alan Shapiro. Jerome Lectures 16. Ann Arbor: University of Michigan Press, 1990.

Women as Leaders in the Gatherings of Early Christian Communities: A Sociohistorical Analysis

Valeriy A. Alikin

1. Introduction

Most studies that investigate the issue of women's leadership in the gatherings of early Christian communities usually look at the Pauline epistles and the book of Acts and the emphases found there on women who functioned in leadership roles and who held various offices such as apostle, presbyter, and bishop. By using this approach, scholars end up considering various kinds of evidence that only implicitly refer to women conducting the gatherings of early Christian communities. This article analyzes and presents more explicit evidence from the second and third centuries in related early Christian literature that supports the practice of women conducting and presiding at the gatherings of early Christian communities.[1] Rarely do scholars adduce the pertinent evidence from the Greco-Roman world that supports the view that women led and presided at banquets, including the

---

1. The topic of women leading Christian communities is usually studied within the overall approach to women's priesthood and women in early Christianity in general. See Ross Shepard Kraemer, *Her Share of the Blessings: Women's Religions among Pagans, Jews, and Christians in the Greco-Roman World* (Oxford: Oxford University Press, 1992); Karen Jo Torjesen, *When Women Were Priests: Women's Leadership in the Early Church and the Scandal of Their Subordination in the Rise of Christianity* (San Francisco: HarperSanFrancisco, 1993); Kevin Madigan and Carolyn Osiek, *Ordained Women in the Early Church: A Documentary History* (Baltimore: Johns Hopkins University Press, 2005); Lynn H. Cohick, *Women in the World of the Earliest Christians: Illuminating Ancient Ways of Life* (Grand Rapids: Baker Academic, 2009).

banquets of various associations.² From a sociohistorical point of view, the local early Christian community functioned as a voluntary religious association that conducted communal meals. In the Greco-Roman world, numerous religious communities had women who held leadership roles presiding over communal meals and symposia. The Christian communities were no exception. The analysis of the pertinent evidence shows that during the second and third centuries women could serve as leaders in the gatherings of the Christian communities.

2. Women Presiding over Meals and Communal Gatherings in the Greco-Roman World

During the past ten years, the study of the periodic gatherings of the early Christians has undergone a substantial shift. A predominantly literary approach has given way to a more sociological approach.³

The essence of this new approach can be formulated as follows: the local early Christian community, as a sociocultural phenomenon, functioned as a voluntary religious association, not unlike many other associations in the Greco-Roman world of the first century CE. There is firm evidence from the first two centuries CE to support this view.⁴

---

2. Exceptions are Riet van Bremen, *The Limits of Participation: Women and Civic Life in the Greek East in the Hellenistic and Roman Periods*, Dutch Monographs on Ancient History and Archaeology 15 (Amsterdam: Gieben, 1996); and Bernadette J. Brooten, *Women Leaders in the Ancient Synagogue*, BJS 36 (Chico, CA: Scholars Press, 1982).

3. This more sociological approach to early Christianity was initiated in about 1975 by such scholars as Wayne A. Meeks, *The First Urban Christians: The Social World of the Apostle Paul* (New Haven: Yale University Press, 1983); and Gerd Theissen, *Soziologie der Jesusbewegung: Ein Beitrag zur Entstehungsgeschichte des Urchristentums*, Theologische Existenz heute 194 (Munich: Kaiser, 1977); Theissen, *Studien zur Soziologie des Urchristentums*, WUNT 19 (Tübingen: Mohr Siebeck, 1979).

4. In 55 CE, for instance, Paul compares the local Christian community meal with the pagan religious association meal in Corinth (1 Cor 10:16–21). In about 112 CE, Pliny the Younger, in his correspondence with the Roman Emperor Trajan (Pliny, *Ep.* 10.96) equates Christian communities with associations. In the second century CE, Lucian refers to leaders of Christian communities as *thiasarchai*, that is, leaders of cult associations (Lucian, *Peregr.* 11). About 200 CE, Tertullian compares the Christian community meal with the meal consumed by various pagan religious associations, such as the *collegia Saliorum* and the Dionysus and Serapis cults (Tertullian, *Apol.* 39).

The main activity of both the Greco-Roman associations and Christian communities was a communal banquet that comprised a supper and a contiguous symposium. Numerous passages in works by Christian authors show that until the middle of the third century, Christian communities, too, had a communal meal and convivial gatherings on Sunday evening as their main assembly.[5] The origins of the Christian gathering should be studied, therefore, in the context of the banquet practices of voluntary religious associations in the Greco-Roman world.[6]

Religious or cult associations conducted their own gatherings, which were led by various functionaries. The question is whether women could perform the leading role at meals in general and at meals of religious associations in the Greco-Roman world.[7] There is enough evidence to substantiate the view that they did.

Pagan Greek women could certainly organize and preside over banquets in their houses.[8] This can be illustrated by a passage in Apuleius's

---

5. 1 Cor 11:17–14:40; Did. 9–10, 14; Justin, *1 Apol.* 67; Irenaeus, *Haer.* 1.13; Clement of Alexandria, *Strom.* 6.113; Athenagoras, *Leg.* 3, 31; Theophilus of Antioch, *Autol.* 3.4; Acts Pet. 13; Minucius Felix, *Oct.* 8.4; 9.6; 31.1, 5; Tertullian, *Apol.* 7, 39; Tertullian, *Nat.* 1.2; 1.7; Hippolytus, *Trad. ap.* 25–29; Origen, *Cels.* 1.1; 8.32; Cyprian, *Ep.* 63. When describing Christian gatherings, the author of Acts (2:44 and 4:32) used the symposium proverb κοινὰ τὰ φίλων ("friends have things in common"; see, e.g., Plutarch, *Quest. conv.* 2.10.2 [644D], 5.5.2 [679D], 9.14.1 [743E]; Iamblichus, *VP* 6.32). This shows again that the context of Christian gathering was a communal symposium.

6. See Valeriy A. Alikin, *The Earliest History of the Christian Gathering: Origins, Development and Content of the Christian Gathering in the First to Third Centuries*, VCSup 102 (Leiden: Brill, 2010), 17–39.

7. On the role of women in leading positions in Jewish voluntary religious associations, see Brooten, *Women Leaders*, 134; Brooten, "Female Leadership in the Ancient Synagogue," in *From Dura to Sepphoris: Studies in Jewish Art and Society in Late Antiquity*, ed. Lee I. Levine and Zeev Weiss, JRASup 40 (Portsmouth, RI: Journal of Roman Archaeology, 2000), 215–23. See also Peter Richardson and Valerie Heuchan, "Jewish Voluntary Associations in Egypt and the Roles of Women," in *Voluntary Associations in the Graeco-Roman World*, ed. John S. Kloppenborg and Stephen G. Wilson (London: Routledge, 1996), 226–51.

8. The designation *pagan* is problematic for describing religious aspects in Greco-Roman antiquity. Originally there was no common term for various forms of traditional religion in the Greco-Roman world. The idea of *paganism* was a creation of Christians who wanted to define their religious rivals as a coherent group. Paganism described traditional Greco-Roman beliefs and practices that included polytheism, the use of idols, and animal sacrifices. Another helpful explanation of the term pagan is "the people of the place"; that is, pagans were people rooted in local customs of an

Metamorphoses (2.18-19). In this passage, the main character of the book, Lucius, attends a supper and drinking party in the house of Byrrhaena, a distinguished lady at Hypata, a small town in Thessaly (2.18).[9] Another example of a woman who exercised power and extended hospitality to representatives from a Lycian *koinon* is Junia Theodora in Corinth. She was a prominent member of Corinth's social elite during the second quarter of the first century CE.[10] Pausanias describes the public and secret rites to Demeter performed by elderly women in Corinth in the middle of the second century CE. From the description it is clear that both men and women participate in these rites, and there was an old woman who performed the leadership role in the ceremony (Pausanias, *Descr.* 35.6-8).[11]

Evidence from inscriptions shows that women functioned as presidents (*prostatides*)[12] of associations and performed the leading roles at the communal banquets. This is evidenced by a dedication of a statue by an association of women in Alexandria dated to the early first century CE: "The high priestess and president (*prostatis*) Tetiris dedicated this to the Apollonian (?) women's synod (*synodos*) in the ... xth year of Caesar, on the first of the month Pachon."[13] A prominent role was played by women in various religious cults. A good example is the *Bona Dea* cult, the rites of which took place in the homes of leading statesmen. Most of the cult

---

ancient religious landscape. See Pierre Chuvin, *A Chronicle of the Last Pagans*, trans. B. A. Archer, Revealing Antiquity 4 (Cambridge: Harvard University Press, 1990), 7-9; Jaclyn Maxwell, "Paganism and Christianization," in *The Oxford Handbook of Late Antiquity*, ed. Scott Fitzgerald Johnson (Oxford: Oxford University Press, 2012), 852-53; Christopher P. Jones, *Between Pagan and Christian* (Cambridge: Harvard University Press, 2014), 5-8.

9. "Forte quadam die de me magno opere Byrrhena contendit apud eam cenulae interessem, et, cum impendio excusarem, negavit veniam."

10. Steven J. Friesen, "Junia Theodora of Corinth: Gendered Inequalities in the Early Roman Empire," in *Corinth in Contrast: Studies in Inequality*, ed. Steven J. Friesen, Sarah A. James, and Daniel N. Schowalter, NovTSup 155 (Leiden: Brill, 2014), 203-26, esp. 206-7. The *koinon* was a regional league of cities that served as an institution to mediate Roman influence.

11. See Ross Shepard Kraemer, ed., *Women's Religions in the Greco-Roman World: A Sourcebook*, rev. ed. (Oxford: Oxford University Press, 2004), 39-40, no. 17A.

12. In Rom 16:2, Paul introduces Phoebe to the Roman Christians and identifies her as patron (*prostatis*) both to himself and to many other Christians in Cenchreae.

13. See Richard S. Ascough, Philip A. Harland, and John S. Kloppenborg, eds., *Associations in the Greco-Roman World: A Sourcebook* (Waco, TX: Baylor University Press, 2012), 169-70, no. 282 (from which the translation comes).

officials were women, who performed various functions at the festivals, which involved music and the drinking of wine.[14] The literary sources, such as Juvenal, Ovid, and Plutarch, portray the role exercised by women from aristocratic circles in the cult activities. Lynn Cohick states that, according to inscriptions, there were more slaves than freedwomen who participated in the cult's activities. Inscriptions also reveal several types of women leaders in the cult, among whom there was the title *magistra* that refers to a woman who led a religious collegium. The *magistra* of the *Bona Dea* was responsible for overseeing the sacrifices and offerings, as well as leading the cultic meal.[15] Other inscriptions testify to women holding religious offices in various religious cult associations and sponsoring lavish banquets.[16]

Another example of women performing leadership roles is in the cult of Dionysos. Diodorus of Sicily describes the gatherings of the cult that included the offering of sacrifices, eating, the drinking of mixed wine, hymns, and frenzied revelry. The gatherings were led by matrons, who "forming in groups, offer sacrifices to the god and celebrate his mysteries and, in general, extol with hymns the presence of Dionysus."[17] After the meal, they held a *symposion*, where they passed around the cup of wine mixed with water and, while drinking, made exclamations to Zeus the Savior (Diodorus Siculus, *Bib. hist.* 4.3.2–5).[18] Participation in the cult's activities was not restricted to women. Livy claims that by allowing men and women to worship together, the cult introduced practices that were unfamiliar and foreign to Romans (*Ab urbe cond.* 39.8–19).[19] An inscription from Miletus in western Turkey describes the duties of the priestess in the Dionysos cult (*thiasos*):[20]

---

14. Cohick, *Women in the World*, 168–69.
15. Ibid., 172–73.
16. Kraemer, *Her Share of the Blessings*, 84–85.
17. Text cited in Kraemer, *Women's Religions*, 27, no. 12.
18. See Kraemer, *Women's Religions*, 27–28.
19. See Cohick, *Women in the World*, 176.
20. The Greek term *thiasos* (Latin equivalent *collegium*) was used to designate a type of voluntary religious association in Greco-Roman antiquity. For the taxonomy of cult associations, see John S. Kloppenborg, "Collegia and *Thiasoi*: Issues in Function, Taxonomy and Membership," in Kloppenborg and Wilson, *Voluntary Associations*, 16–30.

> Whenever the priestess performs the holy rites on behalf of the city ... it is not permitted for anyone to throw pieces of raw meat [anywhere], before the priestess has thrown them on behalf of the city, nor is it permitted for anyone to assemble a band of maenads [*thiasos*] before the public *thiasos* [has been assembled].[21]

This priestess performed holy rites not only on behalf of the cult members, but even for the whole city. The rites included public sacrifices with men and women feasting, drinking wine, and singing. These activities were led by women as well as by men, as is indicated in the second-century inscription (150 CE) that praises Pompeia Agrippinilla, priestess of the *thiasos*.[22] She was a patron of a second-century Dionysiac association near Rome that boasted more than three hundred members, who gratefully erected a statue to its patron and priestess.[23] It should be noted that almost a third of the different titles and functions in that association were allotted to women, and most importantly they were represented at the highest level of the cult association's hierarchy: Agrippinilla's daughter Cornelia was the torch bearer, and Agrippinilla herself was the priestess of the association. This seems to be consistent with the general trend in the first and second centuries CE toward more active involvement of women in the high-priestly offices of various cult associations.[24]

---

21. *LSAM* 48. The text can be seen in Franciszek Sokolowski, *Lois sacrées de l'Asie Mineure*, Travaux et mémoires (Ecole française d'Athènes) 9 (Paris: de Boccard, 1955). The English translation is from Kraemer, *Women's Religions*, 21.

22. For additional evidence of women holding leading positions as priestesses in Greco-Roman cultic associations, see John S. Kloppenborg and Richard S. Ascough, *Greco-Roman Associations: Texts, Translations, and Commentary*, BZNW 181 (Berlin: de Gruyter, 2011), especially nos. 28 (*IG* 2.1314), 44 (*IG* 2.1337), 45 (*IG* 2.1334), 77 (*IG* 10.2.1.255), and 81 (*IG* 10.2.1.260).

23. Bradley H. McLean, "The Agrippinilla Inscription: Religious Associations and Early Church Formation," in *Origins and Method: Towards a New Understanding of Judaism and Christianity; Essays in Honour of John C. Hurd*, ed. Bradley H. McLean (Sheffield: JSOT Press, 1993), 239. Carolyn Osiek also provides evidence about Sergia Paullina, who hosted a burial society in her house in Rome (*CIL* 6.9148); see Osiek, "*Diakonos* and *Prostatis*: Women's Patronage in Early Christianity," *HvTSt* 61 (2005): 357–58.

24. Gennadi A. Sergienko, *Our Politeuma Is in Heaven! Paul's Polemical Engagement with the "Enemies of the Cross of Christ" in Philippians 3:18–20* (Carlisle: Langham Monographs, 2013), 33–34. In his work, Sergienko also provides ample evidence for women priestesses in cultic associations in Macedonia (see 34–35).

Another second-century CE inscription from Aphrodisias speaks about Tata, who was a priestess of Hera for life and at least twice served as priestess of the imperial cult:

> The council and the people and the senate honour with first-rank honours Tata, daughter of Diodoros son of Diodoros son of Leon, reverend priestess of Hera for life, mother of the city, who became and remained the wife of Attalos son of Pytheas the *stephanephorus*, herself a member of an illustrious family of the first rank, who, as priestess of the imperial cult a second time, twice supplied oil for athletes in hand-bottles, filled most lavishly from basins for the better part of the night as well [as in the day], who became a *stephanephorus*, offered sacrifices throughout the year for the health of the imperial family, who held banquets for the people many times with couches provided for the public, who herself, for dances and plays, imported the foremost performers in Asia and displayed them in her native city (and the neighbouring cities could also come to the display of the performance), a woman who spared no expense, who loved honour, glorious in virtue and chastity.[25]

From the inscription it is obvious that Tata held and presided over banquets for the people many times, with couches provided for the public. She is described as priestess with the added description of esteem: "reverend" (ἀγνή). Two more examples of women presiding at banquets of religious associations are Nikippa Pasia and Phaena Antigonika. Both of them exercised leadership roles in religious associations. Nikippa participated in the associations of the worshippers of Kore. She assisted male priests in financing the adornment of the cult's sanctuary and carried some religious responsibilities. Additionally, she hosted the cult and celebrated certain rituals in her house. Phaena provided the worshipers of Demeter with lavish meals as well as other benefactions.[26] These women acted as the cult's benefactors, and this gave them opportunity to perform leadership functions along with male leaders. As Riet van Bremen maintains: "Wealth had become a precondition for office-holding, and office-holding seemingly an excuse for public spending, to be taken on by whoever could afford it."[27]

---

25. *MAMA* 8.492. For the English translation, see Kraemer, *Women's Religions*, 249.
26. *IG* 5.2.265–66. These inscriptions contain decrees from Mantineia that are dated 64–63 BCE and 46–45 BCE. See van Bremen, *Limits of Participation*, 27–28.
27. Van Bremen, *Limits of Participation*, 29.

Having analyzed numerous Jewish inscriptions that mention the titles of a leader (*archēgisa*) female elder (*presbytida*), and mother of the synagogue (*mētēr synagōgēs*), Bernadette Brooten came to the conclusion that those titles were not merely honorific and that women performed functions of female heads or elders of synagogues similar to male leadership roles. Therefore, it is not impossible to imagine women performing leadership functions by sitting in councils of elders, teaching, and arranging religious services.[28]

Thus, both literary and epigraphic sources indicate that women could perform high-level leadership roles in pagan religious cults and associations. As far as the social status of women holding position in religious cults and associations is concerned, they represent a cross section of Greco-Roman society. Freeborn women generally held more prestigious positions than freed women or slaves. Those of lower social status were more likely to serve as *ministrae*.[29] Therefore we can assert that various titles and positions held by women were not merely honorific and women were in charge of the communal banquets of certain groups of both women and men. The conclusion of Carolyn Osiek is completely warranted: the available "evidence makes clear that both personal and public patronage were widely practiced by women in much the same way that it was practiced by men. The older interpretation that public offices and titles when held by men were actual, but when held by women were honorary, is no longer tenable."[30] Thus it can be stated that in the Greco-Roman world women performed leadership roles by presiding over communal banquets of religious associations.

3. Women Presiding over Gatherings of Christian Communities in the Second and Third Centuries

As householders, women, too, could perform leadership roles and possibly even conduct Christian gatherings, serving as matrons or hosts of Christian communities. Mary, mother of John Mark, hosted a gathering

---

28. Brooten, "Female Leadership," 217–20, 223.
29. Celia E. Schultz, *Women's Religious Activity in the Roman Republic* (Chapel Hill: University of North Carolina Press, 2006), 142. Note also two *ministrae* from the Christian community in Bithynia who were tried by Pliny (*Ep* 10.96.8).
30. Carolyn Osiek, "*Diakonos* and *Prostatis*," 358.

of Christ's believers in Jerusalem (Acts 12:12).[31] Another case in point is Lydia, who, according to Luke, hosted a church in her house in Philippi. When Paul and Silas were released from this town's prison, they went to Lydia's house, where they met and encouraged the brothers and sisters (Acts 16:40).[32] Lydia, as the head of the household and a businesswoman, played an important role. As the head of the household and a dealer in purple cloth, she might very likely have presided over the gatherings of Christians in her home. Regardless of the historicity of the specific instances, Luke is completely at home in presenting women in these "hosting" roles. It suggests that at the end of the first century (when Luke was writing) such practices were regarded as acceptable and, probably, not exceptional. On the basis of Luke's account of Lydia in Acts 16 and of a close analysis of the letter to the Philippians, Gennadi Sergienko has argued that women played an important role in the life of Christian communities. He points out: "The elevated role of women in the Philippian Christian community may have been due to the fact that women in other cults of the time played similarly elevated roles.... It was almost natural for women of high status and means to assume the role of priestesses and/or patrons in different Graeco-Roman cults."[33]

Nympha in Laodikeia, too, is presented as hosting a church that met in her house (Col 4:15).[34] It is most likely that Apphia, together with two

---

31. "As soon as he realized this, he went to the house of Mary, the mother of John whose other name was Mark, where many had gathered and were praying" (NRSV).

32. "After leaving the prison they went to Lydia's home; and when they had seen and encouraged the brothers and sisters there, they departed" (NRSV).

33. Sergienko, *Our Politeuma Is in Heaven*, 107.

34. Ἀσπάσασθε τοὺς ἐν Λαοδικείᾳ ἀδελφοὺς καὶ Νύμφαν καὶ τὴν κατ' οἶκον αὐτῆς ἐκκλησίαν. Whether a man, Nymphas, or a woman, Nympha, is meant depends on what one considers to be the original reading for the personal pronoun. Perhaps an original "her" was subsequently changed to "his," because at a later stage it could not be conceived of that a woman might be responsible for an entire house church; see Eduard Schweizer, *The Letter to the Colossians: A Commentary* (Minneapolis: Augsburg, 1982), 241. James Dunn also indicates that Νυμφαν can be accented either Νύμφαν (from the feminine Nympha) or Νυμφᾶν (from the masculine Nymphas): "Since both names are attested in papyri and inscriptions ... the decision depends on the gender of the following possessive pronoun." The feminine pronoun "her" is best attested as in the earliest manuscripts (B and others). The masculine readings can be explained in part, at least, by the later scribal assumption that the leader of a house church could not have been a woman. For the argument and for the citation of Dunn

other leaders, presided over a house church in Colossae (see Phlm 2).[35] True, the person who hosted a church in her or his house does not always need to have been the conductor of that church's gatherings. But there is no reason to assume that Christian women could not preside over a meal of the church meeting in her house.[36] Osiek contends: "the assumption can be made that they [households and church gatherings] were conducted in the same way that any other patronage situation was done, with deference, respect, and submission owed to the patronal figure who expected to be the center of attention and of honor except at those times when founding apostles were present."[37] Thus it is very likely that women performed leadership roles in the gatherings of the early Christian communities in the first century. How did the situation develop in the second and third centuries?

As the church moved towards further organization and institutionalization in the second century, the roles played by women in the earliest communities in the first century began to be suppressed. This is reflected in several New Testament writings dating from the end of the first century and the beginning of the second century, for example, the Pastoral Epistles (see, for e.g., 1 Tim 2:11–13).[38] The letters of Ignatius of Antioch do not provide direct evidence for women presiding at the gatherings of Christian communities. However, one can imply from his references to women that they could have hosted church gatherings in their homes. In his letter to Polycarp, Ignatius mentions the unnamed wife of Epitropos. It might be

---

above, see James D. G. Dunn, *The Epistles to the Colossians and to Philemon: A Commentary on the Greek Text*, NIGTC (Grand Rapids: Eerdmans, 1996), 274.

35. "To Apphia our sister, to Archippos our fellow soldier, and to the church in your house," even allowing that κατ' οἶκόν σου suggests Philemon as the owner (cf. Dunn, *Epistles*, 275).

36. This is the tenor of Carolyn Osiek, *A Woman's Place: House Churches in Earliest Christianity* (Minneapolis: Fortress, 2006), 159–63. Epigraphic evidence dating from 27 BCE to the sixth century CE shows that women could be called leaders in a number of synagogues in Italy, Asia Minor, Egypt, and Palestine. See Brooten, "Female Leadership," 215–23.

37. Osiek, "*Diakonos* and *Prostatis*," 363.

38. "Let a woman learn in silence with full submission. I permit no woman to teach or to have authority over a man; she is to keep silent. For Adam was formed first, then Eve" (NRSV).

that she was the materfamilias who exercised patronage toward a Christian group independent of her unbelieving husband (Ignatius, *Pol.* 8.2).[39]

In the second century, during Anicetus's episcopate in Rome, a certain Marcellina, a woman who held gnostic views, came to Rome and by her teaching influenced many people to depart from the right confession (Irenaeus, *Haer.* 1.25.6).[40] Marcellina probably conducted gatherings of her own group, but our informant, Irenaeus, does not explicitly say so.[41]

Irenaeus provides us with one more piece of evidence of women who, together with the founder of another gnostic group in the mid-second century, Marcus the Magician, led proceedings. Marcus, after whom this movement is called, taught about the feminine dimension of God and attracted numerous female followers.[42] Some of those women functioned as prophetesses and performed the rites of prayer, consecrating the elements of the eucharistic meal (Irenaeus, *Haer.* 1.13.2).[43]

Another example of women leading Christian gatherings comes from Hippolytus, who in his *Refutation of All Heresies*, writes about the Montanist prophetesses Maximilla and Priscilla. Though Hippolytus concentrates on describing their prophetic activities and tries to find faults in their teaching and doctrines, he nevertheless points out that these women influenced Montanist congregations to introduce feasts and meals of parched food (*Haer.* 8.12).[44] It is most likely that by introducing feasts and meals, they presided over those gatherings. The apocryphal Acts of Paul

---

39. "I greet all by name, and the wife of Epitropos, along with the entire household of her and her children." See Osiek, "*Diakonos* and *Prostatis*," 364.

40. "From among these also arose Marcellina, who came to Rome under [the episcopate of] Anicetus, and, holding these doctrines, she led multitudes astray" (*ANF*).

41. Irenaeus, *Haer.* 1.13.2, also mentions gatherings of Valentinian gnostics, in which the leader, Marcus the Magician, allowed women to say eucharistic prayers and to prophesy, but only under his supervision.

42. Patricia Cox Miller, *Women in Early Christianity: Translations from Greek Texts* (Washington, DC: Catholic University of America Press, 2005), 31.

43. "Again, handing mixed cups to the women, he [Marcus] bids them consecrate these in his presence. When this has been done, he himself produces another cup of much larger size than that which the deluded woman has consecrated, and pouring from the smaller one consecrated by the woman into that which has been brought forward by himself" (*ANF*).

44. "They introduce, however, the novelties of fasts, and feasts, and meals of parched food, and repasts of radishes, alleging that they have been instructed by women." See Kraemer, *Women's Religions*, 263 no. 94.

and Thecla, written probably in the second half of the second century, describes Tryphaena, who exercised a form of Christian patronage and acted as benefactor for Christians, as utilizing her house as a meeting place for a local Christian community (Acts Paul Thecl. 39).[45] In addition, the Acts of Paul and Thecla portrays Thecla as a model for women's leadership roles in the church.[46] Thecla is said to teach in the gatherings of Christian communities and to conduct baptisms (34, 42, 45). Her teaching activity definitely shows that she took the leading role in Christian gatherings, as it is evident that itinerant teachers sometimes did in the second century.[47] Thecla's teaching of the word of God and the presence of joy in Tryphaena's house point to a Christian gathering similar to the meeting that took place in the house of Onesiphoros earlier in the narrative (5).

In his treatise *De baptismo*, Tertullian expressed his knowledge of the existence of the Acts of Paul and Thecla and criticized the practice of women teaching and baptizing (*Bapt.* 17). At the same time he stated that there were some Christian circles that had adduced the Acts of Paul and Thecla as evidence for the justification for women to teach and to baptize in their gatherings. In *De praescriptione haereticorum*, Tertullian also criticized certain "heretics" for permitting women to teach, engage in disputes, perform exorcisms, and "perhaps to baptize" (*Praescr.* 41.5).[48] Tertullian did not reproach the heretics for allowing women to preside over eucharistic gatherings. In his own circles, the possibility of women fulfilling priestly functions, such as conducting the Eucharist, was regarded as an

---

45. "And Tryphaena, having received the good news, went with the multitude to meet Thecla. After embracing her she said, 'Now I believe that the dead are raised! Now I believe that my child lives. Come inside and all that is mine I shall assign to you.' And Thecla went in with her and rested eight days, instructing her in the word of God, so that many of the maidservants believed. And there was a great joy in the house." See J. K. Elliott, *The Apocryphal New Testament: A Collection of Apocryphal Christian Literature in an English Translation* (Oxford: Clarendon, 2005), 371. See also Magdalena Wilhelmina Misset-van de Weg, "A Wealthy Woman Named Tryphaena: Patroness of Thecla of Iconium," in *The Apocryphal Acts of Paul and Thecla*, ed. Jan N. Bremmer, Studies on the Apocryphal Acts of the Apostles 2 (Kampen: Kok Pharos, 1996), 28.

46. Miller, *Women in Early Christianity*, 155.

47. Did. 10, 15; Acts Pet. 5, 7, 8, 9, 20 demonstrate that itinerant teacher functioned as leaders when they ministered in a given local Christian community.

48. *Ipsae mulieres haereticae, quam procaces! quae audeant docere, contendere, exorcismos agere, curationes repromittere, fortasse an et tingere.*

outrage (*Virg.* 9.2).[49] However, his outrage against women conducting the Eucharist suggests that some were doing this.

Thus, it would seem that women had a better chance of obtaining leading positions and the presidency of communal gatherings in "heterodox" circles than in mainstream Christianity. This is illustrated by the following episode recorded in a letter sent by Bishop Firmilian of Caesarea to Cyprian of Carthage around 256 CE:

> Suddenly, a certain woman started up in our midst: she presented herself as a prophetess, being in a state of ecstasy and acting as if she were filled with the Holy Spirit. But she was so deeply under the sway and control of the principal demons that she managed to disturb and deceive the brethren for a long time by performing astonishing and perpetual feats.... Among the other practices by which she deceived many, she frequently dared to use this one: employing a by no means despicable form of invocation, she would pretend to sanctify the bread and celebrate the Eucharist, and she would offer the sacrifice to the Lord not without the sacred recitation of the wonted ritual formula. And she would baptize many also, adopting the customary and legitimate wording of the baptismal interrogation. And all this she did in such a way that she appeared to deviate in no particular from the ecclesiastical discipline. (Cyprian, *Ep.* 75)[50]

This evidence reveals that shortly after 235 CE, among the Christians in the provinces of Cappadocia and Pontus, an unnamed woman arose who, according to Firmilian, pretended to be a prophetess. This prophetess was most likely Montanist, but strangely enough Firmilian describes her as a deviant within the church itself. She attracted many followers by her ecstatic teachings. She often conducted gatherings in which she herself said the eucharistic prayers, sanctified the bread, and offered the sacrifice to God. She also held baptismal services and baptized many people. In all this, she used the customary liturgical formulas of the prevailing church, so that nothing might seem to be different from the rules established in the church. This is a clear case of a woman conducting church gatherings

---

49. *Non permittitur mulieri in ecclesia loqui, sed nec docere nec tinguere nec offerre nec ullius virilis muneris, nedum sacerdotalis officii sortem sibi vindicarent.*

50. See Anne Jensen, *God's Self-confident Daughters: Early Christianity and Liberation of Women*, trans. O. C. Dean Jr. (Louisville: Westminster John Knox, 1996), 182–83.

and the eucharistic meal, albeit outside of the prevailing church. This practice of women holding high-level leadership positions in churches in the third century is supported by the Epitaph of Ammion, found in Uçak (Phrygia) and dated by scholars around 200–210 CE, which names a woman presbyter: "Διογᾶς ἐβίσκοπος Ἀμμίῳ πρεσβυτέρᾳ μνήμης χάριν."[51] Despite some scholars identifying it as a Montanist inscription, Eisen questions this identification, which is primarily based on the tendency to consider evidence for Christian women office holders as coming from heretical groups.[52] Another epigraphic source mentions Kale, a woman presbyter in Sicily in the fourth or fifth centuries: "Here lies Kale the elder [πρε(σ)β(ύτις)]. She lived fifty years blamelessly. She completed her life on September 14."[53] Thus, the possibility cannot be ruled out that in the third to fifth centuries, female presbyters conducted the Eucharist.[54] Epiphanius, writing in the fourth century against the Quintillians, actually speaks about Montanism, a charismatic movement that arose in Phrygia in the second half of the second century and spread around the Mediterranean world:

> They use both the Old and New Testament and also speak in the same way of a resurrection of the dead. They consider Quintilla together with Priscilla as founders, the same as the Cataphrygians. They bring with them many useless testimonies, attributing a special grace to Eve because

---

51. "Diogas, *episkopos*, (commissioned this tomb) for Ammion, *presbytera*, in memory." Greek text and English translation from William Tabbernee, *Montanist Inscriptions and Testimonia: Epigraphic Sources Illustrating the History of Montanism*, Patristic Monograph Series 16 (Macon, GA: Mercer University Press, 1997), 66.

52. Ute Eisen, *Women Officeholders in Early Christianity: Epigraphical and Literary Studies* (Collegeville, MN: Liturgical Press, 2000), 117. For scholars who identify the inscription as Montanist, see, e.g., Ulrich Huttner, *Early Christianity in the Lycus Valley*, Ancient Judaism and Early Christianity 85; Early Christianity in Asia Minor 1 (Leiden: Brill, 2013), 312.

53. Kraemer, *Women's Religions*, 256–57. See G. H. R. Horsley, "Women Office-Holders in the Church," *NewDocs* 1:121.

54. This could probably be confirmed by material evidence. On the early third century fresco from the catacombs of Priscilla in Rome, one can see a woman breaking bread at an early Christian Eucharist. The clothing and hairstyle of people depicted on the fresco suggest that most participants are women. One more example of a woman presiding over a Christian gathering is the fresco from the catacombs of Saints Marcellinus and Peter depicting a Christian celestial agape meal where the participants are astonished that it is led by a woman. See Torjesen, *When Women Were Priests*, 52, 154.

she first ate of the tree of knowledge. They acknowledge the sister of Moses as a prophetess as support for their practice of appointing women to clergy. Also, they say, Philip had four daughters who prophesied. Often in their assembly seven virgins dressed in white enter carrying lamps, having come in to prophesy to the people.... Women among them are bishops, presbyters, and the rest, as if there were no difference of nature. For in Christ Jesus there is neither male nor female. These are the things we have learned. They are called Artotyritai because in their mysteries they use bread and cheese and in this fashion they perform their rites. (*Pan.* 49.2.1–3)[55]

From this passage one can infer that in the Montanist groups called Quintillians and Cataphrygians, women held leadership positions such as bishop and presbyter.[56] These groups consider Priscilla and Quintilla as their founders and adduce evidence from both the Old Testament (Exod 15:20) and the New Testament (Acts 21:9 and Gal 3:28) to justify their practice of ordaining women. In addition, Epiphanius speaks about a Montanist liturgical ritual, mentioning the use of bread and cheese in their sacramental meal practices that most likely take place in the evening. Further he condemns the Arabian Christian women of Thracian descent called Kollyridians. Those women baked cakes to the Virgin Mary and functioned as priests: "They prepare a kind of cake in the name of the ever-Virgin, assemble together, and in the name of the holy Virgin they attempt to undertake a deed that is irreverent and blasphemous beyond measure—in her name they function as priests for women" (Epiphanius, *Pan.* 78.23.4).[57] Epiphanius's argument against the Kollyridians serves as

---

55. See Madigan and Osiek, *Ordained Women*, 164–65.

56. Stephen Benko suggests that the Montanist movement was powerfully influenced by the Cybele cult in Asia Minor. Therefore, the role of women as priestesses in the Cybele cult was accommodated by Montanism and so it was logical for women in this movement to assume and perform leadership roles. See Stephen Benko, *The Virgin Goddess: Studies in the Pagan and Christian Roots of Mariology*, SHR 59 (Leiden: Brill, 1993), 17–18, 149–50, 160, 168, 191. This influence did not arise only in the second, third, and fourth centuries, but was present from the beginning of Christianity in the first century. As Valerie Abrahamsen has also suggested, women who, prior to their conversion to Christianity, had played leadership roles in pagan cults and religious associations would have easily assumed those roles in Christian communities. See Valerie Abrahamsen, "Women at Philippi: The Pagan and Christian Evidence," *JFSR* 3 (1987): 17–30.

57. Cited in Kraemer, *Women's Religions*, 86, no. 38.

a refutation that women might legitimately function as Christian priests.[58] Epiphanius's description shows that those women conducted the eucharistic service and offered bread: "For some women prepare a certain kind of little cake with four indentations, cover it with a fine linen veil on a solemn day of the year, and on certain days they set forth bread and offer it in the name of Mary. They all partake of the bread; this is part of what we refuted in the letter written to Arabia" (*Pan.* 79.1.7).[59] "Furthermore, these women of this sect 'renew the drink offering to Fortune and set the table for a demon,' not to God, as it is written, and they feast on the food of impiety" (79.8.1).[60]

Then Epiphanius gives various reasons why women cannot perform priestly duties. The first reason is based on the popular opinion on the nature of women that the female sex is easily mistaken, fallible, and poor in intelligence. The second argument is from the Old Testament, where no woman ever exercised priesthood. The third reason is based on the New Testament. Epiphanius states that if women had been allowed priesthood, the mother of Jesus would have performed this role. Additionally, there were no women among those whom Jesus chose to be his apostles. Finally, Paul mentioned only the office of widows for women. Nowhere did he write about women as presbyters or priestesses (Epiphanius, *Pan.* 79.4.1). The fact that Epiphanius writes about Christian groups with women priests and his vehement condemnation of it confirms the existing practice of women presiding over the gatherings of communities in early Christianity as well as his own (majority) position, refuting such women and their practice as part of the masculinization and institutionalization of the church.

---

58. Kraemer, *Her Share of the Blessing*, 166. The name "Kollyridians" is derived from the Greek word κολλυρίς, denoting the bread which the women sacrificed to Mary. The term κολλυρίς usually refers to a small loaf of bread, a cake which, in addition to secular usage, often figures in sacrifices. According to Stephen Benko, this group doubtless believed that they represented a legitimate form of Christian worship. It was difficult to distinguish between traditional Christians and fringe groups because as Justin Martyr, referring to gnostic groups, complained in his *First Apology* (7.26), "all are called Christians." See Benko, *The Virgin Goddess*, 174.

59. Cited in Kraemer, *Women's Religions*, 86, no. 39.

60. Αὗται δὲ πάλιν ἀνακαινίζουσι τῇ Τύχῃ τὸ κέρασμα καὶ ἑτοιμάζουσι τῷ δαίμονι καὶ οὐ θεῷ τὴν τράπεζαν, κατὰ τὸ γεγραμμένον, καὶ σιτοῦνται σῖτα ἀσεβείας. English translation from Benko, *The Virgin Goddess*, 172.

4. Conclusion

Women in the Greco-Roman world could occupy positions of leadership at meals and gatherings of religious associations during the emergence and early development of Christianity. This is evidenced by various literary and epigraphic texts cited in this paper. In many respects, the gatherings of Christians followed the format of the Greco-Roman banquets, such as those held by pagan as well as Jewish individuals, voluntary associations, and cult societies where women could exercise authority and leadership. In the first century, women played an active role in hosting, leading, and performing leadership tasks in the gatherings of Christian communities. There are numerous examples of women playing leading roles in Christian communities in the first, second, and the third centuries. Roman and Greco-Roman societies were predominantly dominated by men, but women of status held leadership positions both in the pagan environment and in Christian circles.

In the second and third centuries, there was a growing tendency to exclude women from leading roles in Christian communities. However, there were charismatic groups where women exercised a certain degree of freedom in performing leadership roles. This is supported by various "orthodox" sources that present a negative picture of this practice. The sheer amount of evidence in the available sources demonstrates that there were a considerable number of Christian groups who followed the first century practice of women in leadership roles in communities, as advocated by the apostle Paul. In the course of time, however, these groups were banned as heretical, together with the leading roles of women in the gatherings of Christian communities.

Bibliography

Abrahamsen, Valerie. "Women at Philippi: The Pagan and Christian Evidence." *JFSR* 3 (1987): 17–30.

Alikin, Valeriy A. *The Earliest History of the Christian Gathering: Origins, Development and Content of the Christian Gathering in the First to Third Centuries.* VCSup 102. Leiden: Brill, 2010.

Ascough, Richard S., Philip A. Harland, and John S. Kloppenborg, eds. *Associations in the Greco-Roman World: A Sourcebook.* Waco, TX: Baylor University Press, 2012.

Benko, Stephen. *The Virgin Goddess: Studies in the Pagan and Christian Roots of Mariology.* SHR 59. Leiden: Brill, 1993.

Bremen, Riet van. *The Limits of Participation: Women and Civic Life in the Greek East in the Hellenistic and Roman Periods.* Dutch Monographs on Ancient History and Archaeology 15. Amsterdam: Gieben, 1996.

Brooten, Bernadette J. "Female Leadership in the Ancient Synagogue." Pages 215–23 in *From Dura to Sepphoris: Studies in Jewish Art and Society in Late Antiquity.* Edited by Lee I. Levine and Zeev Weiss. JRASup 40. Portsmouth, RI: Journal of Roman Archaeology, 2000.

———. *Women Leaders in the Ancient Synagogue.* BJS 36. Chico, CA: Scholars Press, 1982.

Chuvin, Pierre. *A Chronicle of the Last Pagans.* Translated by B. A. Archer. Revealing Antiquity 4. Cambridge: Harvard University Press, 1990.

Cohick, Lynn H. *Women in the World of the Earliest Christians: Illuminating Ancient Ways of Life.* Grand Rapids: Baker Academic, 2009.

Dunn, James D. G. *The Epistles to the Colossians and to Philemon: A Commentary on the Greek Text.* NIGTC. Grand Rapids: Eerdmans, 1996.

Eisen, Ute. *Women Officeholders in Early Christianity: Epigraphical and Literary Studies.* Collegeville, MN: Liturgical Press, 2000.

Elliott, J. K. *The Apocryphal New Testament: A Collection of Apocryphal Christian Literature in an English Translation.* Oxford: Clarendon, 2005.

Friesen, Steven J. "Junia Theodora of Corinth: Gendered Inequalities in the Early Roman Empire." Pages 203–26 in *Corinth in Contrast. Studies in Inequality.* Edited by Steven J. Friesen, Sarah A. James, and Daniel N. Schowalter. NovTSup 155. Leiden: Brill, 2014.

Horsley, G. H. R. "Women Office-Holders in the Church." *NewDocs* 1:121.

Huttner, Ulrich. *Early Christianity in the Lycus Valley.* Ancient Judaism and Early Christianity 85; Early Christianity in Asia Minor 1. Leiden: Brill, 2013.

Jensen, Anne. *God's Self-Confident Daughters: Early Christianity and the Liberation of Women.* Translated by O. C. Dean Jr. Louisville: Westminster John Knox, 1996.

Jones, Christopher P. *Between Pagan and Christian.* Cambridge: Harvard University Press, 2014.

Kloppenborg, John S. "Collegia and *Thiasoi*: Issues in Function, Taxonomy and Membership." Pages 16–30 in *Voluntary Associations in the Graeco-Roman World.* Edited by John S. Kloppenborg and Stephen G. Wilson. London: Routledge, 1996.

Kloppenborg, John S., and Richard S. Ascough. *Greco-Roman Associations: Texts, Translations, and Commentary.* BZNW 181. Berlin: de Gruyter, 2011.

Kraemer, Ross Shepard. *Her Share of the Blessings: Women's Religions among Pagans, Jews, and Christians in the Greco-Roman World.* Oxford: Oxford University Press, 1992.

———, ed. *Women's Religions in the Greco-Roman World: A Sourcebook.* Rev. ed. Oxford: Oxford University Press, 2004.

Madigan, Kevin, and Carolyn Osiek. *Ordained Women in the Early Church: A Documentary History.* Baltimore: Johns Hopkins University Press, 2005.

Maxwell, Jaclyn. "Paganism and Christianization." Pages 852–53 in *The Oxford Handbook of Late Antiquity.* Edited by Scott Fitzgerald Johnson. Oxford: Oxford University Press, 2012.

McLean, Bradley H. "The Agrippinilla Inscription: Religious Associations and Early Church Formation." Pages 239–70 in *Origins and Method: Towards a New Understanding of Judaism and Christianity; Essays in Honour of John C. Hurd.* Edited by Bradley H. McLean. Sheffield: JSOT Press, 1993.

Meeks, Wayne A. *The First Urban Christians: The Social World of the Apostle Paul.* New Haven: Yale University Press, 1983.

Miller, Patricia Cox. *Women in Early Christianity: Translations from Greek Texts.* Washington, DC: Catholic University of America Press, 2005.

Osiek, Carolyn. "*Diakonos* and *Prostatis*: Women's Patronage in Early Christianity." *HvTSt* 61 (2005): 347–70.

———. *A Woman's Place: House Churches in Earliest Christianity.* Minneapolis: Fortress, 2006.

Richardson, Peter, and Valerie Heuchan. "Jewish Voluntary Associations in Egypt and the Roles of Women." Pages 226–51 in *Voluntary Associations in the Graeco-Roman World.* Edited by John S. Kloppenborg and Stephen G. Wilson. London: Routledge, 1996.

Schultz, Celia E. *Women's Religious Activity in the Roman Republic.* Chapel Hill: University of North Carolina Press, 2006.

Schweizer, Eduard. *The Letter to the Colossians: A Commentary.* Minneapolis: Augsburg, 1982.

Sergienko, Gennadi A. *Our Politeuma Is in Heaven! Paul's Polemical Engagement with the "Enemies of the Cross of Christ" in Philippians 3:18–20.* Carlisle: Langham Monographs, 2013.

Sokolowski, Franciszek. *Lois sacrées de l'Asie Mineure*. Travaux et mémoires (Ecole française d'Athènes) 9. Paris: de Boccard, 1955.

Tabbernee, William. *Montanist Inscriptions and Testimonia: Epigraphic Sources Illustrating the History of Montanism*. Patristic Monograph Series 16. Macon, GA: Mercer University Press, 1997.

Theissen, Gerd. *Soziologie der Jesusbewegung: Ein Beitrag zur Entstehungsgeschichte des Urchristentums*. Theologische Existenz heute 194. Munich: Kaiser, 1977.

———. *Studien zur Soziologie des Urchristentums*. WUNT 19. Tübingen: Mohr Siebeck, 1979.

Torjesen, Karen Jo. *When Women Were Priests: Women's Leadership in the Early Church and the Scandal of Their Subordination in the Rise of Christianity*. San Francisco: HarperSanFrancisco, 1993.

Weg, Magdalena Wilhelmina Misset-van de. "A Wealthy Woman Named Tryhaena: Patroness of Thecla of Iconium." Pages 16–35 in *The Apocryphal Acts of Paul and Thecla*. Edited by Jan N. Bremmer. Studies on the Apocryphal Acts of the Apostles 2. Kampen: Kok Pharos, 1996.

The Political Charges against Paul and Silas in Acts 17:6–7: Roman Benefaction in Thessalonica[*]

Jeffrey A. D. Weima

Introduction

The success of Paul and Silas during their mission-founding ministry in Thessalonica in winning some converts from Judaism and even more from paganism not surprisingly caused a negative reaction from both the Jewish and the larger pagan community.[1] At first, opposition to the fledgling Jesus movement was spontaneous and unorganized. This changed, however, when the success of the apostles in securing converts from the synagogue caused the remaining Jews to pursue a planned course of action: "But the Jews were jealous, and taking some bad characters from the marketplace,

---

[*] This paper is dedicated to Dennis Smith, with whom until his untimely illness I shared the honor of being the two participants who attended the highest number of COMCAR study tours.

1. Paul testifies to the opposition that he, as well as his converts, faced during the founding of the Thessalonian church: the apostle, along with Silas and Timothy, needed "courage in our God to declare to you the gospel of God in the face of great opposition" (1 Thess 2:2); and the Christians in that city also "received the word in much affliction" (1 Thess 1:1) with the result that "you indeed suffered ... from your own fellow citizens" (1 Thess 2:14). Although there is uncertainty over the precise meaning of "fellow citizens" (συμφυλέται), there are good grounds for understanding this term not in an ethnic sense (i.e., it has in view only the Gentile citizens of the city) but a geographical sense of referring to all the inhabitants of Thessalonica, the vast majority of whom would have been gentiles but some of whom would have been Jews (see discussion in Jeffrey A. D. Weima, *1–2 Thessalonians*, Baker Exegetical Commentary on the New Testament [Grand Rapids: Baker, 2014], 167–68). This sense agrees with Acts 17:5–9, which claims that local Jews and Greeks were both involved in the events that ultimately led to the forced departure of Paul and Silas from Thessalonica.

they formed a mob and started a riot in the city" (Acts 17:5a).² The loss of even a few synagogue members naturally would have aroused the jealousy and anger of Jewish leaders; how much more intense these hostile feelings must have been towards the apostles for stealing both a great number of God-fearers ("devout Greeks") and several women from rich and powerful families ("not a few of the leading women"; Acts 17:4).

The Jewish leaders, therefore, came up with a strategy for removing Paul and Silas from their city.³ The plan involved hiring "some bad characters from the marketplace" (τῶν ἀγοραίων ἄνδρας τινὰς πονηρούς)—a phrase that, with the addition of the adjective "bad," refers not in a neutral sense to common day laborers or marketplace traders but in a pejorative sense to louts, loafers, and lowlifes, those who hang around public spaces with nothing to do but get into trouble.⁴ These good-for-nothing men were nevertheless good at something: they were able to help the Jews form a crowd and to get their gentile fellow citizens to join them in a riot based on trumped-up charges against Paul and Silas.⁵ The agitated mob "attacked the house of Jason" (Acts 17:5b), who was providing housing for the missionaries. The original plan was to bring the pair to the "citizens' assembly" (δῆμος)—the lowest level of city governance, which handled such matters as financial affairs, festivals, issues connected to the various local cults, and certain judicial concerns.⁶ However, when they could not find Paul and Silas, the plan changed: they seized Jason and a few other converts and brought them instead to a higher power—the "politarchs" (πολιτάρχες).⁷

---

2. Translations are mine unless noted otherwise.

3. Jewish involvement in the apostles' exodus from Thessalonica cannot be dismissed as a Lukan creation, since Paul himself claims that it was "the Jews who ... drove us out" (1 Thess 2:15).

4. Aristophanes, *Ran.* 1015 [1047]; Plato, *Prot.* 347c; Theophrastus, *Char.* 6.2; Herodotus, *Hist.* 2.141; Xenophon, *Hell.* 6.2.23.

5. The historical plausibility of this scenario is supported by Plutarch, who describes a similar situation of "men who were of low birth and had lately been slaves but who were hanging around the marketplace (ἀγοραίους—the same term used in Luke's account) and able to gather a mob and to force all issues by means of solicitations and shouting" (*Aem.* 38.4).

6. Robert M. Evans, *Eschatology and Ethics: A Study of Thessalonica and Paul's Letters to the Thessalonians* (Princeton: McMahon, 1968), 13.

7. It is often claimed that the term *politarch* does not occur in any extant Greek writing other than its twofold reference in Acts 17:6 and 17:8. Consequently, many biblical scholars prior to the late nineteenth century and some even in the early twen-

It is before these city leaders that the unruly crowd raised two charges against the apostles—the first, a general charge of disturbing the peace; the second, a specific charge of disobeying the decrees of Caesar:

> 17:6bThe ones who have caused trouble all over the world, these men have now come here, 7whom Jason has welcomed, and they are all acting against the decrees of Caesar, saying that there is another king—Jesus.

Scholars have struggled to understand precisely what these two charges involve, especially the accusation of violating the decrees of Caesar, and this has in turn caused some to question the accuracy of Luke's account of this episode. A. N. Sherwin-White, for example, who examined certain episodes in the New Testament through the eyes of Roman law, concluded that "the accusation brought against the apostles at Thessalonica is somewhat obscure" and that "this is one of the most confused of the various descriptions of charges in Acts."[8] Karl P. Donfried asks: "What are these *dogmata Kaisaros* which Paul and his associates violated? Is Luke here spinning an entertaining story or is he faithfully describing the reality of

---

tieth century questioned the historical accuracy of these two references in the Acts account. The claim about the term not occurring in any literary source other than Acts, however, is incorrect, as the word does, in fact, occur in the fourth century BCE Greek writer on the art of war, Aeneas Tactitus (*Polior.* 26.12). Furthermore, while literary evidence for the existence of this city office may be weak, with only one additional occurrence outside of Acts, inscriptional evidence has become increasingly impressive, as more and more references to politarchs have been discovered. Although at the close of the nineteenth century nineteen inscriptions attested to the office of politarch (E. D. Burton, "The Politarchs," *AmJT* 2 [1898]: 598–632), there are currently as many as seventy nonliterary references to these unique city officials (G. H. R. Horsley, "The Politarchs," in *The Book of Acts in Its Greco-Roman Setting*, vol. 2 of *The Book of Acts in Its First Century Setting*, ed. David W. J. Gill and Conrad Gempf [Grand Rapids: Eerdmans, 1994], 422; Rainer Riesner, *Paul's Early Period: Chronology, Mission Strategy, Theology* [Grand Rapids: Eerdmans, 1998], 355). Twenty-eight of these inscriptions (40 percent) are from Thessalonica, while the majority of the remaining attestations are from various communities in Macedonia (Amphipolis, Lete, Derriopus, Pella, and Edessa).

8. A. N. Sherwin-White, *Roman Society and Roman Law in the New Testament*, Sarum Lectures 1960–1961 (Oxford: Clarendon, 1963), 96, 103; cited in Justin K. Hardin, "Decrees and Drachmas at Thessalonica: An Illegal Assembly in Jason's House (Acts 17.1–10a)," *NTS* 52 (2006): 30 n. 3.

the Thessalonian situation?"[9] Richard I. Pervo pessimistically comments: "Learned efforts to specify the decrees in question are probably in vain."[10]

The purpose of this essay is to bring greater clarity concerning the charges brought against Paul and Silas. It will be demonstrated that the charges were highly political in nature and that such accusations of anti-Roman activity were extremely dangerous in a city like Thessalonica, which enjoyed a favored relationship with Rome and engaged in a variety of activities to strengthen that relationship, thereby securing political and financial benefits from the empire.

2. Roman Benefaction in Thessalonica

The seriousness of the two charges, as well as their political character, cannot be fully appreciated unless one places those charges within the broader context of a long history of Roman benefaction in Thessalonica.[11] The city of Thessalonica enjoyed a favored relationship with Rome—a relationship that it deliberately fostered in the hopes of political and financial gain. After the fall of Macedonia as an independent kingdom in the battle at Pydna in 168 BCE, the victorious Romans followed the strategy of divide and conquer, splitting the region into four "districts" (μερίδες; see Acts 16:12) with Thessalonica becoming the capital of the second.[12] The following years of Roman rule witnessed sporadic rebellions which were finally suppressed in 146 BCE, at which time the Romans expanded the boundaries of the region and reorganized Macedonia as a province where Thessalonica alone was elevated to the privileged status of capital city and became the home base of Rome's representative, the governor.

Rome's choice of Thessalonica as provincial capital was based not solely on the city's size and wealth but also on its loyalty to the Roman Empire rather than to the local leaders heading up the rebellions. One

---

9. Karl P. Donfried, "The Imperial Cults of Thessalonica and Political Conflict in 1 Thessalonians," *Paul and Empire: Religion and Power in Roman Imperial Society*, ed. Richard A. Horsley (Harrisburg, PA: Trinity, 1997), 215.

10. Richard I. Pervo, *Acts: A Commentary*, Hermeneia (Minneapolis: Fortress, 2009), 420.

11. The following section draws heavily from my commentary; see Weima, *Thessalonians*, 3–7.

12. Livy, *Ab urbe cond.* 44.32; 45.29.9; Diodorus Siculus, *Bib. hist.* 31.8.6–9; Strabo, *Geogr.* 7, fr. 47.

inscription records how the Thessalonians honor Metellus, the Roman praetor, who quelled the insurrection, identifying him as the city's "savior and benefactor" (*IG* 10.2.1.134). Several other inscriptions honor "Roman benefactors" (Ρωμαῖοι εὐεργέται). These are individuals who financed local cultural institutions (e.g., the gymnasium and its activities), helped protect the city from hostile neighbors and anti-Roman invaders, promoted the interests of Thessalonica in Rome, or provided aid in other ways. These honorific inscriptions reveal that a pro-Roman attitude existed in Thessalonica and that at least some of its leading citizens were willing not merely to endure but to embrace eagerly Roman rule in order to enjoy more fully the benefits that this relationship brought.[13] This positive view of Rome was enhanced by Thessalonica's need for the empire's help in fending off the frequent raids by the barbarian tribes in northern Macedonia.[14] Thus, Cicero, the famous Roman statesman, who spent six months in Thessalonica in exile in 58 BCE, referred to Macedonia as "a loyal province, friend to the Roman people" (*Font.* 44).

The close relationship between Thessalonica and Rome can also be seen in the key role that the city played in the empire's civil wars, even though this role all too often involved initially backing the losing side. The city supported Pompey in his quest for power against Julius Caesar. Prior to his inglorious defeat at Pharsalus in 48 BCE, Pompey prepared for battle by gathering in Thessalonica with the two consuls and over two hundred senators, turning the city into a kind of second Rome where the "true" Senate was now held (Dio Cassius, *Hist. rom.* 41.18.4-6; 41.43.1-5). Some six years later Thessalonica was again at the center of the Roman internal wars when the armies of Brutus and Cassius, the two leaders responsible for the assassination of Julius Caesar, faced off in battle in the plains of nearby Philippi against the armies of Marc Antony and Octavian (who later became Caesar Augustus), the two avengers of Caesar's murder. Thessalonica initially supported Brutus and Cassius but, between the two battles on the Philippian plains, switched their allegiance to Marc Antony and Octavian, causing Brutus to promise his soldiers the right to plunder Thessalonica following their anticipated victory (Appian, *Bell. civ.* 4.118; Plutarch, *Brut.* 46.1). Fortunately for Thessalonica, that victory never

---

13. See especially Holland L. Hendrix, "Thessalonians Honor Romans" (ThD diss., Harvard University, 1984); also Gene L. Green, *The Letters to the Thessalonians*, PNTC (Grand Rapids: Eerdmans, 2002), 16–17.

14. A. Papagiannopoulos, *History of Thessaloniki* (Thessaloniki: Rekos, 1982), 36.

came, as both Brutus and Cassius went down to defeat at the hands of Marc Antony and, to a lesser extent, Octavian. A triumphal arch celebrating the two victors was built at the Vardar Gate, one of the major gates of the city wall, and commemorative medals were circulated with the inscription "for the freedom of the people of Thessaloniki."[15] A coin series was produced, presenting on the obverse a veiled female head with the inscription ΟΜΟΝΟΙΑ ("concord, harmony, like-mindedness") and on the reverse a horse galloping free with the inscription ΘΕΣΣΑΛΟΝ[ΙΚΗΣ] / ΡΩΜ[ΗΣ] ("Thessalonica/Rome"), thereby celebrating how the victory of Antony and Octavian had restored concord between the two cities.[16]

The city and the province came under the control of Marc Antony, who in 42 BCE rewarded its citizens for their support by granting Thessalonica the status of a "free city" (*civitas libera*: Pliny, *Nat.* 4.17 [10]).[17] This favored classification meant that the inhabitants enjoyed a measure of autonomy over local affairs, the right to mint their own coins, freedom from military occupation within the city walls, and certain tax concessions. Holland Hendrix notes that this privileged status was "granted only to people and cities which had displayed remarkable loyalty to the interests of the Roman people."[18] Nine years later the city found itself again backing the losing side in Rome's internal wars, as Marc Antony fell at the hands of Octavian in the battle at Actium in 31 BCE. Nevertheless, the city quickly either erased the name of Antony in inscriptions honoring the defeated general (a standard way of effecting *damnatio memoriae*—erasing the memory of someone formally esteemed who was now dishonored) or replaced his name with that of Octavian (*IG* 10.2.1.6, 83, 109), thereby ensuring good relations with Rome and maintaining their favored status as a free city.

The city's intimate relationship with Rome was fostered further with the establishment during this time period of a new cult of Roma and the Roman benefactors.[19] Several inscriptions are addressed to "the gods and

---

15. Papagiannopoulos, *History of Thessaloniki*, 39.
16. Hendrix, "Thessalonians Honor Romans," 162–65.
17. Evidence of Thessalonica's "freedom" is found in one inscription (*IG* 10.2.1.6) and in a series of coins issued by the city inscribed ΘΕΣΣΑΛΟΝΙΚΕΩΝ ΕΛΕΥΘΕΡΙΑΣ ("Freedom of the Thessalonians"). See discussion in Hendrix, "Thessalonians Honor Romans," 159–60.
18. Hendrix, "Thessalonians Honor Romans," 251.
19. C. Edson, "Macedonia," *HSCP* 51 (1940): 133, dates the founding of this new

the Roman benefactors" (*IG* 10.2.1.4), "the priest of the gods … and of the priest of Roma and the Roman benefactors" (*IG* 10.2.1.133, 226), "of both Roma and the Roman benefactors" (*IG* 10.2.1.128) and "Roma and Romans" (*IG* 10.2.1.32). Once the cult to honor the goddess Roma and the Roman benefactors was established, it was natural to extend such honors to the most powerful and most important Roman benefactor, the emperor. A temple in honor of Caesar was built near the end of the first century BCE, and a priesthood to service this temple was established: an important inscription refers to "the temple of Caesar" and the "priest and *agōnothetēs* ('games superintendent') of the Imperator Caesar Augustus son [of god]" and the "priest of the gods … and priest of Roma and of the Roman benefactors" (*IG* 10.2.1.31). This inscription, along with others (*IG* 10.2.1.32, 132, 133), also suggests the preeminence of officials connected with the imperial cult over other priesthoods.[20]

Coinage from the city reveals that Julius Caesar and his adoptive son, Octavian, received divine honors. In one series minted about 27 BCE, the laureate head of Julius Caesar appears with the inscription "God." The reverse side of coins from this series has the image of Octavian and, though they do not have the similar inscriptions "God" or "son of god," his divinity is implied by his pairing with the divine Julius and by the title *Sebastos*, or "Augustus," often found. A statue of Augustus, discovered in Thessalonica in 1939 just north of the Serapeion, depicts the emperor in a divine posture: he is slightly larger than life-sized, semi-naked, and a voluminous robe wraps around his waist and over his left arm; his right arm is raised with closed fist and finger pointed upward as he strides forward.[21] It is "one of the best examples of the imperial propaganda statues—and is, indeed, one of the first of the series—that the Romans erected in various nerve-centres of their boundless empire."[22] In contrast to the *Prima Porta*

---

cult to 41 BCE, while Hendrix ("Thessalonians Honor Romans," 22) dates it to 95 BCE or earlier.

20. In every extant instance in which the "priest and *agōnothetēs* of the imperator" is mentioned, he is listed first in what appears to be a strict observance of protocol. The imperator's priest and *agonothete* assumes priority, the priest of "the gods" is cited next, followed by the priest of Roma and of Roman benefactors (Hendrix, "Thessalonians Honor Romans," 312).

21. Archaeological Museum, Thessaloniki, no. 1065, "Statue of Oktavianus Augustus," Odysseus: Ministry of Culture and Sports, http://tinyurl.com/SBL4522s.

22. J. Vokotopoulou, *Guide to the Archaeological Museum of Thessaloniki* (Athens: Kapon, 1996), 85.

exemplar, where Augustus is in full military garb, the Thessalonian statue of him omits these symbols of power and instead conveys the emperor as a man of not war but peace. Another statue—this one headless but likely that of Claudius—was discovered close to that of Augustus; it also portrays this later emperor in a divine pose.[23]

The good relations that existed between Macedonia, including its leading city of Thessalonica, and Rome can also be seen in the so-called Augustan Settlement of 27 BCE, when the emperor regulated the governance of the provinces, classifying them as either senatorial or imperial. Senatorial provinces were those considered to be peaceful and loyal to Rome that consequently were placed under the control of the Senate, governed by proconsuls (governors) who held office for only a one-year term. Imperial provinces were those typically located on the boundaries of the empire and whose commitment to Rome was considered weak or questionable that consequently were placed under the direct control of the emperor, who appointed procurators or prefects with military authority to hold office and govern these areas as long as the emperor desired. The fact that Augustus designated Macedonia as a senatorial province (Dio Cassius, *Hist. rom.* 53.12.4), therefore, is significant. It also suggests that the act of the subsequent emperor, Tiberius, in reclassifying Macedonia as an imperial province in 15 CE and placing this region under his direct control (Tacitus, *Hist.* 1.76.4) would have been viewed with alarm by those in Macedonia and Thessalonica who were concerned with maintaining good relations with Rome. Pro-Roman sensibilities in the region and capital city were encouraged, however, when Claudius in 44 CE annulled the decision of his predecessor and restored Macedonia's status as a senatorial province and Thessalonica as the dwelling place of the governor (Dio Cassius, *Hist. rom.* 60.24.1).

This historical survey makes clear that Thessalonica enjoyed a favored relationship with Rome and engaged in a variety of activities to strengthen that relationship, thereby securing political and financial benefits from the empire. As Craig Steven de Vos notes: "In light of this history, the city [Thessalonica] seems to have developed an attitude of strong dependence on Roman, and especially, Imperial, benefaction."[24] What this historical

---

23. Archaeological Museum, Thessaloniki, no. 2467.

24. Craig Steven de Vos, *Church and Community Conflicts: The Relationship of the Thessalonian, Corinthian, and Philippian Churches with Their Wider Civic Communities*, SBLDS 168 (Atlanta: Scholars Press, 1999), 125.

overview also makes clear is how important Thessalonica's favored status would have been to both its city leaders and citizens, and how they would naturally be upset and deal aggressively with anyone or any group within the community whom they feared might jeopardize their favored status and bring an end to the Roman benefaction from which they benefited greatly. Especially with the memory still fresh in their mind of the loss of their senatorial status under Tiberius and its recovery just five or six years earlier under Claudius, it is understandable why the crowd and the politarchs "were disturbed" (Acts 17:8) when hearing about the anti-Roman charges brought against Paul and Silas as well as about those local citizens who had embraced their teachings.[25]

3. The Political Charges against Paul and Silas

The angry crowd lodged two charges[26] against Paul and Silas, both of which were political and threatened the Roman benefaction enjoyed by Thessalonica and thus were very serious. In fact, such charges were cleverly chosen to ensure the missionaries' arrest, severe punishment, and almost certain expulsion from the city.

The first charge accused Paul and Silas of disturbing the peace: "The ones who have caused trouble all over the world, these men have now come here" (Acts 17:6b). C. K. Barrett correctly observes: "The charge is much more dangerous than 'They have upset everyone' or even than 'they have

---

25. Riesner, *Paul's Early Period*, 357.

26. Although the vast majority of commentators see two specific charges (that of disturbing the peace [Acts 17:6b] and of violating the decrees of Caesar [17:7b]), a few have argued for the presence of three charges, with the extra charge involving either that of Jason's hosting those involved in disturbing the peace (17:7a) or of proclaiming the existence of another king (17:7c); see, e.g., G. Krodel, *Acts* (Minneapolis: Augsburg, 1986), 319–20; John B. Polhill, *Acts: An Exegetical and Theological Exposition of Holy Scripture*, New American Commentary 26 (Nashville: Broadman & Holman, 1992), 362; Joseph A. Fitzmyer, *The Acts of the Apostles*, AB 31 (New York: Doubleday, 1998), 596. The grammar of the Greek text of the Acts account works against this possibility, however, as the supposed third charge in neither case involves an independent clause: the claimed charge against Jason for hosting troublemakers is part of a brief relative clause, and the claimed charge of proclaiming Jesus as king is given in the form of an adverbial participle that is dependent upon and thus closely connected with the second charge of violating the decrees of Caesar.

turned the world upside down.'"[27] This is because there is a clear political aspect to the charge that modern readers can easily miss.[28] The anti-Roman character of the first charge is better captured by Luke Timothy Johnson's translation in which the missionaries are accused of "subverting the empire."[29]

The gravity of this charge becomes clearer when one recognizes that the Romans actively and aggressively promoted themselves as providing "peace and security" (1 Thess 5:3), and they did so through various public media. The minting of coins, the building of public monuments, the engraving of official proclamations, and the dissemination of literary works all served the common purpose of shaping public opinion and convincing the populace about the peace and security that Roman rule supplied.[30] The charge of disturbing the peace, therefore, accuses Paul and Silas of undermining the main benefit that Rome supposedly provided. Furthermore, as demonstrated above, the fact that Thessalonica had a lengthy and close relationship with Rome would cause both the crowd and the city officials to be especially alarmed at such a charge (Acts 17:8).[31] It is ironic, of course, that Paul and Silas are accused of disturbing the peace by an angry mob which is guilty of the very thing with which they are charging the two missionaries.

The second charge has proven stubbornly hard thus far to identify with specificity: "and they all are acting against the decrees of Caesar, saying that there is another king—Jesus" (Acts 17:7). Five possibilities have been proposed thus far.

---

27. C. K. Barrett, *A Critical and Exegetical Commentary on the Acts of the Apostles*, 2 vols., ICC (London: T&T Clark, 1994–1998), 815.

28. As Pervo (*Acts*, 420 n. 23) notes, the NRSV's rendering of the key verb ἀναστατάνω in the first charge as "turning the word upside down" "removes the political significance of the term."

29. Luke Timothy Johnson, *The Acts of the Apostles* (Collegeville: Glazier, 1992), 307.

30. Jeffrey A. D. Weima, "'Peace and Security' (1 Thess. 5.3): Prophetic Warning or Political Propaganda?," *NTS* 58 (2012): 331–59.

31. Most commentators fail to appreciate the gravity of the first charge, with some thereby asserting that the second charge is the more serious of the two (e.g., Ben Witherington III, *1 and 2 Thessalonians: A Socio-rhetorical Commentary* [Grand Rapids: Eerdmans, 2006], 507; Darrell L. Bock, *Acts*, Baker Exegetical Commentary on the New Testament [Grand Rapids: Baker, 2007], 552).

3.1. Treason

The traditional answer is that the claims of Paul and Silas about the kingship of Jesus were interpreted as an attempt to overthrow the current emperor, Claudius, and that the two missionaries were therefore accused of breaking the Roman law of treason (*maiestas*).[32] Ernst Haenchen is typical of many commentators when he states: "Secondly, the Christians are accused of high treason: instead of the βασιλεύς in Rome, they acknowledge only the βασιλεὺς Ἰησοῦς!"[33] The charge of treason would have been an easy and effective one to make against Paul and Silas, since their accusers could have appealed for support to the various claims connected with the apostles' preaching ministry in Thessalonica.[34] The letters written to the Thessalonians provide a window into the content of the gospel message originally preached in that city (see 1 Thess 5:2; 2 Thess 2:5, 15). This gospel message contains several elements that could be used to support the charge of treason against Paul and Silas:[35]

1. Their gospel resulted in local citizens abandoning idols (1 Thess 1:9: "how you turned from idols to serve a living and true God"), which would involve their refusal not just to offer sacrifices to the various Greek, Roman, and Egyptian deities but also to participate in the imperial cult in Thessalonica and to venerate publically various Caesars, whether past or present.
2. Their gospel proclaimed the existence of a "kingdom" (1 Thess 2:12) distinct from that of Rome, which supports the clarifying charge of sedition brought against Paul and Silas, namely, their "saying that there is another king—Jesus" (Acts 17:7c).
3. Their gospel describes the "coming" (1 Thess 2:19; 4:15) of Jesus and his "reception" (1 Thess 4:17) in technical language (παρουσία,

---

32. *Maiestas* is an abbreviation for the fuller phrase *maietas populi romani minuta*, which means "minimizing the majesty of the Roman people."
33. Ernst Haenchen, *The Acts of the Apostles: A Commentary*, trans. B. Noble and G. Shinn (Oxford: Blackwell, 1971), 510.
34. Bruce notes: "In the present instance there was just enough colour of truth in the charge to make it plausible and deadly." See F. F. Bruce, *The Book of the Acts*, NICNT (Grand Rapids: Eerdmans, 1977), 344–45.
35. Witherington, *Thessalonians*, 508. Also Craig S. Keener, *Acts: An Exegetical Commentary; 15:1–23:35* (Grand Rapids: Baker, 2014), 2553–54.

ἀπάντησις) that refers to the coming of a king and his royal welcome.
4. Their gospel is presented as the true source of "salvation" (1 Thess 5:9) on the day of the Lord in contrast to the "peace and security" (1 Thess 5:3) supposedly provided by Rome and its Caesars.
5. Their gospel contains politically charged language of the Lord Jesus, whose coming will destroy "the man of lawlessness ... the one who opposes and exalts himself over every being called god or every object of worship" (2 Thess 2:3–4), which could be understood as a veiled reference to the emperor and the imperial cult.

The charge of treason brought against Paul and Silas would gain still further strength if their opponents highlighted the fact that the Jesus whom the apostles proclaim had himself been executed by Roman authorities on exactly the same charge. As F. F. Bruce observes: "The fact that the rival emperor whom Paul and the others were accused of proclaiming had been sentenced to death by a Roman judge on a charge of sedition—as anyone could ascertain who took the trouble to inquire—spoke for itself."[36]

It is important to recognize that the shift from the Roman democracy to the Principate was accompanied by a broadening of the law of treason so that crimes against the Roman state were equated with actions or words against the head of the Roman state, the emperor. C. W. Chilton, who examines the Roman law of treason in the early Principate, observes:

> The actual enlargement of the scope of *maiestas* was left to Augustus, and the *Lex Iulia* referred to by later jurists is almost certainly his. The actual terms of this law, too, are unknown, but events show that the *crimen minutae maiestatis* was extended to include, as well as the abuse of the divinity of Julius, verbal abuse and slander of the *Princeps* and sometimes even slander of members of his family. It was this extension of the meaning of *maiestas* by Augustus—showing as it did the shift in the balance of power in the State—that was so significant.[37]

---

36. F. F. Bruce, *1 and 2 Thessalonians*, WBC 45 (Waco, TX: Word, 1982), xxiii.
37. C. W. Chilton, "The Roman Law of Treason under the Early Principate," *JRS* 45 (1955): 75 (cited by H. W. Tajra, *The Trial of St. Paul: A Juridical Exegesis of the Second Half of the Acts of the Apostles*, WUNT 2/35 [Tübingen: Mohr Siebeck, 1989], 38). See also Richard A. Bauman, *The Crimen Maiestatis in the Roman Republic and Augustan Principate* (Johannesburg: Witwatersrand University, 1967), 155–68, 266–92.

This expansion of the law of treason continued under the reign of Tiberius, who "enforced them most rigorously" (Suetonius, *Tib.* 58; see also Tacitus, *Ann.* 1.72). This situation can also be assumed for the reign of Claudius and the time of the mission-founding preaching in Thessalonica by Paul and Silas.

The general context of the charges brought against the two missionaries, then, involved the charge of treason. In fact, all four of the remaining proposals concerning the precise reference in the charge of violating the decrees of Caesar are closely connected to the accusation of treason. But while treason clearly involves the *general* context of the charges brought against Paul and Silas, it does not likely account for the very *specific* accusation of their transgressing the decrees of Caesar.

The major weakness of this proposal is that treason was forbidden by general public law, so there was no need for a specific decree by Caesar to make it illegal. As Rainer Riesner aptly observes: "Although earlier commentators drew attention to the charge of the *crimen maiestatis*, this was already forbidden as a breach of public peace, and not just by special ordinances of the emperor, of which Luke seems to be thinking here."[38]

There are also additional problems with the traditional view that the charge against the apostles involved a charge of treason. Judge has noted that "the law of treason seems to have been framed specifically to cater for the offences of the Roman nobleman who enjoyed the opportunities of command and whose pretensions normally called for trial amongst their peers in the senate" and that "there were more summary means of dealing with disturbances caused by persons of lower status."[39] Although, as noted above, the law against treason was broadened in the early Principate to include not just a greater diversity of activities but also all classes of citizens, it was directed primarily at wealthy senators in Rome who had both the means and opportunity to overthrow the current emperor. The law of *maiestas* did not have first and foremost in view lower-class Roman citizens of foreign nationality in a free city of the Greek East—people like Paul and Silas.[40]

---

38. Riesner, *Paul's Early Period*, 356. See also Sherwin-White, *Roman Society*, 103; E. A. Judge, "The Decrees of Caesar at Thessalonica," *RTR* 30 (1971): 2; Karl P. Donfried, "The Cults of Thessalonica and the Thessalonian Correspondence," *NTS* 31 (1985): 343.

39. Judge, "Decrees," 2. See also Hardin, "Decrees and Drachmas," 31–32.

40. Hardin, "Decrees and Drachmas," 32.

3.2. Jewish Messianic Agitation

Another possibility is that the charge of violating the decrees of Caesar refers to an imperial edict dealing with Jewish messianic agitation.[41] The emperor Claudius wrote a letter (P.Lond. 1912) in 41 CE to Alexandria in response to three issues raised by a delegation sent from that city: (1) congratulations to the emperor on his accession; (2) requests for certain favors; and (3) apologies for recent anti-Jewish disturbances in Alexandria. On the third matter, Claudius sent the city the following response:

> I explicitly order the Jews not to agitate for more privileges than they formerly possessed, and not in the future to send out a separate embassy as if they lived in a separate city, a thing unprecedented, and not to force their way into gymnasiarchic or cosmetic games, while enjoying their own privileges and sharing a great abundance of advantages in a city not their own, and not to bring in or admit Jews who come down the river from Syria or Egypt, a proceeding which will compel me to conceive serious suspicions; otherwise I will by all means take vengeance on them as fomenters of what is a general plague infecting the whole world.

Some eight years later in 49 CE—just a year or so prior to the ministry of Paul and Silas in Thessalonica—Claudius passed a decree in which Jews were banished from Rome because of their rioting over a certain Chrestus, that is, Christ. The Roman historian Suetonius reports: "Since the Jews continually made disturbances at the instigation of Chrestus, he [Claudius] expelled them from Rome" (*Claud.* 25.4; see also Acts 18:2).[42] These two acts of Claudius, therefore, point to the possible existence of an official decree by the emperor against any kind of Jewish disturbance over the messiah—a decree which Paul and Silas are accused of disobeying. As David G. Peterson puts it: "The reference may have been to a special edict, such as the decree of Claudius (about AD 49), banishing Jews from Rome

---

41. So, e.g., E. A. Erhardt, *The Acts of the Apostles* (Manchester: Manchester University Press, 1969), 96; Colin J. Hemer, *The Book of Acts in the Setting of Hellenistic History* (Winona Lake, IN: Eisenbrauns 1990), 167; David G. Peterson, *The Acts of the Apostles*, PNTC (Grand Rapids: Eerdmans, 2009), 482. See also Riesner, *Paul's Early Period*, 357.

42. Keener (*Acts*, 2708): "The most common view among scholars is that Suetonius includes a garbled reference at his source to the Jewish 'Christ' (whether or not Suetonius recognized it), whom he mistakenly thought to be in Rome personally."

because of their rioting 'at the instigation of Chrestus.'"⁴³ Riesner makes the same assertion, but in the form of a rhetorical question: "News of this [Claudius'] edict reaches Thessalonica at precisely that time (perhaps only one or two days after Paul's departure). Could it be that after this edict became known, the agitated Gentile Thessalonians now preferred to avoid any connection with the Jewish community, and now formulated their accusation against the background of the new imperial decree?"⁴⁴

This possible referent to the decrees of Caesar is undermined, however, by a couple of factors. First, the actual charge against the missionaries does not include any claim about Jesus being "Christ" or "messiah" but instead that Jesus is "another king." Second, the attack against Paul and Silas was instigated by local Jews, and it is unlikely that they would have brought a specific charge of messianic agitation, since such a charge might well cause a negative reaction against not merely the two missionaries but also their own Jewish community as a whole.

3.3. Oath of Loyalty to Caesar

A third possibility is that the decrees of Caesar have in view the oath of loyalty to Caesar that many Roman and non-Roman citizens made.⁴⁵ One example (*ILS* 8681) of such an oath comes from an inscription in Paphlagonia, a province located in north Anatolia along the Black Sea, and dates to 3 BCE:

> I swear to Zeus, Earth, Sun, all the gods and goddesses, and to Augustus himself, that I will be loyal to Caesar Augustus, his children and descendants all through my life, both in words, deed, and thought, holding as friends those they hold as friends and considering as enemies whom they judge to be such, that with regard to things that concern them I will not be sparing of my body or my soul or my life or children, but will face every peril with respect to things that affect them. If there is anything that I should recognize or hear as spoken, plotted, or done contrary to

---

43. Peterson, *Acts*, 482.
44. Riesner, *Paul's Early Period*, 357. See also Erhardt (*Acts*, 96), who asks and answers: "What decrees were they? The most likely answer is that they were the very ones by which the Jews had been banished from Rome because of their rioting *impulsore Chresto*."
45. This view was first forwarded by Judge ("Decrees," 5–6), who ultimately rejects it.

this, I will report this and be an enemy of the person speaking, plotting or doing any of these things. Whomever they judge to be enemies, I will pursue and defend against them by land and sea with arms and steel. If I should do anything contrary to this oath or fail to follow up what I have sworn, I impose a curse upon myself encompassing the destruction and total extinction of my body, soul, life, children, my entire family, and everything essential down to every successor and every descendant of mine, and may neither earth nor sea receive the bodies of my family and descendants nor bear fruit for them.[46]

This inscription concludes with a note that the same oath was sworn "by all throughout the regions in the countryside at the temples to Augustus by the altars to Augustus."

There are two features of this oath that are notable with respect to the charges brought against Paul and Silas. First, people were required to commit themselves to be loyal not to the city of Rome, the Roman Senate, or, more broadly, the Roman Empire but narrowly to Caesar Augustus and his family. Second, it is striking how citizens, both Roman and non-Roman alike, despite being geographically far removed from Rome nevertheless were closely connected to the emperor by means of a very personal oath. If this happened in a rather remote place like Paphlagonia, then it could well have happened also in a major city like Thessalonica, especially given that city's aggressive acts in developing close ties with Rome. Such loyalty oaths to Augustus, in fact, appear to have been quite common in that day, as suggested by Josephus's reference that "the whole Jewish nation took an oath to be faithful to Caesar," with the exception of over six thousand members from the Pharisees (*A.J.* 17.42). An inscription from the island of Samos dating to 5 BCE, though not containing the actual text of the oath, records the arrangements for the swearing of such an expression of loyalty.[47] Most significant is the claim of Augustus himself in his *Res Gestae* that "the whole of Italy voluntarily took an oath of allegiance to me.... The provinces of the Spaniards, the Gauls, Africa, Sicily, and Sardinia took the same oath of allegiance" (25.2–3).

---

46. Translation from Tim G. Parkin and Arthur John Pomeroy, *Roman Social History: A Sourcebook*, Routledge Sourcebooks for the Ancient World (London: Routledge, 2007), 9.

47. See P. Herrmann, "Die Inschriften römischer Zeit aus dem Heraion von Samos," *MDAIA* 75 (1960): 68–193, esp. 73–75.

Loyalty oaths to the emperor continued after the reign of Augustus. An inscription discovered near the site of Palaipaphos on the island of Cyprus records the oath of loyalty that local citizens made to Tiberius (*SEG* 19.578):

> We, ourselves and our children, swear to listen to and obey, by land and sea, to regard with loyalty and to worship Tiberius Caesar Augustus, son of Augustus, with all his house, to have the same friends and the same enemies as they, to propose the voting of divine honors to Rome and to Tiberius Caesar Augustus, son of Augustus, and to the sons of his blood—to these only, together with the other gods, and to none other at all. [If we keep this oath, may prosperity be ours; if we break it, may the opposite befall us].[48]

A loyalty oath from the inhabitants of Assos to Caligula (Gaius), dating to his accession in 37 CE, has also been discovered (IAssos 26 = *IMT* 573):

> We swear to Zeus Soter ("Saviour"), god Caesar Augustus, and the ancestral holy Maiden (i.e., Athena) to have good will towards Gaius Caesar Augustus and his whole household and to consider as friends whomever he may choose as friends and to consider as enemies whomever he accuses. If we swear truly, may it go well for us, but if we swear falsely, the opposite will happen.[49]

Yet another loyalty oath to Caligula (Gaius), also given on the occasion of his accession to power in 37 CE, was made by the people of Aritium in Spain (*ILS* 190):

> On my conscience, I shall be an enemy of those persons whom I know to be enemies of Gaius Caesar Germanicus, and if anyone imperils or shall imperil him or his safety by arms or by civil war I shall not cease to hunt him down by land and by sea, until he pays the penalty to Caesar in full. I shall not hold myself or my children dearer than his safety and I shall consider as my enemies those persons who are hostile to him. If consciously I swear falsely or am proved false may

---

48. For more on this oath, see T. B. Mitford, "A Cypriot Oath of Allegiance to Tiberius," *JRS* 50 (1960): 75–79.

49. Text taken from Richard S. Ascough, Philip A. Harland, and John S. Kloppenborg, eds., *Associations in the Greco-Roman World: A Sourcebook* (Waco, TX: Baylor University Press, 2012), 78.

Jupiter Optimus Maximus and the deified Augustus and all the other immortal gods punish me and my children with loss of country, safety, and all my fortune.[50]

It is possible, then, that the charge of violating the decrees of Caesar is connected to the pledge made in loyalty oaths to report any kind of disloyalty to the emperor or potential threat to his well-being. A number of commentators, in fact, have found this possibility convincing.[51] Ben Witherington III, for example, says of the charges brought against Paul and Silas, "in all likelihood ... that what is being referred to is an oath of loyalty to Caesar and Rome."[52] James R. Harrison also adopts this explanation, claiming: "In the view of the Thessalonian Jews, the apostles were preaching a pretender king, Jesus, and had urged the Thessalonian and Berean citizens to violate their oaths of allegiance to the emperor."[53]

As attractive as this explanation is, it suffers from a couple of weaknesses. First, the extant documents dealing with these loyalty oaths do not provide any grounds for describing such texts with the specific term used to accuse the apostles, namely, *decrees*. In fact, the loyalty oaths appear to be done at the instigation of the local citizens rather than stemming from any command or decree from the emperor. Second, there is evidence that the violation of these loyalty oaths fell under the jurisdiction not of

---

50. Cited from James R. Harrison, *Paul and the Imperial Authorities at Thessalonica and Rome: A Study in the Conflict of Ideology*, WUNT 273 (Tübingen: Mohr Siebeck, 2011), 54.

51. So, e.g., Robert Jewett, *The Thessalonian Correspondence: Pauline Rhetoric and Millenarian Piety* (Philadelphia: Fortress, 1986), 125; C. U. Manus, "Luke's Account of Paul in Thessalonica (Acts 17,1–9)," in *The Thessalonian Correspondence*, ed. Raymond F. Collins, BETL 87 (Leuven: Leuven University Press, 1990), 34; de Vos, *Church and Community Conflicts*, 156–57; Victor Paul Furnish, *1 Thessalonians, 2 Thessalonians* (Nashville: Abingdon, 2007), 28. There are also a few commentators who, following the lead of Judge, combine this position with viewing the decrees as bans against predictions (see position no. 5 below), which Judge claimed were enforced through local administration of oaths of loyalty; so, e.g., Hemer, *Book of Acts*, 167; Bruce, *Book of Acts*, 371–72; Peterson, *Acts*, 482; Barrett, *Acts*, 816. Hardin ("Decrees and Drachmas," 36) rightly criticizes this combination of two positions: "Judge amalgamates two distinct issues: restrictions on astrology and the oath of loyalty to the emperor.... As a result, one is left wondering which phenomenon—bans on astrology or oath of loyalty—Judge identifies as the decrees of Caesar in Acts 17.7."

52. Witherington, *Thessalonians*, 7.

53. Harrison, *Paul and the Imperial Authorities*, 54.

THE POLITICAL CHARGES AGAINST PAUL AND SILAS 259

the local authorities (such as the politarchs in Thessalonica) but of the emperor himself.[54] Judge cites a case from the province of Cyrene where three individuals who claimed to know something affecting the safety of Augustus were sent by the proconsul of that province, Sextius, directly to the emperor—an action which Augustus commends ("Sextius acted rightly and conscientiously in this").[55] If Paul and Silas were, in fact, charged with violating a loyalty oath to the emperor, such a charge should have been brought not to the politarchs but to the proconsul, who was conveniently located in Thessalonica and who would have in turn passed on such a serious charge to the emperor himself.

3.4. Prohibition against Unapproved Voluntary Associations

Yet another possibility is that the decrees of Caesar refer to imperial laws against voluntary associations (*collegia*). This explanation was first proposed by Hardin, who argues that "the imperial regulations of voluntary associations, which were aimed precisely at curbing such groups, provide a possible identification of these two charges brought before the politarchs."[56]

The political instability of Rome during the final decades of the Republic caused the Roman Senate to rule against voluntary associations, especially those whom it deemed were disruptive and threatened peace and order. This concern about voluntary associations continued under both Julius Caesar and Augustus, who banned all clubs except those that were clearly nonpolitical and had been established many years earlier (Suetonius, *Jul.* 42.3; *Aug.* 32.1). Although the laws against associations were relaxed under the brief reign of Caligula, this new openness was brought to a halt by Claudius, who disbanded the clubs introduced by his predecessor (Dio Cassius, *Hist. rom.* 60.6.6). The level of fear Roman emperors had that voluntary associations might pursue political purposes and threaten the *pax Romana* is illustrated in Trajan's preference to let the city of Nicomedia burn rather than approve the request of Pliny, his proconsul in Bithynia, to form an association of fire fighters:

---

54. Contra Donfried ("Imperial Cults of Thessalonica," 216), who asserts: "In all likelihood the politarchs in Thessalonica were responsible for administering the oath of loyalty and for dealing with violations of the oath."
55. Judge, "Decrees," 6–7.
56. Hardin, "Decrees and Drachmas," 39.

But it is to be remembered that these sorts of societies have greatly disturbed the peace of your province in general, and of those cities in particular. Whatever title we give them, and whatever our object in giving it, men who are banded together for a common end will all the same become a political association before long. (Pliny, *Ep.* 10.34)

Hardin thus argues that the Roman prohibitions against unlawful voluntary associations provide the proper backdrop for the legal proceedings before the politarchs in Thessalonica. He strengthens his proposal by citing an inscription from Irnitania in Spain dating to the Flavian period (69–76 CE) in which those breaking the law against unauthorized clubs will be penalized with a financial penalty, similar to the security payment the politarchs required from Jason and others in the Thessalonian house church:

> Concerning gatherings, clubs, and *collegia*. No one in this municipality must form a political gathering, nor have a club or collegium for that purpose, nor conspire that it may be held, nor form in such a way that any of these things may occur. Anyone who forms contrary to this is condemned to pay 1,000 sesterces to the municipes of the Municipium Flavium Irnitanum.[57]

Such evidence for empire-wide prohibitions against volunteer associations, however, is offset by the epigraphic evidence that *collegia* continued not merely to exist during the Principate but to flourish as a wide-spread, popular institution.[58] Arnaoutoglou argues for a more nuanced understanding of the historical situation in which voluntary associations were not indiscriminately banned, but suppressed only on a local level and only in specific situations where the concern for maintaining public peace and order required it.[59] Richard S. Ascough similarly comments: "Despite the prohibition against such associations, 'these measures do not seem to have been uniformly enforced. If Claudius, Nero, and Trajan are seen to

---

57. Hardin, "Decrees and Drachmas," 46. The text of this inscription comes from J. Gonzalez, "The *Lex Irnitana*: A New Flavian Municipal Law," *JRS* 76 (1986): 172; the translation is that of Hardin.

58. This point is recognized by Hardin, "Decrees and Drachmas," 41.

59. Ilias N. Arnaoutoglou, "Roman Law and *collegia* in Asia Minor," *RIDA* 49 (2002): 27–44.

suppress the collegia, it is because these clubs continued to spring up and grow whenever the political climate allowed them to do so."[60]

The biggest difficulty with viewing the background the charges of Acts 17:6-7 as that of an illegal voluntary association is that it shifts the focus in the two accusations away from Paul and Silas and redirects them to Jason and the rest of the church. Hardin recasts the situation whereby the crowd brings charges not against the two apostles but Jason and the other Christ-followers: "In sum, Jason and his companions were dragged from Jason's house to stand trial before the politarchs. Jason was charged in the first instance with harboring those who had been upsetting the world (17.6b–7a). Then the entire group was indicted for acting contrary to Caesar's decrees by being a politically orientated group (17.7b)."[61]

The grammar of the text, however, reveals that the first charge is aimed squarely at Paul and Silas rather than Jason, since they are the subjects of the main clause ("These men who are subverting the whole empire have now come here"; οἱ τὴν οἰκουμένην ἀναστατώσαντες οὗτοι καὶ ἐνθάδε πάρεισιν), while the reference to Jason is relegated to a short relative clause ("whom Jason has received"; οὓς ὑποδέδεκται Ἰάσων). In addition, the fact that the charge of actively disturbing the peace is more serious than that of housing those engaged in such anti-Roman activity also suggests that the object of the first charge is not, as Hardin proposes, Jason, but instead Paul and Silas. Finally, the parallel with the immediately preceding story further strengthens this view: charges were brought against the two missionaries before the city authorities in Philippi, and the more natural way of reading the account in Acts 17:6-7 is that the same thing is happening to Paul and Silas again in Thessalonica. It is true that the second charge broadens the scope to include Jason and others in the church: "and they are *all* acting against the decrees of Caesar" (17:7b). But this second charge, like the first, has in view primarily Paul and Silas rather than excluding them. All this makes it unlikely that the decrees of Caesar refer to laws forbidding unauthorized voluntary associations.

---

60. Richard S. Ascough, *Paul's Macedonian Associations: The Social Context of Philippians and 1 Thessalonians*, WUNT 2/161 (Tübingen: Mohr Siebeck, 2003), 46, citing Wendy J. Cotter, "The Collegia and Roman Law: State Restrictions on Voluntary Associations, 64 B.C.E.–200 C.E.," in *Voluntary Associations in the Graeco-Roman World*, ed. John S. Kloppenborg and Steven G. Wilson (London: Routledge, 1996), 88.

61. Hardin, "Decrees and Drachmas," 39.

3.5. Prediction of a Change of Ruler

A fifth and final proposal is that the decrees of Caesar refer to imperial edicts against predictions about the emperor, especially those dealing with his health, death, and successor.[62] In 11 CE, the seventy-four-year-old Augustus responded to widespread questions about his health and heir by passing an imperial edict that forbade astrologers, diviners, prophets, and all others against predicting anyone's death, especially that of the emperor (Dio Cassius, *Hist. rom.* 56.25.5–6):

> The seers were forbidden to prophesy to any person alone or to prophesy regarding death even if others should be present. Yet so far was Augustus from caring about such matters in his own case that he set forth to all in an edict (διάταξιν) the aspect of the stars at the time of his own birth. Nevertheless, he forbade this practice.

This prohibition was reaffirmed and extended by Tiberius five years later in 16 CE:

> But as for all the other astrologers and magicians and such as practiced divination in anyway whatsoever, he put to death those who were foreigners and banished all the citizens that were accused of still employing the art [of divination] at this time after the previous decree [δόγμα] by which it had been forbidden to engage in any such business in the city." (Dio Cassius, *Hist. rom.* 57.15.8)

The ban by Tiberius is referred to in a couple of ancient sources that, despite raising complicating factors, nevertheless ultimately confirm this prohibition. Suetonius states: "He [Tiberius] also expelled the astrologers; but upon suing for pardon and promising to renounce their profession, he revoked his decree" (*Tib.* 36). Tacitus locates the ban not narrowly with

---

62. Judge, "Decrees," 3, whose proposal is followed by many commentators; see, e.g., Bruce, *Thessalonians*, xxiv; I. Howard Marshall, *The Acts of the Apostles: An Introduction and Commentary*, TNTC (Grand Rapids: Eerdmans, 1980), 279; D. J. Williams, *Acts* (Peabody, MA: Hendrickson, 1985), 296; Donfried, "Cults of Thessalonica," 342–44; Hemer, *Book of Acts*, 167; Witherington, *Acts*, 508; Barrett, *Acts*, 815–16; Riesner, *Paul's Early Period*, 356–57; Green, *Thessalonians*, 50. Several of these commentators, however, as observed above (see n. 53), take the problematic step of combining this view with the "oath of loyalty" option.

Tiberius but with the Senate under his reign: "Decrees of the Senate were passed to expel from the city astrologers and magicians" (*Ann.* 2.32). This action of the Senate took place in response to the case of Libo Drusus, who "was accused of revolutionary schemes" and who used "astrologers' promises, magical rites, and interpreters of dreams" (*Ann.* 2.27).

The ban against astrologers and prophets in general, and against predictions concerning the health or well-being of the emperor in particular, continued to be in effect well after the time of the apostles Paul and Silas. The celebrated Roman lawyer, Julius Paulus, who served under Septimius Severus (193–211 CE) outlines the legislation against magicians, astrologers, and prophets as well as the death penalty for those violating this legislation: "Those who consult astrologers, male or female soothsayers, or diviners, with reference to the life of the emperor or the safety of the state, shall be punished by death, together with the party who answered their questions" (*Sent.* 5.21). Just a short time later in the early third century CE, the Roman jurist Ulpian (ca. 170–223) states: "For those who have sought advice about the health of the emperor suffer either capital punishment or some other penalty" (*De officio proconsulis libri* x). The fact that Ulpian's statement occurs in a document dealing with the office of the proconsul led Judge to conclude that the ban was not limited to Rome or even to Italy but was an empire-wide restriction.[63]

These statements from Roman historians and jurists led Bruce to summarize the historical context as follows: "The practice of magic and divination in general was banned as well as of astrology; in particular, consultation about the emperor's health or about high matters of state was apparently forbidden under the severest penalties."[64] In such a setting, Paul's eschatological preaching in Thessalonica about a resurrected Lord who will soon reappear on earth as a universal king and judge could have been interpreted as a prediction about a change of ruler and thus a violation of the decrees of Caesar.

The strength of this proposal lies in the fact that the decree of Caesar Augustus against predicting a change of ruler that was shortly thereafter confirmed by Tiberius is referred to as a "dogma" (δόγμα; Dio Cassius, *Hist. rom.* 57.15.8), which is the same term used in Acts 17:7. Furthermore, the ongoing nature of the ban by subsequent emperors for many

---

63. Judge, "Decrees," 4–5.
64. Bruce, *Thessalonians*, xxiv.

years after Augustus and Tiberius testifies to the very real fear of Roman emperors in the possibility that prophecies might be used to overthrow those in power and to claim the right to the throne. Such a fear was, in fact, well grounded, as evidenced by Vespasian's use of the prophecy concerning his own rise to power by the Jewish general and later client of his, Josephus (*B.J.* 3.401–402; Suetonius, *Vesp.* 5). It is not hard in such an historical context to see how opponents of Paul and Silas in Thessalonica could cleverly use the apostles' preaching about "another king—Jesus" (Acts 17:7b),[65] who would soon come to "rescue" his followers (1 Thess 1:10) and establish his "kingdom" (1 Thess 2:12) as a prediction for a change of ruler and thus a violation of the decrees of Caesar.

4. Conclusion

Thessalonica enjoyed a long history of Roman benefaction in which the city engaged in a variety of activities to strengthen its relationship with Rome, thereby securing political and financial benefits from the empire. The two charges brought against Paul and Silas were highly political—since they threatened to destroy the favored status that Thessalonica enjoyed with Rome—and were thus also extremely serious. The first charge of disturbing the peace was cleverly constructed to accuse Paul and Silas of undermining one of the main benefits that Roman rule supposedly provided. The Julio-Claudian line of emperors skillfully used a variety of public media—coins, public monuments, official proclamations, and literary works—to shape public opinion and to convince its subjects about the peace that Roman rule provided, thereby making the first charge a most severe offence. The gravity of the second charge of violating the decrees of Caesar also becomes more apparent in light of Thessalonica's strong

---

65. The clarification of the charge against the two apostles, namely, their "saying that there is another king—Jesus" (Acts 17:7b), agrees with Paul's claim in his letter that he preached during his mission-founding visit in Thessalonica about the "kingdom" (1 Thess 2:12). As Karl P. Donfried observes: "Paul's categorical statement in 1 Thess 2:12 that he did speak to the Thessalonians about the kingdom during his presence in the city should help us understand the relative accuracy of the Acts 17 account, not only with regard to Paul's use of king/kingdom language but also with regard to the fact that this language may well have served as a catalyst for the animosity he and his co-workers aroused in Thessalonica." See Donfried, "The Kingdom of God in Paul," in *The Kingdom of God in 20th-Century Interpretation*, ed. Wendell L. Willis (Peabody: Hendrickson, 1987), 188.

dependency on Roman benefaction. Even if the specific referent of these decrees of Caesar remains tentative, it is clear that a charge of violating these decrees—at minimum an insult and at maximum a direct challenge to the authority of the emperor himself—would be viewed with the greatest alarm by both the citizens and the city officials. It made no difference that the nascent Christian movement involved only a small percentage of the overall population of a large, provincial capital city like Thessalonica. The anti-Roman nature of the two charges leveled against the church's founders would cause local citizens and authorities alike to fear that the presence of such a movement within their city, however small, might cost them their privileged status as a free city as well as their favorable, and thus profitable, relationship with Rome.[66] This fear would have been exacerbated by the fact that in recent times they had lost some administrative privileges under Tiberius and did not get them back until six years earlier through the personal favor of Claudius himself. When this specific historical context is kept in mind, the accusations brought against Paul and Silas should not be judged either as "one of the most confused of the various descriptions of charges in Acts" or Luke "spinning an entertaining story" but instead as an entirely plausible account.

Bibliography

Arnaoutoglou, Ilias N. "Roman Law and *collegia* in Asia Minor." *RIDA* 49 (2002): 27–44.

Ascough, Richard S. *Paul's Macedonian Associations: The Social Context of Philippians and 1 Thessalonians.* WUNT 2/161. Tübingen: Mohr Siebeck, 2003.

Ascough, Richard S., Philip A. Harland, and John S. Kloppenborg, eds. *Associations in the Greco-Roman World: A Sourcebook.* Waco: Baylor University Press, 2012.

Barrett, C. K. *A Critical and Exegetical Commentary on the Acts of the Apostles.* 2 vols. ICC. London: T&T Clark, 1994–1998.

Bauman, Richard A. *The Crimen Maiestatis in the Roman Republic and Augustan Principate.* Johannesburg: Witwatersrand University, 1967.

---

66. Keener, *Acts*, 2555: "As a free city and the seat of the governor (who might well hear about these charges), Thessalonica would not be willing to risk its favored status by allowing talk of another king."

Bock, Darrell L. *Acts*. Baker Exegetical Commentary on the New Testament. Grand Rapids: Baker, 2007.
Bruce, F. F. *The Book of the Acts*. NICNT. Grand Rapids: Eerdmans, 1977.
———. *1 and 2 Thessalonians*. WBC 45. Waco, TX: Word, 1982.
Burton, E. D. "The Politarchs." *AmJT* 2 (1898): 598–632.
Chilton, C. W. "The Roman Law of Treason under the Early Principate." *JRS* 45 (1955): 73–81.
Cotter, Wendy J. "The Collegia and Roman Law: State Restrictions on Voluntary Associations, 64 BCE–200 CE." Pages 74–89 in *Voluntary Associations in the Graeco-Roman World*. Edited by John S. Kloppenborg and Steven G. Wilson. London: Routledge, 1996.
De Vos, Craig Steven. *Church and Community Conflicts: The Relationship of the Thessalonian, Corinthian, and Philippian Churches with Their Wider Civic Communities*. SBLDS 168. Atlanta: Scholars Press, 1999.
Donfried, Karl P. "The Cults of Thessalonica and the Thessalonian Correspondence" *NTS* 31 (1985): 336–56.
———. "The Imperial Cults of Thessalonica and Political Conflict in 1 Thessalonians." Pages 215–23 in *Paul and Empire: Religion and Power in Roman Imperial Society*. Edited by Richard A. Horsley. Harrisburg, PA: Trinity, 1997.
———. "The Kingdom of God in Paul." Pages 175–90 in *The Kingdom of God in 20th-Century Interpretation*. Edited by Wendell L. Willis. Peabody: Hendrickson, 1987.
Edson, C. "Macedonia." *HSCP* 51 (1940): 126–36.
Erhardt, E. A. *The Acts of the Apostles*. Manchester: Manchester University Press, 1969.
Evans, Robert M. *Eschatology and Ethics: A Study of Thessalonica and Paul's Letters to the Thessalonians*. Princeton: McMahon, 1968.
Fitzmyer, Joseph A. *The Acts of the Apostles*. AB 31. New York: Doubleday, 1998.
Furnish, Victor Paul. *1 Thessalonians, 2 Thessalonians*. Nashville: Abingdon, 2007.
Gonzalez, J. "The *Lex Irnitana*: A New Flavian Municipal Law," *JRS* 76 (1986): 147–243.
Green, Gene L. *The Letters to the Thessalonians*. PNTC. Grand Rapids: Eerdmans, 2002.
Haenchen, Ernst. *The Acts of the Apostles: A Commentary*. Translated by B. Noble and G. Shinn. Oxford: Blackwell, 1971.

Hardin, Justin K. "Decrees and Drachmas at Thessalonica: An Illegal Assembly in Jason's House (Acts 17.1–10a)." *NTS* 52 (2006): 29–49.
Harrison, James R. *Paul and the Imperial Authorities at Thessalonica and Rome: A Study in the Conflict of Ideology*. WUNT 273. Tübingen: Mohr Siebeck, 2011.
Hemer, Colin J. *The Book of Acts in the Setting of Hellenistic History*. Winona Lake, IN: Eisenbrauns 1990.
Hendrix, Holland L. "Thessalonians Honor Romans." ThD diss., Harvard University, 1984.
Herrmann, P. "Die Inschriften römischer Zeit aus dem Heraion von Samos." *MDAIA* 75 (1960): 68–193.
Horsley, G. H. R. "The Politarchs." Pages 419–31 in *The Book of Acts in Its Greco-Roman Setting*. Vol. 2 of *The Book of Acts in Its First Century Setting*. Edited by David W. J. Gill and Conrad Gempf. Grand Rapids: Eerdmans, 1994.
Jewett, Robert. *The Thessalonian Correspondence: Pauline Rhetoric and Millenarian Piety*. Philadelphia: Fortress, 1986.
Johnson, Luke Timothy. *The Acts of the Apostles*. Collegeville: Glazier, 1992.
Judge, E. A. "The Decrees of Caesar at Thessalonica." *RTR* 30 (1971): 1–7.
Keener, Craig S. *Acts: An Exegetical Commentary; 15:1–23:35*. Grand Rapids: Baker Academic, 2014.
Krodel, G. *Acts*. Minneapolis: Augsburg, 1986.
Manus, C. U. "Luke's Account of Paul in Thessalonica (Acts 17,1–9)." Pages 27–38 in *The Thessalonian Correspondence*. Edited by Raymond F. Collins. BETL 87. Leuven: Leuven University Press, 1990.
Marshall, I. Howard. *The Acts of the Apostles: An Introduction and Commentary*. TNTC. Grand Rapids: Eerdmans, 1980.
Mitford, T. B. "A Cypriot Oath of Allegiance to Tiberius," *JRS* 50 (1960): 75–79.
Papagiannopoulos, A. *History of Thessaloniki*. Thessaloniki: Rekos, 1982.
Parkin, Tim G., and Arthur John Pomeroy, *Roman Social History: A Sourcebook*. Routledge Sourcebooks for the Ancient World. London: Routledge, 2007.
Pervo, Richard I. *Acts: A Commentary*. Hermeneia. Minneapolis: Fortress, 2009.
Peterson, David G. *The Acts of the Apostles*. PNTC. Grand Rapids: Eerdmans, 2009.

Polhill, John B. *Acts: An Exegetical and Theological Exposition of Holy Scripture.* New American Commentary 26. Nashville: Broadman & Holman, 1992.

Riesner, Rainer. *Paul's Early Period: Chronology, Mission Strategy, Theology.* Grand Rapids: Eerdmans, 1998.

Sherwin-White, A. N. *Roman Society and Roman Law in the New Testament.* Sarum Lectures 1960–1961. Oxford: Clarendon, 1963.

"Statue of Oktavianus Augustus." Odysseus: Ministry of Culture and Sports. http://tinyurl.com/SBL4522s.

Tajra, H. W. *The Trial of St. Paul: A Juridical Exegesis of the Second Half of the Acts of the Apostles.* WUNT 2/35. Tübingen: Mohr Siebeck, 1989.

Vokotopoulou, J. *Guide to the Archaeological Museum of Thessaloniki.* Athens: Kapon, 1996.

Weima, Jeffrey A. D. *1–2 Thessalonians.* Baker Exegetical Commentary on the New Testament. Grand Rapids: Baker, 2014.

———. "'Peace and Security' (1 Thess. 5.3): Prophetic Warning or Political Propaganda?" *NTS* 58 (2012): 331–59.

Williams, D. J. *Acts.* Peabody, MA: Hendrickson, 1985.

Witherington, Ben, III. *1 and 2 Thessalonians: A Socio-Rhetorical Commentary.* Grand Rapids: Eerdmans, 2006.

Paul's Walk to Assos:
A Hodological Inquiry into Its Geography, Archaeology, and Purpose

Glen L. Thompson and Mark Wilson

The authors wish to congratulate Dennis Smith for his contributions to biblical scholarship and his passion for understanding the world in which the New Testament emerged. It was our privilege to become acquainted with Smith at the first COMCAR gathering at Ephesus in 2008. We have renewed that friendship at the COMCAR alumni receptions held annually at the Society of Biblical Literature meetings. A fond memory of our time at Ephesus is the photo taken of some of us reclining on the mosaic floor around the triclinium in the Marble Hall of the Terrace Houses. Smith always has dining on his mind, it seems, even during our Ephesus visit. The Anatolian Biblical Roads Initiative first presented there has now developed into The Anatolian Roads Project (TARP). What follows is the fruit of a portion of our second research trip in Turkey in 2013.[1]

1. Introduction

The essay begins by laying out briefly the background for the walk in the context of Paul's third journey discussed in Acts 20. It next presents the likely route from Alexandria Troas to Assos by examining the material remains along the way, such as a bridge and roadways. Part of the route followed the Sacred Way linking Troas to the temple of Smintheus, and the

---

1. This research trip in June 2013 was conducted under the auspices of Wisconsin Lutheran College, Milwaukee, and the Asia Lutheran Seminary, Hong Kong, and supported financially by Jerry and Kay Fischer and the Fischer Family Foundation. Many thanks are extended to them as well as to the students who also participated.

findings of recent excavations at the Smintheum are presented. Finally, the various reasons for Paul's walk proposed by scholars will be examined with our own proposals, concluding the article.

For many Christians today a detailed discussion of Paul's walk to Assos might have minimal interest. But, as Craig Keener notes, Paul's itinerary "would have interested educated readers in antiquity. The latter often appreciated 'travel literature.'"[2] There is a small but growing group of individuals who wish to experience Anatolia in the same way that the early apostles did—by walking. Throughout Turkey now a network of culture routes has sprung up that includes the St. Paul Trail, the St. Nicholas Way, the Phrygian Way, the Hittite Way, and Abraham Path.[3] In fact, several scholars have expressed interest in recreating Paul's walk from Troas to Assos. We hope that the research forming this essay will assist in making such a walk a future reality.

2. The Walk in the Context of Paul's Third Journey

Troas was an important transit point for Paul on his second and third journeys as he traveled from Asia to Macedonia.[4] Here on his second journey he received the vision of the Macedonian man directing him to Macedonia (Acts 16:8–10).[5] After the riot in Ephesus on his third journey, Paul passed

---

2. Craig Keener, *Acts: An Exegetical Commentary*, 4 vols. (Grand Rapids: Baker Academic, 2014), 3:2980. Ben Sira extolled the benefits of travel for gaining understanding (Sir 34:9–13). And the merchant Titus Flavius Zeuxis boasted on his tomb in Hierapolis that he had safely navigated Cape Malea seventy-two times while traveling to Italy; see Tullia Ritti, *An Epigraphic Guide to Hierapolis (Pamukkale)* (Istanbul: Ege, 2006), 67–70.

3. See the website "Culture Routes in Turkey," Cultural Routes Society, http://tinyurl.com/SBL4522a, featuring all of these.

4. A postcaptivity visit is possible if 2 Tim 4:13 preserves a memory of a later Pauline visit through Troas. The synthesis of Acts with Paul's letters in developing a chronology of the apostle's life and ministry has challenged interpreters. For an excellent discussion of the issues, see Loveday C. A. Alexander, "Chronology of Paul," in *Dictionary of Paul and his Letters*, ed. Gerald F. Hawthorne, Ralph P. Martin, and Daniel G. Reid (Downers Grove, IL: InterVarsity Press, 1993), 115–23.

5. For a discussion of the Lukan presentation of the supernatural guidance that directed Paul and his companions to Troas, see Glen L. Thompson and Mark Wilson, "The Route of Paul's Second Journey in Asia Minor: In the Steps of Robert Jewett and Beyond," *TynBul* (forthcoming).

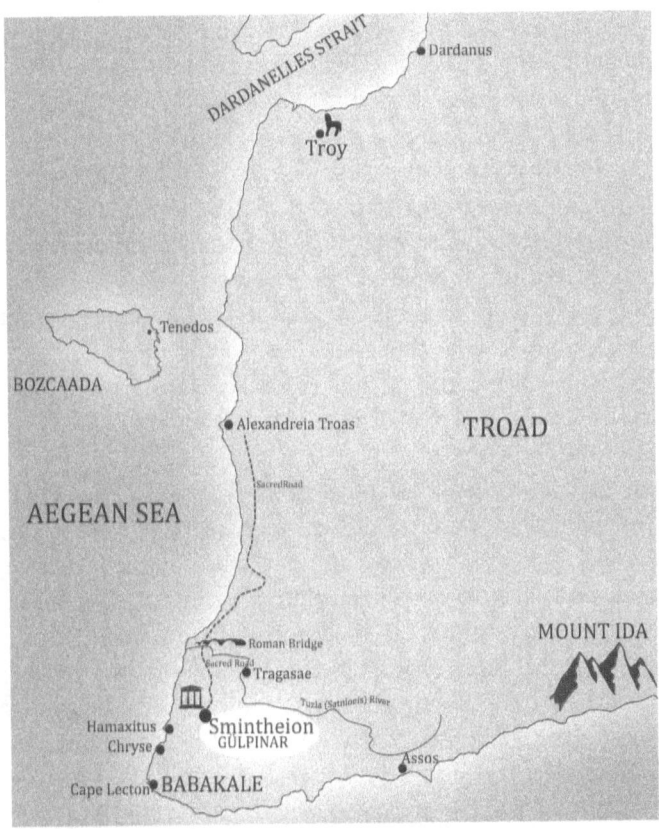

Figure 12.1. Map of the Troad. Used with permission of Ege Yayınları.

through Troas[6] again on his way to Macedonia (fig. 12.1). This time he came to the city for a reason: εἰς τὸ εὐαγγέλιον (2 Cor 2:12). English translations take this as a purpose clause and translate as "to preach/proclaim

---

6. There is discussion whether the city or the Troad region should be understood in Acts 16:8, 20:6, and 2 Cor 2:12 (εἰς τὴν Τρῳάδα); see BDAG, s.v. "Τρῳάς," 1019. Contra BDAG, Murray J. Harris, *The Second Epistle to the Corinthians*, NIGTC (Grand Rapids: Eerdmans, 2013), 236, argues that 2 Cor 2:12–13 must refer to the city because "Paul would be likely to arrange to meet Titus in a city, not in a region," and when he said goodbye, the believers were "presumably people in a single location." The prevalent ethnic name in Troas since its foundation as a Roman colony was Τρῳαδεύς; see Marijana Ricl, "Two New Inscriptions from Alexandreia Troas," *Tekmeria* 5 (2000): 130.

the gospel" (cf. Phil 2:22). Apparently no church yet existed in Troas, or the number of believers was small. Paul's diversion through Troas suggests that perhaps he had been invited to preach in the city while still in Ephesus. Even though God opened a door of ministry there, he felt anxious about Titus's failure to arrive from Corinth. So Paul left what appeared to be a productive place of ministry[7] and said goodbye to them (ἀλλὰ ἀποταξάμενος αὐτοῖς; 2 Cor 2:13). The referent of the pronoun "them" is never identified, but apparently these must be individuals who heard the gospel during Paul's brief stay. Murray J. Harris speculates whether these believers came to faith at this time or on Paul's previous visit to Troas.[8] Since earlier on his second journey Paul had been forbidden by the Spirit to preach in Asia (Acts 16:6),[9] these believers are more likely the spiritual fruit of this second visit.

The return leg of Paul's third journey began with a forced land journey from Corinth due to a plot against him (Acts 20:3).[10] With Jerusalem as his final destination, he revisited the churches in Macedonia that he had started on the second journey (Acts 20:3). Seven men accompanied him, representing various churches in Macedonia and Asia Minor that had contributed to the Jerusalem collection.[11] The men sailed from Neapolis (cf. Acts 16:11) and shipped across the northern Aegean to Alexandria Troas.[12] Paul, however, remained behind in Philippi to celebrate the

---

7. George H. Guthrie, *2 Corinthians*, BECNT (Grand Rapids: Baker, 2015), 146, argues that, while the "open door" could refer to ministry in the Troad region, "the text could also be understood as referring to an open door to move on to Macedonia." But this reading is forced since the door is connected grammatically to Troas, and Macedonia is not even introduced until the final word of the following sentence.

8. Harris, *Second Epistle*, 240.

9. For more on these prohibitions, see Thompson and Wilson, "Route."

10. Responding to Hans Conzelmann's claim that the itinerary described in Acts 20 was constructed by the author of Acts, Dieter Georgi, *Remembering the Poor: The History of Paul's Collection for Jerusalem* (Nashville: Abingdon, 1992), 208, writes, "The itinerary in Acts 20–21 is best understood as a historically correct rendering precisely because of its 'incoherence.'"

11. These companions show the geographical diversity of Paul's ministry efforts: Sopater from Berea, Aristarchus and Secundus from Thessalonica, Gaius from Derbe, Timothy from Lystra, and Tychicus and Trophimus from Asia. The Jerusalem collection is never mentioned in chapter 20 and only hinted at in Acts 24:17. Paul's own writings from this period, Rom 15:25-27 and 2 Cor 8-9, provide the most information on the collection.

12. Georgi, *Remembering the Poor*, 124, makes the improbable suggestion that

Feast of Unleavened Bread, which in 57 CE fell on April 7–14.[13] These events are located in the second "we" section of Acts, so Luke himself was probably an eyewitness.[14] Paul and Luke later sailed to Troas, a journey of five days (Acts 20:6). Since their earlier crossing in the opposite direction took only two days (Acts 16:11), Paton J. Gloag notes rightly that "they were perhaps hindered by contrary winds or by a calm."[15] The vagaries of spring travel therefore caused Paul to miss the main Sunday Christian gathering in Troas. Despite his hurry to reach Jerusalem by Pentecost, he decided to stay an additional seven days so that he could take part in the citywide gathering of believers on the following Sunday evening.[16] During the intervening days he could then minister to the believers he had left so hastily just a few months before. The delay also allowed the party to secure passage on a coasting vessel, particularly one that could provide security for the collection, and to complete other arrangements for the journey.[17]

3. Troas in Paul's Day

Alexandria Troas in the first century CE was an important city in the Roman province of Asia (fig. 12.1).[18] A bustling port city, Bernhard Tenger notes:

---

the first group left Philippi early because they were traveling by land to Troas to await Paul there. Unless the sea lane connecting Europe to Asia was impassable because of weather, it is highly unlikely that a longer land journey would be undertaken. Plus, the group would still need to cross the Dardanelles Strait at Sestos to reach Abydos and Troas farther south.

13. See Colin J. Hemer, *The Book of Acts in the Setting of Hellenistic History* (Winona Lake, IN: Eisenbrauns, 1990), 169, and Keener, *Acts*, 3:2960–61, for a discussion of the calculation of this date.

14. For a discussion of these "we" sections, see Stanley E. Porter, "The 'We' Passages," in *The Book of Acts in Its Greco-Roman Setting*, vol. 2 of *The Book of Acts in Its First Century Setting*, ed. David W. J. Gill and Conrad Gempf (Grand Rapids: Eerdmans, 1994), 559–73.

15. Paton J. Gloag, *A Critical and Exegetical Commentary on the Acts of the Apostles*, 2 vols. (London: T&T Clark, 1870), 2:234.

16. Keener, *Acts*, 3:2967, argues convincingly that this meeting did not take place on Saturday evening after the Jewish Sabbath ended but on Sunday evening, with Luke following the Roman reckoning of days from dawn to dawn.

17. For more on this, see Mark Wilson, "The Lukan *Periplus* of Saint Paul's Third Journey with a Textual Conundrum in Acts 20:15," *Acta Theologica* 36 (2016): 229–54.

18. For a brief summary of the city's history see Glen L. Thompson, "Alexandria Troas: Greek Synoecism, Roman Colony, Christian Center," Academia.edu, http://

"Die verkehrsgeographische Bedeutung der Region demonstriert der Missionweg des Apostle Paulus."[19] Troas was founded after 311 BCE as Antigoneia by Antigonus on the site of Sigia. Through the synoecism of six neighboring towns it became an important regional center.[20] It had the only functioning harbor on the Troad's west coast, and the inner harbor is still visible.[21] However, it was renamed soon after by Lysimachus in honor of his former king, becoming one of the many cities named Alexandria in the Hellenistic world.[22] Augustus founded a Roman colony here—Colonia Augusta Troadensium—whose full title appears on civic inscriptions[23] and late Roman semiautonomous coinage.[24] Unfortunately, there is a paucity of information in ancient sources about Troas.[25] Strabo, a contemporary of Paul and usually a helpful informant, is largely silent about Troas (*Geogr.* 13.1.26). As Colin J. Hemer writes, "Yet he dismisses Troas, the largest city of the area in his day, in a few words, and only gives information about it in a confused parenthesis when dealing with Ilium.... Strabo was more interested in the historical glories of Troy than in this upstart commercial seaport."[26]

---

tinyurl.com/SBL4522c; Mark Wilson, *Biblical Turkey*, 3rd ed. (Istanbul: Ege, 2014), 384–86; and J. M. Cook, *The Troad* (Oxford: Oxford University Press, 1973), 198–204.

19. Bernhard Tenger, "Zur Geographie und Geschichte der Troas," in *Die Troas: Neue Forschungen III*, Asia Minor Studien 33, ed. Elmar Schwertheim (Bonn: Habelt, 1999), 170.

20. Getzel M. Cohen, *The Hellenistic Settlements in Europe, the Islands, and Asia Minor* (Berkeley: University of California Press, 1995), 145–46; and Thompson, "Alexandria Troas." Due to its geographic distance from the new urban center, one of the six cities, Skepsis, was soon detached and reverted to its independence.

21. See Stefan Feuser, *Der Hafen von Alexandria Troas* (Bonn: Habelt, 2009).

22. For a list of nineteen of these, see "The Many Alexandrias of Alexander the Great," The Basement Geographer: Scattershot Slices of the World from Å to Zzyzx, http://tinyurl.com/SBL4522d.

23. For inscriptions, see Marijana Ricl, *The Inscriptions of Alexandreia Troas*, Inschriften griechischer Städte aus Kleinasien 53 (Bonn: Habelt, 1997). A Latin inscription (51–52 §11) dates to the reign of Caracalla before 212 CE, while a Greek inscription (78 §46) dates to the third century CE. A Latin inscription (227 §T120) found in Adriatic Italy dates to Tiberias in the first century CE.

24. The coinage dates from the second century CE because "no coins were minted at Alexandria Troas during the first century A.D."; see Peter Lewis and Ron Bolden, *The Pocket Guide to Saint Paul: Coins Encountered by the Apostle on His Travels* (Kent Town, S. Australia: Wakefield, 2002), 105.

25. For more details, see Thompson, "Alexandria Troas."

26. Colin J. Hemer, "Alexandria Troas," *TynBul* 26 (1975): 80. Strabo's source was

The archaeological history is likewise negligible compared to other nearby cities such as Troy and Assos. Through the centuries it served as a quarry for stone, so the site today is largely desolate except for the abundant Valonia oak trees populating the fields within its fallen walls. The most visible ruin today, a bath-gymnasium complex, dates to around 135 CE, when it was built by the procurator of Asia, the notable Athenian Herodes Atticus.[27] The depression of a stadium, which dates to the Hellenistic period and is the only stadium in the Troad, is also observable.[28] Archaeological survey work at Troas by the University of Münster began in 1993 under the leadership of Elmar Schwertheim.[29] The findings of their excavation have been published in three volumes in the series Asia Minor Studien.[30] Since 2011, a Turkish excavation team headed by Erhan Öztepe of Ankara University has been excavating at Troas.[31]

When Paul visited Troas, he was entering a major population center in Asia Minor, if the conclusion of the Oxford Roman Economy Project (OREP) is sustained. J. W. Hanson has made the controversial assertion

---

Demetrius, a resident of its neighboring rival Scepsis (modern Kurşunlutepe), who perhaps begrudged Troas for absorbing his city during the synoecism.

27. A. C. G. Smith, "The Gymnasium at Alexandria Troas: Evidence for an Outline Reconstruction," *AS* 29 (1979): 23–50; also Manfred Klinkott, *Die Ruinen von Alexandreia Troas: Bestandsaufnahmen der "Thermen des Herodes Atticus" und des "Maldelik" mit Vorberichten der Untersuchungen durch R. Koldewey und A. C. G. Smith*, Asia Minor Studien 72 (Bonn: Habelt, 2014).

28. Robert Mechikoff, Barbara Rieger, and Athena Trakadas, "Alexandria Troas Stadium Survey: Report on the First Campaign," in vol. 7 of *Studien zum antiken Kleinasien*, ed. Elmar Schwertheim, Asia Minor Studien 66 (Bonn: Habelt, 2011), 181–97.

29. Some of the results of their work at Troas are available online (in German); see "Grabung in Alexandria Troas," Westfälische Wilhelms-Universität Münster: Forschungsstelle Asia Minor, http://tinyurl.com/SBL4522e.

30. The first three volumes published by Rudolf Habelt (Bonn) are: Elmar Schwertheim and Hans Wiegartz, eds., *Neue Forschungen zu Neandria und Alexandria Troas*, Asia Minor Studien 11 (Bonn: Habelt, 1994); Schwertheim and Wiegartz, eds., *Die Troas: Neue Forschungen zu Neandria und Alexandria Troas II*, Asia Minor Studien 22 (Bonn: Habelt, 1996); Schwertheim, ed., *Die Troas: Neue Forschungen III*, Asia Minor Studien 33 (Bonn: Habelt, 1999). A fourth volume has since been published that Schwertheim coedited with Georg Petzl, *Hadrian und die dionysischen Künstler: Drei in Alexandria Troas neugefundene Briefe des Kaisers an die Künstler-Vereinigung*, Asia Minor Studien 58 (Bonn: Habelt, 2006).

31. The annual results of the excavations at Troas, Smintheum-Gülpınar, and Assos are published (in Turkish) online by the Turkish Ministry of Culture and Tourism, "Kazı Sonuçları Toplantıları," http://tinyurl.com/SBL4522f.

that Troas was the second most populated city in Asia, even ahead of Ephesus and Pergamon.[32] He estimated its population at 111,200 persons within a civic area of 278 hectares.[33] The OREP has sought to develop a more scientific methodology to determine civic populations in antiquity by coupling population density figures (e.g., population at 100, 150, 200, or 400 persons per hectare) with the known area of the cities. Such area-based estimates, according to Hanson, "call a number of long-held views in the existing literature into question regarding the population of the larger cities in Asia."[34] Hanson notes that a primary reason for Troas's importance was that it acted as a nodal point "between road systems from the east and maritime routes to the south and west."[35] It was the main port for ships waiting to enter the Hellespont on the way to the Black Sea since a westerly wind was necessary to fight the strong current coming out of the Hellespont.[36] A *decumanus maximus*, unmarked on the map, led from

---

32. J. W. Hanson, "The Urban System of Roman Asia Minor and Wider Urban Connectivity," in *Settlement, Urbanisation and Population*, ed. Alan K. Bowman and Andrew Wilson, Oxford Studies in the Roman Economy (Oxford: Oxford University Press, 2011), 254, table 9.1. Smyrna is not included in the study because its area was apparently unknown to Hanson. Akın Ersoy, the archaeologist leading the Smyrna agora excavation, calculates the city's area as 193 hectares (personal communication, 18 January 2016). In the same volume, Andrew Wilson in his article "City Sizes and Urbanization in the Roman Empire," in Hanson, *Settlement*, 187, table 7.11, uses Hanson's data to extrapolate a conservative population density for civic populations in Asia Minor.

33. This calculation allows for a density of 400 persons per hectare, the densest of four possible calculations. Walter Leaf, *Strabo on the Troad* (Cambridge: Cambridge University Press, 1923), 236, similarly estimated a population of 100,000 but within an area of 1,000 acres (= 405 ha) or 100 persons to the acre (247 per ha). Leaf's estimated area is 69 percent higher than Hanson's. If the density were 250 persons per hectare, Hanson estimates Troas's population at 69,500.

34. Hanson, "Urban System," 252. This particularly challenges the figures given by T. R. S. Broughton, "Roman Asia," in *An Economic Survey of Ancient Rome*, ed. Tenney Frank, 4 vols. (Baltimore: Johns Hopkins University Press, 1938), 812–16. Troas does not even reach a population of 30,000 in Rodney Stark's two studies, *The Rise of Christianity: How the Obscure, Marginal Jesus Movement Became the Dominant Religious Force in the Western World in a Few Centuries* (San Francisco: HarperCollins, 1997), 131–32, and *Cities of God: The Real Story of How Christianity Became an Urban Movement and Conquered Rome* (New York: HarperOne, 2006), 61.

35. Hanson, "Urban System," 259.

36. Thompson, "Alexandria Troas," 4.

Figure 12.2. Decumanus Maximus, Troas. Photo by Mark Wilson.

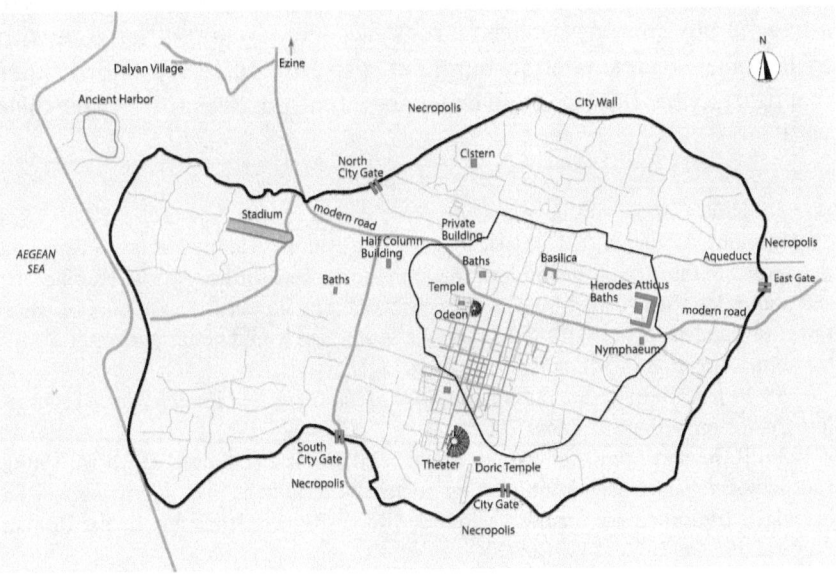

Figure 12.3. City Plan of Troas. Design by Tutku Tours;
http://tutkutours.com/MAP_02_Ancient-city-plans.asp. Used with permission.

the harbor to the central civic area; excavations have recently revealed a section of it near the Agora Temple.

A cardo, shown on the map of Troas (fig. 12.3, above) and visible as a dirt track on Google Earth, ran through the city's western quadrant. This street led to the south gate from which Paul would have exited the city.[37] The road then passed through the city's southern necropolis before descending to the coastal plain called in antiquity the Halesion (or Alesion) Plain.[38]

4. The Logistics of Paul's Walk and of His Friends' Sea Journey

Paul made an arrangement with his companions to travel πεζεύειν (Acts 20:13), translated "on foot" (NIV, NKJV) or "by land" (NRSV, ESV, NLT). R. Martin Pope observes that "it is an open question whether Paul walked the distance of over twenty miles to Assos or rode a mule."[39] Hemer argues that Paul probably used a horse or vehicle for the journey and that "πεζεύειν is not to be pressed in an etymological sense."[40] He cites Polybius's reference to πεζεύειν μετὰ τῶν ἵππων (*Hist.* 10.48.6) as an example of πεζεύειν being used "explicitly sometimes of travel on horseback."[41] But Polybius is not making such a point. Rather he is describing how the Apasiacae make a treacherous crossing between a rock face and a waterfall "on foot with their horses" (trans. of Shuckburgh; cf. also *Hist.* 16.29.11). Shortly after that he describes how, through dry spaces along the river, they "make their

---

37. Fatih Cimok, *Journeys of Paul: From Tarsus "to the Ends of the Earth,"* 3rd ed. (Istanbul: A Turizm, 2010), 193, suggests that Paul left via the Neandria Gate and descended to the area of the modern road junction where the hot springs (Kaplıcalar) still stand. He then turned toward the coast. But why go out the east gate, oriented toward Neandria, when exiting through the south gate would better correspond with the actual direction in which Paul was traveling?

38. R. J. A. Talbert, *The Barrington Atlas of the Greek and Roman World* (Princeton: Princeton University Press, 2000), 56.

39. R. Martin Pope, *On Roman Roads with St. Paul* (London: Epworth, 1939), 120. Donkeys and mules were used for travel but usually as pack animals involved in official transport; see Stephen Mitchell, "Requisitioned Transport in the Roman Empire," *JRS* 66 (1976): 119, 122–23.

40. Hemer, *Book of Acts*, 268.

41. Hemer, "Alexandria Troas," 105. Hemer's suggestion is often repeated in the literature, apparently without his reference in Polybius being checked. See, e.g., Paul Trebilco, "Asia," in Gill and Gempf, *Greco-Roman Setting*, 360.

way on horseback" (ποιεῖσθαι τὴν δίοδον ἐπὶ τῶν ἵππων; *Hist.* 10.48.8). The definition in the Greek-English Lexicon of Liddell and Scott, "go or travel on foot, walk," and in its abridged version, which adds "opp. to riding," negates any suggestion of animal conveyance.[42]

The route of Paul's walk is largely derived from archaeological *realia* along its path. After crossing the Halesion Plain and the Roman bridge to the Smintheum (both discussed below), J. M. Cook notes that "the Roman road will have struck inland from the Smintheum to cross the Figureau to Assos."[43] Ben Witherington III premises Paul's decision to walk on the fact that Assos "was an easy day's journey of twenty miles."[44] Using a Scalex digital MapWheel on the *Barrington Atlas*, a distance of 31 miles (50 km) was calculated.[45] A similar distance was calculated on Google Earth Pro (see fig. 12.4, below).[46] Thus the distance is 50 percent higher than Witherington's estimate and therefore at least a two-day walk.[47] The distance from Troas to the Smintheum was 16 miles (25.7 km), while the distance from the Smintheum to Assos was 15 miles (24.3 km). The Smintheum was a probable stopover point for Paul who, after preaching through the previous night, was undoubtedly exhausted.

---

42. Confirming this view are S. R. Llewelyn and R. A. Kearsley, *A Review of the Greek Inscriptions and Papyri Published in 1982-1983*, NewDoc 7:88. See Mark 6:33, where those following Jesus arrived by foot (πεζῇ).

43. Cook, *The Troad*, 234.

44. Ben Witherington III, *Acts of the Apostles* (Grand Rapids: Eerdmans, 1998), 608, who derives this distance from F. F. Bruce, *The Acts of the Apostles: Greek Text with Commentary and Introduction*, 3rd ed. (Grand Rapids: Eerdmans, 1990), 427.

45. My (Wilson's) inaccurate suggestion to Keener (*Acts*, 3:2981) of a distance of 38 miles was an overestimate based on measuring along the modern highway rather than the shorter ancient route.

46. Charles Fellows, *A Journal Written during an Excursion in Asia Minor* (London: Murray, 1839), 56, reckoned the distance at 30 miles based on an 8.5 hour horseback ride between the two cities in 1838. Peter Walker, *In the Steps of Paul: An Illustrated Guide to the Apostle's Life and Journeys* (Grand Rapids: Zondervan, 2008), 142, likewise estimates 30 miles (50 km) without citing supporting evidence.

47. W. J. Conybeare and J. S. Howson, *The Life and Epistles of St. Paul*, 2nd ed., 2 vols. (London: Longman, Brown, Green, Longmans, & Roberts, 1855-1856), 2:258, present this cozy scenario: "If the vessel sailed from Troas at seven in the morning, she would easily be round Cape Lectum before noon. If Saint Paul left Troas at ten, he might arrive at Assos at four in the afternoon; and the vessel might be at anchor in the roads of Mitylene at seven." These commentators presume that Paul is an apostolic superman who could cover the distance in six hours with no sleep!

Figure 12.4. Route of Paul's Walk from Troas to Assos.

Calculations related to distance and time for this journey of Paul have been relatively straightforward.[48] Keener expresses a truism found in discussions of ancient travel that "a strong but ordinary traveler could probably traverse fifteen to twenty miles per day (twenty to thirty kilometers)."[49] Hiking guides suggest that a walking speed of 4–5 kilometers an hour is possible for a fit walker, thus achieving 20–24 miles (32–40 km).[50] Perhaps the best source discussing "normal" travel times in antiquity is Gaius, *On the Provincial Edict* 1, quoted in Justinian's *Digest* 2.11.1. Here it states that the time allocated for a party to appear in court is based on a travel day of 20,000 paces, or 20 Roman miles. This would be the equivalent of 18.3 miles (29.6 km).[51]

---

48. Because the distance was so short and the rise in altitude only 1,000 feet, there was no need to employ the new three-dimensional modeling for travel in antiquity introduced by Tønnes Bekker-Nielsen in his presentation "Ancient Roads in the Third Dimension" at the symposium "Roads and Routes in Anatolia: Pathways of Communication from Prehistory to Seljuk Times" sponsored by the British Institute in Ankara in 2014.

49. Keener, *Acts*, 1:587.

50. See, for example, the discussion of Roger Caffin, "FAQ–Navigation," BushwalkingNSW.org, http://tinyurl.com/SBL4522g.

51. Under Agrippa the Roman pace (*passus*) was standardized at five Roman

The sailing distance for the ship carrying Paul's companions was slightly longer: 18 nautical miles (20.75 mi. / 33.25 km) from Troas to Cape Lectum and 15 nautical miles (17.25 mi. / 27.75 km) from Lectum to Assos, totaling 33 nautical miles (38 mi. / 61 km).[52] Depending on wind conditions, the distance would take almost two days to accomplish.[53] Thus Paul would join the ship in Assos late in the afternoon of the second day, sometime after the coasting vessel had anchored for the night in the harbor of Assos.[54] Commentators typically discuss the difficulty of sailing in the Troad. F. F. Bruce states that the longer time for the sea journey was "since the prevailing wind was the stormy northeaster."[55] However, Jamie Morton cautions: "In the Aegean there was very little differentiation between coastal and open-sea sailing, the many long promontories and chains of islands there being used to minimize sailing distances between landfalls."[56] On his return from Troy, Nestor utilized the strong northerly winds and currents in springtime to reach Tenedos opposite Troas. From Tenedos, Nestor continued past Cape Lectum before arriving at Lesbos, thus showing that such a sail was known in antiquity (Homer, *Od.* 3.159–174).

---

feet, about 4 feet 10 inches (1.48 m). The Roman mile had 1,000 paces (mille *passus* or *passuum*). We thank Tønnes Bekker-Nielsen for pointing out Gaius's statement in the *Digest*.

52. Eckhard Schnabel, *Acts*, ZECNT 5 (Grand Rapids: Zondervan, 2012), 837, estimates 43 miles (70 km) for the boat trip that could be covered in eight to seventeen hours.

53. Conybeare and Howson, *Life and Epistles*, 253 n. 1, aptly remind us "that many commentators write on the nautical passages of the Acts as if the weather were always the same and the rate of sailing uniform, or as if the Apostle travelled in steam-boats."

54. The length of this journey is commonly given between 20 miles (cf. Bruce, *Acts*, 427) and 22 miles: Brian Rapske, "Acts, Travel and Shipwreck," in Gill and Gempf, *Greco-Roman Setting*, 17. While this was the distance directly, the Roman road followed the coast past the Smintheum before turning southeastward to Assos. Therefore walking would not have saved any time, although this is the reason usually given for Paul's decision.

55. Bruce, *Acts*, 427.

56. Jamie Morton, *The Role of the Physical Environment in Ancient Greek Seafaring* (Leiden: Brill, 2001), 173. In figure 22, "Currents in the Aegean," Morton shows a northerly current passing along the western coast of the Troad.

5. Satnioeis Roman Bridge

A well-preserved Roman bridge with ramps stands in a field 13 miles (21 km) south of Troas and below the modern channel of the Tuzla River (fig. 12.5).[57] The riverbed of the ancient Satnioeis River has shifted some 197 feet (60 m) northward over the centuries, something Diller had already noted in 1881.[58] The Tuzla Bridge was first investigated by Prokesch von Osten in 1826.[59] Cook provides a description, drawing, and five photographs of the bridge from his 1966 survey.[60] Fifty years ago, seven arches of the bridge were visible. A. Coşkun Özgünel and his archaeological team did extensive work excavating and documenting the bridge in 1986–1987.[61] It was determined that the bridge was 305 feet (93 m) long with a width of 21.3 feet (6.5 m) resting on nine semicircular arches. (The ninth and most northern arch cannot be seen at present, having been buried subsequent to the river's change of course.) Özgünel was unable to determine the bridge's height because, after soundings of 9.8 feet (3 m), his team reached the water table. The three central arches are higher and larger than the others because they apparently spanned the main channel of the river. The lack of any ruts made by metal-wheeled carts and chariots between Troas and the Smintheum suggested to Tayyar Gürdal that "the bridge was intended for pedestrian traffic along the Sacred Way between these two sites where the cult of Apollo Smintheus was worshipped."[62] The bridge has been dated

---

57. Vittorio Galliazzo, *I Ponti Romani*, 2 vols. (Treviso: Canova, 1994), 2:420 §874, with drawing. Unfortunately this bridge is omitted in the twenty ancient bridges of Turkey listed in "Roman Bridges in Turkey," *Wikipedia*, http://tinyurl.com/SBL4522h; as well as in Colin O'Connor, *Roman Bridges* (Cambridge: Cambridge University Press, 1993).

58. J. S. Diller, "The Geology of Assos," in *Report on the Investigations at Assos, 1881*, ed. Joseph T. Clarke, Papers of the Archaeological Institute of America: Classical Series 1 (Boston: Williams, 1882), 215.

59. Anton Prokesch von Osten, *Denkwürdigkeiten und Erinnerungen aus dem Orient*, 3 vols. (Stuttgart: Hallberger'sche, 1836–1837), 3:363–64.

60. Cook, *Troad*, 225–26. The drawing is figure 10, and the photographs are 26a–28a.

61. The bridge is discussed and illustrated in A. Coşkun Özgünel, "Gülpınar: The Roman Bridge in Tuzla Valley," in *60. Yaşında Sinan Genim'e Armağan Makaleler*, ed. Oktay Belli and Belma Barış Kurtel (Istanbul: Ege, 2005), 516–25; Tayyar Gürdal, "A Roman Bridge on the Satnioeis (Tuzla) River," in *Smintheion: In Search of Apollo Smintheus*, ed. A. Coşkun Özgünel (Istanbul: Ege, 2015), 125–35.

62. Gürdal, "Roman Bridge," 131. The construction technique of the bridge's

Figure 12.5. Satnioeis Roman Bridge. Photo by Mark Wilson.

to the late first century BCE, during the reign of Augustus, based on comparisons with other Roman bridges built during this period. Thus Paul would have crossed this bridge with other pedestrians while walking along the Sacred Way.[63]

6. The Smintheum in Paul's Day

As Paul approached the southern end of the Halesion Plain, the road would have entered a valley leading to the forty-four-columned pseudodipteral Ionic temple located today in modern Gülpınar (fig. 12.6).[64] The distance

---

rough-hewn ashlars and voussoirs resembles that used in other Roman structures at the Smintheum, thus suggesting a similar source (the hills between them) and a similar time for their construction.

63. Later along his journey to Jerusalem, Paul walked on another sacred way at Miletus; see Mark Wilson, "The Ephesian Elders Come to Miletus: An Annaliste Reading of Acts 20:15–18a," *Verbum et Ecclesia* 34 (2013): 6–7.

64. For a discussion of the temple and its relationship with Homer, see A. Coşkun Özgünel, "The Temple of Apollo Smintheus and the Iliad," in Özgünel, *In Search of Apollo*, 15–63.

Figure 12.6. Temple of Apollo Smintheus. Photo by Mark Wilson.

from the bridge to the Smintheum was a short 3 miles (5 km).[65] The original settlement was at Chrysa, named eponymously after a priest, Chryses, whose daughter Chryseis was seized by Agamemnon (*Il.* 1.1–52).[66] Chrysa has been localized at Göztepe, 2.5 miles (4 km) southwest of the Smintheum at a headland on the coast.[67] The temple was dedicated to Apollo Smintheum, that is, "Apollo the Mouse God" (Strabo, *Geogr.* 13.1.48).[68] By the Roman period, Homeric Chrysa was no longer important, for as Ricl states: "In Roman Itineraries, the Smintheum, not Chrysa, features as a station on the inland road from Alexandreia to Assus."[69]

---

65. Gürdal, "Roman Bridge," 127, states twice that the distance is 9 kilometers (5.6 mi.), but measuring between the bridge and the temple on Google Earth yields the shorter distance.

66. For a brief history of the site, see Henry Matthews, *Greco-Roman Cities of Aegean Turkey: History, Archaeology, Architecture* (Istanbul: Ege, 2014), 62–65.

67. See Cook, *Troad*, 231–32; Musa Tombul, "Apollon Smintheus'a Hizmet veren İki Kent: Hamaksitos ve Khrysa," in *Smintheion: Apollon Smintheus'un İzinde*, ed. A. Coşkun Özgünel (Istanbul: Ege, 2013), 151–55.

68. For the tradition related to the mouse's association with this temple, see Thompson, "Alexandria Troas," 6.

69. Marijana Ricl, "Alexandreia Troas in the Hellenistic Period," *Mélanges d'histoire et d'épigraphie: Offerts à Fanoula Papazoglou par ses élèves á l'occasion de son quatre-vingtième anniversaire*, ed. Miroslava Mirković et al. (Belgrade: Université de Belgrade, 1997), 99.

Figure 12.7. Sacred Road leading to the Smintheum. Photo by Mark Wilson.

A 164 foot (50 m) section of the road upon which Paul would have approached the temple complex was excavated in 2005–2006. It was paved with well-cut rectangular slabs framed on both sides with elevated rectangular curbing (fig. 12.7). Its width ranges from 3.55 to 3.85 meters (11.65 to 12.63 ft.), slightly wider that the 3.25 meter standard used for Roman and Byzantine roads.[70] The road's engineering resembles the stone-paved Roman road excavated near the Agora Temple in Troas, thus suggesting a similar date of construction for both in the early first century CE.[71] Along this sacred road were found votive inscriptions on the bases of statues or columns honoring the prophets and priests of Apollo Smintheus and dedicated by the citizens of Troas and other neighboring cities. Tolga Özhan suggests the strong likelihood that this road "was decorated along the course of its route with artifacts including such dedications as these."[72] Luke has already shown Paul's interest in such dedicatory inscriptions in Athens (Acts 17:23), so it is likely Paul would have read these as he walked

---

70. David H. French, "A Road Problem: Roman or Byzantine?" *IstMitt* 43 (1993): 446.

71. For a comparative picture of the two road sections, see Gürdal, "Roman Bridge," 128–29, figs. 1 and 2.

72. For a fuller discussion of these inscriptions, see Tolga Özhan, "New Inscriptions from Smintheion: Dedications, Epitaphs, and Fragments," in Özgünel, *In Search of Apollo*, 107.

along. Also found near the sacred road was Roman Bath II. Its location "implies that visitors arriving on foot along this sacred road benefited from the bath by purifying their bodies with the water from the sacred spring, before entering the sacred space of the sanctuary."[73] This bath as well as nearby Bath I were in use from the first century BCE through the fourth century CE. Along the monumental street leading to Bath I, twenty-four inscribed statue bases were found, all in Greek except for one in Latin. These inscriptions, honoring the athletes victorious in the *Smintheia Pauleia* games held at the sanctuary, "provide substantial insight into the previously little-known athletic competitions."[74]

The relationship between Troas and the Smintheum was also evident through the former's coinage. As Otto Mørkholm explains, "In cases where we find both a city name and the name of a deity, as for instance Apollo Smintheus at Alexandria Troas, the coinage may be regarded as a normal civic issue, expressing the devotion of the population to its main god."[75] An early bronze coin dating from 301–281 BCE (BMC 9.1) shows Apollo Smintheus facing right with a mouse at his left foot.[76]

Images of Apollos Smintheus appeared later on the reverse of didrachms and tetradrachms issued from 176 to 65 BCE (cf. Bellinger Troy A133cf). However, Lewis and Bolden think it is "unlikely that Paul would have seen these tetradrachms."[77] Images of the temple itself (Bellinger Troy A273) only appear during Caracalla's reign (198–217 CE).[78] Of

---

73. Davut Kaplan, "Roman Baths and Related Structures," in Özgünel, *Apollon Smintheus*, 83.

74. Özhan, "New Inscriptions," 107. Ricl, *Inscriptions*, 82–84 §§52–54, has previously published inscriptions related to these games, but all date to the third century CE. The name *Smintheia Pauleia* is generally believed to preserve the memory and possible cult of Paullus Fabius Maximus, proconsul of Asia in 11 CE. But as Ricl (*Inscriptions*, 83) notes: "Robert, however, preferred to seek the origin of this name in a later period, when an unknown citizen of Alexandreia Troas could have instituted a foundation for the celebration of these games."

75. Otto Mørkholm, *Early Hellenistic Coinage from the Accession of Alexander to the Peace of Apamaea (336–188 B.C.)* (Cambridge: Cambridge University Press, 1991), 29.

76. "Alexandreia (BC 301–281) AE 14," Asia Minor Coins: Ancient Greek and Roman Coins from Asia Minor, Photo Gallery, http://tinyurl.com/SBL4522i.

77. Lewis and Bolden, *Pocket Guide*, 106.

78. "Alexandreia (AD 198–217) AE: Caracalla," Asia Minor Coins: Ancient Greek and Roman Coins from Asia Minor, Photo Gallery, http://tinyurl.com/SBL4522j.

the coins found during excavations at the Smintheum, 90 percent (18 out of 20) dating to the Hellenistic period and 82 percent (190 out of 231) from the Roman period were minted at Alexandria Troas.[79] Thus Peter Lewis and Ron Bolden conclude, "So whether through coins or through his surroundings at Alexandria Troas, Paul would have come under the influence of Apollo."[80]

After an overnight stop near the Smintheum, Paul turned southeastward to continue the second half of his walk to Assos. Mark Fairchild has proposed alternatively that "Paul could have boarded the ship at Chryse (modern Gülpınar) where the temple of Apollo Smintheus existed.… The road would have taken Paul right past the site."[81] The road turned inland at the Smintheum and not toward the coast at Chryse (see fig. 12.1), located 1.2 miles (2 km) to the west at Göztepe.[82] Also, Chryse's harbor was no longer in use in the Roman period.[83] Because the road did not run to the coast at Chryse and its harbor was inactive, this scenario is unlikely.[84]

7. The Road between the Smintheum and Assos

The excavators of the Smintheum have focused on the road's function for pilgrimage rather than considering its larger role in the Troad's road network. Based on its appearance in the Tabula Peutingeriana, Cook saw its extension to Assos as a natural part of the system.[85] During our research trip in 2013, we documented several sections of road between the Smintheum

---

79. Zeynep Çizmeli Özgün, "The Sanctuary of Apollo Smintheus in the Light of Numismatic Evidence," in Özgünel, *In Search of Apollo*, 93–103, esp. 100–101.

80. Lewis and Bolden, *Pocket Guide*, 106.

81. Mark Fairchild, *Christian Origins in Ephesus and Asia Minor* (Istanbul: Arkeoloji ve Sanat, 2015), 110.

82. Özgünel, "Temple of Apollo," 17.

83. Note the deprecatory comments about the functionality of this harbor localized at Akliman in Cook, *Troad*, 233.

84. The closest serviceable harbor was probably at Cape Lectum (Babakale). Takeko Hareda and Fatih Cimok, *Roads of Ancient Anatolia*, 2 vols. (Istanbul: A Turizm, 2008), 1:24–25 figs. 10–11, show pictures of the cape and a section of road that connected it to the Smintheum, approximately 8 miles (12.9 km) to the northeast. However, no date for this road is given.

85. Cook, *Troad*, 25. For a recent discussion of this thirteenth century CE copy of a fourth–fifth century CE map that is critical for hodological research on the Roman

and Assos, a section not a part of the Sacred Way. North of Kocaköy, the track of the road ran parallel to the modern highway on its eastern side. The surface was deteriorated, with only a few paving stones remaining; curbstones were disrupted and scattered to the side of the bed. At Koyunevi a road trace was detected south of the highway. West of Balabanlı a section of road is visible, ascending toward the village on the north of the highway. The road is paved with stones, but little curbing remains (fig. 12.8).

The best-preserved section of road exists just east of Korubaşı (fig. 12.9).[86] It begins at the southeastern entrance of the village, with the main track running 0.68 miles (1.1 km) to the southeast, parallel to and located below the highway. Its pavement contains various sizes of stones, with

Figure 12.8. Road Section at Balabanlı, with Halesion Plain in background. Photo by Mark Wilson.

---

cursus publicus, see Richard Talbert, *Rome's World: The Peutinger Map Reconsidered* (Cambridge: Cambridge University Press, 2010).

86. A picture of this road section graces the cover of Ronald Brownrigg's *Pauline Places: In the Footsteps of Paul through Turkey and Greece* (London: Hodder & Stoughton, 1989). Strangely, the memory of this place for Étienne de Mesmay, *Sur les routes de l'apôtre Paul en Turquie*, Cahiers de l'École Cathédrale 67 (Paris: Parole et Silence, 2005), 121, is not of a road but large stone buildings that resemble prehistoric tombs: "Juste après Korubasi, une grande étendues très rase est parsemée de constructions rondes faites en très grosses pierres."

Figure 12.9. Road section at Korubaşı with Acropolis of Assos in center background. Photo by Mark Wilson.

larger stones flush with the surface functioning as curbing; however, in some places the curbing is raised on both sides. Also, the center is ridged to provide better drainage. No wheel ruts are visible on the road surface. Several branches of the road are evident, with one descending to the ravine below that was apparently crossed by a small bridge no longer extant. Dating of the road is difficult since the present surface is certainly a repaving. Its width varies from 7.05 feet (2.15 m) to 10.66 feet (3.25 m).[87]

This route between Troas and Assos is not shown on David H. French's *Conspectus Map* 5.1.[88] The *Barrington Atlas* does show a road connecting the Smintheum and Assos, but it is located farther north along the southern bank of the Satnioeis River.[89] Brill's *New Pauly Atlas* shows a less detailed route here, but its broken line puts it in the "documented or

---

87. For the difficulties of dating a road, see French, "Road Problem," 445–54. The width of the roads north of Tarsus and of Antalya that French discusses varied from 3 to 3.5 meters (9.84 to 11.38 ft.).

88. David H. French, *Milestones: Asia*, vol. 3.3.5 of *Roman Roads and Milestones of Asia Minor / Küçük Asya'daki Roma yolları ve miltaşları* (Ankara: British Institute at Ankara, 2014), 25.

89. Talbert, *Barrington Atlas*, 56.

conjectured" category.⁹⁰ The W. M. Calder and G. E. Bean map, although dated, does depict a route close to what we documented.⁹¹

8. Assos in Paul's Day

From the road section at Korubaşı the acropolis of Assos was now in Paul's view. Its massive walls running 2 miles (3.2 km)—today the world's most complete fortification preserved from the Hellenistic period—loomed before him (fig. 12.10). The archaeological history of the city is more developed than Troas and spans almost 150 years. It was the first expedition made by the Archaeological Institute of America, and Joseph T. Clarke and Francis H. Bacon excavated there from 1881 to 1883.⁹²

As Paul approached the city, he must have been aware that Aristotle had lived in Assos for three years and that his wife Pythias was from there.⁹³ Nearing the city from the west, the road split. One fork bypassed the city to the southwest and proceeded directly to the port, a distance of approximately .9 mile (1.45 km; fig. 12.11).

The other fork passed through the West Necropolis (fig. 12.12) and led to the Western Gate. It "was paved with 5–6 m wide polygonal stones in the Archaic period, possibly before 500."⁹⁴ Hundreds of graves from

---

90. Anne-Maria Wittke et al., eds., *Brill's New Pauly: Historical Atlas of the Ancient World*, NeuePaulySup 3 (Leiden: Brill, 2010), 197.

91. W. M. Calder and G. E. Bean, *A Classical Map of Asia Minor* (London: British Institute of Archaeology in Ankara, 1958).

92. The publications resulting from this excavation include Clarke, *Assos 1881*; Joseph T. Clarke, ed., *Report on the Investigations at Assos, 1882, 1883*, Papers of the Archaeological Institute of America: Classical Series 2 (New York: Macmillan, 1898); and Joseph T. Clarke, Francis H. Bacon, and Robert Koldewey, *Investigations at Assos* (Cambridge: Archaeological Institute of America, 1902). Publications on Assos in Habelt's series, *Asia Minor Studien*, include Ümit Serdaroğlu, Reinhard Stupperich, and Elmar Schwertheim, eds., *Ausgrabungen in Assos*, Asia Minor Studien 2 (Bonn: Habelt, 1990); Serdaroğlu and Stupperich, eds., *Ausgrabungen in Assos 1990*, Asia Minor Studien 5 (Bonn: Habelt, 1992); Serdaroğlu and Stupperich, eds., *Ausgrabungen in Assos 1991*, Asia Minor Studien 10 (Bonn: Habelt, 1993); Serdaroğlu and Stupperich, eds., *Ausgrabungen in Assos 1992*, Asia Minor Studien 21 (Bonn: Habelt, 1996); Stupperich, ed., *Ausgrabungen in Assos 1993*, Asia Minor Studien 57 (Bonn: Habelt, 2006).

93. For a summary of the history of the city, see Wilson, *Biblical Turkey*, 357–64.

94. Tuna Şare Ağturk and Nurettin Arslan, *A Terracotta Treasure at Assos* (Istanbul: Ege, 2015), 13–14. For an aerial view and drawing of the road, see their fig. 3.

Figure 12.10. City plan of Assos. Courtesy Ege Yayınları.

the Archaic, Classical, and Hellenistic periods lined this 820-foot-long (250 m) road with an additional one hundred sarcophagi and monumental tombs that date to the Roman period. The most conspicuous of these, shaped like a pyramid and sitting to the left of the Western Gate, was that of Publius Varius, dating from the first century BCE.[95] Which spur of the road Paul chose is unknown: he might have passed through the city to observe its monuments and citizens, or he might have gone directly to the harbor to be reunited with his companions on the ship.

In Paul's day Assos was an important port on the Troad's southern coast. Speaking of its importance, Michael Grant makes this curious statement, "The larger of the town's two (artificially created) harbors was used by ships in order to avoid the strong currents off the west coast of the

---

95. Nurettin Arslan and Beate Böhlendorf-Arslan, *Assos: An Archaeological Guide* (Istanbul: Homer, 2010), 108–13.

Figure 12.11. Road to the harbor of Assos.
Photo by Mark Wilson.

Troad—across which vessels were also conveyed from Assus by land."⁹⁶ He continues, "The city suffered from the competition of Alexander [sic] Troas … and lost its position as a land portage terminal, concentrating henceforth on agriculture instead."⁹⁷ Grant seems to be envisioning a sort of *diolkos*, like that at Corinth which spanned the narrow 3.9-mile-long isthmus between the Gulf of Corinth and the Saronic Gulf.⁹⁸ Grant's undocumented statement seems highly unlikely since the city stands over 500 feet (152 m) above sea level and is situated approximately fifteen miles

---

96. Michael Grant, *A Guide to the Ancient World* (New York: Barnes & Noble, 1997), 77.

97. Ibid. Grant also mistakenly states about Assos: "The ship which took St. Paul to Italy called at its port."

98. Only two other *diolkoi* for ships are known in antiquity, and both were in Egypt. These are mentioned by Oribasius (*Coll. med.* 2.58.54–55 [*CMG* 6.1.1]) and Ptolemy (*Geogr.* 4.5.10).

Figure 12.12. Road through Necropolis to Western Gate of Assos. Photo by Mark Wilson.

from the nearest harbor on the western coast.[99] The steep descent to its port was known to be so dangerous that Stratonicus is quoted ironically by Strabo (*Geogr.* 13.1.57 [Jones]): "Go to Assus, in order that thou mayest more quickly come to the doom of death." Would anyone really drag a ship uphill along such a steep road from the harbor to avoid a strong current off the Troad's west coast? As David Pettegrew observes, "It was neither easy nor wise to haul a ship overland in antiquity.... The transfer presented very real danger to ships, and land was obviously an incredible hindrance to their movement."[100] The idea that Paul might have followed such a portage or its remains must be rejected.

The harbor of Assos was situated on a narrow shoreline, so no settlement developed there (fig. 12.13). It was not natural but was formed by a mole built in antiquity. Despite Grant's claim of two artificial harbors, archaeologists have identified only one. Ümit Serdaroğlu observes that "the sill stones of the ancient mole, each measuring 90 cm. in width and more than 2 m. in length can be clearly seen if one looks down."[101] A small mole sill 164 feet (50 m) west of these can also be seen. The size of the harbor

---

99. The *diolkos* at Corinth climbed to only 262 feet (80 m) above sea level.

100. David Pettegrew, "The *Diolkos* of Corinth," *AJA* 115 (2011): 563.

101. Ümit Serdaroğlu, *Assos: Behramkale*, Antique Cities Series 1a (Istanbul: Arkeoloji ve Sanat, 1995), 91.

Figure 12.13. Harbor of Assos with Acropolis in background.
Photo by Mark Wilson.

"was large enough to provide shelter for quite a number of modestly-sized ships."[102] Clarke provides a drawing of the Turkish mole as it looked in 1881, which was rebuilt in the nineteenth century. He claims it was one-fifth the size of the original but gives no support for that calculation.[103]

9. Suggested Reasons for Paul's Walk

Why did Paul walk from Troas to Assos? Verlyn Verbrugge and Keith R. Krell conclude that "we simply do not know, and any suggestion is pure speculation."[104] Commentators, however, have suggested a number of reasons for Paul's walk, and the following discussion summarizes the main ones. Luke provides hints in the narrative regarding the reasons, and the final two suggestions present our conclusions based on these clues; these, we believe, are more than speculation.

---

102. Arslan and Böhlendorf-Arslan, *Archaeological Guide*, 130.
103. Clarke, *Assos 1881*, 130.
104. Verlyn D. Verbrugge and Keith R. Krell, *Paul and Money: A Biblical and Theological Analysis of the Apostle's Teachings and Practices* (Grand Rapids: Zondervan, 2015), 191.

9.1. Ministry Concerns in Troas

William Mitchell Ramsay suggested that Paul stayed on until the last moment, "perhaps to be assured of Eutychus's recovery, while the other delegates went on ahead in the ship."[105] Witherington likewise concurs that Paul needed more time to complete his ministry in Troas and that the delay was "to complete his final exhortation to this congregation."[106] Since Paul already had a week in Troas to take care of ministry affairs, why would a few extra hours be needed now? Eutychus's physical situation could have been ascertained in the six or so hours after his fall, following which Paul continued to speak until sunrise (ἄχρι αὐγῆς; Acts 20:11).[107]

Ernst Haenchen strangely introduces the reading ἕως αὐγῆς, interpreting this as daybreak before sunrise. He thus conjectures that Paul "continues preaching until about five o'clock in the morning" and then departed.[108] There are two problems related to Haenchen's reading. The first is a lexical one. The *Greek-English Lexicon* of Liddell and Scott (1968) notes that αὐγή means "light of the sun" and in the plural "rays, beams," hence, sunrise.[109] The second problem is astronomical. In late April, civil twilight—that period when there is enough sunlight to conduct outdoor activities without the aid of artificial lighting—begins around 5:50 a.m. Based on

---

105. William Mitchell Ramsay, *St. Paul the Traveler and Roman Citizen*, ed. Mark Wilson (Grand Rapids: Kregel, 2001), 222.

106. Witherington, *Acts of the Apostles*, 608; see also John B. Polhill, *Acts: An Exegetical and Theological Exposition of Holy Scripture*, New American Commentary 26 (Nashville: Broadman & Holman, 1992), 420. So also John McRay, *Paul: His Life and Teaching* (Grand Rapids: Baker Academic, 2003), 198: "Perhaps Paul needed more time in Troas to establish and instruct the infant church there."

107. Isaiah 59:9 is the only verse in which αὐγή is used in the Old Testament; μείναντες αὐγήν is translated "having waited for sunlight" by Moisés Silva in *A New English Translation of the Septuagint* (Oxford: Oxford University Press, 2007).

108. Ernst Haenchen, *The Acts of the Apostles: A Commentary* (Philadelphia: Westminster, 1971), 585–86. He is following Kirsopp Lake and Henry J. Cadbury, eds., *The Acts of the Apostles: English Translation and Commentary*, ed. F. J. Foakes-Jackson and Kirsopp Lake, 5 vols., The Beginnings of Christianity 1 (London: Macmillan, 1932), 4:257, who note that αὐγή means daylight before the sunrise in modern Greek and suggest that it probably has the same meaning here.

109. The English translations "daylight" (NIV), "daybreak" (ESV, NKJV), and "dawn" (NRSV, NLT) are ambiguous in their meaning and carry the connotation of civil twilight rather than sunrise. Paul uses the verbal form metaphorically in 2 Cor 4:4: αὐγάσαι τὸν φωτισμόν.

Figure 12.14. Harbor of Troas with island of Tenedos in background. Photo by Mark Wilson.

Haenchen's projection, Paul would begin his walk in the dark. The sun rose around 6:20 a.m. on April 26, so his walk probably began around that time.[110] After the meeting broke up, those departing by ship went to the harbor (fig. 12.14) while Paul left on foot (Acts 20:11, 13). The coasting vessel's departure was contingent on the breezes arising around dawn, so there was little reason to go to the ship earlier.[111]

---

110. The date calculation of April 26 is based on the chart in Wilson, "Lukan *Periplus*," .237 The times for civil twilight and sunrise are calculated for nearby Bozcaada (Tenedos); see "Sunrise and Sunset Bozcaada," Sunrise-and-Sunset.com, http://tinyurl.com/SBL4522k.

111. Ramsay, *St. Paul*, 222–23. Ramsay strangely discusses wind conditions in the summer in the Aegean when, as he acknowledges, Paul is traveling in the spring. He goes on to suggest that "it would be necessary for all passengers to go on board soon after midnight in order to be ready to sail with the first breath from the north." Since coastal vessels typically did not sail at night, it is problematic to think the crew and passengers would spend most of the night aboard the vessel. Civil twilight occurred about thirty minutes before sunrise and would be the earliest that such a vessel could depart.

9.2. Danger of Jewish Enemies

Some suggest that the collection conducted by Paul in Corinth was illegal.[112] This is the reason Luke never mentions the Jerusalem collection in Acts. The plot then by the Corinthian Jews was to intercept Paul and prevent its delivery (Acts 20:3). For this reason Verbrugge and Krell regard the itinerary in Acts 20 as "somewhat convoluted" because Paul "kept trying to keep his enemies guessing as to what his plans were and where he might be."[113] Charles Fellows suggests that Paul and his team made the circuitous diversion through Macedonia because "Philippi and Troas are the cities where he would have been safest from the plot of the Jews."[114] However, Thessalonica was the likely port to which the party sailed from Corinth, and a synagogue of the Jews existed there (Acts 17:2). Fellows explains the reason for Paul's walk: "Knowing that he was under more suspicion (i.e., from Jewish opponents) than the delegates, he sent them ahead to Troas with the money. Later, he walked from Troas to Assos, as a diversionary tactic, while the others took the money in the boat." This seems an overly complex reading of the pericope, and it is doubtful that Paul's enemies would have continued their pursuit into Asia from Achaia and Macedonia.

9.3. Danger of Cape Lectum

Joseph A. Fitzmyer suggests that Paul walked to Assos because he wished to avoid sailing around the treacherous coastal waters of Cape Lectum (Babakale; fig. 12.15).[115] Hemer also points out that Paul's travel overland was "appropriate to local circumstances, where the ship had to negotiate an exposed coast and double Cape Lectum before reaching Assos."[116]

---

112. For a discussion of this issue, see, for example, Keith F. Nickle, *The Collection: A Study in Paul's Strategy*, SBT 48 (London: SCM, 1966), 148–50 and Margaret F. Thrall, *Commentary on 2 Corinthians 8–13*, vol. 2 of *The Second Epistle to the Corinthians*, ICC (London: T&T Clark, 2000), 2:517–18.

113. Verbrugge and Krell, *Paul and Money*, 191.

114. Richard Fellows, "The Plot against Paul (Acts 20:3)," *Paul and Co-Workers* (blog), 5 December 2009, http://tinyurl.com/SBL45221.

115. Joseph A. Fitzmyer, *Acts of the Apostles*, AB 31 (New York: Doubleday: 1998), 671. Like us, Schnabel, *Acts*, 837, rightly asks "why his travel companions travel by ship" if the coast is so treacherous.

116. Hemer, *Book of Acts*, 125. "Double" is a nautical term meaning to sail around a cape or promontory.

Figure 12.15. Cape Lectum with Lesbos in background.
Photo by Mark Wilson.

Upon this reading, Paul seemingly had no compunction about sending his co-workers into harm's way. Strabo describes the "doubling" of Lectum matter of factly: κάμψαντι δὲ τὸ Λεκτόν (*Geogr.* 13.1.49). However, when Strabo warns about the hazards of doubling Cape Malea, he quotes this proverb: Μαλέας δὲ κάμψας ἐπιλάθου τῶν οἴκαδε (*Geogr.* 8.6.20). It seems that doubling Lectum posed only a normal navigational threat, unlike Malea. An exposed coast characterizes the entire Aegean coastline of western Asia Minor, thus to avoid it Paul would have needed to walk the entire distance.[117] Interestingly, the only warnings that the *Mediterranean Pilot* gives for this journey is that the coast near the mouth of the Tuzla River should be given a wide berth because of shoals and that the shoals east of the Sivrice lighthouse (7.5 mi. / 12 km east of Lectum) should also be avoided. There are no warnings given for rounding Lectum, and assurance is given that the water in the area "is all along deep."[118]

---

117. Darrell Bock, *Acts*, BECNT (Grand Rapids: Baker, 2008), 621, makes the unhelpful comment: "A boat ride is long and potentially dangerous, given its route around Cape Lectum." Since the group's journey by boat to Caesarea Maritima had only just started, they still had approximately 900 miles to travel. Bock ultimately concludes, "We do not know, however, why the different route is taken."

118. United States Hydrographic Office, United States Navy Department, *From Cape Matapan (Greece) Eastward, the Mediterranean Archipelago, and the Southern*

9.4. A Bad Sailor

Kirsopp Lake and Henry J. Cadbury admit that the reason for Paul's walk is obscure but then suggest a possible reason: "He was a bad sailor, and to such the open water from Troas to Assos in the stormy north-east wind, prevalent about five days out of seven, can be most unpleasant in a small boat."[119] Responding to such a suggestion, C. K. Barrett writes, "The suggestion that he was liable to sea sickness is exegetical despair."[120] Jerome Murphy-O'Connor calls such speculation "rather farfetched."[121] Because Paul had already suffered three shipwrecks as well as drifting at sea for a day and night (2 Cor 11:25), could he have developed aquaphobia? Charles L. Quarles suggests that Paul opted to walk so that he would never again have the experience of "examining the fins in distant water to determine whether they marked the approach of sharks or dolphins."[122] That Paul boarded the ship again in Assos shows that any apparent paranoia about seasickness and the jaws of sharks was rather short-lived.

9.5. Ministry Training

Another suggestion is that Paul walked so as to continue his training of Troas's church leaders. Fairchild expands this to include leaders of the church in Assos.[123] Yet this suggestion is based on a number of hypotheticals. First, the presence of a church in Assos must be assumed, for which there is no evidence. As we have argued elsewhere, Paul bypassed Assos on his second journey and probably on his third journey after he left Ephesus

---

Shore of the Mediterranean Sea, Eastward of Ras Ashdir (Libia), vol. 4 of *Mediterranean Pilot* (Washington, DC: Government Printing Office, 1916), 370, online at Internet Archive, http://tinyurl.com/SBL4522n. For a satellite map of the coastline with the various Turkish names of the points, see "Babakale Haritası Çanakkale," Harita TR, http://tinyurl.com/SBL4522o.

119. Lake and Cadbury, *Acts*, 4:257–58.

120. C. K. Barrett, *A Critical and Exegetical Commentary on the Acts of the Apostles*, 2 vols., ICC (London: T&T Clark, 1994–1998), 2:957.

121. Jerome Murphy-O'Connor, *Paul: A Critical Life* (Oxford: Oxford University Press, 1997), 346.

122. Charles L. Quarles, *Illustrated Life of Paul* (Nashville: B&H, 2014), 181. Pliny (*Nat.* 9.70.26) does warn about the danger of dogfish, the ancient name for the whole genus of sharks, but this in the context of a warning to divers (cf. Aelian, *Nat. an.* 1.55).

123. Fairchild, *Christian Origins*, 110.

by taking the inland road instead.[124] So we have no evidence that Paul preached there prior to his visit in Acts 20. If a church did exist, it was perhaps started by believers in Troas. Connected to this, Fairchild also suggests that the reason that Paul's companions preceded him to Troas was to gather Christian leaders from around the Troad to meet Paul in Troas. However, Luke never suggests this. Rather, Paul remained in Philippi to celebrate the Feast of Unleavened Bread. Because his companions were gentiles, there was no need for them to wait for the Passover. Undoubtedly Paul did send them ahead for a reason, but as suggested elsewhere, it was for the purpose of arranging transportation on a coasting vessel to reach a Mediterranean transit point.[125] His companions expected Paul to follow shortly after them; however, unfavorable winds caused a day delay in his arrival (cf. Acts 16:11). It is unlikely that Paul's companions would have left Troas to make a four-day trip around the Troad to gather leaders when they expected Paul to arrive in Troas shortly. As stated earlier, the delay in Paul's arrival forced him to stay in Troas an extra seven days. Surely any leadership training could have been accomplished during this week. Fairchild concludes, "It is unimaginable to think that Paul took the journey from Troas to Assos alone."[126] But that is exactly what Luke presents him as doing, leaving the believers in Troas behind and sending his companions by ship to Assos.

9.6. Ministry Tour

D. L. Burdick postulates that Paul, after he left Ephesus, evangelized in the cities between Assos and Troas, then suggests that "it is at least possible that Paul chose to go by foot from Troas to Assos because there were converts on that route who needed his continued ministry."[127] Eckhard J. Schnabel speculates similarly about the walk, especially if "there were churches in the towns that he would have passed through—Kolonai, Larisa, Hamaxitos, Smintheion."[128] As appealing as this proposal seems, it

---

124. Thompson and Wilson, "Route."
125. See Wilson, "Lukan *Periplus*," 232–33.
126. Fairchild, *Christian Origins*, 110. Since other people would be traveling along this route, especially between Troas and the Smintheum, Paul's aloneness was relative.
127. D. L. Burdick, "With Paul in the Troad," *Near East Archaeological Society Bulletin* 12 (1978): 42.
128. Schnabel, *Acts*, 837.

is doubtful that these villages contained believers at this time. Barrett more realistically states, "There is nothing to suggest that he made an evangelistic tour through the district,"[129] and we concur with his opinion.

9.7. Penny-Pincher

Although Luke does not explicitly mention that Paul and his companions were carrying the collection for Jerusalem (see above), this is the probability. Despite Paul having a surfeit of funds, Quarles suggests that Paul took the land route because it "was more direct, nearly as fast, and would save one fare."[130] This characterization depicts Paul as a penny-pincher who would walk 30 miles (48 km) to save the funds needed for his boat passage. That a lack of money was the reason behind his decision to walk does not fit the New Testament picture of Paul.

9.8. Macho Man

Paul's decision to walk to Assos, according to Peter Walker, illustrates "his physical robustness."[131] Likewise, Burdick speculates: "Our modern stress on physical exercise might cause us to wonder if he was a physical fitness buff."[132] Since Luke has portrayed Paul walking significant distances on various earlier journeys, his walk need not be construed as a demonstration of his machismo to his younger companions and that the "old man" (Phlm 9) still had what it takes. I. Howard Marshall concurs that "it is highly unlikely that Luke wanted to show the tremendous physical resilience of Paul as a man capable of a long tramp after a sleepless night."[133] This is not to say, of course, that Paul lacked physical stamina. On the contrary, Luke's depiction of his numerous journeys portrays an individual extremely fit for travel.[134]

---

129. Barrett, *Acts*, 2:957.
130. Quarles, *Illustrated Life*, 181.
131. Walker, *In the Steps*, 142.
132. Burdick, "Paul in the Troad," 41.
133. I. Howard Marshall, *The Acts of the Apostles: An Introduction and Commentary*, TNTC (Grand Rapids: Eerdmans, 1980), 327–28.
134. In Acts Paul Thecl. 3, Paul is described as a bandy-legged traveler coming along the royal road to Iconium. Bruce J. Malina and Jerome H. Neyrey, *Portraits of Paul: An Archaeology of Ancient Personality* (Louisville: Westminster John Knox,

9.9. Time for Solitude and Personal Space

W. J. Conybeare and J. S. Howson suggest that Paul walked because of his desire for solitude: "The discomfort of a crowded ship is unfavorable for devotion: and prayer and meditation are necessary for maintaining the religious life, even of an Apostle."[135] Richard N. Longenecker likewise suggests that Paul "may just have wanted to be alone with God on the walk to Assos."[136] Because of the lack of privacy on board the ship, Walker asks whether the walk might have afforded Paul "one of his last opportunities to be on his own before he arrived at Jerusalem." According to him, the purpose was that Paul "needed space to think, to pray, to enjoy his freedom."[137] Interestingly, Walker proposes that Paul's seven companions did not accompany him through Macedonia but sailed to Troas directly from Corinth. If that were the case (and not what the text says), why would Paul need personal space since he had not yet even traveled aboard ship with his companions?

9.10. A Bold Response to the Spirit's "Warnings"

The final two readings, those of Glen L. Thompson and Mark Wilson respectively, both find clues in Paul's address to the elders in Miletus: "And now, compelled by the Spirit [δεδεμένος ἐγὼ τῷ πνεύματι], I am going to Jerusalem, not knowing what will happen to me there. I only know that in every city[138] the Holy Spirit warns me that prison and hardships are facing me" (Acts 20:22–23 NIV). Murphy-O'Connor rightly connects the note of apprehension here with Paul's feeling in Rom 15:31.[139] However, Paul's appeal for prayer to be rescued from his Jewish opponents in Judea seems more a natural precaution than the supernatural warnings to which Paul is referring. Up to this point in his journey from Achaia no specific examples

---

1996), 128–31, suggest that the portrait here, based on ancient stereotypes, portrays Paul as a courageous and bold male who is a resilient, wiry, hard worker.

135. Conybeare and Howson, *Life and Epistles*, 259.

136. Richard N. Longenecker, *The Acts of the Apostles*, vol. 9 of *The Expositor's Bible Commentary*, ed. Frank C. Gaebelein (Grand Rapids: Zondervan, 1981), 510.

137. Walker, *In the Steps*, 142.

138. The NIV translation "in every city" is not supported by the best manuscripts. Both NA^{27} and UBS^4 omit πᾶσαν from the text.

139. Murphy-O'Connor, *Critical Life*, 344.

of warnings by the Holy Spirit have been given. Witherington correctly observes that the warnings here are both retrospective and prospective. However, he goes too far back when he suggests "that the cities Paul may have in mind are those where he previously experienced persecution and plot and imprisonment at the hands of his fellow Jews (e.g., Pisidian Antioch, Iconium, Lystra, Thessalonica, Beroea, Corinth)."[140] More likely is Longenecker's suggestion that the warnings came recently, "probably through Christian prophets he met along the way."[141] Where these prophetic warnings began is unmentioned, but it is probable that they started in Philippi and continued in Troas, Paul's two major stopovers before his speech in Miletus.

Upon initially hearing these warnings, Paul must have immediately begun wrestling with their repercussions for his future ministry. If they had indeed begun before or during his stay in Troas, he would have needed additional time to absorb their implications. While "the prospect of a possible prolonged imprisonment might not be readily welcomed by a free Roman citizen like Paul,"[142] the bold and single-minded apostle would not allow future persecution to alter his focus on preaching the gospel. Nor would he let the machinations of his Jewish enemies distract him from his ministry to gentiles. The walk to Assos provided such time for further prayer and reflection (as in the previous reading, no. 9). Having informed his companions about the warnings, his walk would illustrate that he was still unafraid of "the powers of this dark world" (Eph 6:12). The apostle would boldly walk the Sacred Way straight to and through the most famous pagan center of the region, the precinct of Apollo Smintheus. To his companions taking the sea route, it would demonstrate, even if only symbolically (since he had little time to stop and preach there), Paul's unchanged priorities. It may also have been along the way that the warnings led Paul to another decision—to accelerate the mentoring of his companions and of other church leaders in the days of freedom that still remained. Thus, despite his resolution not to spend much time in Asia but to hurry on to Jerusalem (Acts 20:16), he decided to remain a few days at Miletus in order

---

140. Witherington, *Acts of the Apostles*, 620.
141. Longenecker, *Acts of the Apostles*, 512. Jan Lambrecht, "Paul's Farewell Address at Miletus (Acts 20,17–38)," in *Les Actes des Apôtres: Traditions, rédaction, théologie*, ed. Jacob Kremer, BETL 48 (Leuven: Leuven University Press, 1979), 316, sees Paul's words as predictive.
142. Wilson, *Biblical Turkey*, 362.

to hold a teaching session with the Ephesian church leaders. While the warnings might affect his timetable, what lay ahead in Jerusalem was not going to change his priorities or his message.

9.11. Spiritual Preparation for Arrival in Jerusalem

According to Wilson, the reason for Paul's walk to Assos is to be found in his speech at Miletus.[143] The use of δέω in Acts 20:22, quoted above, introduces an important catchword for this section.[144] That Paul is bound by the Spirit (NKJV, NLT) means that he is compelled (NIV) or constrained (ESV) by the Spirit's instruction and guidance. Additional warnings through the Spirit were again given by believers in Tyre (Acts 21:4). After Paul's arrival in Caesarea, the prophet Agabus came down from Jerusalem and removed his belt and bound (δήσας) him with it before declaring, "The Holy Spirit says, 'In this way the Jewish leaders in Jerusalem will bind (δήσουσιν) the owner of this belt and will hand him over to the Gentiles'" (21:11; NIV). This prophetic act of binding illustrated the compulsion by the Spirit to which Paul had earlier submitted.[145] The walk to Assos gave Paul time to process the Spirit's warnings and perhaps to reflect on Jesus's words before going to the cross: "Nevertheless, not my will, but yours, be done" (Luke 22:42 ESV). As he walked, his prayer was no doubt for clarity about the future as well as for strength to continue his journey and to endure the upcoming persecution of his enemies, perhaps even death. Just as Jesus "set his face to go to Jerusalem" for the purpose of suffering (Luke 9:51; 18:31–33; cf. Matt 16:21), so did Paul, and he *was* going to reach Jerusalem, avoiding no obstacles along the way. Setting one's face (αὐτὸς τὸ πρόσωπον ἐστήρισεν)[146] and being bound in the Spirit (δεδεμένος τῷ πνεύματι) serve as functional equivalents for embracing the divine will

---

143. Mark Wilson, "The Role of the Holy Spirit in Paul's Ministry Journeys," *Ekklesiastikos Pharos* 87 (2005): 89–94. The discussion that follows summarizes those pages.

144. Mark Wilson, "Paul: Bound in the Spirit for Jerusalem, Acts 20:22," in *Devotions on the Greek New Testament: Fifty-Two Reflections to Inspire and Instruct*, ed. J. Scott Duvall and Verlyn D. Verbrugge (Grand Rapids: Zondervan, 2012), 54–55; cf. Stanley E. Porter, *Paul in Acts* (Peabody: Hendrickson, 2008), 86.

145. Verbrugge and Krell, *Paul and Money*, 194 n. 24, note: "The Spirit allows Paul to make his own decision according to the will of the Lord as he felt it in his heart."

146. Joseph A. Fitzmyer, *The Gospel according to Luke, I–IX: Introduction, Translation, and Notes*, AB 28 (New York: Doubleday: 1970), 828, suggests a meaning that

in the Lukan narratives. It was this divine will that Paul tapped into on his walk from Troas to Assos.

10. Conclusion

That Luke, without an explanation, describes Paul's companions traveling to Assos by sea while he walked by land is an observation made by all commentators on Acts 20. Luke's failure to elucidate the reason may indicate that Paul himself never informed anyone else of the motive for his walk. This was the one leg of the trip on which Luke was not present, so his silence should not be exaggerated.

The fact that he left his companions and mentees to sail by themselves is equally interesting. Those representatives from various cities where Paul had ministered were multitasking: (1) observing and assisting their mentor, Paul; (2) making a study trip and pilgrimage to the Holy Land; (3) protecting the funds being transported; and (4) serving as witnesses to their churches that the funds did arrive in Jerusalem and were used for their intended purpose. The third point would have required them to stay together, while Paul did not necessarily need to stay with them day and night (as the Philippi delay had already shown). So some sort of modeling may also have been going on.

In any case, along the way Paul became confident that his trip to Jerusalem accorded with the Spirit's will. This can be seen from his subsequent speech to the Ephesian elders at Miletus, a speech that not only defended his past ministry but expressed his confidence in the Spirit's control of events. His only concern was that he be allowed to "finish the race and complete the task the Lord Jesus has given me—the task of testifying to the good news of God's grace" (Acts 20:24; NIV). He was able to look forward without fear, even though "I know that none of you ... will ever see me again" (v. 25; NIV). A week or so earlier, when he had said goodbye to his companions in Troas, he may still have been assessing the significance of the warnings by the Spirit. But by the time he rejoined his companions in Assos, he apparently had a fuller grasp of the Spirit's reason for this journey. So the purpose of the walk had been realized.

"would express Jesus' resolute determination to face his destiny and any opposition related to it."

Bibliography

Ağturk, Tuna Şare, and Nurettin Arslan. *A Terracotta Treasure at Assos*. Istanbul: Ege, 2015.

Alexander, Loveday C. A. "Chronology of Paul." Pages 115–23 in *Dictionary of Paul and his Letters*. Edited by Gerald F. Hawthorne, Ralph P. Martin, and Daniel G. Reid. Downers Grove, IL: InterVarsity Press, 1993.

"Alexandreia (AD 198–217) AE: Caracalla." Asia Minor Coins: Ancient Greek and Roman Coins from Asia Minor. Photo Gallery. http://tinyurl.com/SBL4522j.

"Alexandreia (BC 301–281) AE 14." Asia Minor Coins: Ancient Greek and Roman Coins from Asia Minor. Photo Gallery. http://tinyurl.com/SBL4522i.

Arslan, Nurettin, and Beate Böhlendorf-Arslan. *Assos: An Archaeological Guide*. Istanbul: Homer, 2010.

"Babakale Haritası Çanakkale." Harita TR. http://tinyurl.com/SBL4522o.

Barrett, C. K. *A Critical and Exegetical Commentary on the Acts of the Apostles*. 2 vols. ICC. London: T&T Clark, 1994–1998.

Bock, Darrell L. *Acts*. BECNT. Grand Rapids: Baker, 2007.

Broughton, T. R. S. "Roman Asia." Pages 499–918 in *An Economic Survey of Ancient Rome*. Edited by Tenney Frank. 4 vols. Baltimore: Johns Hopkins University Press, 1933–1940.

Brownrigg, Ronald. *Pauline Places: In the Footsteps of Paul through Turkey and Greece*. London: Hodder & Stoughton, 1989.

Bruce, F. F. *The Acts of the Apostles: Greek Text with Commentary and Introduction*. 3rd ed. Grand Rapids: Eerdmans, 1990.

Burdick, D. L. "With Paul in the Troad." *Near East Archaeological Society Bulletin* 12 (1978): 31–65.

Caffin, Roger. "FAQ-Navigation." BushwalkingNSW.org. http://tinyurl.com/SBL4522g.

Calder, W. M., and G. E. Bean. *A Classical Map of Asia Minor*. London: British Institute of Archaeology in Ankara, 1958.

Cimok, Fatih. *Journeys of Paul: From Tarsus "to the Ends of the Earth."* 3rd ed. Istanbul: A Turizm, 2010.

Clarke, Joseph T. *Report on the Investigations at Assos, 1881*. Papers of the Archaeological Institute of America: Classical Series 1. Boston: Williams, 1882.

———. *Report on the Investigations at Assos, 1882, 1883*. Papers of the Archaeological Institute of America: Classical Series 2. New York: Macmillan, 1898.

Clarke, Joseph T., Francis H. Bacon, and Robert Koldewey. *Investigations at Assos*. Cambridge: Archaeological Institute of America, 1902.

Cohen, Getzel M. *The Hellenistic Settlements in Europe, the Islands, and Asia Minor*. Berkeley: University of California Press, 1995.

Conybeare, W. J., and J. S. Howson. *The Life and Epistles of St. Paul*. 2nd ed. 2 vols. London: Longman, Brown, Green, Longmans, & Roberts, 1855–1856.

Cook, J. M. *The Troad*. Oxford: Oxford University Press, 1973.

"Culture Routes in Turkey." Cultural Routes Society. http://tinyurl.com/SBL4522a.

Diller, J. S. "The Geology of Assos." Pages 180–215 in *Report on the Investigations at Assos, 1881*. Edited by Joseph T. Clarke. Papers of the Archaeological Institute of America: Classical Series 1. Boston: Williams, 1882.

Fairchild, Mark. *Christian Origins in Ephesus and Asia Minor*. Istanbul: Arkeoloji ve Sanat, 2015.

Fellows, Charles. *A Journal Written during an Excursion in Asia Minor*. London: Murray, 1839.

Feuser, Stefan. *Der Hafen von Alexandria Troas*. Bonn: Habelt, 2009.

Fitzmyer, Joseph A. *The Acts of the Apostles*. AB 31. New York: Doubleday, 1998.

———. *The Gospel according to Luke, I–IX: Introduction, Translation, and Notes*. AB 28. New York: Doubleday: 1970.

French, David H. *Milestones: Asia*. Vol. 3.3.5, of *Roman Roads and Milestones of Asia Minor / Kücük Asya'daki Roma yolları ve miltaşları*. Ankara: British Institute at Ankara, 2014.

———. "A Road Problem: Roman or Byzantine?" *IstMitt* 43 (1993): 445–54.

Galliazzo, Vittorio. *I Ponti Romani*. 2 vols. Treviso: Canova, 1994.

Georgi, Dieter. *Remembering the Poor: The History of Paul's Collection for Jerusalem*. Nashville: Abingdon, 1992.

Gloag, Paton J. *A Critical and Exegetical Commentary on the Acts of the Apostles*. 2 vols. London: T&T Clark, 1870.

"Grabung in Alexandria Troas." Westfälische Wilhelms-Universität Münster: Forschungsstelle Asia Minor. http://tinyurl.com/SBL4522e.

Grant, Michael. *A Guide to the Ancient World*. New York: Barnes & Noble, 1997.

Gürdal, Tayyar. "A Roman Bridge on the Satnioeis (Tuzla) River." Pages 125–35 in *Smintheion: In Search of Apollo Smintheus*. Edited by A. Coşkun Özgünel. Istanbul: Ege, 2015.

Guthrie, George H. *2 Corinthians*. BECNT. Grand Rapids: Baker, 2015.

Haenchen, Ernst. *The Acts of the Apostles: A Commentary*. Philadelphia: Westminster, 1971.

Hanson, J. W. "The Urban System of Roman Asia Minor and Wider Urban Connectivity." Pages 229–75 in *Settlement, Urbanisation and Population*. Edited by Alan K. Bowman and Andrew Wilson. Oxford Studies in the Roman Economy. Oxford: Oxford University Press, 2011.

Hareda, Takeko, and Fatih Cimok. *Roads of Ancient Anatolia*. 2 vols. Istanbul: A Turizm, 2008.

Harris, Murray J. *The Second Epistle to the Corinthians*. NIGTC. Grand Rapids: Eerdmans, 2013.

Hemer, Colin J. "Alexandria Troas." *TynBul* 26 (1975): 79–112.

———. *The Book of Acts in the Setting of Hellenistic History*. Winona Lake, IN: Eisenbrauns, 1990.

Kaplan, Davut. "Roman Baths and Related Structures." Pages 81–100 in *Smintheion: Apollon Smintheus'un İzinde*. Edited by A. Coşkun Özgünel. Istanbul: Ege, 2013.

Keener, Craig. *Acts: An Exegetical Commentary*. 4 vols. Grand Rapids: Baker Academic, 2012–2015.

Klinkott, Manfred. *Die Ruinen von Alexandreia Troas: Bestandsaufnahmen der "Thermen des Herodes Atticus" und des "Maldelik" mit Vorberichten der Untersuchungen durch R. Koldewey und A. C. G. Smith*. Asia Minor Studien 72. Bonn: Habelt, 2014.

Lake, Kirsopp, and Henry J. Cadbury, eds. *The Acts of the Apostles: English Translation and Commentary*. Edited by F. J. Foakes-Jackson and Kirsopp Lake. 5 vols. The Beginnings of Christianity 1. London: Macmillan, 1932.

Lambrecht, Jan. "Paul's Farewell Address at Miletus (Acts 20,17–38)." Pages 307–37 in *Les Actes des Apôtres: Traditions, rédaction, théologie*. Edited by Jacob Kremer. BETL 48. Leuven: Leuven University Press, 1979.

Leaf, Walter. *Strabo on the Troad*. Cambridge: Cambridge University Press, 1923.

Lewis, Peter, and Ron Bolden. *The Pocket Guide to Saint Paul: Coins Encountered by the Apostle on His Travels*. Kent Town, S. Australia: Wakefield, 2002.

Llewelyn, S. R., and R. A. Kearsley. *A Review of the Greek Inscriptions and Papyri Published in 1982–1983. NewDocs* 7. Sydney: Macquarrie University, 1994.

Longenecker, Richard N. *The Acts of the Apostles.* Volume 9 of *The Expositor's Bible Commentary.* Edited by Frank C. Gaebelein. Grand Rapids: Zondervan, 1981.

Malina, Bruce J., and Jerome H. Neyrey. *Portraits of Paul: An Archaeology of Ancient Personality.* Louisville: Westminster John Knox, 1996.

"The Many Alexandrias of Alexander the Great." The Basement Geographer: Scattershot Slices of the World from Å to Zzyzx. http://tinyurl.com/SBL4522d.

Marshall, I. Howard. *The Acts of the Apostles: An Introduction and Commentary.* TNTC. Grand Rapids: Eerdmans, 1980.

Matthews, Henry. *Greco-Roman Cities of Aegean Turkey: History, Archaeology, Architecture.* Istanbul: Ege, 2014.

McRay, John. *Paul: His Life and Teaching.* Grand Rapids: Baker Academic, 2003.

Mechikoff, Robert, Barbara Rieger, and Athena Trakadas. "Alexandria Troas Stadium Survey: Report on the First Campaign." Pages 181–97 in vol. 7 of *Studien zum antiken Kleinasien.* Edited by Elmar Schwertheim. Asia Minor Studien 66. Bonn: Rudolf Habelt, 2011.

Mesmay, Étienne de. *Sur les routes de l'apôtre Paul en Turquie.* Cahiers de l'École Cathédrale 67. Paris: Parole et Silence, 2005.

Mitchell, Stephen. "Requisitioned Transport in the Roman Empire." *JRS* 66 (1976): 106–31.

Mørkholm, Otto. *Early Hellenistic Coinage from the Accession of Alexander to the Peace of Apamaea (336–188 B.C.).* Cambridge: Cambridge University Press, 1991.

Morton, Jamie. *The Role of the Physical Environment in Ancient Greek Seafaring.* Leiden: Brill, 2001.

Murphy-O'Connor, Jerome. *Paul: A Critical Life.* Oxford: Oxford University Press, 1997.

Nickle, Keith F. *The Collection: A Study in Paul's Strategy.* SBT 48. London: SCM, 1966.

O'Connor, Colin. *Roman Bridges.* Cambridge: Cambridge University Press, 1993.

Özgün, Zeynep C. "The Sanctuary of Apollo Smintheus in the Light of Numismatic Evidence." Pages 93–103 in *Smintheion: In Search of Apollo Smintheus.* Edited by A. Coşkun Özgünel. Istanbul: Ege, 2015.

Özgünel, A. Coşkun, "Gülpınar: The Roman Bridge in Tuzla Valley." Pages 516–25 in *60. Yaşinda Sinan Genim'e Armağan Makaleler*. Edited by Oktay Belli and Belma Barış Kurtel. Istanbul: Ege, 2005.

———. "The Temple of Apollo Smintheus and the Iliad." Pages 15–63 in *Smintheion: In Search of Apollo Smintheus*. Edited by A. Coşkun Özgünel. Istanbul: Ege, 2015.

Özhan, Tolga. "New Inscriptions from Smintheion: Dedications, Epitaphs, and Fragments." Pages 105–23 in *Smintheion: In Search of Apollo Smintheus*. Edited by A. Coşkun Özgünel. Istanbul: Ege, 2015.

Pettegrew, David. "The *Diolkos* of Corinth." *AJA* 115 (2011): 549–74.

Polhill, John B. *Acts: An Exegetical and Theological Exposition of Holy Scripture*. New American Commentary 26. Nashville: Broadman & Holman, 1992.

Pope, R. Martin. *On Roman Roads with St. Paul*. London: Epworth, 1939.

Porter, Stanley E. *Paul in Acts*. Peabody: Hendrickson, 2008.

———. "The 'We' Passages." Pages 559–73 in *The Book of Acts in Its Greco-Roman Setting*. Vol. 2 of *The Book of Acts in Its First Century Setting*. Edited by David W. J. Gill and Conrad Gempf. Grand Rapids: Eerdmans, 1994.

Prokesch von Osten, Anton. *Denkwürdigkeiten und Erinnerungen aus dem Orient*. 3 vols. Stuttgart: Hallberger'sche, 1836–1837.

Quarles, Charles L. *Illustrated Life of Paul*. Nashville: B & H, 2014.

Ramsay, William Mitchell. *St. Paul: The Traveler and Roman Citizen*. Edited by Mark Wilson. Grand Rapids: Kregel, 2001.

Rapske, Brian. "Acts, Travel and Shipwreck." Pages 1–47 in *The Book of Acts in Its Greco-Roman Setting*. Vol. 2 of *The Book of Acts in Its First Century Setting*. Edited by David W. J. Gill and Conrad Gempf. Grand Rapids: Eerdmans, 1994.

Ricl, Marijana. "Alexandreia Troas in the Hellenistic Period." Pages 89–116 in *Mélanges d'histoire et d'épigraphie: Offerts à Fanoula Papazoglou par ses élèves á l'occasion de son quatre-vingtième anniversaire*. Edited by Miroslava Mirković, Slobodan Dušanić, Marijana Ricl, and Petar Petrović. Belgrade: Université de Belgrade, 1997.

———. *The Inscriptions of Alexandreia Troas*. Inschriften griechischer Städte aus Kleinasien 53. Bonn: Habelt, 1997.

———. "Two New Inscriptions from Alexandreia Troas." *Tekmeria* 5 (2000): 127–31.

Ritti, Tullia. *An Epigraphic Guide to Hierapolis (Pamukkale)*. Istanbul: Ege, 2006.

"Roman Bridges in Turkey." Wikipedia. http://tinyurl.com/SBL4522h.
Schnabel, Eckhard J. *Acts*. ZECNT 5. Grand Rapids: Zondervan, 2012.
Schwertheim, Elmar, ed. *Die Troas: Neue Forschungen III*. Asia Minor Studien 33. Bonn: Habelt, 1999.
Schwertheim, Elmar, and Georg Petzl. *Hadrian und die dionysischen Künstler: Drei in Alexandria Troas neugefundene Briefe des Kaisers an die Künstler-Vereinigung*. Asia Minor Studien 58. Bonn: Habelt, 2006.
Schwertheim, Elmar, and Hans Wiegartz, eds. *Neue Forschungen zu Neandria und Alexandria Troas*. Asia Minor Studien 11. Bonn: Habelt, 1994.
———. *Die Troas: Neue Forschungen zu Neandria und Alexandria Troas II*. Asia Minor Studien 22. Bonn: Habelt, 1996.
Serdaroğlu, Ümit. *Assos: Behramkale*. Antique Cities Series 1a. Istanbul: Arkeoloji ve Sanat, 1995.
Serdaroğlu, Ümit, and Reinhard Stupperich, eds. *Ausgrabungen in Assos 1990*. Asia Minor Studien 5. Bonn : Habelt, 1992.
———, eds. *Ausgrabungen in Assos 1991*. Asia Minor Studien 10. Bonn : Habelt, 1993.
———, eds. *Ausgrabungen in Assos 1992*. Asia Minor Studien 21. Bonn: Habelt, 1996.
Serdaroğlu, Ümit, Reinhard Stupperich, and Elmar Schwertheim, eds. *Ausgrabungen in Assos*. Asia Minor Studien 2. Bonn : Habelt, 1990.
Shuckburgh, Evelyn S. *The Histories of Polybius*. London: Macmillan, 1889.
Silva, Moisés. *A New English Translation of the Septuagint*. Oxford: Oxford University Press, 2007.
Smith, A. C. G. "The Gymnasium at Alexandria Troas: Evidence for an Outline Reconstruction," *AS* 29 (1979): 23–50.
Stark, Rodney. *Cities of God: The Real Story of How Christianity Became an Urban Movement and Conquered Rome*. New York: HarperOne, 2006.
———. *The Rise of Christianity: How the Obscure, Marginal Jesus Movement Became the Dominant Religious Force in the Western World in a Few Centuries*. San Francisco: HarperCollins, 1997.
Stupperich, Reinhard, ed. *Ausgrabungen in Assos 1993*. Asia Minor Studien 57. Bonn: Habelt, 2006.
"Sunrise and Sunset Bozcaada." Sunrise-and-Sunset.com. http://tinyurl.com/SBL4522k.
Talbert, R. J. A. *The Barrington Atlas of the Greek and Roman World*. Princeton: Princeton University Press, 2000.
———. *Rome's World: The Peutinger Map Reconsidered*. Cambridge: Cambridge University Press, 2010.

Tenger, Bernhard. "Zur Geographie und Geschichte der Troas." Pages 103–80 in *Die Troas: Neue Forschungen III*. Edited by Elmar Schwertheim. Asia Minor Studien 33. Bonn: Habelt, 1999.

Thompson, Glen L. "Alexandria Troas: Greek Synoecism, Roman Colony, Christian Center." Academia.edu. http://tinyurl.com/SBL4522c.

Thompson, Glen L., and Mark Wilson. "The Route of Paul's Second Journey in Asia Minor: In the Steps of Robert Jewett and Beyond." *TynBul* (forthcoming).

Thrall, Margaret. *Commentary on 2 Corinthians 8–13*. Vol. 2 of *The Second Epistle to the Corinthians*. ICC. London: T & T Clark, 2000.

Tombul, Musa. "Apollon Smintheus'a Hizmet veren İki Kent: Hamaksitos ve Khrysa." Pages 151–55 in *Smintheion: Apollon Smintheus'un İzinde*. Edited by A. Coşkun Özgünel. Istanbul: Ege, 2013.

Trebilco, Paul R. "Asia." Pages 291–362 in *The Book of Acts in Its Greco-Roman Setting*. Vol. 2 of *The Book of Acts in Its First Century Setting*. Edited by David W. J. Gill and Conrad Gempf. Grand Rapids: Eerdmans, 1994.

Turkish Ministry of Culture and Tourism. "Kazı Sonuçları Toplantıları." http://tinyurl.com/SBL4522f.

United States Hydrographic Office, United States Navy Department. *From Cape Matapan (Greece) Eastward, the Mediterranean Archipelago, and the Southern Shore of the Mediterranean Sea, Eastward of Ras Ashdir (Libia)*. Vol. 4 of *Mediterranean Pilot*. Washington, DC: Government Printing Office, 1916.

Verbrugge, Verlyn D. and Keith R. Krell. *Paul and Money: A Biblical and Theological Analysis of the Apostle's Teachings and Practices*. Grand Rapids: Zondervan, 2015.

Walker, Peter. *In the Steps of Paul: An Illustrated Guide to the Apostle's Life and Journeys*. Grand Rapids: Zondervan, 2008.

Wilson, Andrew. "City Sizes and Urbanization in the Roman Empire." Pages 161–95 in *Settlement, Urbanisation and Population*. Edited by Alan K. Bowman and Andrew Wilson. Oxford Studies in the Roman Economy. Oxford: Oxford University Press, 2011.

Wilson, Mark. *Biblical Turkey*. 3rd ed. Istanbul: Ege, 2014.

———. "The Ephesian Elders Come to Miletus: An Annaliste Reading of Acts 20:15–18a." *Verbum et Ecclesia* 34 (2013): 1–9.

———. "The Lukan *Periplus* of Saint Paul's Third Journey with a Textual Conundrum in Acts 20:15." *Acta Theologica* 36 (2016): 229–54.

———. "Paul: Bound in the Spirit for Jerusalem, Acts 20:22." Pages 54–55 in *Devotions on the Greek New Testament: Fifty-Two Reflections to Inspire and Instruct*. Edited by J. Scott Duvall and Verlyn D. Verbrugge. Grand Rapids: Zondervan, 2012.

———. "The Role of the Holy Spirit in Paul's Ministry Journeys." *Ekklesiastikos Pharos* 87 (2005): 89–94.

Witherington, Ben, III. *Acts of the Apostles*. Grand Rapids: Eerdmans, 1998.

Wittke, Anne-Maria, Eckart Olshausen, Richard Szydlak, and Christine F. Salazar, eds. *Brill's New Pauly: Historical Atlas of the Ancient World*. NeuePaulySup 3. Leiden: Brill, 2010.

The Baptists of Corinth:
Paul, the Partisans of Apollos, and the History of Baptism in Nascent Christianity

Stephen J. Patterson

1. Christian Baptism: A First Sighting

The earliest mention of baptism in a Christian context is almost always overlooked in the various attempts to tell the story of how baptism came to be a rite practiced within nascent Christian communities. It occurs in a place that is easily missed, at the very beginning of 1 Corinthians:

> For it has been reported to me by Chloe's people that there is quarreling among you, my brothers [and sisters]. What I mean is that each of you says, "I belong to Paul," or "I belong to Apollos," or "I belong to Cephas," or "I belong to Christ." Is Christ divided? Was Paul crucified for you? Or, were you *baptized* in the name of Paul? (1 Cor 1:11–13)[1]

There it is: the first word about baptism in the Jesus tradition. It is not as casual a reference as it may at first seem. For Paul carries on now about baptism rather vehemently:

> I'm thankful that I baptized none of you (except Crispus and Gaius), lest anyone should say that you were baptized in my name. (Oh, I did baptize also the house of Stephanus. Beyond that I don't know if I baptized

---

* This essay is an abbreviated version of "From John to Apollos to Paul: How the Baptism of John Entered the Jesus Movement," to appear in Stanley E. Porter and Andrew W. Pitts, eds., *Christian Origins and the Establishment of the Early Jesus Movement*, ECHC 4 (Leiden: Brill, 2016).

1. All translations are my own unless noted otherwise.

anyone else). For Christ did not send me to baptize, but to preach the gospel, and not with wisdom expressed in words, lest the cross of Christ be emptied of its power. (1 Cor 1:14-17)

If we take this this brief paragraph seriously and at face value, we learn something very surprising. When Paul was in Corinth, he did not do much baptizing.[2] This can only mean that in the Pauline communities baptism was not yet the universal rite of initiation. Only a handful of Paul's correspondents were baptized. In 1 Cor 1:17, he actually goes so far as to renounce baptism. We know that this is hyperbole, for in the later letters, Galatians and Romans, he will appropriate various understandings of baptism to his own cause (Gal 3:26-28; Rom 6:3-11). Still, Paul could not say this at all if baptism was the initiation ritual by which everyone entered his newly formed Christ communities. Baptism must have been, for Paul, as for the Corinthians, something special, something extra.

If Paul himself did baptize, why does he repudiate it here? Because it is obviously related to the dissention now appearing in the Corinthian churches in connection with the wisdom teaching to which Paul is so opposed. This is clear from 1 Cor 1:17, which consists of two pairs of contrasting opposites: baptism versus preaching (v. 17a) and wisdom versus cross (v. 17b). Paul came not to baptize but to preach, and not to preach wisdom but the cross. By contrast, whoever came to Corinth after Paul did baptize, and he taught wisdom. Who was he? His name was Apollos, whom Acts describes as a learned Alexandrian who baptized in the manner of John (Acts 18:25).[3]

The claim that Apollos was the teacher whose ideas are at issue in 1 Corinthians is no longer controversial,[4] so I will pause only long enough

---

2. Compare Hans Dieter Betz's remarks in "Transferring a Ritual: Paul's Interpretation of Baptism in Romans 6," in Betz, *Paulinische Studien: Gesammelte Aufsätze III* (Tübingen: Mohr Siebeck, 1994), 258-62.

3. See especially Richard Horsley, "Wisdom of Word and Words of Wisdom in Corinth," *CBQ* 39 (1977): 231-32.

4. See especially Gerhard Sellin, "Das 'Geheimnis' der Weisheit und das Rätsel der 'Christuspartei' (zu 1 Kor 1-4)," in Sellin, *Studien zu Paulus und Epheserbrief*, FRLANT 229 (Göttingen: Vandenhoeck & Ruprecht, 2009), 9-36; also Sellin, "Hauptprobleme des Ersten Korintherbriefes," *ANRW* 25.4:2940-3044. More recently, rhetorical-critical approaches to the letter have yielded the same consensus. See Joop Smit, "What Is Apollos? What Is Paul? In Search for the Coherence of First Corinthians 1:10-4:21," *NovT* 44 (2002): 231-51. For a history of the long discussion of this ques-

to summarize the evidence for it. First, while Paul may seem to name four possible factions among the assemblies of Corinth (1 Cor 1:12), as Paul's argument unfolds through chapters 1–4, only Apollos plays any further role. Insofar as we may be relatively certain that Apollos actually visited the Corinthian assemblies (see 1 Cor 16:12; Acts 18:27–28), it is altogether plausible that his presence there produced a following. This is why in 1 Cor 3:4 the so-called factions have been reduced now to two; some belong to Apollos, some to Paul.

Second, the discovery that the partisans' language—as much as it may be discerned from Paul's account—reflects the sort of Hellenistic Jewish wisdom theology associated especially with Philo and the Alexandrian tradition, makes it very likely that Apollos, the learned Jew from Alexandria (see Acts 18:24), was its source.

Third, while Paul manages to critique the partisans through chapters 1 and 2 without obvious reference to Apollos, in chapter 3 he makes it clear that the one who has been "watering the crop he planted" is indeed Apollos (1 Cor 3:6). Though Paul maintains a civil and collegial tone through 1 Cor 3:5–9, with 3:10 the collegiality begins to unravel, and it becomes clear that whatever the Corinthians might have felt about Paul and Apollos, *Paul* views Apollos as a rival.[5] First Corinthians 3:12 is not about the gold, silver, and gems, but the wood, hay, and straw. First Corinthians 3:17 is a threat, plain and simple.

Finally, 1 Cor 4:6 indicates that Paul has indeed been talking about himself and Apollos all along. If the effect of μετεσχημάτισα in this much-contested statement is to suggest that Paul has meant it all only hypothetically, the blistering rhetoric of the previous paragraphs and the very real threats that follow betray Paul's poor attempt at deflection. He is truly hurt and angry that some of the Corinthians have admired Apollos and criticized him (especially 1 Cor 4:1–5). Apollos was present in Corinth and his teaching attracted a following. It is this teaching that Paul seeks to undermine in 1 Cor 1–4.

More disputed is the characterization of Apollos in Acts 18:25. The doubts about this passage go back to Ernst Käsemann, who simply found

---

tion, see John C. Hurd, *The Origin of I Corinthians* (New York: Seabury, 1965; repr., Macon, GA: Mercer University Press, 1983), 96–107.

5. *Pace* Corin Mihaila, *The Paul-Apollos Relationship and Paul's Stance Toward Greco-Roman Rhetoric*, LNTS 402 (London: T&T Clark, 2009).

the idea of this kind of John-Jesus hybrid preposterous.[6] His analysis has proven to be remarkably influential: many critical scholars today simply accept that the words ἐπιστάμενος μόνον τὸ βάπτισμα Ἰωάννου ("but he was familiar only with the baptism of John") in Acts 18:25c are Lukan redaction on the authority of Käsemann's 1952 essay. Käsemann just could not imagine people who might have revered both John and Jesus, nor could he imagine a time when Christianity entertained different baptismal practices. This, however, flew in the face of virtually all prior research on the passage.[7] Nevertheless, to Martin Dibelius's earlier notion that here was a kind of "half-Christian," an example of the many diverse movements that Luke's sweeping narrative attempts to pave over, or Herbert Preisker's similar conclusion that here is rare evidence for a time before theological and cultic uniformity had gained a foothold in the nascent church, Käsemann can offer only scorn for what he regards as an overzealous "modern liberal-idealist outlook on the primitive Christian past."[8] Today, of course, the critical scholar can only marvel at what Käsemann regards as the more realistic alternative view:

> For the hypothesis that there was ever a Christianity without cultus or official ministry is not only incapable of proof but contradicts directly the role of apostolate and prophecy on the one side and of the sacraments on the other, as far back as we can see.[9]

---

6. Ernst Käsemann, "The Disciples of John in Ephesus," in Käsemann, *Essays on New Testament Themes*, SBT (Naperville, IL: Allenson, 1962), 136–48.

7. Thus the broad consensus, prior to Käsemann, that Apollos and the mysterious disciples of Acts 19:1–7 were, as Dibelius described them, "halb-Christen." See Martin Dibelius, *Die urchristliche Überlieferung von Johannes dem Täufer*, FRLANT 15 (Göttingen: Vandenhoeck & Ruprecht, 1911), 88–89; also Hans W. Wendt, *Die Apostelgeschichte*, KEK (Göttingen: Vandenhoeck & Ruprecht, 1913), 270; Erwin Preuschen, *Die Apostelgeschichte*, HNT 4.1 (Tübingen: Mohr Siebeck, 1912), 115; Alfred Loisy, *Les actes des apôtres* (Paris: Nourry, 1920), 719–20; Ernst Lohmeyer, *Johannes der Täufer*, vol. 1 of *Das Urchristentum* (Göttingen: Vandenhoeck & Ruprecht, 1932), 26; Herbert Preisker, "Apollos und die Johannesjünger in Ephesus," *ZNW* 30 (1931): 301–4; more recently, see Joan E. Taylor, *The Immerser: John the Baptist within Second Temple Judaism*, Studying the Historical Jesus (Grand Rapids: Eerdmans, 1997), 72–76.

8. Dibelius, *Johannes*, 88–89; Preisker, "Apollos," 301–4; Käsemann, "Disciples," 140.

9. Käsemann, "Disciples," 140–41.

Of course, Käsemann's critical instincts about the historicity of Acts were not faulty, nor his sense that one of Luke's redactional interests was the *una sancta* of the early church. Time and again Luke glides over conflicts known to have characterized the earliest decades of the Jesus movement in favor of a more harmonious picture. If there was a conflict between the Hellenists and the Hebrews, it was not about substantive matters, but merely work assignments, a matter easily resolved (Acts 6:1–6). If Paul and the Jerusalem church feuded over the status of the uncircumcised, Peter explains the matter and concord is achieved (Acts 15:1–35). This happens again and again in Acts. In this way, Luke creates the impression of a unified church tidily following first the leadership of Peter, then of Paul. Can this explain Luke's work in Acts 18:24–28? No.

Käsemann thought that Apollos could not have been a follower of John the Baptist and a follower of Jesus at the same time. This was historically impossible. Luke therefore must have added ἐπιστάμενος μόνον τὸ βάπτισμα Ἰωάννου ("who knew only the baptism of John") in order to push Apollos doctrinally to the margins, thus freeing up space for Paul to assume his dominant role in Ephesus. This, of course, is possible, but it is not at all consistent with Luke's modus operandi. Luke never *creates* the impression of conflict—let alone exacerbates it—only to smooth it out later. Rather, he always does the opposite: he downplays conflict or covers it up entirely. Moreover, if Luke really did toss this theological grenade into the narrative, Acts 18:26 is a fairly anemic repair, and verses 27–28 leave Apollos a free operator, owing nothing to Paul at all.

Käsemann's influence, however, was widely felt, and within a few years the theory was being refined. Eduard Schweizer agreed that a John-Jesus hybrid like Apollos was unlikely.[10] He must have been a Jewish preacher and not a Christian follower of Jesus at all. But when Luke read in his source that Apollos was "alive in the spirit" (ζέων τῷ πνεύματι) and that he had been instructed in "the way of the Lord" (τὴν ὁδὸν τοῦ κυρίου), Luke was mistakenly lead to believe that he was in fact a follower of Jesus. But if Priscilla and Aquila needed to set him straight, he must have been deficient in some way. It must have been, Luke reasoned, that Apollos was like those misguided souls he writes about next (in Acts 19:1–7), who knew only John's baptism. So, Luke added Acts 18:25c to his source. But Schweizer

---

10. Eduard Schweizer, "Die Bekehrung des Apollos, Ag. 18, 24–26," *EvT* 15 (1955): 247–54.

does not explain why, if Apollos was a Jewish preacher and not really a part of the Jesus movement, Luke would have had a source concerning him at all, let alone how he would have misread his source.

Finally, Michael Wolter took one more swing at the passage.[11] He agreed that the hybrid Apollos was unlikely and that Luke must have been responsible for Acts 18:25c. But the issue for Luke was not how to deal with theological outliers. It was, rather, how to deal with political rivals to his hero, Paul. Apollos, as we know from 1 Corinthians, was in fact a rival. Wolter argued that Luke added Acts 18:25c to make Apollos look bad—to push him to the theological margins, so that Paul's disciples could then swoop in and correct him. He leaves behind disciples (Acts 19:1–7), whom Paul then corrects, in his role as Lukan theologian-in-residence. But like Käsemann's theory, Wolter's involves Luke is some very unlikely editorial work. Luke never *heightens* the theological differences of the rivals who appear in his narrative, but softens them. It is unlikely that Acts 18:25c came from his hand, for any imagined reason.

But there is something about Luke's reportage in Acts 18:24–19:7 that is truly out of step with what we otherwise know about Apollos from 1 Corinthians. Together, these two stories imply that the baptism practiced by Apollos in Ephesus had nothing to do with imparting the Holy Spirit. This is highly unlikely. For if there is one thing we know about the teaching of Apollos, it is that it was all about the Spirit. Those who followed him in Corinth claimed to be "spirituals" (πνευματικοί; 1 Cor 3:1); they excelled in spiritual gifts, such as speaking in tongues and prophecy (1 Cor 12 and 14). Therefore, any baptism practiced by Apollos would most certainly have conveyed what people thought of as the Holy Spirit. If Luke brings anything to the passage that is historically unlikely, it is the idea that Apollos's baptism did not convey the Spirit. Why would he do this? It must be because in Luke's scheme—inherited from Mark—the baptism of John did not involve the Holy Spirit, but Christian baptism did.[12] Therefore, if Apollos baptized in the manner of John the Baptist, it must not have involved the Holy Spirit. So reasoned Luke. But all of this, of course, is premised on the idea that Apollos was in fact a follower of both Jesus and John. If Luke could entertain this idea at the end of the first century, or later, there must

---

11. Michael Wolter, "Apollos und die ephesinischen Johannesjünger (Act 18 24–19 7)," *ZNW* 78 (1987): 49–73.

12. See, e.g., Luke 3:16 (cf. Mark 1:8); Acts 1:5; 11:16.

have been such hybrids in his world. They were not, as Käsemann supposed, an impossibility.

So, from Acts we learn that Apollos was a follower of Jesus who baptized like John. If one tries to imagine how baptism first made its appearance in the Jesus movement, when Jesus apparently did not baptize,[13] one will have to posit figures like Apollos, who brought John's rite with them and introduced it to followers of Jesus who, like Paul, had not been followers of John. The conflict in 1 Corinthians can also be imagined as just the sort of dispute that might have arisen in connection with the importation of baptism. Paul, who had not been a follower of John, and who probably did not know or care that Jesus had been, would have viewed baptism with mixed feelings. How important was this *Johannine* rite to the *Jesus* movement? When it appears as the calling card of a rival in his Corinthian churches, he could easily be moved to repudiate it. It follows, then, that to learn more about the origins of baptism in the Jesus movement, we will need to turn not to Paul, but to his rival, Apollos the baptist.

2. Apollos the Baptist in Corinth

So, what may be said about Apollos's teaching on the basis of 1 Corinthians? In what sense might we understand it as continuing and developing the ministry of John the Baptist?

John's baptism was eschatological, anticipating the "greater one who is to come." This appears to have been true for Apollos as well, but in a modified sense. For him, the coming one *had* arrived. This is an aspect of Apollos's teaching that Paul criticizes most vehemently. "Already you are filled! Already you have become rich! Without us you have begun to reign!" (1 Cor 4:8). Apparently, for Apollos, the baptism in the Holy Spirit that John had associated with the one who was to come was already at

---

13. The absence of any reference to Jesus baptizing in the synoptic accounts and the odd rejection of the idea in John 4:2 have produced a mild consensus that Jesus did not baptize. Still, a significant minority has always taken the opposite view. Recently, for example, see Jens Schröter, *Jesus von Nazareth: Jude aus Galiläa—Retter der Welt*, Biblische Gestalten 15 (Leipzig: Evangelische Verlagsanstalt, 2006), 138. For a recent take on the majority view, see Michael Labahn, "Kreative Erinnerung als nachösterliche Nachschöpfung: Der Ursprung der christliche Taufe," in David Hellholm et al., eds., *Ablution, Initiation, and Baptism: Late Antiquity, Early Judaism, and Early Christianity / Waschungen, Initiation und Taufe: Spätantike, frühes Judentum und frühes Christentum*, 3 vols., BZNT 176.1-3 (Berlin: de Gruyter, 2010) 1: 344-47, 350-54.

work, transforming those who had received Apollos's teaching into "spirituals" (πνευμάτικοι); they were the "perfect" (τέλειοι), no longer "children" (νήπιοι), no longer mere "mortals" (ψύχικοι, σάρκινοι).[14] *This eschatological step forward is important to grasp if we are to understand how Apollos's ideas about baptism can be understood to continue and develop those of John.* John spoke of "one who is to come," who would bring a baptism in the Holy Spirit. For Apollos, that future was now; the Holy Spirit was already doing its work.

So, how did Apollos understand the coming of the Spirit and its effects? It must have been in connection with baptism, of course. In chapter 15 Paul mentions something about the partisans' teaching that is very revealing in this respect: the Corinthians practiced something like surrogate baptism—they baptized on behalf of the dead (ὑπὲρ τῶν νεκρῶν; 1 Cor 15:29a). This means that they saw baptism as an answer to the problem of death. Paul does not dispute this! He simply avers that if they believe this, they must grant him the point that there will indeed be a future resurrection of the dead (1 Cor 15:29b). His reasoning is that if surrogate baptism works, that by it the dead are made to live, then where are they? We will see them in the future—at the resurrection of the dead. But the Corinthians must have learned something different from Apollos—that there was no future resurrection of the dead (1 Cor 15:12), that baptism could overcome death already now, in the present. How? We must take our clues from the distinctive language that turns up in Paul's polemical engagement of Apollos's teaching. As Pearson, Horsley, and others have demonstrated, the distinctive *pneumatikos-psychikos* language of the partisans in 1 Corinthians derives from Hellenistic Judaism, such as one finds in Philo, the great sage of Apollos's hometown, Alexandria.[15]

As is well known, Philo engaged in a Platonic exegesis of Gen 1–2 to show that Moses knew all about Platonic anthropology. The man created

---

14. Paul nowhere else uses the terminology that crops up in chapters 2 and 3; it almost certainly derives from his opponents. See Birger A. Pearson, *The Pneumatikos-Psychikos Terminology in 1 Corinthians: A Study in the Theology of the Corinthian Opponents of Paul and Its Relation to Gnosticism*, SBLDS 12 (Missoula, MT: Scholars Press, 1973), 38–39; also Richard A. Horsley, "Pneumatikos vs. Psychikos: Distinctions of Spiritual Status among the Corinthians," *HTR* 69 (1976): 269–88; and Horsley, "'How Can Some of You Say That There Is No Resurrection of the Dead?' Spiritual Elitism in Corinth," *NovT* 20 (1978): 203–31.

15. Pearson, *Pneumatikos-Psychikos Terminology*; Horsley, "Pneumatikos vs. Psychikos;" Horsley, "Words of Wisdom."

from dust in Gen 2:7, he says, is mortal, "consisting of body and soul" (ἐκ σώματος καὶ ψυχῆς συνεστώς; Philo, *Opif.* 134). This is typical Middle Platonic anthropology. The mortal parts of a human being are the body and the (mortal) soul (see, e.g., Plutarch, *Fac.* 28 [943A]). Now, Philo believed that when Genesis tells of God breathing life into the mortal man, Adam (in Gen 2:7), he was imparting to him the *immortal* soul, what Plato called the "mind" (νοῦς), but which Philo calls the "divine Spirit" (πνεῦμα θεῖον) (*Opif.* 135). This is what makes the human being immortal. The mortal human being, created from dust, was mere body and soul. He became truly alive only when God breathed the divine Spirit into him.

Was this something like what Apollos taught the Corinthians, that in baptism the Spirit enters a person and makes them immortal? It is telling that Paul's argument against them consists, finally, in an alternative exegesis of Gen 1–2 (see 1 Cor 15:42–50). By his reading, "the first Adam" was alive, but mortal, as Genesis says (εἰς ψυχὴν ζῶσαν; Gen 2:7); but Christ, the "second Adam," was a "life-giving spirit" (εἰς πνεῦμα ζῳοποιοῦν). Now people bear the image of the man of dust, the first Adam, but soon they *will* bear the image of the second Adam, the "man of heaven," Christ. That "will" is key, for while Philo, Apollos, and many Hellenistic Jews read Genesis protologically, Paul was reading Genesis eschatologically. Between now and immortality there lay, for Paul, the resurrection. For the followers of Apollos, however, baptism brought immortality now, even for those already dead. They are made immortal, like the first Adam, through the gift of the divine Spirit.[16]

One should note, finally, that the baptism of Apollos was accompanied by wisdom teaching—"word wisdom" as Paul calls it (1 Cor 1:17 and passim). Could this have been an aspect of John the Baptist's mission as well? In the cycle of stories about John's baptism of Jesus in Mark and Q, the Spirit drives Jesus into the wilderness to prepare for what is to come. In Q he emerges as a wisdom teacher. Baptism inaugurates him to his calling as a prophet of wisdom, an honor he shares with John (see Q 7:35). Paul characterizes Apollos's teaching as a "higher" wisdom, the "mystery

---

16. For the general background of these ideas in Hellenistic Judaism, especially Philo, see originally Jacques Dupont, *Gnosis: La connaissance religieuse dans les épîtres de Saint Paul*, Universitas Catholica Lovaniensis, Dissertationes ad gradum magistri in Facultate Theologica consequendum conscriptae 2/40 (Paris: Gabalda, 1949), 172–80; also Pearson, *Pneumatikos-Psychikos Terminology*, 17–23; Horsley, "Pneumatikos vs. Psychikos," 274–80.

of God" (1 Cor 2:1). This idea also turns up, surprisingly, in Q 10:21 (the so-called Johannine logion), where Jesus, speaking in the Holy Spirit, is heard to utter words that would have been right at home among the Corinthian "spirituals": "I praise you, Father, Lord of heaven and earth, for you have hidden these things from the wise and learned, and revealed them to children" (νηπίοις).[17]

So, the figure of Apollos, whom Paul engages in 1 Corinthians, offers a plausible scenario for how the baptism of John could have been mediated into the Jesus movement. Jesus, like John, would have been understood as a prophet of wisdom. The Spirit of which John spoke on the banks of the Jordan was the same Spirit that drove Jesus into the wilderness and filled him with wisdom. Now that the Spirit of God had begun to act, baptism became the rite by which it was imparted. Baptism now became something more than an act of *metanoia*. It transformed one into a "spiritual"— a *pneumatikos*—already rich, filled, and prepared to reign in the kingdom of God. Baptism in the Spirit rendered one immortal.

3. The Baptism of Jesus as John's Baptism

Before concluding, I want to visit briefly the story told by Mark and Q about Jesus's baptism at the hands of John. This story is remarkably consistent with what we have been exploring in connection with Apollos. Jesus is immersed in water; this imparts to him the Holy Spirit; he is then transformed into a "son of God." Rudolf Bultmann once argued persuasively that this story was a cult legend based upon early Christian practices, as reflected in Acts, among other places.[18] Now I believe we should modify Bultmann's view. If the story of Jesus's baptism we have in Mark was also present, in some form, in Q,[19] then this story is really very early,

---

17. Q 10:21, after the reconstruction of the SBL International Q Project; see James M. Robinson, Paul Hoffmann, and John S. Kloppenborg, eds., *The Sayings Gospel Q in Greek and English: With Parallels from the Gospels of Mark and Thomas* (Minneapolis: Fortress, 2002), 103.

18. Rudolf Bultmann, *History of the Synoptic Tradition*, trans. John Marsh (New York: Harper and Row, 1963), 251–52.

19. Bultmann believed that the story had its origins in the Hellenistic church and not among the Palestinian followers of Jesus precisely because it does not occur in Q (*History*, 251). But I will follow the Society of Biblical Literature International Q Project in reconstructing a version of the story also in Q. See Robinson, Hoffmann, and Kloppenborg, *Sayings Gospel Q*, 78–79.

too early to reflect that later time when baptism was the universal rite of initiation it would become in Matthew or Acts. If it existed before Q, then some version of it would have circulated roughly contemporaneously with 1 Corinthians. It turns out, then, that it was apparently modeled, not on the later Christian ideas about baptism as reflected in Mark, Matthew, or Luke-Acts, but on a version of John's baptism as it was adapted and mediated into some of the communities of the Jesus movement. In these communities the clock had ticked one more tock forward, the Spirit had come and begun its activity of transformation. Jesus, by their lights, was its first recipient. Baptism had transformed him. He was now immortal, a son of God. In Q, this prepared him to preach the secret and hidden wisdom of God (as Apollos did in Corinth). In Mark, it prepared him to do battle with demons, to suffer and die, but in the end, to be restored to the world of the living. But that, too, is something we learned from 1 Corinthians about the power of baptism. Otherwise, what did they mean by "baptizing on behalf of the dead" (1 Cor 15:29a)?

So, 1 Corinthians and Apollos are a kind of missing link in the history of baptism. Everyone agrees that baptism was a rite imported from circles associated with John the Baptist. But what did it mean? Most have assumed that it signaled repentance, period. But that does not help us understand actual depictions of John's baptism, like those we find in Mark and Q. Nor does it explain baptism's first sighting in the activity of Apollos as reflected in 1 Corinthians. But if Apollos was a baptist who still baptized like John, then the things we can piece together about him and his ritual of baptism should help us say quite a lot more about John's baptism as it was incorporated into the Jesus movement. It was not just about repentance. It was about transformation. It made one a "spiritual," a "son of God," an immortal. It came with instruction, wisdom, "secret and hidden" until now. Eventually baptism would take on a life of its own in the Jesus movement and later become, for Christians, the initiation ritual by which everyone joined the church. The story of how that came to be should now include this first, odd episode. Baptism came not from Christians, like Paul, but baptists, like Apollos, and it must have taken some time for Christians to get used to the idea.

Bibliography

Betz, Hans Dieter. "Transferring a Ritual: Paul's Interpretation of Baptism in Romans 6." Pages 240–71 in *Paulinische Studien: Gesammelte Aufsätze III*. Tübingen: Mohr Siebeck, 1994.

Bultmann, Rudolf. *History of the Synoptic Tradition.* Translated by John Marsh. New York: Harper & Row, 1963.

Dibelius, Martin. *Die urchristliche Überlieferung von Johannes dem Täufer.* FRLANT 15. Göttingen: Vandenhoeck & Ruprecht, 1911.

Dupont, Jacques. *Gnosis: La connaissance religieuse dans les épîtres de Saint Paul.* Universitas Catholica Lovaniensis, Dissertationes ad gradum magistri in Facultate Theologica consequendum conscriptae 2/40. Paris: Gabalda, 1949.

Horsley, Richard A. "'How Can Some of You Say That There Is No Resurrection of the Dead?' Spiritual Elitism in Corinth." *NovT* 20 (1978): 203–31.

———. "Pneumatikos vs. Psychikos: Distinctions of Spiritual Status among the Corinthians." *HTR* 69 (1976): 269–88.

———. "Wisdom of Word and Words of Wisdom in Corinth." *CBQ* 39 (1977): 224–39.

Hurd, John C. *The Origin of I Corinthians.* New York: Seabury, 1965. Repr., Macon, GA: Mercer University Press, 1983.

Käsemann, Ernst. "The Disciples of John in Ephesus." Pages 136–48 in Käsemann, *Essays on New Testament Themes.* SBT. Naperville, IL: Allenson, 1962.

Labahn, Michael. "Kreative Erinnerung als nachösterliche Nachschöpfung: Der Ursprung der christliche Taufe." Pages 337–76 in *Ablution, Initiation, and Baptism: Late Antiquity, Early Judaism, and Early Christianity / Waschungen, Initiation und Taufe: Spätantike, frühes Judentum und frühes Christentum.* Edited by David Hellholm, Tor Vegge, Øyvind Nordeval, and Christer Hellholm. 3 vols. BZNT 176.1–3. Berlin: de Gruyter, 2010.

Lohmeyer, Ernst. *Johannes der Täufer.* Vol. 1 of *Das Urchristentum.* Göttingen: Vandenhoeck & Ruprecht, 1932.

Loisy, Alfred. *Les actes des apôtres.* Paris: Nourry, 1920.

Mihaila, Corin. *The Paul-Apollos Relationship and Paul's Stance toward Greco-Roman Rhetoric.* LNTS 402. London: T&T Clark, 2009.

Pearson, Birger A. *The Pneumatikos-Psychikos Terminology in 1 Corinthians: A Study in the Theology of the Corinthian Opponents of Paul and Its Relation to Gnosticism.* SBLDS 12. Missoula, MT: Scholars Press, 1973.

Porter, Stanley E., and Andrew W. Pitts, eds. *Christian Origins and the Establishment of the Early Jesus Movement.* ECHC 4. Leiden: Brill, 2016.

Preisker, Herbert. "Apollos und die Johannesjünger in Ephesus." *ZNW* 30 (1931): 301–4.
Preuschen, Erwin. *Die Apostelgeschichte.* HNT 4.1. Tübingen: Mohr Siebeck, 1912.
Robinson, James M., Paul Hoffmann, and John S. Kloppenborg, eds. *The Sayings Gospel Q in Greek and English: With Parallels from the Gospels of Mark and Thomas.* Minneapolis: Fortress, 2002.
Schröter, Jens. *Jesus von Nazareth: Jude aus Galiläa—Retter der Welt.* Biblische Gestalten 15. Leipzig: Evangelische Verlagsanstalt, 2006.
Schweizer, Eduard. "Die Bekehrung des Apollos, Ag. 18, 24–26." *EvT* 15 (1955): 247–54.
Sellin, Gerhard. "Das 'Geheimnis' der Weisheit und das Rätsel der 'Christuspartei' (zu 1 Kor 1–4)." Pages 9–36 in Sellin, *Studien zu Paulus und Epheserbrief.* FRLANT 229. Göttingen: Vandenhoeck & Ruprecht, 2009.
———. "Hauptprobleme des Ersten Korintherbriefes." *ANRW* 25.4: 2940–3044.
Smit, Joop. "What Is Apollos? What Is Paul? In Search for the Coherence of First Corinthians 1:10–4:21." *NovT* 44 (2002): 231–51.
Taylor, Joan E. *The Immerser: John the Baptist within Second Temple Judaism.* Studying the Historical Jesus. Grand Rapids: Eerdmans, 1997.
Wendt, Hans W. *Die Apostelgeschichte.* KEK. Göttingen: Vandenhoeck & Ruprecht, 1913.
Wolter, Michael. "Apollos und die ephesinischen Johannesjünger (Act 18 24–19 7)." *ZNW* 78 (1987): 49–73.

A Response

Dennis E. Smith

I am deeply grateful that my colleagues have seen fit to honor me in this way. I cannot claim to be worthy of such an honor, but I am happy to serve as an excuse for putting together such a fine collection of papers from my colleagues and friends. Indeed, the significance of this collection goes beyond honoring a single individual. It also spotlights the achievements of COMCAR as a research seminar. Here New Testament scholars across a wide spectrum of backgrounds and interests engage, and indeed contribute to, the latest perspectives on archaeological interpretation. What is especially impressive is the way in which many of these essays exhibit the interrelationship between the interpretation of material culture and New Testament exegesis. I will spotlight three categories that these essays address.

1. Material Culture

The importance of archaeology to New Testament research has gone through several phases over the last several generations. In earlier years, it was primarily used for illustrative or apologetic purposes. In the 1970s and 1980s, especially through the influence of Helmut Koester at Harvard University, it returned to prominence as an important interpretive tool for New Testament and Christian origins research. COMCAR (Colloquium on Material Culture and Ancient Religion) was formed to continue the Koester legacy by introducing New Testament scholars to the most recent methods of archaeological interpretation by means of site visits led by the excavators and primary interpreters.

The variety of methods exhibited in this collection is striking. For example, Dan Schowalter has contributed an excerpt from a classic field report, a genre that warms my archaeologist's heart. He has surveyed the small finds from the Roman temple excavation at Omrit, Israel, where he serves as dig director, in search of evidence for dining facilities. It is an appropriate search since, as he points out (and I affirm), dining facilities were commonly found at Greek and Roman temple sites. Alas, small finds at an excavation often yield very little, which is the case here as well, but there are tantalizing possibilities in the data he surveys.

Many of the contributors center their arguments on the interpretation of inscriptions; see the essays by Valeriy A. Alikin, Alan H. Cadwallader, Lynn R. Huber, Ma. Marilou S. Ibita, William Rutherford, and Jeffrey A. D. Weima. The work of Cadwallader especially stands out. His skill at developing a thick description analysis of inscriptional data is exceptional. Here he analyzes the meager remains of tombstones from the Colossae necropolis and teases out data about household models in Colossae that establish the normality of nonnuclear household relations.

Proposals about the social class of early Christians have gone through several variations in recent research. Who would have guessed that the latest version would involve stable isotope analysis? Thanks to the methodological precision of Steve J. Friesen, we now have a new method in our toolbox for analyzing diet and its potential connection to inequality in the early Christian world.

I consider myself a competent interpreter of the social data to be found in an archeological site, but I never would have noticed "the social, cultural, and religious discourses with which the [New Testament] text converses" had not Huber brought that perspective to my attention. Indeed, I had always considered the ubiquitous bath-gymnasium complexes to be a dime a dozen until Huber alerted me to their usefulness in denoting how masculinity was defined. Her review of this cultural data provides the semantic background for the concept of "the victor" ("he who conquers") in Rev 2–3: "as the idealized masculine identity to which the audience is called."

Surveying ancient roads in the areas of Paul's travels stretches back a long way in biblical archaeology. Is it still a useful area of research? Indeed it is, as shown by the continuing research of Glen L. Thompson and Mark Wilson. To be sure, one can quibble about whether the example chosen for analysis, a journey of Paul recorded only in Acts 20:13–14, is historically reliable. However, even if one puts together the itinerary of Paul solely on the basis of his letters,[1] one must account for the roads he must have used

---

1. See my article "How Acts Constructed the Itinerary of Paul: Conclusions Excerpted from the Acts Seminar Report," *Forum* 4 (2015): 153–62.

and how long the travel may have been. For this, the work of Thompson and Wilson is invaluable.

Our COMCAR expeditions have taken us to key Roman period sites in Italy and in the eastern Mediterranean, namely, southern Greece, Macedonia, Turkey (twice), Israel, and Jordan. Virtually everywhere we went we came across monuments, inscriptions, public works, and urban spaces that bore the name of Hadrian as benefactor. Rutherford takes on a particular feature of Hadrianic benefaction, namely, what he terms the "politics of patronage." His analysis centers on Athens, where Hadrian's benefaction was especially prominent. He concludes by proposing that the implied political ideology of these benefactions was influential in the argument of Aristides's *Apology*.

2. Meals in the Greco-Roman World

I am particularly gratified that several essays engage in dialogue with, and in many cases enhance, my work on ancient meals.[2]

Ibita specializes in the interpretation of early Christian meals. She is especially known for her convincing argument that the reference to the have-nots at the meal in 1 Cor 11:22 refers to actual hunger among some of the members due to their lower class status. In the essay in this volume, she extends that argument by taking up the issue of a possible famine in Corinth when Paul wrote the letter, thus enlarging on the external factors that may have been in play in Corinth.

Alikin is another contributor who has specialized in meals research. His essay illustrates how an understanding of the protocols of the ancient banquet can enhance our interpretation of women leaders in early Christian communities. That is to say, since women can be shown to have hosted banquets and served as leaders in associations, their leadership in early Christian communities as banquet hosts and benefactors is consistent with practices in the culture.

I have for some time relied on Friesen's proposals about the probable poverty level of early Christian communities. Thus I have had to imagine the setting whereby such a class of people could celebrate a reclining meal together as described in the literary data. Now Friesen has proposed

---

2. See especially Dennis E. Smith, *From Symposium to Eucharist: The Banquet in the Early Christian World* (Minneapolis: Fortress, 2003).

a means to define the types and amount of food their communal tables might have held, another valuable perspective on our reconstructions of early Christian meetings at the dinner table.

Two papers deal with the vocabulary of ancient meals. First Keith Dyer collects the vocabulary of eating in the New Testament and inquires how we might imagine their meals. He raises significant questions about how slaves and the poor could have managed to recline at the early Christian meals since they would not have had the resources or the social position to do so. I would note that in the gospel tradition reclining together became a potent symbol for inclusion in the kingdom (Mark 2:15–17 and parallels). Yet Dyer's questions remain troubling. For my part, I think it is quite likely that more often than not slaves were relegated to secondary status at early Christian meals, especially in the period of the household codes.

Jorunn Økland surveys the vocabulary for wining and dining in the Greek version of Esther as part of her research as a member of the team that is producing a new Norwegian translation of the Bible. She notes the often-overlooked importance for translators to be familiar with material culture. I could not agree more; indeed, a pet peeve of mine is the misleading NRSV translation of New Testament terms for reclining with the phrase "sit at table," thus erasing for the English reader all contact with the ancient culture of the reclining banquet (see, e.g., Mark 2:15; 6:39–40; 8:6; 14:3; 14:18; and parallels). Similarly, Økland has recognized that the Greek version of Esther, while purporting to describe drinking parties in Persia, is imbued with Greek wine-drinking culture, thus presenting a challenge for translators who wish to give due regard to the semantic background for the wine-drinking terminology.

3. New Testament and Christian Origins

When an exegete immerses herself in the material evidence at an archaeological site, how might that change or enhance the exegesis? Several essays demonstrate the difference it can make. I have already mentioned Huber's intriguing arguments on the construction of the male in Rev 2–3 and Alikin's detailed study on women leaders in early Christian communities. Friesen's study lays the groundwork for what promises to be a long-term investigation of inequality in the early Christian world. Cadwallader's study of Colossian epitaphs manages to put a different spin on the household codes in Colossians, namely, that they "had little to do with the membership of the Colossian congregation."

According to Dominika Kurek-Chomycz and Reimund Bieringer, the phrase καινὴ κτίσις ("new creation") in 2 Cor 5:17 can be read differently if one takes into account the cultural identity of the Corinthian recipients of the letter. In a detailed analysis that warms my exegete's heart, they note how the phrase was commonly used to refer to the founding/refounding of a city. Given the importance of the refounding of Corinth as a Roman colony in the material evidence at the site, the recipients would likely have understood the phrase "as a challenge to the ideology underlying the Roman new creation of the ancient Hellenic city, offering an alternative model to the way this ongoing re-creation of Corinth was being put into practice."

A couple of essays reference Acts as a reliable source of historical data regarding the travels of Paul. In my own work, I have opposed that view.[3] Nevertheless, the challenges of these papers remain substantial.

Weima makes a case for the historical reliability of the charges against Paul and Silas in Thessalonica according to Acts 17:6–7. The charges, he argues, should be interpreted as treason and disloyalty to the emperor, and they resonate historically because of the positive view toward Roman benefaction that existed in first century CE Thessalonica. He concludes that the Acts story is "an entirely plausible account." One can also argue for the plausibility that the Acts story correlates with historical data because of the author's skill at verisimilitude. Even so, Weima's research is fundamental for understanding Acts 17:6–7.

Stephen J. Patterson's essay imagines a moment in Christian origins when the definition and practice of baptism were still being debated. The center of that debate, he argues, was between Paul and Apollos, with Apollos representing a baptism associated with Hellenistic Jewish wisdom theology (as in 1 Cor 1:11–17) as well as deriving from the baptism of John (as in Acts 18:24–19:7). This is a welcome addition to our renewed assessments of Christian origins, although I would tend to place the Acts debate about the baptism of John not in the time of Paul but in the early second century CE when Acts was written.

This is an impressive collection of essays, demonstrating in a variety of ways how our interpretation of the New Testament in its social and cultural context is enhanced by informed analysis of the material evidence.

---

3. Dennis E. Smith and Joseph B. Tyson, eds., *Acts and Christian Beginnings: The Acts Seminar Report* (Salem, OR: Polebridge, 2013).

It functions also as an affirmation of the COMCAR experience. I am very proud to have contributed to this effort and honored to have provided an occasion for this publication.

Bibliography

Smith, Dennis E. *From Symposium to Eucharist: The Banquet in the Early Christian World*. Minneapolis: Fortress, 2003.

———. "How Acts Constructed the Itinerary of Paul: Conclusions Excerpted from the Acts Seminar Report." *Forum* 4 (2015): 153–62.

Smith, Dennis E., and Joseph B. Tyson, eds. *Acts and Christian Beginnings: The Acts Seminar* . Salem, OR: Polebridge, 2013.

CONTRIBUTORS

Valeriy A. Alikin is President and Chair of the Department of Theology and Church History at St. Petersburg Christian University, Russia. He is the author of *The Earliest History of the Christian Gathering: Origins, Development and Content of the Christian Gathering in the First to Third Centuries* (2010) and various publications in the field of the New Testament and early Christianity. He has recently contributed and edited several volumes of Transactions of SPbCU in Russian.

Reimund Bieringer is Professor of New Testament Exegesis at the Faculty of Theology and Religious Studies, Katholieke Universiteit Leuven, Belgium. The main areas of his research are the New Testament and Judaism, 2 Corinthians, the Gospel of John, and biblical hermeneutics. He is a Past President of the European Association of Biblical Studies. His publications include *Studies on 2 Corinthians* (1994), written with Jan Lambrecht; *When Love Is Not Enough: A Theo-ethic of Justice* (2002), written with Mary Elsbernd; and *Normativity of the Future: Reading Biblical and Other Authoritative Texts in an Eschatological Perspective* (2010), also written with Mary Elsbernd.

Alan H. Cadwallader is Senior Lecturer in Biblical Studies at the Australian Catholic University, Canberra. He has edited and authored a number of books, most especially focused on ancient Colossae (*Colossae in Space and Time*, 2011; *Fragments of Colossae*, 2015) and on Mark's Gospel (*Beyond the Word of a Woman*, 2008). He is currently preparing a volume on the testimonia, numismatics, and inscriptions of Colossae and a commentary on Mark in the Earth Bible series.

Keith Dyer is Associate Professor of New Testament at Whitley College, within the University of Divinity in Melbourne, Australia. His research interests include the Gospel of Mark, the book of Revelation, and Pauline eschatology. Recent publications include contributions to *Oxford Bibliographies in Biblical Studies* (2015); *Colonial Contexts and Postcolonial Theologies: Storyweaving in the Asia-Pacific* (2014), and *Resurrection and Responsibility* (2009).

Steven J. Friesen is the Louise Farmer Boyer Chair in Biblical Studies in the Department of Religious Studies at the University of Texas at Austin. His research foci include apocalypticism and the book of Revelation, the use of archaeological material, and forms of inequality in the Roman Empire. He is the author of *Imperial Cults and the Apocalypse of John: Reading Revelation in the Ruins* (2001) and coeditor of *Corinth in Context: Comparative Studies on Religion and Society* (2010).

Lynn R. Huber is Professor of Religious Studies at Elon University, where she is also department chair. Huber's research focuses on the book of Revelation, specifically the text's gendered imagery. Her most recent book is *Thinking and Seeing with Women in Revelation* (2013), and she is currently working on a project exploring Revelation through queer interpretive lenses.

Ma. Marilou S. Ibita is a postdoctoral fellow at the Faculty of Theology and Religious Studies, Katholieke Universiteit, Leuven, Belgium. Her doctoral dissertation is entitled "If Anyone Hungers, He/She Must Eat in the House" (1 Cor 11:34): A Narrative-Critical, Socio-historical and Grammatical-Philological Analysis of the Story of the Lord's Supper" (2012). She has also recently contributed to ecological hermeneutics in *Gender Agenda Matters* (2015) and is currently working on an interdisciplinary project, *New Hermeneutics for Renewed Dialogues*, dealing with the Gospel of John, pneumatology, and Jewish-Christian dialogue.

Dominika Kurek-Chomycz is Lecturer in New Testament Studies at Liverpool Hope University, UK, and currently serves as acting Executive Officer of the European Association of Biblical Studies. She coauthored *2 Corinthians: A Bibliography* (2008) and coedited *Theologizing in the Corinthian Conflict: Studies in Exegesis and Theology of 2 Corinthians* (2013). Her doctoral dissertation on Paul's olfactory metaphor in 2 Cor 2:14–16 and the motif of scent in ancient Jewish literature is forthcoming with Brill. Her research interests include the Pauline letters, material culture, emotions, sense perception and sense imagery, women and masculinity in early Judaism and Christianity, and biblical hermeneutics.

Jorunn Økland is the Director of the Norwegian Institute at Athens and Professor of Gender Studies in the Humanities, University of Oslo. She coedited *Biblical Spatiality and the Sacred* (2015), which included her chapter "Carnelian and Caryatids: Stone and Statuary in the Heavenly Sanctuary"; she contributed "Feminist Readings of the Bible" to vol. 4 of *The New Cambridge History of the Bible* (2015).

Stephen J. Patterson is the Atkinson Professor of Religious Studies at Willamette University; he is a historian of religion specializing in the beginnings of Christianity. His most recent books are *The Lost Way* (2014) and *The Gospel of Thomas and Christian Origins* (2013).

William Rutherford received his doctorate in New Testament and Christian Origins from the University of Edinburgh. He has authored articles on early Jewish-Christian relations in *Harvard Theological Review* and *Studia Patristica* and has contributed to several conference volumes, including *Justin Martyr and His Worlds* (2007) and *Peter in Early Christianity* (2015). He presently serves as Assistant Headmaster at Great Hearts Monte Vista in San Antonio, Texas, where he also teaches Latin and Western Humanities.

Daniel N. Schowalter is a Professor in the Classics and Religion departments at Carthage College. He is codirector of the excavation of a three-phase Roman Temple at Omrit in northern Israel. He serves on the steering committee for the *Colloquium on Material Culture and Ancient Religion*, the "Archaeology of Religion in the Roman World" section of the Society of Biblical Literature, and is a member of the editorial board for Oxford Biblical Studies Online. He is coeditor of *Corinth in Contrast: Studies in Inequality* (2013), and *The Architecture*, vol. 1 of *The Temple Complex at Roman Omrit* (2016).

Hal E. Taussig retired in June of 2016 from seventeen years as Visiting Professor of New Testament and Early Christianity at Union Theological Seminary. He is Professor of Early Christianity at the Reconstructionist Rabbinical College, board member of the Westar Institute and cochair of its Christianity Seminar, ongoing theologian in residence at Holden Village and the Boulder United Methodist Church, and board chair of the Tanho Center for a new New Testament. The most recent of his fourteen books are *Meals in Early Judaism: Social Formation at the Table* (2014), *Re-reading the Gospel of Mark amidst Pain and Trauma* (2013), and *A New New Testament: A Bible for the 21st Century* (2013).

Glen L. Thompson serves as Academic Dean and Professor of New Testament and Historical Theology at Asia Lutheran Seminary in Hong Kong. Besides documenting the Roman road system in Anatolia, his research interests and publications include Tang era Christianity in China and the early papacy. The first volume of his critical edition and translation of the earliest surviving papal correspondence has recently appeared: *The Correspondence of Pope Julius I* (2015).

Jeffrey A. D. Weima is Professor of New Testament at Calvin Theological Seminary, where he has taught for the past twenty-four years. He has published five books: *Neglected Endings: The Significance of the Pauline Letter Closings* (1994); *An Annotated Bibliography of 1 and 2 Thessalonians* (1998); *1 and 2 Thessalonians* (2002); a major commentary on 1 and 2 Thessalonians (2014); and, most recently, *Paul the Ancient Letter Writer: An Introduction to Epistolary Analysis* (2016). He is the author of numerous scholarly articles, academic essays, and book reviews. He has taught courses all over the world and leads biblical study tours to Greece, Turkey, Israel/Jordan, and Italy.

Mark Wilson is the director of the Asia Minor Research Center in Antalya, Turkey. His academic affiliations include Research Fellow in the Department of Biblical and Ancient Studies, University of South Africa; and Adjunct Lecturer in New Testament, Ridley College, Melbourne, Australia. He is the author of *Biblical Turkey: A Guide to the Jewish and Christian Sites of Asia Minor* (2010) and of "The Synagogues of Asia Minor and the Western Diaspora during Late Antiquity" in the forthcoming *Cambridge World History of Religious Architecture*. His research interests include, especially, early Jewish and Christian communities and Roman roads.

Index of Ancient Sources

Hebrew Bible/Old Testament

Genesis
- 1–2   322, 323
- 1:7   199
- 2:7   323
- 14:19   199
- 14:22   199

Exodus
- 15:20   235

Judges
- 6   74

2 Samuel (2 Reigns)
- 22:32   199

Esther
- 1   97
- 1:3   90, 92
- 1:5   90, 92
- 1:7   94, 97
- 1:8   90, 92
- 1:9   90, 92
- 1:10   92
- 1:11   91
- 2:18   90, 92
- 3:22   93, 95
- 4:45   91, 93
- 5–7   97
- 5:4   91, 92, 94
- 5:6   91, 92, 94
- 6:14   91, 92, 94
- 7:1   94
- 7:1–2   91
- 7:1–10   94
- 7:2   92, 94
- 7:7   91, 94
- 7:11   91, 94
- 8:16   91, 92, 94, 95
- 8:17   97
- 9:17   92
- 9:18   92
- 9:19   92

Isaiah
- 26:20   214
- 28:15   214
- 43:18–19   196, 214
- 43:19   214
- 54:16–17   214
- 59:9   295
- 61:4   215

Deuterocanonical Works

1 Esdras
- 4:53   201
- 6:12   201

Judith
- 16:14   215

Wisdom
- 19:6   197

Sirach
- 34:9–13   270

INDEX OF ANCIENT SOURCES

Bel and the Dragon	74

3 Maccabees

3:61	97

4 Maccabees

6:1–12	118

Pseudepigrapha

1 Enoch

72:1	197

Jubilees

1:29	197
4:26	197

Liber Antiquitatum Biblicarum

3.10	197

New Testament

Matthew

4:18–22	27
9:9–13	75
14:16–21	27
15:27	74
16:21	304
22:1–14	76
25:32–33	27

Mark

1:8	320
1:16–20	27
2:15	332
2:15–17	75, 332
6:14–29	75
6:33	279
6:35–44	27
6:39	76
6:39–40	332
7:28	74
8:6	332
14:3	332
14:18	332

Luke

3:16	320
5:9–11	27
7:36–50	75, 81
9:12–17	27
9:51	304
10:38–42	81
11:37–52	81
14:1	75
14:1–24	81
14:7–11	71, 76
16:21	74
17:7–10	72
18:31–33	304
19:1–27	81
19:5–7	75
22:15–20	76
22:21	74
22:26	178
22:26–27	76
22:30	74
22:42	304

Q

	325
7:35	323
10:21	324

John

4:2	321
6:8–14	27
13:1–20	81
21:1–14	27

Acts

1:5	320
2:44	223
4:32	223
6	27
6:1–6	319
6:2	74
11:16	320
11:26	77
12:12	229
12:20–23	28, 75
15:1–35	319

INDEX OF ANCIENT SOURCES

16	229	Romans	
16:6	272	6:3–11	316
16:8	271	8	200
16:8–10	270	8:35	42, 49
16:11	244, 272, 273, 300	13:5	41
16:12	244	14	78
16:34	74	15:25–27	272
16:40	229	15:31	302
17	264	16:2	47, 224
17:2	297		
17:4	242	1 Corinthians	316, 320–22, 324
17:5	242	1–2	317
17:5–9	241	1–4	317
17:6	242–43, 249	1:11–13	315
17:6–7	241–65, 333	1:11–17	333
17:7	249–51, 258, 261, 263–64	1:12	317
17:8	242, 249, 250	1:14–17	315–6
17:23	285	1:17	316, 323
18	202	2:1	324
18:2	254	3	317
18:12–17	211	3:1	320
18:24	317	3:4	317
18:24–28	319	3:5–9	317
18:24–19:7	320, 333	3:6	317
18:25	316–20	3:10	317
18:26	319	3:12	317
18:27–28	317, 319	3:17	317
19:1–7	318, 319	4:1–5	317
20	272, 297, 300, 305	4:6	317
20–21	272	4:8	321
20:3	272, 297	6–7	72
20:6	271, 273	6:11	72
20:11	295, 296	7:1	47
20:13	272, 278, 296	7:7	181
20:13–14	330	7:21–24	78
20:16	303	7:26	41, 49
20:22	304	8–11	78
20:22–23	302	8:10	77, 79
20:24	305	9:16	41
20:25	305	9:24–27	210
21:4	304	10:16–21	222
21:9	235	10:21	74, 79
21:11	303	11:2	331
24:17	272	11:17–34	33–49
27:27–37	27	11:17–14:40	223

1 Corinthians (cont.)

11:18	47
11:20–21	77
11:20–27	76
11:21	77
11:21–22	45
11:22	44–45, 47–49, 77
11:30	41, 46, 48–49
11:33–34	46, 48–49, 76
11:34	44–45, 48, 49
12	320
14	78, 320
15	322
15:12	322
15:29	322, 325
15:42–50	323
16:12	317

2 Corinthians

2:12	203, 211
2:12–13	271
2:13	271
2:14	272
4:4	211
5	295
5:10	210–11, 216
5:14	196, 211–12
5:14–15	210
5:14–21	210
5:16	213
5:17	210
5:20	195–217, 333
8–9	211
8:12–15	272
11:25	44
11:27	299
	41, 42, 49

Galatians

2:11–14	76
3:26–28	316
3:28	235
6:15	197–98

Ephesians

6:12	303

Philippians

2:22	272
3:20	196

Colossians

2:1	183
4:7	182
4:9	182
4:10	182
4:10–12	182
4:15	182, 229

1 Thessalonians

1:1	241
1:10	264
2:2	241
2:12	264
2:14	241
2:15	242
2:19	251
3:7	41
4:15	251
4:17	251
5:2	251
5:3	252
5:9	252

2 Thessalonians

2:3–4	252
2:5	251
2:15	251

1 Timothy

2:11–13	230
5:1–16	27

2 Timothy

4:13	270

Philemon

2	230
9	301
10	181

INDEX OF ANCIENT SOURCES 343

Hebrews	
12:1	118

James	
2:14–17	27

Revelation	
1:3	124
1:9	122
1:12	120
1:20	120
2–3	101–25
2:1	120
2:2	122
2:3	122
2:7	123
2:10	123
2:11	123
2:13	103, 122
2:17	123
2:19	122
2:25	122
2:26–28	123
3:1	120
3:2–3	122
3:3	122
3:5	124
3:8	120
3:10	122
3:11	123
3:12	104
3:16	104
3:21	123
6:9	124
7:13–14	124
13:7	124
13:10	122
14:1	124
14:12	122
14:12–13	124
20:4–6	124
22:2	124
22:4	124

EARLY CHRISTIAN WRITINGS

Acts of Barnabas	182

Acts of Paul and Thecla	
3	301
5	232
34	232
39	231–32
42	232
45	232

Acts of Peter	
5	232
7	232
8	232
9	232
13	223
20	232

Aristides, *Apologia* 129, 130–32, 151–52

Athenagoras, *Legatio pro Christianis*	
3	223
31	223

Clement of Alexandria, *Stromata*	
6.113	223

Cyprian, *Epistulae*	
63	223
75	233

Didache	
9–10	223
10	232
13	27
15	232

Epiphanius, *Panarion*	
49.2.1–3	234–35
78.23.4	235
79.1.7	236
79.4.1	236
79.8.1	236

Eusebius, *Chronicon*	129–30	Origen, *Contra Celsum*	
2.152	39	1.1	223
ad ann. Hadr. 5	141	8.32	223
ad ann. Hadr. 6	149		
ad ann. Hadr. 7	141	Orosius, *Historiarum adversus Paganos*	
ad ann. Hadr. 8	129	7.6.17	39
ad ann. Hadr. 9	143–44		
		Shepherd of Hermas, *Similitudes*	
Eusebius, *Historia ecclesiastica*		2.1–10	27
4.3	132	5.3.7	27
Hippolytus, *Refutatio omnium haeresium*		Syncellus, *Ecloga Chronographica*	
8.12	223, 231	659.9	149
Hippolytus, *Traditio apostolica*		Tertullian, *Ad nationes*	
25–29	223	1.2	223
		1.7	223
Ignatius, *To Polycarp*			
8.2	230–1	Tertullian, *Adversus Marcionem*	
		1.20.4	197
Irenaeus, *Adversus haereses*			
1.13	223	Tertullian, *Apologeticus*	
1.13.2	231	7	223
1.25.6	231	39	222–23
Jerome, *De virus illustribus*		Tertullian, *De baptismo*	
20	129	17	232
Jerome, *Epistulae*		Tertullian, *De praescriptione haereticorum*	
70.4	129	41.5	232
Justin, *Apologia 1*			
7.26	236	Tertullian, *De virginibus velandis*	
67	223	9.2	232–3
Martyrdom of Polycarp		Theophilus of Antioch, *Ad Autolycum*	
17	118	3.4	200, 223
		3.27	200
Minucius Felix, *Octavius*			
8.4	223	INDEX OF CLASSICAL TEXTS	
9.6	223		
31.1	223	Aelian, *De natura animalium*	
31.5	223	1.55	299

INDEX OF ANCIENT SOURCES

Aeneas Tactitus, *Poliorcetica*	
26.12	243
Appian, *Bella civilia*	
4.118	245
Apuleius, *Metamorphoses*	
2.18–19	223–24
2.18	224
11	211
Aristophanes, *Ranae*	
1015 [1047]	242
Aristotle, *Ethica nichomachea*	
1161b	177
Arius Didymus (*apud* Stobaeus)	
2.7.26	180
Athenaeus, *Deipnosophistae*	
4.143e	70
4.143f	74
10.420e–11	95
10.422e–11	95
10.422e	85
10.433b	95, 98
10.434	96
11.483b	96
11.484c	96
Aulus Gellius, *Noctes atticae*	
16.13.8–9	206
Cicero, *De legibus*	
2.63	157
Cicero, *Epistulae ad Atticum*	
14.21.4	75
16.2.6	75
Cicero, *Pro Fonteio*	
44	245

Dio Cassius, *Historia romanae*	
41.10	40
41.18.4–6	245
41.43.1–5	245
53.12.4	248
56.25.5–6	262
57.15.8	262–63
60.6.6	259
60.24.1	248
69.16.1–2	131
69.16.1	132, 144, 148
69.16.2	135, 141, 149
Dio Chrysostom, *Orationes*	
29.9	113
29.10–11	122
Diodorus Siculus, *Bibliotheca historica*	
4.3.2–5	225
31.8.6–9	244
Epictetus, *Diatribai (Dissertationes)*	
4.4	118
Galen, *De alimentorum facultatibus*	
K 523	45
K 620	45
Galen, *De usu partium*	
14:6–7	108
Galen, *Protrepticus ad artes addiscendas*	
9	118
Herodotus, *Historiae*	
2.141	242
Historia Augusta	
Hadrianus	
1.5	132
2.8	149
13.1	144
13.6	142
19.1	132
26.1	144

INDEX OF ANCIENT SOURCES

Gallienus	
11.3–4	132
Homer, *Ilias*	
1.1–52	284
14.675	162
Homer, *Odyssea*	
3.159–74	281
Horace, *Carmina*	
3.6	180
Iamblichus, *Vita Pythagorae*	
6.32	223
Isaeus, *Orationes*	
8.33	177
Josephus, *Antiquitates judaicae*	88
17.42	256
18.373	201
Josephus, *Bellum judaicum*	
3.401–2	264
4.533	201
Josephus, *Vita*	
222	71
Julius Paulus, *Sententiae*	
5.21	263
Justinian, *Digesta*	
2.11.1	280
7.2 pref.	171
7.2.5	171
7.2.6	174
7.2.9	171
7.4	171, 178
7.6	178
7.12.4	178
47.22.4	176
Livy, *Ab urbe condita*	201
39.8–19	225
44.32	244
45.29.9	244
Lucian, *De morte Peregrini*	
11	222
Martial, *Epigrammata*	
2.37	75
3.23	75
Orabasius, *Collectiones medicae*	
2.58.54–55	292
Pausanias, *Graeciae descriptio*	
1.18.6–9	131
1.18.6	131
1.18.9	143
1.20.7	133
1.29.6	149
2	202
35.6–8	224
Philo, *De opificio mundi*	
134	323
135	323
Philo, *De vita Mosis*	
2.51	201
Philostratus, *Vitae sophistarum*	
2.1	134
Philostratus, *Vita Apollonii*	
4.17	138
Plato, *Leges*	
12.958d	158
12.958e	157
12.959d	171, 174
Plato, *Protagoras*	
347c	242

INDEX OF ANCIENT SOURCES

Pliny the Elder, *Naturalis historia*	
4.17 [10]	246
9.70.26	299
36.69	22
Pliny the Younger, *Epistulae*	
10.34	260
10.96	222
10.96.8	228
Plutarch, *Aemilius Paullus*	
38.4	242
Plutarch, *Brutus*	
46.1	245
Plutarch, *Caesar*	
57	173
Plutarch, *De facie in orbe lunae*	
28 [943A]	323
Plutarch, *De fraterno amore*	
8 [481F]	177
Plutarch, *Quaestionum convivialum libri IX*	
2.10.2 [644D]	223
5.5.2 [679D]	223
7.1 [697C]	69
9.14.1 [743E]	223
Plutarch, *Romulus*	
13.1	201
Plutarch, *Solon*	
19.1	134
24.1	149
Polybius, *Historiae*	
10.48.6	278
10.48.8	279
16.29.11	278

Pseudo-Aurelius Victor, *Epitome de Caesaribus*	
14.2	132
Ptolemy, *Geographia*	
4.5.10	292
Res gestae divi Augusti	
25.2–3	256
Sibylline Oracles	
12.173–74	135
Soranus, *Gynaecia*	
3.3	108
Strabo, *Geographica*	
7, fr. 47	244
8.6.20	298
13.1.26	274
13.1.48	284
13.1.49	298
13.1.57	293
Suetonius, *Augustus*	
32.1	259
Suetonius, *Claudius*	
18.1–2	40
18.2	39
25.4	254
25	147
Suetonius, *Tiberius*	
36	262
58	253
Suetonius, *Vespasianus*	
5	264
Tacitus, *Annales*	
1.72	253
2.27	263
2.32	263
12.43	39, 40

INDEX OF ANCIENT SOURCES

Tacitus, *Historiae*
  1.76.4 — 248

Theophrastus, *Characteres*
  6.2 — 242

Ulpian, *De officio proconsulis*
  x [apud *Mosaicarum et romanarum legume collatio* 15.2] — 263

Velleius Paterculus, *Historiarum Libri Duo*
  2.103.5 — 180

Virgil, *Aeneid*
  6.808–12 — 149

Virgil, *Eclogae*
  4 — 205

Xenophon, *Cyropaedia*
  1.2.8 — 96

Xenophon, *Hellenica*
  6.2.23 — 242

Index of Inscriptions and Papyri

ALA
  180i — 178

AltHierapolis
  64 — 174
  103 — 174
  269 — 175

BGU
  2.655 — 172

CBP
  181–2.69 — 179
  385.231 — 174
  385.232 — 174
  385.236 — 174

CIG
  3.3955 — 161, 166, 184–85
  3.4380k^3 — 169, 186–87

CIJ
  755 — 178

CIL
  6.9148 — 226
  8.21 — 163
  10.5624 — 163

CIRB
  266 — 168
  372 — 168
  400 — 168
  443 — 168
  1283 — 182

EAD
  30.143 — 175

EKM
  Beroia
  1 — 112

GIBM
  905 — 178

IArykanda
  67 — 182

IBoubon
  102 — 160, 169, 177

IDelos
  5.2535–2537 — 135

IG
  2.1100 — 137, 140
  2.1102 — 136, 143
  2.1103 — 138
  2.1104 — 139
  2.1314 — 226
  2.1337 — 226

INDEX OF ANCIENT SOURCES

2.1334		226	IKilikiaBM		
2.1764B		136	2.201b		182
2.2024		132			
2.2049		136	IKorinthKent		
2.2245		173	23		206
2.3286		132	127		37
2.3301		141	138		37
2.3503		139	140		37
2.3620		143	142		37
2.4210		136	143		37
2.12113		173	157		212
4.1.678		177	158		37, 38
5.1.21		140	159		38
5.2.265–66		227	160		37, 38
10.2.1.4		247	161		38
10.2.1.6		246	162		37, 38
10.2.1.31		247	163		38
10.2.1.32		247	164		37
10.2.1.83		246	169		37
10.2.1.109		246	170		37
10.2.1.128		247	177		37
10.2.1.132		247	188		37
10.2.1.133		247	227		37
10.2.1.134		245	234		37
10.2.1.226		247	235		37
10.2.1.255		226	236		37
10.2.1.260		226	238		37
10.2.1.824		182	306		212
12.2.141		204	322		212
12.2.163		204	503		204
12.2.165		204			
12.3.581/1437		173	IKorinthMeritt		
			76		37
IGBulg			94		37
3.2.1690		177			
			IKorinthWest		
IGRR			73		37
4.617		182	83		37
4.731		174	86		37, 38
4.870		164	87		37, 38
4.871	163, 170, 172, 184–85		88		37, 38
4.1682		115	89		37, 38
			90		37, 90
IHadrianoi			91		37
77		113			

INDEX OF ANCIENT SOURCES

IKyzikos		6.48	164, 176, 184–85
324	168	6.49	164
		6.50	160, 164, 180
ILipara		6.51a	160, 162
422	173	6.51b	160, 162
		6.74	178
ILS		6.276	170
1.190	257–58	6.306	170
1.337	141	7.404	177
2.2.8681	255–56	7.507	177
		8.237	178
IMT		8.492	227
573	257	9.86	175
IPerge		MDAIA	
1.317	182	1893.206.3	165, 169, 170, 175
		1908.379–81.2	114
ISmyrna			
1.440	160, 186–87	OGIS	
		573	175
Katalog der Inschriften von Philippi			
301–4	203	P. Lond.	
		1912	254
LBW			
3.1693b	164	P. Oslo	
		3.130	163
LSAM			
48	226	P. Oxy.	
		12.1458	172
MAMA			
4.27	170	PfuhlMöbius	
4.114	170	236	161
4.299	175	1607	161
4.343	174	1634	161
6.24	178	1665b	161
6.38	164	1920	161, 169
6.39	161, 164, 186–87	1973	161, 179
6.40	164	1974	176, 177
6.41	164	2005	161
6.42	161, 164, 172, 186–87	2104	167
6.43	163, 170, 175, 184–85		
6.44	162, 169, 176, 184–85	Ritti	
6.45	166, 174, 184–85	59	161
6.46	161, 186–87	73	176
6.47	158, 164, 175, 184–85	113	158

INDEX OF ANCIENT SOURCES

167	170

SB

18.13176	163

SEG

3.111	143
3.693	204
15.416	168
16.653	178
19.172	139
19.578	257
28.840	178
28.1125	174
28.1154	170
32.1169	175
32.1170	175
32.1185	175
35.1337	185
37.526	200
38.935	173
40.1241	175
50.528	176
53.293	176
54.1275	145

SGO

1.02.15.01	168
2.16.31.91	177

SIG

2.985	183

SPP

22.56	163

TAM

2.46	178
3.703	173
4.109	174
4.231	178
4.283	178

Index of Place Names

Abydos 273
Achaia 35–36, 39–40, 142, 147, 297, 302
Acmoneia 180–81
Actium 212, 246
Aegean 272, 281, 296, 298
Africa 163, 256
Alexandria 224, 322
Alexandria Troas 284, 286
Amphipolis 112, 243
Anatolia 164, 255, 269–70
Ankyra 110
Antigoneia 274
Antioch 76, 77, 198
Antioch of Pisidia 303
Apameia 175, 181
Aphrodisias 178, 227
Apollonia Pontica 18, 19
Appa 165
Arabia 236
Aritium 257
Asia 124, 142, 158–59, 227, 270, 272–73, 275–76, 297, 303
Asia Minor 101, 109–11, 113, 117, 121, 123, 125, 158, 180, 230, 272, 275–76, 298
Assos xix, 257, 269–305
Athens xix, 129–52, 285
Attica 137
Attouda 161, 166
Balabanlı 288
Beroia 112, 113, 303
Bithynia 259
Black Sea 255, 276
Boubon 160, 169
Britain 211
Cadmus, Mount 164
Caesarea 233
Caesarea Philippi 72
Caesarea Maritima 5, 72, 298, 304
Cappadocia 233
Carthage 233
Casal Bertone 23
Cenchreae 47, 224
Cephallenia 141
Cephisus River 141
Chania 58
Chrysa 284
Colossae 157–87
Corinth xix, 5, 9, 33–49, 72, 77, 195–217, 222, 272, 292, 293, 297, 302, 303, 315–25
Crete 58, 70, 74
Cyprus 182, 257
Dardanelles Strait 273
Delphi 132
Derbe 272
Derriopus 243
Dokimeia 162
Edessa 243
Egypt 230
Eleusis 130, 136, 138, 141, 143, 147, 150
Ephesus 1, 16–17, 21, 82, 101, 110, 117, 122, 124, 142, 269–70, 299–300, 319, 320
Eumeneia 166, 181
Galilee, Sea of 72
Glevum 17, 22, 25
Hadriani 113
Halesion Plain 278, 279, 283, 288
Hamaxitos 300

INDEX OF PLACE NAMES

Hellespont	276	Pella	82, 243
Hierapolis	104, 158, 161	Pergamon	82, 101, 103, 110–11, 114–15, 117, 122, 124, 276
Honaz	164, 165, 166		
Hypata	224	Persepolis	86, 95
Iconium	301, 303	Persia	86, 88, 91, 94, 96, 98
Ilissos River	141	Pharsalus	245
Ilium	274	Philadelphia	101, 104, 120, 122–23
Irnitania	260	Philippi	72, 203, 229, 261, 272–73, 297, 300, 303, 305
Isola Sacra	15, 25		
Isthmia	212	Phrygia	162, 167, 183, 234
Italy	163, 230, 263, 270, 274, 292	Piraeus	138
Jerusalem	201, 229, 272–73, 283, 297, 301–4, 319	Pontus	233
		Portus	15
Kocaköy	288	Poundbury Camp	15, 23
Kolonai	300	Priene	110, 115, 116
Korubaşı	288	Pydna	244
Kos	58	Rome	15, 17, 20–21, 23, 25, 39, 44, 49, 142, 147–49, 159, 200–201, 208, 226, 231, 234, 244–46, 248, 250–59, 263–65
Koyunevi	288		
Laodikeia	101–2, 104, 110, 123, 161, 164–66, 229		
		Samos	256
Larisa	300	Sardinia	256
Lechaion	204	Sardis	101, 110, 114–15, 120, 124
Lectum, Cape	279, 281, 297, 298	Sargalassos	14
Leptiminus	15–19, 24	Satnioeis River	282–83, 289
Lesbos	281	Sepphoris	72
Lete	243	Sestos	273
Lycus River	162	Sicily	256
Lystra	272, 303	Sidon	28
Macedonia	82, 112, 243, 270–72, 297, 302	Sigia	274
		Smintheion	271, 300
Magnesia	110	Smyrna	101–2, 117, 122–23, 160
Malea, Cape	270, 298	Spain	256, 260, 276
Mantineia	227	Sparta	132, 147
Miletus	110, 225, 283, 302–5	Stratonikeia	158
Mitylene	204	Susa	86, 90, 92–93
Neapolis	272	Tenedos	281, 296
Nicomedia	259	Termessos	122
Nikopolis	200	Thassos	82
Oinoanda	158	Thessalonica	241–65
Omrit	xix, 55–65	Thessaly	224
Ostia	15, 19	Thyatira	101, 122
Palestine	230	Tiber River	15
Patara	117	Tiberias	72
Palaipaphos	257	Tralles	142
Paphlagonia	255–56	Trapezopolis	161

Troas	269–305
Tunisia	15
Tuzla (Satnioeis) Bridge	282, 298
Tyre	28, 304
Vagnari	20, 24
Velia	15, 18, 24

Index of Modern Authors

Aasgaard, R.	47	Bauman, R. A.	252
Abrahamsen, V.	235	Bayhan, A. A.	165
Ağturk, T. S.	290	Beale, G. K.	104, 121, 124
Ahrens, S.	159	Bean, G. E.	290
Aichele, G.	89	Bekker-Nielsen, T.	280–81
Aitken, E. B.	71	Bell, G.	165
Aland, B.	89	Bengel, J. A.	33, 41
Aland, K.	89	Benjamin, A. S.	131, 145
Alexander, L. C. A.	203, 270	Benko, S.	235, 236
Alexander, P. J.	134	Bermann, S.	87
Alikin, V.	223	Berns, C.	158
Allison, P. M.	61, 106, 107	Betz, H-D.	316
Amandry, M.	207	Bieringer, R.	211
Anderson, W.	159, 174	Bijovsky, G.	62
Anderson, J. G. C.	168	Bispham, E.	204–5
Anderson-Stojanović, V.	61	Blount, B. K.	104, 121, 123
Appadurai, A.	106	Blue, B. B.	33, 38, 41, 44, 47
Apter, E.	87	Boardman, J.	178
Arnaoutoglou, I. N.	176, 260	Boatwright, M. T.	130–32, 138, 142, 146–47
Arslan, N.	290–91, 294		
Arundell, F. J.	164, 166	Bock, D. L.	250, 298
Ascough, R.	71, 224, 226, 257, 260–61	Bodel, J.	163
Aulock, H. von	173	Bodnar, E. W.	146
Aune, D. E.	119	Böhlendorf-Arslan, B.	291, 294
Bacon, F. H.	290	Bolden, R.	274, 286–87
Bagnall, R. S.	112–14	Bons, E.	199–200
Bain, K.	110–11	Bookidis, N.	208–9
Bakhtin, M.	76, 105	Bourbou, C.	46
Balabanski, V.	181	Boyle, A. J.	75
Balch, D.	183	Bremen, R. van	222, 227
Barclay, J. M. G.	216	Breytenbach, C.	210
Barrett, C. K.	34, 40, 41, 250, 258, 262, 299, 301	Bridges, E.	88
		Brooten, B. J.	222–23, 228, 230
Bash, A.	211	Broughton, T. R. S.	276
Baughan, E. P.	179	Brownrigg, R.	288

INDEX OF MODERN AUTHORS

Bruce, F. F. 251–52, 258, 262–63, 279, 281
Brueggemann, W. 76
Buckler, W. 162, 175, 177, 179
Bultmann, R. 324
Burdick, D. L. 300–301
Burton, E. D. 243
Butler, J. 107–8
Cadbury, H. J. 295, 299
Cadwallader, A. H. 24–25, 74, 82, 129, 160–64, 166, 169–70, 173–76, 183
Calder, W. M. 162, 166, 175, 177, 179, 290
Caldwell, L. 111
Champion-Smith, V. A. 133
Chandler, R. 165
Chenery, C. 12, 17, 22
Cheung, C. 17, 22, 23
Chilton, C. W. 252
Christophilopoulos, A. P. 135
Chun, S. 205–6
Chuvin, P. 224
Cimok, F. 278, 287
Clarke, J. T. 179, 290, 294
Cobb, L. S. 109, 118, 125
Cohen, G. M. 150, 274
Cohen, H. 150
Cohick, L. H. 221, 225
Conway, C. 108, 109
Conybeare, W. J. 279, 281, 302
Conzelmann, H. 272
Cook, J. M. 274, 278, 282, 284, 287
Cormack, S. 159
Corsten, T. 177
Cotter, W. J. 261
Coulton, J. J. 158, 174
Craig, O. E. 12, 14–15, 17–18, 24
Crouch, A. 216
Crowe, F. 22
Croy, N. C. 122, 123
Cummings, C. 12
Danylak, B. N. 33, 36–38, 40–41, 43
Das, A. A. 42
Davidson, J. N. 96
Day, J. 131, 137, 141
Deissmann, A. 216–17
Dell'Acqua, A. P. 199, 200
Demargne, J. 161
Demirkök, F. 167
Derderian, K. 160
Derow, P. 112–14
DeSilva, D. A. 120–21
Dibelius, M. 318
Dieulafoy, J. 86
Dieulafoy, M. A. 86
Diller, J. S. 282
Dittenberger, W. 132
Donfried, K. P. 244, 253, 259, 264
Dönmez, E. S. 167
Drew-Bear, T. 167
Duff, P. B. 120, 211
Dunbabin, K. M. D. 117
Duncan-Jones, R. 163
Dunn, J. D. G. 33, 38, 229–30
Dupont, J. 323
Eckardt, H. 12, 19, 21–22
Eckhel, J. H von 150
Edson, C. 246
Eisen, U. 234
Ellis, R. S. 63
Engels, D. 34–35
Erdkamp, P. 37, 39, 45
Erdmann, H. 164–65
Erdmann, K. 164–65
Erhardt, E. A. 254, 255
Ersoy, A. 276
Ertuğrul, F. 164
Evans, R. M. 242
Fairchild, M. 287, 299–300
Fee, G. D. 41
Fellows, C. 279
Fellows, R. 297
Feuser, S. 274
Fewster, P. 200
Fitzgerald, J. T. 42
Fitzmyer, J. A. 42, 249, 297, 304
Folch, M. 157–58
Follet, S. 129, 131–32, 134, 141–42, 144
Foucart, P. 144
Foucault, M. 114

INDEX OF MODERN AUTHORS

Fox, S. C.   11, 12, 46
French, D. H.   285, 289
Friesen, S. J.   10, 34, 44, 47, 72, 102–3, 105, 120, 224
Fuller, B. T.   14, 18
Furnish, V. P.   33, 214, 258
Gaetringen, F. H. von   115
Galliazzo, V.   282
Gardiner, E. N.   110
Garland, R.   157
Garnsey, P.   34, 36–37, 39–46
Geagan, D. J.   131, 133, 135–36, 140, 144, 146, 148
Georgi, D.   272
Ghenery, C.   22
Gill, D. W. J.   33, 36, 38
Glancy, J. A.   71, 72, 82
Gleason, M. W.   102, 109
Gloag, P. J.   273
Gonzalez, J.   260
Gounaropoulou, L.   112
Graindor, P.   131, 133, 135, 137–38, 141–42
Grant, M.   292
Green, G. L.   245, 262
Grundmann, W.   41
Gürdal, T.   282, 284–85
Guthrie, G. H.   272
Haenchen, E.   251, 295–96
Hall, A. S.   158
Hammerstaedt, J.   158
Hansen, M. H.   34
Hanson, J. W.   275–76
Hardin, J. K.   253, 258–61
Hareda, T.   287
Harland, P. A.   175–76, 224, 257
Harris, M. J.   214, 271–72
Harrison, J. R.   258
Hatzopoulos, M. B.   112
Hedges, R. E. M.   17
Heilig, C.   211
Hemer, C. J.   103, 254, 258, 262, 273–74, 278, 297
Henderson, S. W.   46
Hendrix, H. L.   245–47
Herrmann, P.   256
Hesse, R.   59–60
Heuchan, V.   223
Hodgson, R.   42
Hoffmann, P.   324
Horrell, D. G.   47
Horsley, G. H. R.   196, 234, 243
Horsley, R.   316, 322
Howson, J. S.   279, 281, 302
Hubbard, M. V.   198
Huber, L. R.   102
Hunt, G. R.   63
Hurd, J.   317
Huttner, U.   176, 181, 234
Ibita, M. M. S.   44, 47–48
Jackson, T. R.   198, 205–6
Jacobsthal, P.   63
Jeal, R. R.   182
Jensen, A.   233
Jensen, R. M.   27
Jewett, R.   258
Johnson, L. T.   250
Jones, A. H. M.   37
Jones, C. P.   131, 142
Jongman, W.   43–44
Joyce, R.   105–6
Judge, E. A.   182, 253, 255, 258–59, 262–63
Kahl, B.   75
Kantor, G.   159
Kaplan, D.   286
Käsemann, E.   317–19, 320
Kearsley, R. A.   279
Keenan, J. G.   172
Keener, C. S.   103, 104, 254, 265, 270, 273, 280
Keenleyside, A.   16–18, 24
Kelp, U.   160, 162, 170
Kent, J. H.   37
Kienast, D.   147
Killgrove, K.   17, 20–21, 23–25
Klinkott, M.   275
Kloppenborg, J. S.   224–26, 257, 324
Koester, C. R.   102, 103, 104–5
Koester, H.   5, 329

Kokkos, A.	142	Marshall, I. H.	262, 301
Koldeway, R.	290	Matthews, H.	284
König, J.	111, 118, 122	Mattingly, H.	150
Kontoleon, A. E.	161	Maxwell, J.	224
Kraemer, R. S.	221, 224–25, 231, 234–36	Mechikoff, R.	275
Krell, K. R.	294, 297, 304	Meeks, W.	222
Krodel, G.	249	Meggitt, J. P.	43
Krsmanovic, D.	159, 174	Mell, U.	198
Kubínska, J.	174	Meritt, B. D.	36, 139
Kutlu, M.	164–65	Mesmay, E. de	288
Kwok, C. S.	19	Metcalf, W. E.	131
Labahn, M.	321	Meyboom, P. G. P.	161
Laes, C.	111, 113–14	Mihaila, C.	317
Lake, K.	295, 299	Miller, P. C.	231–32
Lambrecht, J.	303	Milner, N. P.	158
Lampakis, G.	161, 164	Misset-van de Weg, M.	232
Laqueur, T.	108	Mitchell, S.	278
Lavan, L.	115–16	Mitford, T. B.	257
Leaf, W.	276	Möbius, H.	161, 167, 177
Leigh, S.	141	Modica, J. B.	216
Lewis, P.	274, 286–87	Moo, D. J.	42
Liu, L.	87	Moore, S. D.	121
Llewellyn, S. R.	279	Mørkolm, O.	286
Loftus, W. K.	86	Morton, J.	281
Lohmeyer, E.	318	Müldner, G.	12, 14–15, 22
Loisy, A.	318	Murphy-O'Connor, J.	46, 299, 302
Longenecker, B. W.	44, 46, 72	Nelson, M.	59, 61, 62
Longenecker, R. N.	302–3	Neyrey, J. H.	301–2
Longfellow, B.	64	Newby, Z.	110, 113, 115
Lopez, D. C.	75	Nickle, K. F.	297
Lopiparo, J.	105–6	Nida, E. A.	80
Lösch, S.	16, 17, 22	Nongbri, B.	10
Louw, J. P.	80	Notopoulos, J. A.	136
Ma, J.	114, 115	O'Connor, C.	282
MacDonald, M. Y.	182–83	Oakes, P.	196
McGowan, A. B.	70, 73, 76–78	Oliver, J. H.	131, 133–36, 138–40, 146, 148
McKnight, S.	216		
McLean, B.	226	Osborne, G. R.	103
McRay, J.	295	Osiek, C.	47, 221, 226, 228, 230–31, 235
Madigan, K.	221, 235	Osten, A. P. von	282
Maier, H. O.	121	Owens, M. D.	198, 205
Malina, B.	301–2	Özgün, Z. C.	287
Manus, C. U.	258	Özgünel, A. C.	282–83, 287
Manuwald, G.	75	Özhan, T.	285–86
Mare, W. H.	161	Papagiannopoulos, A.	245–46
Marks, S.	71	Papathanasiou, A.	11, 15

INDEX OF MODERN AUTHORS

Paris, P.	139	Robert, J.	177
Parkin, T. G.	256	Robert, L.	164, 175, 177, 286
Pasquinicci, M.	35	Robinson, J. M.	324
Passoni Dell'Acqua, A.	199	Roueché, C.	163
Patterson, S. J.	315	Roussopoulos, A. S.	133
Pearce, J.	158	Royalty, R. M.	102–3, 123
Pearson, B.	322–23	Ruschenbusch, E.	149
Perrot, J.	86, 93	Russell, B.	163
Pervo, R. I.	244, 250	Rutgers, L. V.	11, 19, 24
Peterson, D. G.	254–55, 258	Rutherford, W.	132, 151
Petersen, J. M.	182	Saller, R.	36–37, 39
Petzl, G.	275	Sanders, G. D. R.	34–35, 39, 44, 48
Pettegrew, D.	293	Sarre, F. T. P.	165
Pfuhl, E.	161, 167, 177	Shear, T. L.	131
Pierre, M-J.	132	Scheidel, W.	10
Pilhofer, P.	203	Schepartz, L. A.	46
Pococke, R.	165	Schmidt, E. F.	86, 95
Polhill, J. B.	249, 295	Schnabel, E.	281, 297, 300
Pomeroy, A. J.	256	Schoeninger, M. J.	12
Pomeroy, S. B.	158	Schowalter, D.	34, 55, 59, 63, 65
Pope, R. M.	278	Schroder, H.	17
Porter, S. E.	196, 273, 304	Schroeter, J.	321
Potter, D.	112	Schultz, C. E.	228
Pouderon, B.	132	Schüssler Fiorenza, E.	119–20, 123
Preisker, H.	318	Schweizer, E.	229, 319–20
Preucel, R. W.	105–6	Schwertheim, E.	275, 290
Preuschen, E.	318	Scranton, R. L.	34, 213
Price, S. R. F.	206	Segre, M.	177
Prowse, T. L.	12, 14–15, 17–20, 24–25	Sellin, G.	316
Putzeys, T.	115–16	Serdaroğlu, Ü.	290, 293
Quarles, C. I.	299, 301	Sergienko, G. A.	226, 229
Rabinowitz, A.	96	Shear, J.	131
Ramelli, I. L. E.	46	Shear, T. L. Jr.	131
Ramsay, W. M.	102–3, 119, 179, 295–296	Sherwin-White, A. N.	243, 253
		Shogren, G. S.	69
Rapske, B.	281	Silva, M.	295
Raubitschek, A. E.	136	Simmonds, A.	75
Remijsen, S.	110, 117, 122	Şimşek, C.	162
Renan, E.	164	Sirks, B.	37
Richards, M. P.	11, 15, 23	Slingerland, D.	203
Richardson, P.	223	Smit, J.	316
Rickman, G.	37, 43	Smith, A. C. G.	275
Ricl, M.	178, 271, 274, 284, 286	Smith, D. E.	3–9, 26, 28, 55, 57, 59, 65, 69–71, 73, 76, 78, 85, 98, 101, 129, 157, 183, 241, 269, 330, 333
Rieger, B.	275		
Riesner, R.	243, 249, 253–55, 262		
Ritti, T.	176, 270	Smith, M. F.	158

Smith, R. R. R.	162–63	Vernant, J-P.	160
Smith, W. C.	10	Vischer, W.	133
Söğüt, B.	158	Vokotopoulou, J.	247
Sokolowski, F.	226	Vos, C. S. de	248, 258
Sørensen, M. L. S.	106	Vout, C.	144
Spawforth, A. J.	131, 141–42	Wacker, M-T.	88, 92, 97
Standhartinger, A.	71, 157, 179, 183	Walbank, M. E. H.	35, 204, 206–8, 212
Stark, R.	276	Walker, P.	279, 301–2
Stevenson, G. M.	117, 123	Walker, S.	131, 141–42
Strelan, R.	159	Wallace-Hadrill, A.	109
Strobel, A.	41	Walters, J. C.	206
Strubbe, J.	111, 113–14, 164	Ward, R. B.	110
Stuhlmacher, P.	198	Webb, G. R.	76
Stupperich, R.	290	Weber, G.	161, 165, 169–71, 175
Swift, E.	115–16	Weima, J. A. D.	241, 244, 250
Sydenham, E. A.	150	Wendt, H. W.	318
Syme, R.	132	West, A. B.	33
Tabbernee, W.	234	Wiegartz, H.	275
Tajra, H. W.	252	Wilhelm. A.	138
Talbert, R. J. A.	278, 288–89	Willers, D.	131–32, 135, 141–43, 145
Tarán, L.	157	Williams, D. J.	262
Taussig, H.	69–70, 71	Williams, M. E.	4
Taylor, C.	115	Wilson, A.	276
Taylor, J. E.	318	Wilson, M.	270, 272–74, 279, 283, 290, 296, 300, 303–4
Tenger, B.	273–74		
Theissen, G.	222	Wilson, R. McL.	181–82
Thiselton, A. C.	33, 40–41	Winter, B. W.	33, 38–41, 47
Thomas, C.	160, 167, 209	Wiseman, J.	33, 34, 38
Thompson, G. L.	270, 272, 273, 274, 276, 284, 300	Witherington, B.	40, 250–51, 258, 262, 279, 295, 303
Thonemann, P.	159, 164–65, 168, 174–75, 180–81	Woloch, G. M.	146
		Wolter, M.	320
Thrall, M. E.	41, 211, 297	Wood, M.	87
Todd, S. C.	178	Wood, R.	161
Tombul, M.	284	Woodward, A.	63
Torjesen, K. J.	221, 234	Woodward, P.	63
Traill, J. S.	134–35	Wright, N. T.	216
Trakadas, A.	275	Wujeski, T.	179
Trebilco, P.	278	Yegül, F.	110, 114–15
Troyer, K. de	88, 92, 97	Yıldız, H.	162, 166
Tykot, R. H.	17, 23–25	Yıldızturan, M.	167
Tyson, J. B.	4, 333	Zanker, P.	144, 213
Vallat, F.	86	Zizioulas, J.	182
Van Nijf, O.	110–11, 117, 122, 209–10	Zuiderhoek, A.	137, 142
Verbrugge, V. D.	294, 297, 304		

Index of Subjects

Achaemenids, 86, 88, 95
Acts of the Apostles
　history and, 5, 241, 243, 264, 272–73, 330, 333
　purpose, 4, 333
Alexander the Great, 204
Anicetus of Rome, 231
Apollos, 315–25, 333
　the Baptist, 325
artifacts
　gender and, 106–8, 110, 115
　text and, 102–6, 107, 123
　texts as, 101
Aristides, *Apology* of, 129, 130–32, 151–52, 331
Augustus Caesar, 205–7, 212–13, 216
　Ara Pacis, 205
baptism, 232, 233, 325. See also Apollos, Paul
　of John, 75, 316, 318–22, 323–5, 333
　Spirit and, 319, 320–5
baths
　ephebes, 110–13
　gymnasium and, 108–19, 330
benefaction, 43, 46–47, 114, 130, 132–33, 137, 145–48, 151–52, 241–65, 331
body, bodies
　athletes, 110, 113, 115–18, 122–24, 209–10, 227
　female, 108–11, 180
　male, 108–19
　Revelation and, 101–25
bones, study of, 9, 15, 46
　animal, 59–60
　stable isotope analysis, 10, 11–13, 330

teeth, 12, 20, 21, 46
Caligula, emperor, 257, 259
children, 70, 169, 174–75, 177–80
　food consumption, 18–19, 44
church, 10–11, 27–28, 316, 318–20, 324
　sibling-ethics and, 47–49
city, cities, 130–32, 142, 145, 147
　food supply, 33–35, 39, 43, 136–38, 141–42
　offices, officials, 36–39, 43
Claudius, emperor, 36, 39–41, 147, 208, 211, 248–49, 251, 253–55, 259–60, 264–65
coins, 63, 172–73, 207–8, 247, 250, 264
　homonoia, 246
Colossae, 157–87
　Ak Khan and, 164–65
　fortress, 164
　höyük, 161–62, 164
COMCAR, xix–xx, 55, 82, 101, 269, 329, 331, 334
Corinth, 9, 33–49, 195–217
　Acrocorinth, 209
　Bema/rostrum, 212–13
　Hellenic city, 196, 205, 216
　refoundation, 35, 195–217, 333
　Roman colony, 35, 202–10
Cyprian of Carthage, 233
Dionysos, cult of, 225–6
　the Dionysia, 132, 137, 144, 147–48
disease, 36, 45–46, 174
drink, drinking, 70, 85–98, 332
　types, 90–94
　vessels, 94–96
　water, 96

-361-

INDEX OF SUBJECTS

drink, drinking (cont.)
  wine, 97, 332
Epiphanius, 234–36
epitaphs, 157–59, 161, 165–66, 168–70, 173–76, 179–81, 184–87, 234
  family relationships and, 160, 166, 174–75, 181–82
Esther, book of, 85–98, 332
Eucharist, 3, 26, 70, 73, 76–78, 81, 231–34
family, 10, 115, 133, 157–87, 205, 208, 227, 242, 252, 255–56
  household, 159–60, 166, 174
  structure, 24, 27, 175, 180–82
Firmilian of Caesarea, 233
food
  charity, 27, 46–48, 141–42, 145, 147
  crises, 33–49
  the *curator annonae*, 36–39, 48
  famine, 34, 39–40, 44, 138, 331
  hunger, 45–46, 48, 331
  in Corinth, 34–36, 43
  Paul and, 41–42, 44–45, 48–49
  production, 47, 136, 138
  types, 12–16, 23, 27, 39, 44–45
Forum/agora, 74, 75, 82, 117, 137–39, 207, 209, 212–13, 241–42
God, Christian, 151, 214
  creation, 195–217, 333
gods, 58, 65, 82, 103, 113, 132–33, 137, 144, 147–48, 179, 207–9, 224–25, 227, 285–87
graves, funerary monuments, 23–24, 158, 160, 171, 175, 290–91, 330
  bōmos, 161–62, 165–76, 184, 186
  chamosorion, 163, 168, 170
  costs, 163–4, 185, 187
  reliefs, 158–60, 165–67, 175–76, 178–80, 184, 186
  types, 24, 161–62, 174, 178
Hadrian, 129–52, 204, 331
  Athens, 129–52
  Eleusinian mysteries, 129–30, 132, 137–38, 140, 143–44, 147, 150
  Hellenism, 130, 132–33

  Panhellenica, 131, 141–43, 145, 147
  household code, 181–83, 330, 332
Ignatius of Antioch, 230–31
imperial cult, 206–9, 246–47, 251–52
inscriptions, 36–39, 55–59, 113–15, 117, 121, 123, 157–87, 204, 224–27, 234, 243, 245, 247, 255–57, 260, 330
Irenaeus, 231
Jesus, 27, 72, 87, 108, 120–21
  Adam and, 195, 323
  carnivalesque and, 76
  Christ, 197, 198, 202, 235, 255
  dining and, 75–76, 81
  as king 216, 241, 243, 250–52, 255, 258
  resurrection, 124, 195, 210, 216
Jews, 26, 91, 97, 151, 228, 323
  agitation, 93, 94, 241–42, 254, 255
  god-fearers, 242
  in Rome, 254
Josephus, 73, 80, 81
Julius Caesar, 202, 206–7, 212, 245, 247, 252, 259
Kore, cult of, 209, 227
land, 203, 205, 213
  centuriation, 35
  fertility, 34, 36
  holdings, 137, 141–42, 147
law, law codes, 131, 134, 136–39, 140–41, 143, 147, 149–51
  law-givers, 134–35
Lydia of Philippi, 229
Marcus the Magician, 231
Mary of Jerusalem, 228–9
masculinity, 102, 107, 112, 119, 330
  maintenance of, 109, 114–15, 332
  the victor, 102, 112, 114, 117–18, 120–25, 330
meals, dining, 1–5, 69–82, 85. *See also* drinking, eucharist
  diet, 9, 10, 14, 25, 74
  facilities, 57, 61–62
  gender and, 16–18, 331
  hosting, 90–94, 331

INDEX OF SUBJECTS

reclining, 57, 69, 71, 73–74, 77, 179, 332
  status, 9, 15, 23, 46–47, 71–72, 77–78
  tables, 57–59, 73, 77
  temples and, 55, 61–65, 73, 79, 82
  terminology, 78–81, 332
  triclinium, 70
migration, 19–21
  labor and, 20, 71
military, 246, 248
  triumph, 211
Montanism, 231, 233–36
  Cataphrygians, 234–35
  Maximilla, 231
  Priscilla, 231
  Quintilians, 234
names, ancient
  Agais, 114
  Agrippa, 280
  Agrippina, 65
  Ahasuerus, 89,
  Ammion, 234
  Anot-, 173
  Antiates, 212
  Aphias, 169
  Apphia, 181
  Apollonides, 173
  Apollonios, 115, 173
  Appas, 176
  Aquila, 319
  Archippos, 181
  Aristarchus
  Ariste, 168–70
  Artaxerxes, 86, 88–89
  Artos, 177
  Asinos, 165
  Attalus, 149, 227
  Avidius Quietus, 145
  Barnabas, 182
  Bartos, 177
  Biartos, 177
  Byrrhaena, 224
  Cephas, 76
  Chloe, 315
  Cladus, 113

Claudia Antonia Sabina, 115
Claudius Hipparchus, 137
Cleisthenes, 149
Commodus, 146
Cornelia, 226
Crispinus, 161
Crispus, 315
Cyrus, 96
Damokrates, 161, 173
Darius, 86, 93
Demaretos, 200
Dikaia, 200
Dinippus, 36–39, 42–43
Diodoros, 227
Diogas, 234
Diogenes, 158
Dion, 171–72, 175
Dionyseios, 175
Dios, 172
Domitian, 110
Draco, 149
Epaphras, 183
Epictetus, 168–70
Epieikes, 173
Epieikeia, 173
Epitropos, 230
Erastus, 47
Eugenetoriane, 173
Flavia Pollitta, 115
Fuscus, 37
Gaius, 47, 315
Gallio, 211
Glykon, 175, 179
Haman, 91, 93, 94
Hamaxitos
Hermogenes, 204
Herod Agrippa I, 28
Herod Antipas, 75
Herodes Atticus, 133, 275
Hieikis, 172–75, 177–78, 181
Hieikokoula, 173
Hierokles, 158
Hipparchus, 139
Julius Paulus, 263
Juncus, 135, 136

INDEX OF SUBJECTS

names, ancient (cont.)
  Junia Theodora, 224
  Kale, 234
  Karpon, 170
  Kastor, 168
  Korymbos, 174
  Leon, 227
  Libo Drusus 262–63
  Lucius, 224
  Lucius Antonius Priscus, 37
  Lucius Septimius Theronides, 117
  Lysimachus, 274
  Marcellina, 231
  Marcus Annius Pythodorus, 135
  Marcus Antonius Achaicus, 37
  Marcus Aurelius, 138
  Marcus Porcius Cato, 146
  Mark Antony, 207, 212
  Markos, 182
  Melancomas, 113
  Menandros, 115
  Meniadas, 173
  Meniandros, 172–75, 178
  Menias, 173
  Mênias, 173
  Menodotos, 115
  Mithridates, 115
  Mokeas, 173
  Nikippa Pasia, 227
  Onesimus, 78
  Phaena Antigonika, 227
  Philemon, 78, 181
  Phoebe, 47
  Pompeia Agrippinilla, 226
  Pomponius Atticus, 146
  Prisca / Priscilla, 319
  Priscus, 212
  Ptolemy Euergetes, 149
  Publius Vedius Antoninus, 115
  Pulcher, 37
  Pytheas, 227
  Pythodorus, 135
  Quintus Trebellius Rufus, 146
  Rufus, 146
  Salvius, 75
  Secundus, 272
  Sergia Paullina, 226
  Silas, 333
  Skeparnos, 173
  Solon, 149
  Sopater, 272
  Sospes, 37
  Stephanas, 47
  Stephanus, 315
  Tata, 227
  Tatas, 170
  Tatianos, 176–77, 180–82
  Tetiris, 224
  Theophanes, 204
  Theophilos, 115
  Tiberius, 110, 207–8
  Timothy, 272
  Titus, 272
  Trophimos, 272
  Tryphion, 173
  Tryphonionos, 173
  Tryphaena, 232
  Tychicus, 272
  Vashti, 92, 93, 97
  Vedius, 115
  Xerxes, 86, 88, 91, 95–96
  Zenon, 173–4
  Zenonis, 172–5
necropolis/cemetery, 15, 23, 157–87
Nero, emperor, 36, 48, 250
Norwegian Bible Society, 85, 89
Nympha of Laodikeia, 182–83, 229
Omrit, 55–65, 329–30
occupations, 21–23
  gladiators, 16–17, 21–22, 118
panopticon, 120
Paul of Tarsus, 181
  address to elders, 302, 305
  charges against, 241–65
  at Corinth, 36, 38, 41–42, 78–79, 195–217, 297, 315–25
  dining, 76–77
  Judaism, 195, 197, 241, 323
  opposition, 241, 252, 264, 297, 303

INDEX OF SUBJECTS

and Roman ideology, 196, 205–6, 209, 216, 217
travels, 269–305, 330–31
Philip of Macedon, 203
Polycarp, 230
Pompey the Great, 204, 245
ports, 15, 17, 24, 34, 46, 138
poverty, the poor, 9–10
roads, 35, 134, 141, 143, 150, 161, 269–305
   journey time, 165, 270, 279–71, 295–96
   travel, 141, 278, 330–31
Rome, 15, 17, 20–21, 23, 25, 39, 44, 49, 121, 142, 147–49, 200–201, 208, 226, 231, 234, 244–46, 248, 250–59, 263–65
Roman Empire, 244–45, 247–48, 250, 256, 264
   imperial ideology, 205–6, 209, 211, 216–17, 331, 333
Romanization, 140, 145–46, 183, 202, 204–5, 209–10, 212–13
Silas, 241–65, 333
Serapis, cult of, 247
slaves, slavery, 24, 26, 44, 71–72, 109, 112, 115–16, 137, 170, 180–82, 225, 228, 242, 332
stele, stelai, 111–13
temples, 55, 57, 62–65, 73, 82, 131, 142–44, 150, 201–2, 207–9, 212, 247
   sacrificial deposit, 59–63
   Smintheum, 269–71, 275, 279, 281–87, 289, 300, 303
Tertullian, 197, 222, 232–3
Thecla, 231–3
Thessalonica, 241–65, 333
   history of, 244–9
Tiberius, emperor, 248, 249, 253, 257, 262, 263, 265
Trajan, emperor, 259, 260
translation, 85–89, 119–20, 332
   Septuagint, 198–200, 203, 215
tribe, tribes, 133, 134, 136
unguentaria, 60–61, 107

Vespasian, emperor, 264
voluntary associations, 24, 73, 224, 226, 259–61
   banquet practices, 26, 221–23, 225–28
   presiding, 224, 226, 230, 235, 237, 331
   titles, 228
water, 12, 20, 21, 36, 65, 104, 141, 225, 324
   fountains, 63–65
wisdom, 109, 316–17, 323–25, 333
women, 175. *See also* Montanism
   church leadership, 221–37, 331
   food consumption, 26–28, 74, 224
   households, 169, 180, 181–82, 223, 233, 332
   Kollyridians, 235–36
   priesthood, 221, 224–27, 229, 232–34, 235–36
Zeus, 103, 131, 142–43, 150, 225